*Publications of the*
CENTRE FOR REFORMATION AND RENAISSANCE STUDIES

Essays and Studies, 1

Victoria Uni'
in the
University o

# The Premodern Teenager

## Youth in Society 1150–1650

Edited by
Konrad Eisenbichler

Toronto
Centre for Reformation and Renaissance Studies
2002

CRRS Publications
Centre for Reformation and Renaissance Studies
Victoria University in the University of Toronto
Toronto, Ontario M5S 1K7
Canada

tel: 416/585-4465
fax: 416/585-4430
email: crrs.publications@utoronto.ca
www.crrs.ca

**National Library of Canada Cataloguing in Publication Data**

Main entry under title:
  The premodern teenager : youth in society, 1150–1650

(Essays and studies ; 1)
Includes bibliographical references and index.
ISBN 0-7727-2018-5

1. Teenagers—Europe, Western—History. I. Eisenbichler, Konrad
II. Victoria University (Toronto, Ont.). Centre for Reformation and
Renaissance Studies. III. Series: Essays and studies (Victoria University
(Toronto, Ont.). Centre for Reformation and Renaissance Studies) ; 1.

HQ799.E8P74 2002

305.235'094'0902        C2002-900289-3

Cover illustration: Francesco del Cossa, "The Month of April" (detail), Sala dei
Mesi, Palazzo Schifanoia, Ferrara, Italy

by permission of: Ferrara, Civica Fototeca

Cover design: Ian MacKenzie, Paragraphics

Typesetting and print production: Becker Associates

# Contents

# Illustrations

# Contributors

Christopher Carlsmith taught history to adolescents for seven years prior to completing his Ph.D. at the University of Virginia in 1999. With the assistance of a Fulbright Grant to Italy, he has conducted research on the history of education in Renaissance Italy and has published articles in both Italian and English. He currently teaches in the History Department at the University of Massachusetts-Lowell.

Victoria Cole is a Reference and Digital Services Librarian at Cornell University currently finishing a Ph.D. in history at Binghamton University.

Philip Collington completed his University of Toronto Ph.D. dissertation, '"O Word of Fear": Imaginary Cuckoldry in Shakespeare's Plays' in 1998. In 1999–2000 he was a SSHRC Postdoctoral Fellow at the University of Michigan, Ann Arbor. He is currently an Assistant Professor in the Department of English at Niagara University in Lewiston, NY. He has published articles in *Shakespeare Yearbook*, *English Language Notes*, and *English Literary Renaissance*.

Kelly DeVries is the author of several books on medieval military history and technology: *A Cumulative Bibliography of Medieval Military History and Technology* (2001), *Joan of Arc: A Military Leader* (1999), *The Norwegian Invasion of England* (1999), *Infantry Warfare in the Early Fourteenth Century* (1996), and *Medieval Military Technology* (1992). He teaches history at Loyola College in Maryland.

Konrad Eisenbichler is Professor of Renaissance Studies and Italian at the University of Toronto. He has published on Italian theatre, literature, and confraternities. His monograph *The Boys of the Archangel Raphael. A Youth Confraternity in Florence, 1411–1785* (Toronto, 1998) won the Howard R. Marraro Prize from the American Catholic Historical Association.

Ruth Mazo Karras is Professor of History at the University of Minnesota. She is the author of *Common Women: Prostitution and Sexuality in Medieval England*, and many articles on gender and sexuality. She is currently completing a book on competing models of masculinity in the late Middle Ages.

Carol Lansing is Professor of History at the University of California, Santa Barbara. She is the author of *The Florentine Magnates* (Princeton, 1991), a study which examined the aristocratic male youth culture in thirteenth-century Florence, *Power and Purity: Cathar Heresy in Medieval Italy* (Oxford, 1998), and has just completed *The Lament for the Dead: Gender and Civil Society in Medieval Italy*.

Mark Lawhorn has taught at the University of Hawaii since 1992. He has published articles on children in Shakespearean drama and is currently completing a book on children in early modern English drama.

John L. Leland is Associate Professor in the Department of Humanities and Social Sciences at Salem International University. He earned a doctorate in medieval studies at Yale University and has published a number of articles on politics and crime in the reign of Richard II of England, particularly on pardons.

Ottavia Niccoli teaches history at the Università di Trento (Italy). She is particularly interested in cultural, religious and social history in the sixteenth and seventeenth centuries. She has published *Rinascimento al femminile* (Bari, 1998), *Infanzie. Funzioni di un gruppo liminale dal mondo classico all'età moderna* (Firenze, 1993), *Putti, fanciulli e mammoli nell'Italia fra Cinque e Seicento* (Bari, 1995), and *Storie di ogni giorno in una città del Seicento* (Bari, 2000).

John Carmi Parsons has taught at the Pontifical Institute of Medieval Studies (Toronto), the University of Toronto, and the University of Texas at Dallas. His publications include *Eleanor of Castile: Queen and Society in Thirteenth-Century England* (New York, 1995), an edited volume titled *Medieval Queenship* (New York, 1993), and three co-edited volumes, *Medieval Mothering* (New York, 1996), *Eleanor of Aquitaine: Lord and Lady* (New York, 2002), and *Capetian Women* (New York, 1992). He is currently preparing a contracted monograph on *Queens and Queenship in the Middle Ages* (London, 2003).

Ursula Potter was awarded a Ph.D. from the University of Sydney in 2001 for a thesis titled *Pedagogy and Parenting in English Drama 1560–1610*. Analysing Tudor school texts, school records, and sixteenth-century writings on education, the thesis discusses issues of pedagogy, gender, and parenting in English drama. Dr. Potter has previously published on *Love's Labour's Lost*, and has a book chapter forthcoming on mothers and schools in Tudor school drama, as well as an article on an Elizabethan Patient Griselda play as political allegory for Anne Boleyn.

Marian Rothstein, Professor of Modern Languages at Carthage College, is author of *Reading in the Renaissance: Amadis de Gaule and the Lessons of Memory* (Newark DE, 1999) and many articles relating Renaissance prose fiction to the history of ideas. Her work on teen knights is part of a continuing interest in the idea of the noble and how it is understood and represented in sixteenth-century French fact and fiction.

Ludovica Sebregondi teaches art history in the Faculty of Architecture at the Università degli Studi di Firenze. Previously, she taught at the Universität Innsbruck (Austria). Sebregondi has published several books and many articles on confraternities and other lay religious associations in Medieval and Renaissance Florence. She has also published on the iconology of several important figures (Savonarola, Pico della Mirandola, Poliziano, Iacopone da Todi, Giordano Bruno), on whom she has produced books, articles, and CD-ROMs. Her work combines art-historical, historical, and socio-anthropological approaches.

Fiona Harris Stoertz is an Associate Professor in the Department of History at Trent University in Peterborough, Ontario. She has previously published on childhood and adolescence and obstetrics and gynaecology in medieval England and France.

Ilaria Taddei teaches history at the Université de Pierre Mendès France, Grenoble II (France). She has published two books on youths, one *Fête, jeunesse et pouvoirs. L'Abbaye des Nobles Enfants de Lausanne* (Lausanne, 1991), the other *Fanciulli e giovani. Crescere a Firenze nel Rinascimento* (Firenze, 2001). She is particularly interested on youth organizations in early modern Europe.

Roni Weinstein completed a Ph.D. at the Hebrew University of Jerusalem (1995) on marriage rituals of Italian Jews during the early modern period (forthcoming in Brill Series of Judaic Studies). His main publications deal with different aspects of social and cultural history of Jewish Italian communities, such as family life, childhood, sexuality, social control, and Ghetto life. In 2000–01 he was a fellow at the Villa I Tatti, Florence.

Robert Zajkowsi has taught at Binghamton University, Ithaca College, and Syracuse University. He is now completing his doctoral dissertation on the hagiographical traditions surrounding the cult of St. Edmund of East Anglia. He is particularly interested in the role the lives of saints play in the moral and ideological formation of young monks. He is exploring in particular the way in which the figure of Edmund is used as a model for the young King Henry VI.

# Introduction

## Konrad Eisenbichler

The place of adolescents, teenagers, and youths in premodern European culture has not yet been studied in depth. While a lot of excellent work has been carried out in the past four decades on premodern children and childhood—especially in the wake of Philippe Ariès's ground-breaking work, *L'Enfant et la vie familiale sous l'ancien régime*, very few scholars indeed have focused on post-pubescent youth in the Middle Ages and the Renaissance. This unexplainable lacuna became painfully clear to me when I was preparing my monograph on a lay religious organization for young males, 13–24 years old;[1] there simply was no body of critical studies on what it meant to be a youth in premodern Europe or what such youths contributed to their society.

Perhaps one of the reasons for such scholarly silence can be gleaned from a witty remark by a learned colleague as we were having a beer at the annual Kalamazoo Congress of Medieval Studies: 'To speak of the medieval teenager is like speaking of the medieval week-end.' The man was right; I was trying to talk about a concept, 'teenage,' that simply was not expressed at that time. And yet, as we see from the explosion of works on homosexuality in the Middle Ages and the Renaissance, a concept need not have been articulated quite the same way as we do today in order for it to have existed and for us to study it. As Joseph Cady has brilliantly shown in his article on 'The "Masculine Love" of the "Princes of Sodom." "Practising the Art of Ganymede" at Henry III's Court,' we first need to be wary of falling prey to the desire to find our own modern terminology in the texts of our predecessors and, second, we need to be a lot more sensitive to the terminology current at the time.[2]

---

[1] Konrad Eisenbichler, *The Boys of the Archangel Raphael. A Youth Confraternity in Florence, 1411–1785* (Toronto: University of Toronto Press, 1998).

[2] Joseph Cady, 'The "Masculine Love" of the "Princes of Sodom." "Practising the Art of Ganymede" at Henry III's Court: The Homosexuality of Henry III and His *Mignons* in Pierre de L'Estoile's *Mémoirs-Journaux*' pp. 123–154 in *Desire*

Words change over time, though phenomena may not. To be gay in the 1890s did not mean the same as to be gay in the 1990s. Similarly, there certainly were individuals in the 1890s whose sexual interests lay with their own kind, though they did not call themselves 'gay.' In the sixteenth century, King Henry III of France was a homosexual no matter what terminology people at that time used to describe his attraction to men. Along the same line, although the term 'teenager' did not exist in premodern England (as it does not exist today in languages other than English), there certainly was a post-pubescence period and people were aware that individuals from their early teens to their early twenties were in a phase of their life-cycle that lay somewhere between childhood and adulthood. And they had a vocabulary to describe it. Latin used the term *adulescens*; English had *adolescent* and *youth*; Italian had *fanciullo* and *giovane*; and so forth.

Once we notice the vocabulary, we can also notice the presence of youths. When we look closely, we discover that teenaged men and women were active at all levels and in all areas of premodern society. There are plenty of examples of teenagers who became rulers: Charles VIII of France became king at thirteen (1483); Charles I of Spain at sixteen (1516); Francis II of France at fifteen (1559); Henry VIII of England at eighteen (1509); John of Bohemia at fourteen (1410); John III of Portugal at nineteen (1521). Teenaged girls were not excluded from the throne. Elisabeth Valois became queen consort of Spain at fourteen (1559); Joanna I became queen of Naples at seventeen (1343); Mary Stuart, already queen of Scotland from infancy (1542), became queen consort of France at sixteen (1559); Mary of Austria became queen consort of Hungary at seventeen (1522). And at least one teenager became emperor: Charles V von Hapsburg, elected Holy Roman Emperor at nineteen years of age (1519). This is not to mention all the teenagers who ascended to princely and ducal thrones or the myriad that were anointed bishop or cardinal while in their teens.

In the military, we find that premodern armies had youths not only in their ranks, as we would expect, but also at their head. At sixteen, Edward the Black Prince commanded the centre of the English army at the battle of Crécy (1346) and gained not only

---

*and Discipline. Sex and Sexuality in the Premodern West*, eds. Jacqueline Murray and Konrad Eisenbichler (Toronto: University of Toronto Press, 1996).

immense fame for his bravery and actions, but also induction into the newly established chivalric Order of the Garter. At seventeen Joan of Arc led her troops against the impregnable boulevard of the Augustins during the siege of Orléans and, defeating the English, contributed to the relief of the city. Before becoming *le roi* Henry III, the sixteen-years-old Prince Henry was appointed lieutenant-general of France (1567) and two years later won brilliant victories against the Huguenots at Jarnac and Moncontour (1569).

If we turn our eyes to the middle class, we find that teenagers were present in the business and commercial worlds both at home and abroad. Merchants regularly sent their young sons on missions abroad, put them in charge of subsidiaries of the family business, or set them to apprentice with a large firm. The young Marco Polo travelled deep into Asia, while the teenaged Boccaccio went to Naples to learn banking from the Bardi. Some enterprising youths with plenty of initiative went abroad on their own in search of work. At the age of fifteen the orphaned Francesco di Marco Datini left Tuscany for Avignon to seek his fortune and found it, so much so that he was later able to return to his hometown a successful and wealthy merchant; today we know him as 'the merchant of Prato.'

Young women also had their work cut out for them. In the middle and upper classes (in Italy, especially) they generally married in their teens and were entrusted with the management of the house-hold. Those who were not married were often placed in convents and more or less obliged to take orders. A few had sincere vocations and some even became saints, revealing their enormous spiritual strengths already in their teenage years. St Catherine of Siena (1347–80) is but one example of a fervently religious young woman. St Elizabeth of Hungary (1207–31), queen consort of her country at the age of fourteen, is another; as a teenaged monarch she dedicated herself to charitable works and then, when widowed and expelled from court by her brother-in-law, the twenty-one-year-old queen became a Franciscan tertiary and continued her previous charitable activities. For a similar saintly adolescent on the male side, we need only look to St Luigi Gonzaga (1568–91), now patron saint of youths.

In scholarship and the arts, many important contributions were made by talented individuals still in their teens. At fourteen Angelo Poliziano translated the *Iliad* into Latin hexameters (1473), at six-teen he became private secretary to Lorenzo the Magnificent (1475), between the ages of sixteen and nineteen he composed the *Stanze per la giostra* (1475–78) and a number of works in Latin, and by the age of twenty he was private tutor to Lorenzo's children, including Giovanni de' Medici, the future Pope Leo X. By the time he was twenty, Michelangelo had already carved the *Madonna of the Stairs*, the *Battle of the Centaurs*, the *St Petronius*, the *St Proclus*, and several other works now lost (a life-size statue of Hercules, a St John the Baptist, a sleeping Cupid). His *Bacchus* and his *Vatican Pietà* were both completed before he was twentyfour years old. At thirteen Albrecht Dürer drew a delicate *Self-Portrait* (1484) that foreshadowed not only his technical skill, but also his profound interest in the self, an interest he would share with Michel de Montaigne, himself a precocious youth. In his late teens and early twenties Hans Holbein painted his *Nativity* and *Adoration of the Kings* (Freiburg im Breisgau), the *Passion Altar* (Basel), and the *Dead Christ in the Tomb* (Basel).

Youths, in short, contributed significantly to Western civilization in medieval and early modern times. Their contribution, however, has generally not been examined in light of their adolescence. This volume intends to do just that, at least within the limits inherent in a small collection of diverse articles. It draws our attention to an age group that has generally been ignored by the scholarly community and re-examines important moments in the history, literature, and art of premodern Europe by taking into consideration their participants' youth. Some of these considerations range from problems of terminology to problems of sources, from the symbolic role of youths as voices of innocence to their sometimes violent behaviour as a group, from their sexual/hormonal changes to their political power, and from the independence of male teenagers to the restrictions imposed on their female counterparts.

A few of these issues have been taken as sign-posts for the present collection. The first is the question of terminology and definitions. What is a premodern youth? What is the difference between a *puer* and an *adulescens*, or between a *fanciullo* and a *giovane*? The second is the ritual role given to youth in what was, in most cases across Europe, a gerontocracy that governed not only the state but the culture of the time. The third is the question of education. How does one educate an adolescent prince, for example? Or, how does one provide educational opportunities to gifted youths who cannot afford to go to school? Or how does the imaginary world of literature help form the young. The fourth is the fascination young people have for the military; and here we meet teenaged soldiers, knights, and leaders. The fifth is the irrepressible interest they have for sex.

And the last section looks at the inevitable problem of teens in trouble, be it medical, social, or legal.

There is no over-all, unified methodology in this volume. This collection of articles is not intended to argue in favour of a particular critical or scholarly school, but in favour of a new look, from a variety of angles, at a little studied area. We see this volume and its eclecticism as a tantalizing array of entry points into the question of adolescence, or 'teenagers' in pre- and early modern times. And since we are all, generally, word-smiths, it would be best to start with a close look at words themselves.

Ilaria Taddei's contribution thus opens the volume with a careful examination of the terminology used in fifteenth- and sixteenth-century Florentine documents to identify and differentiate young persons as fanciulli, *adolescenti*, or *giovani*. She observes that such terms were not always used interchangeably and that, although it is not possible to associate each term with a precise range in years without taking into consideration its specific documentary context, nonetheless it is possible to identify distinct age groups according to the terminology used. In a republic such as Florence, age differentiation was important not only because it marked an individual's journey through the various stages of life from infancy through childhood, youth, and adulthood to senility, but also because it regulated that individual's integration into the social and political structure of the *polis*. Florentine citizens were franchised and gained access to various government offices (and, therefore, to socio-political power) on the basis, among others, of their age. It was thus crucially important to be absolutely clear about actual age (the Florentines were among the first to set up an official birth registry) and about age categories. In order to reconstruct the significance of age in the attribution of socio-political roles to these *fanciulli*, *adolescenti*, and *giovani*, Taddei begins with considerations on the theoretical classifications of the ages of life and then proceeds to an evaluation of the importance given to age in social practices and in the establishment of legal categories for individuals.

Ludovica Sebregondi moves Taddei's inquiry from the legal and philosophical to the visual and everyday as she turns our attention to the actual clothes Florentine males wore at the height of the Renaissance. In so doing, she seeks to determine whether young males wore garments specific to their age (as they often do today, one might add), or not. Her evidence is drawn from the visual record, sumptuary legislation, and moralistic literature, occasionally combining the three to give us a fuller picture not only of contemporary fashions, but also of responses to these fashions. Under the cloak of public morality, religious reformers such as Savonarola and Bernardino of Siena, or laymen such as Francesco Valori, sought to restrict the conspicuous consumption of the moneyed classes and the irrepressible sexuality of the young. In fact, as she points out, while the rich used clothing as a mark of social distinction and elevation, the young used it to highlight their youthfulness and sexual vitality. Sebregondi looks at the ensemble of clothes a man wore in fifteenth-century Florence and then sorts it out for us to highlight not only specific items and their use, but also the use of, and prohibition against, certain materials and colours. Class differences emerge not only in the type of garment used, but also in the manner certain common garments are worn. For example, Sebregondi finds that upper class males wore their doublets and hose tight fitting and well laced, while working class youths wore them looser and partly unlaced, the first to stress elegance and gentility, the second to facilitate movement during work.

Roni Weinstein draws this first section to a close by looking at youths from a subculture. Premodern Europe, we must remember, was not a monolith, nor did cultural uniformity exist even within well defined regional or civic boundaries. Then, as today, the continent was a mosaic where in any given area a dominant group set the primary colour, but a variety of minority groups provided the rich palette of shades and hues that gave it sparkle. Jews were one such minority group. Focusing on youths of the Jewish subculture of Italy, Weinstein asks whether Jewish-Italian teenagers were like their Christian-Italian counter-parts. In many respects they were, bonding and cavorting together as youths from the dominant Christian culture did, even adopting some typically Christian-Italian elements, such as the traditions of the *Mattinata*, or the idea of lay religious confraternities, or the sense of neighbourhood or family honour. As Weinstein points out, Jewish and Italian youths were, on the whole, a product of the wider 'Italian' context in which they were born and lived. Ironically, if we overlook the obvious matter of religion, the most striking differences existed not between Jews and Christians, but between native Italian Jews and immigrant Jews from other parts of Europe or the Mediterranean basin. The newcomers brought with them social practices and expectations that were at odds with the native Italian ones. In other words, the customs of the minority Jewish youth culture caused more consternation to Jews from other cultures than to Christians and Jews from Italy. Weinstein's observations suggest that the sociology of youth is predicated, to a large extent, by the social context dominant in a given place at a given time, and this influence overcomes even fundamental religious differences.

The second section, on ritual and youths, opens with Ottavia Niccoli's fundamental observations on the interplay of love, play, and violence in the daily life of premodern adolescents. In perusing the criminal records of Bologna in the High Renaissance, Niccoli is able to identify and extract a variety of behavioural patterns among the local youth and to reconstruct veritable sociological models for them. Ironically, however, her examination is made possible by the simple fact that such behaviour, no longer considered acceptable in late Cinquecento Bologna, landed its exponents in court and thus recorded their misdeeds for posterity. Niccoli's research is doubly significant because it points not only to youth culture, but also to the tremendous changes that affected Italian society in the second half of the sixteenth century when a variety of political and religious developments dramatically altered the cultural status quo. On the cusp between the Medieval/Renaissance world and the new dispensation of the 'Ancient Regime' the changing attitudes towards, and criminalization of, certain aspects of the conduct of the young reveals an array of youthful behaviour whose 'normality' would have attracted little attention and even less recorded description in earlier times, but whose 'undesirability' in the new cultural climate of Tridentine Italy now drew scrutiny and suppression.

Moving back in time to late-medieval England and from a middle class into a regal context, Virginia Cole examines a different use of ritual: the conscious attempts by one teenager, the future King Edward II (1284–1327), to use carefully orchestrated religious rituals as a venue for asserting his own individuality and claim a degree of independence from a powerful and overpowering royal father. Prince Edward's own large household generated a multitude of records that provide ample documentation for the study of his daily activities or of his relationship with Piers Gaveston. This rich collection also sheds light on young Edward's personal sense and political use of ritual. When viewed in this light, the documents expose the tensions inherent in the heir's position in the realm as well as the specific tensions in this particularly difficult father/son relationship.

Robert Zajkowski turns our attention to another English royal adolescent nearly two centuries earlier, King Henry VI (1421–71), and on the efforts of some of his subjects to 'instruct' or 'educate' him through subtle manipulation of traditional public ritual. As a case in point, Zajkowski studies the February 1432 royal entry into London. One the most important themes enunciated in the elaborate pageants staged by the officials of the city on the route of the royal entourage was that of the education of a ruler in the seven liberal arts, in virtue, and in the law. The imagery thus reflected both the general fifteenth-century taste for works of practical and moral advice and the more specific wishes of the minority council for the young king's instruction in virtue through an 'apprenticeship' in service.

Mark Lawhorn continues the focus on spectacle by examining closely Samuel Rowley's *When You See Me, You Know Me*, a play on the relationship between the young Prince Edward, son of Henry VIII of England, and his whipping boy, Edward Browne. The play was composed in 1604 for Prince Henry's Men and mounted for the young Prince Henry Stuart, son and heir of King James I. Lawhorn addresses two issues raised by Rowley's play. The first is the question of the education of the young prince: as the play's prince and the current prince hover between childhood and youth, the play's subtle messages betray political and cultural hopes, not to mention expectations, for the political 'coming of age' of Prince Henry, the first direct male heir to the English throne in sixty years. The second concerns the place of corporal punishments in the education of premodern youths both in a specific manner (on the youth who received the whipping) and in a general manner (on other youths who are witness to, or aware of, the whipping). As Lawhorn points out, the play's physical violence on a young body raises questions that were part of the current debate on education and gives birth, within the play's action, to a special bond between the heir and his 'proxy for correction.'

A much kinder approach to education is examined by Christopher Carlsmith in his article on a confraternity's material and economic support of deserving youths in sixteenth-century Italy. By focusing on Bergamo, a provincial town in the Veneto, Carlsmith provides us with a glimpse into the educational resources available to youths in an ordinary, mid-sized Italian town. And although many of the Bergamasque students were bright and well deserving of support, not all of them, however, were model youths. By looking at those who misbehaved and at their sponsoring confraternity's response to such behaviour, Carlsmith rounds out the picture by illustrating contemporary societal norms not only for instruction, but also for social disciplining on the eve of the Counter-Reformation.

Marian Rothstein brings us back to the pedagogical aspect of literature with her analysis of sixteenth-century French *romans d'aventure*. In these stories, the young hero typically matures more rapidly than other children do. He sets off on his adventures early in his teens and then, after some years of knight-errantry during which time his strength and loyalty are thoroughly and variously tested, he marries and settles down to rule his kingdom in plain domestic bliss. Although these heros were not expected to embody exceptional standards of moral behaviour, they did have some moral usefulness in presenting their reading public with models to be imitated or shunned. The wide appeal such stories enjoyed allows us not only to gain an insight into the fantasy world of the literary imagination of the time, but also into contemporary views on adolescence as a special, 'glorious' time of testing and learning in preparation for a more sedate and responsible adulthood.

Dashing young knights are the subject of Ruth Mazo Karras's article, as well. In this case, however, Karras turns the traditional view on its head to argue that the way literary scholars and contemporary chroniclers configured a knight's interest in a fair lady did not, in fact, correspond to how it actually functioned within the idealogy of chivalry. The usual claim is that chivalric culture was geared to the female gaze: not only were tournaments and pageants supposedly held in order to earn the love of ladies, but chroniclers reported that the wish to gain the attention of the fair sex was a strong motivation for chivalric activity as a whole. Karras rejects this view and claims, instead, that such deeds and, indeed, a knight's efforts to gain a lady's eye were not meant to elicit a woman's praise, but a man's. In other words, knights sought to attract a woman's  gaze only in order to gain approval from their male peers. Consequently, the aristocratic women around these valiant knights were merely a component part of a larger male-designed system for measuring masculine prowess within the firmly contained parameters of male culture. Karras concludes that in the later Middle Ages women and the idea of woman served to ratify masculine hierarchy and prestige, not to determine it. Young knights sought and bestowed approval among themselves, and fair ladies served a tangential role that did not determine the criteria whereby a young knight gained the respect of his peers.

A young knight could gain the respect of his fellow males not only on the jousting field under the supposed female gaze, but also on the battle field by dint of arms. As Kelly DeVries points out, there were a number of youths both in the rank and file of medieval armies and in the leadership. DeVries, however, challenges traditional views by suggesting first that these 'youths' may not have been as young or as numerous as we might think and, second, by arguing that their young age was not necessarily noticed by their fellow soldiers and contemporaries. Their success 'proved' they were adults. On the other hand, had they lost, contemporaries would have been quick to blame it on their tender years and inexperience.

After Mars, we turn to Venus. Fiona Harris Stoertz opens the discussion on sex by pointing out that moralists and medical writers agreed that it was in the nature of adolescents to be consumed by lust. She then examines how society sought to respond to this perceived threat to the morality of its young. To simplify matters, Stoertz focuses on adolescents in four specific groups: monks, nobles, apprentices, and university students. In monasteries, adolescent sexuality was kept in check by constant vigilance, careful training, and segregation of younger from older monks. Among the nobility, instead, young males were given a much freer rein to express their sexuality and were, in fact, expected to be sexually active. Those who were not, or who wished to remain chaste, became a serious concern for their families. Unlike their male counterparts, young noble women were expected, instead, to restrain their sexuality and remain chaste. Families ensured female chastity by keeping careful vigilance over their daughters, by engaging them in appropriate occupations, and by marrying them off as soon as possible after menarche. While early marriage might have been a solution for young women, it did not work for university students and male apprentices. These young men were discouraged from consorting with 'honest' women for fear that they might marry them and thus bring to an early close their scholarly career or their apprenticeship. Kept away from 'honest' women, university students and young apprentices had frequent recourse to prostitutes, much to the dismay of contemporary moralists.

All this sexual repression and conflicted activity naturally led to profound anxieties about sex. In *The Two Gentlemen of Verona*, the young lover Valentine spends much of his time not so much pursuing his beloved Silvia as fearfully guarding her from rival suitors. His possessiveness seems to contradict the standard assumption that only married men feared being cuckolded. In fact, when we look closely at Shakespeare's unmarried young men in love, we discover that they behave like jealous husbands, anxiously guarding their beloved from potential rivals. In his contribution to the volume, Philip Collington examines this contradiction and the processes whereby early modern young men were not only acculturated into the lore of cuckoldry, but also conditioned to suspect all women of potential infidelity. Using two of Shakespeare's most idealistic young lovers as case studies and drawing on recent sociological work on youth, Collington demonstrates that sexual precocity brought along the onset of sexual anxieties that would remain with pre-modern males for the rest of their adult life.

Young women's anxieties were different. For early modern society one of these revolved around greensickness, or cholorisis. The disease was recognised by sixteenth-century physicians as a condition affecting mainly pubescent girls; its symptoms included anaemia, melancholy, hysteria, and a pale and greenish complexion. For many lay authors greensickness was closely linked to the state of virginity in young women, as its Latin name, *morbus virgineus*, clearly suggests. In the eyes of these male writers greensickness came to represent an unstable state of mind in adolescent girls and an expression of their emerging sexuality. The cure was generally accepted to be sexual intercourse.

Ursula Potter examines sixteenth-century understanding of greensickness and cures for it. She surveys a number of lay and medical authors for their views on the condition, including John Hall, a physician and son-in-law to Shakespeare. For some, such as Juan Luis Vives, prevention was better than cure; this required abstention from certain foods, from society and dancing, and, of course, from the sight and company of men. For Erasmus, on the other hand, marriage was the cure. As Tudor schoolboys read his colloquy *Courtship*, they learned that a young girl who was pale and run down probably needed only a good dose of sex to give her some colour and energy. Elizabethan dramatists presented greensickness as a comedic element: a concerned father might naively diagnose his daughter's disturbed state of mind and prescribe quick marriage as the cure. Old Capulet is one such father; for a sixteenth-century theatre audience, his diagnosis of Juliet's suddenly altered state, incorrect as it is, is not without reasonable medical grounds. While Shakespeare's use of the 'greensickness' trope in *Romeo and Juliet* goes beyond the merely humorous to expose the limitations of male attitudes towards female sexuality, it also endorses a premodern view on the female body that was generally held at the time and remained largely unquestioned both in the cultural and in the professional literature.

If sex was the cure for greensickness, then some young women in Bologna did not need to worry about it. In Carol Lansing's study of teenaged girls in late medieval Bologna we encounter a motley crew of survivors. These are young women who, for lack of powerful families and an influential support network, were left to fend for themselves in daily life and, as we meet them, in front of a court of law. To paraphrase the Bard, the courtroom becomes a theatre where the life of these young women in trouble is carefully constructed and played out. Different characters from the working poor step into the spotlight of Lansing's scholarship to tells us of a desperate world of daily struggle and danger. Tales of assault, rape, kidnapping and abuse mix with accusations of *mala fama*, concubinage, seduction, and desertion. The picture that emerges is rather bleak.

Not only the working poor, but noble young women and even teenaged queens occasionally had to step in front of a court and defend themselves. John Parsons takes us to France and then to Holland in order to examine two aristocratic teenagers as they stepped forcefully in front of the court of public opinion to save themselves from potential destruction. Upon hearing that her husband, King Philip II of France, was planning to repudiate her, the fourteen-year-old Isabelle of Hainaut (1170–90), removed her royal robes and, clad only in her shift, walked barefoot as a penitent through Senlis. When the town's poor rioted in her support, King Philip promised them that Isabelle would remain his wife. A century later the fifteen-year-old Elizabeth, Countess of Holland, rushed in despair to the marketplace of The Hague to beg the people to save her husband, the count, kidnapped by the unpopular regent Frank van Borselen. The people rallied to her cause, caught the fleeing regent, summarily beheaded him, and freed the count. By focusing on these particular examples of adolescent female agency, Parsons considers what these spectacular moments reveals not only about roles young women might assume at an early age, but also what they tells us about their training. In particular, Parsons examines how the young women appealed to disruptive marginal elements (the poor) or to the general population (the merchants in the market) for help to save themselves and their crown.

The run-away youths John Leland examines in fourteenth-century England also took a desperate situation in hand and sought to resolve it expeditiously. These were young men and women who, after some time in service, fled from their masters before the termination of their contract and sought refuge and employment elsewhere. Occasionally these youths left the city and returned to the country where, in many cases, they re-entered their natal home and worked for the family. By examining the use of pardons for violations to the Statute of Labourers, Leland brings into focus the difficult lives of these young servants and apprentices. He describes the pull of family loyalties and the push of unsatisfactory work environments, the family connections that provided initial employment, as well as the opportunities these youths in post-plague England suddenly enjoyed. In so doing, Leland introduces a small but significant variant to the accepted theories on youth work experience and migration in the late Middle Ages, that of a reverse labour flow from the city to the country.

From this array of articles, a mere sampling of what can be done and of perspectives or approaches that can be adopted when studying youths in premodern Western civilization, it is clear that post-pubescent young men and women were a vital element of Medieval and Renaissance society. Because the category 'teenager' had not yet been formulated, other words were used to identify persons who were no longer children but not yet adults: among the Latin reading public, at puberty a *puer* became an *adulescens* and then, a few years later, a *iuvenis*; in Italy, a *bambino* became a *fanciullo*, and then an *adolescente* and eventually a *giovane*; similar categories mark out the stages of life before adulthood in other linguistic areas. Given the social, legal, and ritualistic structures of premodern society, it is not surprising to find that these categories could be both firm and fluid. Males generally enjoyed a long, leisurely period of adolescence and youth that reached well into their mid-twenties, whereas females generally had adulthood thrust upon them in their mid-teens by early marriage, childbearing, and household responsibilities. Young males dressed to attract, and attract they did—though sometimes this also brought upon them the censure of moralists and the force of the law. Working and lower class young women were more likely to have to contend with direct sexual aggression, while their aristocratic sisters faced political threats to their security and person. Royal teenagers lived in a world where ceremonial rituals and festive entertainments were used to convey subtle messages about status, power, and responsibility. Education, then as now, came in various guises and was intimately connected with the culture and ideals of the time. Young people read the signs and learned the lessons accordingly. Some were harsh—they placed youths in critical situations and forced them to fight for survival, they made unnatural demands that gave rise to anxieties with deep and long-lasting effects, they forced them to make choices that ran afoul of the law. To be young was to find oneself stuck between the innocence of childhood and the responsibilities of adulthood, sometimes with none of the benefits of either. Nonetheless, the undeniable fascination of Renaissance artists, for one, with the figure of a teenaged youth points to an interest that has not yet been fully studied by modern scholars. Neither has the meaning of being young, nor its obligations. This collection of essays, in its variety and eclecticism, fills some of these needs and leaves the question wide open for further, more extensive examination of what it meant to be a teenager in premodern Europe.

*Victoria College*
*University of Toronto*

# Puerizia, adolescenza *and* giovinezza: *Images and Conceptions of Youth in Florentine Society During the Renaissance*

## Ilaria Taddei

The lexicon used by fifteenth- and sixteenth-century Florentine sources reveals that the terminology applied to infancy and youth was not as blurred or as ambiguous as some scholars, following pioneer work of Philippe Ariès, have often pointed out.[1] As is the case today, words for childhood and youth contain an overlay of meanings that does not exclusively depend on physical age. In this article, therefore, I will examine the relationship between language and the theoretical classification of the stages of human life, and I will point to the influence of cultural models on the periodization of human ages. I will then refer to the typical characteristics of childhood, adolescence, and youth and, finally, I will show that in Renaissance Florentine society the passage from infancy to adulthood was clearly perceived.

There are many words used to indicate childhood and youth in fifteenth- and sixteenth-century Florentine sources: *infans, puer, adulescens, iuvenis* in Latin, and *infante, putto, bambino, fanciullo, adolescente, giovane, garzone,* and *ragazzo* in the vernacular. Within this variety, the more common words were *fanciullo* and *giovane,* so I will focus my analysis on them.

Depending on the various contexts of the documents, the Latin term *puer* (boy) and its Italian equivalent *fanciullo* acquired different meanings and could refer either to a child in his early infancy or to an adolescent. For example, in his *Diario fiorentino*, the chronicler Luca Landucci uses the term *fanciullo* to refer to earliest infancy; and so do some official Florentine documents.[2] A 1497 sumptuary law that used

---

[1] Ariès, *L'Enfant et la vie familiale sous l'Ancien Régime.*

[2] Landucci, p. 13; ASF, Prov. Reg., 206, anno 1527, fol. 15r: 'Item che e fanciulli o fanciulle che si portano a battezzare non possino havere adosso oro, ariento o gioie d'alchuna sorte'; ASF, Compagnia poi magistrato del Bigallo, 1459, 76, s.n.: 'Io raccomando a vostra signoria la causa di Pandolfo de' Medici che vorrebbe mettere i' nelli abbandonati un fanciullo piccolo, di età d'anni due incirca, anzi

age to determine appropriate clothing for Florentine citizens, used the term *fanciulli* for those under the age of fourteen.[3] The same word, however, could be used also for older youths. The *ricordi* of the adult confraternity of San Paolo, under whose aegis the youth confraternity of San Giovanni Evangelista operated, claimed that the members of the Vangelista who had reached the age of twenty had to leave the youth confraternity and refers to them interchangeably as *fanciulli* and as *giovani*.[4]

In fact, the word *fanciullo* could replace the less common terms *infante*, *putto*, and *bambino*. Drawing upon a traditional subdivision that went back to Isidore of Seville, *infanzia*, the first age bracket in human life, gathered persons under the age of seven. A government disposition of 1434, referring to the Ufficiali dei Pupilli (the officers in charge of the protection of children), called *infanti* those children who were under seven years of age, 'who did not have the intellectual capacity to distinguish their needs.'[5]

Despite the ambiguity of language, however, as Ottavia Niccoli has indicated, the term *fanciulli*, especially if used in the plural, was the word that indicated clearly a group's age. In fact, *fanciulli* belonged to the *puerizia* (childhood), that age period that, again according to Isidore of Seville, began at the end of infancy, that is, at seven years of age, and finished at fourteen years of age.[6] *Fanciulli*, therefore, constituted a category with a defined identity, that was associated with specific ritual functions and to their society's concept of *puerizia*.

The third age category, *giovinezza* (youth), instead, is much more difficult to identify. For one, the category *giovani* (young men) was particularly large and, therefore, not easy to circumscribe. Normative sources, such as government deliberations, specified that *giovani* who participated in public rituals, such as embassies or the welcoming of illustrious visitors, were to be between twenty-five and thirty-five or forty years of age.[7] In fact, in fifteenth- and sixteenth-century documents,

---

credo che e' dicesse 28 mesi.'

[3] ASF, Prov. Reg., 187, fol. 111r: 'Che per virtù della presente provisione tutti e fanciulli della ciptà di Firenze insino metà d'anni 14 sieno tenuti et debbino observare tucte le cose infrascritte.'

[4] ASF, Compagnie religiose soppresse da Pietro Leopoldo, 1579, fasc. 2, fols. 60v–63v.

[5] ASF, Prov. Reg., 185, fol. 23r.

[6] Niccoli, *Il seme della violenza*, pp. 17–19.

[7] ASF, Prov. Reg., 189, fols. 17v–18r and Prov. Reg., 208, fol. 34v; ASF, Carte di Corredo 52, 'Constituto per gli ambasciatori,' fols. 20r, 27v, 29r.

the term *giovane* (youth) often did indicate this extended age bracket of twenty-four to thirty-five/forty.[8] However, while it would have been difficult to define someone over the age of forty as a *giovane*, it was very common to use this term to indicate someone under the age of twenty-four. Saint Bernardine of Siena considered *giovinezza* as a period that started at age eighteen and ended at age thirty and was characterized by dissolute and irrational behaviour.[9] Having done so, however, Bernardine then used the term *giovane* also to indicate individuals between the ages of fourteen and twenty-five.[10]

This lexical ambivalence or fluidity is evident in other sources as well. When compiling lists of *giovani*, contemporary sources often included *fanciulli* and *adolescenti*. Filippo Strozzi, recalling the communal legislation against games of chance, wrote that in 1473: 'The previous Signoria passed many laws limiting pomp at funerals and banquets, which go on a long time, and it also passed new prohibitions against games of chance, and it especially prohibited *giovani* up to the age of twenty-four from playing any card or dice game, and others from playing prohibited card or dice game such as *zara* and other such games.'[11] A sumptuary law of 1527, regulating apparel according to

---

[8] For some examples of the term *giovane* in a variety of contemporary sources, see: Cambi, *Istorie*, 3:201–2, anno 1502: 'Ora fu schoperto questo tratato, e preso qui Iacopo di Gio. Batista da Ghiacieto, giovane d'anni 25 e legieva in istudio hopera d'umanità, ed era precietore [. . .]. Alli 7 di giugno inanzi fu mozzo la testa a dua giovani d'anni 24 nella congiura di sopra [. . .].' The Venetian ambassador in Florence, Marco Foscari, considering the chances of Giovanni de' Medici's election to the papacy, noted that: 'In Firenze fu nuove de 5, 6, 7, 8 di marzo sempre che il favore de' Medici cresceva, il che dava speranza, pur l'essere d'anni 38 giovane la togliexa assai'; Foscari, *Discorsi*, p. 77. See the well known communal legislation of December 1494 that allowed youths over the age of twenty-four to participate in the Consiglio Maggiore; ASF, Prov. Reg., 185, fol. 12r: 'Et più ancora accioché tucti e giovani beneficiati siano stimolati dalla virtù si provede che una volta l'anno et del mese di gennaio . . . si traghino a sorte 24 di tale consiglio Maggiore e quali debbino nominare 24 giovani beneficiati cioè uno per uno et non minori d'anni 24.' When Francesco di Alessandro Capponi died in 1582, he was called a 'giovane di anni 34 in circa'; ASF, Manoscritti, 129, Francesco Settimanni, 'Memorie fiorentine dall'anno 1532 all'anno 1737,' vol. 4, fol. 262v.

[9] Bernardine of Siena, *Le prediche volgari*, 3:44.

[10] Bernardine of Siena, *Prediche volgari sul Campo di Siena*, 2:1246.

[11] 'La Signoria passata à fatto molti statuti circa la modestia de' moritori e de' conviti, sono chose lunghe, e anche sopra il giuocho nuove prohibizioni et maxime

age, referred to 'giovani up to eighteen years of age completed.'[12] In 1560, on the occasion of the baptism of the son of Duke Cosimo I, 'thirty couples of youths aged sixteen to eighteen all magnificently dressed followed closely upon many courtiers.'[13]

Often fanciulli and adolescenti were indicated by way of the diminutive giovanetti (little youths), a term much more frequently used than its synonym adolescenti. Both expressions, giovanetti and adolescenti, generally referred to individuals around twenty years of age.[14] At this age, half-way between puerizia (childhood) and giovinezza (youth), the members of the youth confraternity of the Arcangelo Raffaello, studied by Konrad Eisenbichler, left their confraternity's subgroup of the pueri and joined its subgroup of the 'iuvenes huiusmodi etatis medie' (young men of a medium age), that is, of the 'adolescentes postquam decimumnonum aut vicesimum annum' (adolescents over the nineteenth or twentieth year of age).[15]

Evidently, it is not possible to associate each term with a precise age category without taking into consideration its specific documentary context. Nonetheless, it is possible to identify distinct age groups according to the terminology used in fifteenth/sixteenth-century Florentine sources. One must therefore revise the hypothesis advanced by Philippe Ariès that the medieval and Renaissance lexicon for infancy and youth is imprecise.[16] The fact is, that fifteenth- and sixteenth-century Florentine sources do not use an ambiguous terminology, not any

---

che i giovani insino in 24 anni non possino giuocare a niuno giuoco di carte o dadi, gli altri a niuno giuoco vietato di carte o dadi chome sono condannati zara et simili.' ASF, Carte Strozziane, serie III, 178, fol. 11r.

[12] 'a giovani infino all'età d'anni 18 forniti'; ASF, Prov. Reg., 206, fol. 15r.

[13] 'trenta coppie di giovani di età di anni 16 a 18 e tutti vestiti magnificamente seguivano appresso molti cortigiani'; ASF, Manoscritti, 127, Francesco Settimanni, Memorie fiorentine dall'anno 1532 all'anno 1737, vol. 2, fol. 488r.

[14] See: ASF, Compagnie religiose soppresse da Pietro Leopoldo, 160, fasc. 6/7, fols. 14v, 26v and fasc. 8, fols. 12v, 110r. At the age of twenty one Cardinal de' Medici is called a giovanetto by Cambi in his Istorie, 2:62–63 and by Landucci in his Diario fiorentino, p. 75. Along the same lines, Cardinal Ippolito d'Este, passing through Florence in 1497, is called a 'giovanetto di circa 22 anni'; Landucci, Diario fiorentino, p. 160.

[15] ASF, Diplomatico, Patrimonio Ecclesiastico, 24 June 1442, cit. in Trexler, Public Life in Renaissance Florence, p. 371 and in Eisenbichler, The Boys of the Archangel Raphael, p. 422. The correct date is the one cited by Eisenbichler (24 June 1442).

[16] Ariès, L'Enfant et la vie familiale, p. 43.

more, that is, than today's terminology could be deemed to be ambiguous. Indeed, the ages' delimitation depended, at least in theory, on clear scientific categories and on juridical definitions that first had been formulated by Roman law and then had been integrated into canon law.

Contrary to what Ariès affirmed, the Florentine lexicon was in fact quite rich. It even provided a specific term, *adolescente*, to indicate a person aged somewhere between *puerizia* (boyhood) and *giovinezza* (youth). Admittedly, other terms such as *fanciullo* and *giovane* could be used in place of *adolescente*, but this versatility is not a sign of a vague or indistinct perception of adolescence; if anything, it reveals the lack of a clear demarcation point between infancy and youth. The situation remains the same today.

Medieval and Renaissance speculation on the ages of life took as its reference point Isidore of Seville's *Etymologiae Origines*, which presented juridical notions integrated into the *Decretum Gratiani* and reconstructed the meaning of terms on the basis of their etymology (which, sometimes, is completely arbitrary).[17] Drawing upon Saint Augustine, who had correlated the days of Creation with the ages of the world and the course of human life, Isidore proposed a six-stage cycle of life. The first stage, infancy, whose etymology came from the expression *non fari*, extended from birth to age seven.[18] As Saint Augustine had indicated, it was defined by the individual's incapacity for speech. The infant was devoid of intellect and reason, and his blood, like that of an old or of a crazy person, was dominated by the cold humour. *Puerizia*, Isidore's second stage of life, extended from seven to fourteen years. According to Isidore this term found its origin in the adjective *purus*: purity was in fact this period's principal characteristic.[19] In the case of both *infanzia* and *puerizia*, Isidore accepted the boundaries established by Roman law whereby seven was the end of infancy and juridical immunity and fourteen was the end of puberty and the beginning of the intellectual capability of action.[20] The third stage of life as defined by Isidore was adolescence, which extended

---

[17] Isidore of Seville, *Etymologiarum sive originum*, vol. 2, l. XI.ii. See also: Fontaine, *Isidore de Seville*; R. Naz, 'Isidore de Séville' 1:315–48.

[18] Isidore of Seville, *Etymologiarum*, vol. 2, l. XI.ii: 'Infans dicitur homo primae aetatis; dictus autem infans quia adhuc fari nescit, id est loqui non potest.' On the first period of Isidore's schema see Nagel/Vecchio, 'Il bambino,' pp. 719–763.

[19] Isidore of Seville, *Etymologiarum*, vol. 2, l. XI.ii: 'Puer a puritate vocatus, quia purus est.'

[20] Burdese, 'Età. Diritto Romano.'

from fourteen to twenty-eight years of age and coincided with the period of growth and concupiscence.[21] The fourth, *iuventus* (youth), extended from twenty-eight to fifty years of age.[22] The fifth, *aetas senioris* or *gravitas*, reached from fifty to seventy years of age when, finally, the sixth, *senectus*, extreme old age, appeared.[23]

Isidore's cycle enjoyed great success. It influenced both the imagination and the conception of the various stages of life, both within the legal confines of medieval canon law and the general expectations of pre-modern social roles. The humanist Matteo Palmieri in his treatise *Della vita civile* followed Isidore's pattern not only in its numerical aspects, but also in the qualities that were associated with each age group.[24] Taking his reference from the concept of the fork in the road where an individual is obliged to chose between virtues and the vices, Palmieri identified the course of human life with the letter Y. He associated infancy, which he characterized as 'ignorant and without understanding,' with the stem of the letter Y because it proceeded 'simply and along one path, without dividing between vices here and virtue there, for it does not yet have knowledge of them.'[25]

In the memoirs of Florentine merchants and in fifteenth-century civic or religious treatises, this view was not unusual: according to Isidore's concept of *infirmitas*, *infanzia* was characterized by the inability to understand and to express oneself. This cognitive weakness of the individual stretched past infancy and reached to the end of *puerizia* when, finally, the age of reason, or rationality, began. The imperfect use of the intellect linked *infanzia* and *puerizia*, the joint age that Palmieri defined as the 'the age of ignorance.'[26] Indeed, the two ages were often joined together in fifteenth-century Florentine documents and the characteristics of one transferred easily to the other. A different, yet similar characterization of childhood and boyhood as *infirmitas* is found in Filippo di Niccolò Capponi, who picked up the image of the midget that Aristotle had applied to the newborn

---

[21] Isidore of Seville, *Etymologiarum*, vol. 2, l. XI.ii: 'Adulescens dictus, eo quod sit ad gignendum adultus, sive a crescere et augeri.'

[22] Isidore of Seville, *Etymologiarum*, vol. 2, l. XI.ii: 'Iuvenis vocatus, quod iuvare posse incipit.'

[23] Isidore of Seville, *Etymologiarum*, vol. 2, l. XI.ii: 'Senes autem quidam dictos putant a sensus diminutione, eo quod iam per vetustatem desipiant.'

[24] Palmieri, *Vita Civile*, pp. 30–31.

[25] Palmieri, *Vita Civile*, p. 32.

[26] Palmieri, *Vita Civile*, p. 33.

and extended it to older children saying that *fanciulli*, like midgets, were physically deformed (the upper part of their body was more developed than the lower part) and this led to an imbalance of the humours that, in turn, led to their intellectual deficiency.[27]

A positive consequence to this *infirmitas* was the belief that a child was unable to do evil. The innocence of childhood had been established in Roman and in canon law, both of which, finding the child incapable of doing harm, had proclaimed his juridical immunity until the legal end of *puerizia* (fourteen years of age).[28] The *infirmitas* of infancy and childhood was therefore seen not only in negative terms, but, according to the time and the context, as a virtue, as well. The Greco-Roman world had already granted a sacred dimension to the innocence of children. Infancy was bestowed with superhuman powers that conferred prophetic abilities on children: their gestures and their words became the object and the means for many divinatory practices.[29]

The religious and cultural climate of the fifteenth century picked up on these beliefs and praised the ideal virtues of the child, and especially its purity. In the fifteenth century the image of *puer* was always ambiguous, because it recalled both the child's lack of intellectual ability and his innocence. Between the two, however, the positive conception of childhood prevailed because the purity of the child was exalted as a virtue that granted children a social role as mediators between God and Humanity.

In Matteo Palmieri's description of the ages of life, one can clearly identify a specific dimension of adolescence, one that is associated as early as the eleventh century with the period of personal crisis that characterizes the process of sexual development and maturity.[30] Palmieri saw adolescence as a particularly difficult moment in an individual's life, a moment when human life forked and broke into two diverging directions, towards virtue or towards vice. This, for Palmieri, was represented by the point where the letter Y divided into two branches. At this fork on the road of life, the child had to chose between right

---

[27] Aristotle, *Parts of Animals*, book IV, 10, 686b, pp. 367–71. *Libro intitolato facile est inventis addere*, fol. 107r.

[28] Néraudau, 'Il bambino nella cultura romana,' p. 54; Nagel/Vecchio, 'Il bambino,' p. 722.

[29] On the sacredness of children in antiquity see Grottanelli, 'Bambini e divinazione,' pp. 23–72 and Néraudau, 'Il bambino nella cultura romana,' pp. 30–60.

[30] Goodich, *From Birth to Old Age*, p. 126.

and wrong.[31] However, the young person was not yet mature enough to confront, alone, the dangers on the road ahead. It was therefore necessary that the adolescent be controlled and instructed with particular severity by his father while, at the same time, he be separated from the company of older youths. The danger was that these older youths 'of greater malice' could transfer reprehensible behaviour unto the younger adolescent, who was still wrapped in 'puerile softness' and therefore could be easily seduced.[32]

This perceived need to separate youths by age groups was widespread in fifteenth-century Florentine society and was based on an understanding of the nature and needs of adolescents. Separation into homogeneous age groups was seen as a way to facilitate the difficult passage through adolescence, that is, through sexual maturity. It was also seen as a way to prevent younger adolescents from being corrupted by contact with older ones. Although younger adolescents had not yet lost all the purity of their childhood, they were nonetheless already exposed to sexual instincts and these, according to Saint Bernardine, made all young men, fourteen to twenty-five years old, incapable of rational behaviour.[33]

In his *Forbidden Friendships*, Michael Rocke has demonstrated that in same-sex relationships, male adolescents generally abandoned the passive role sometime between the ages of eighteen and twenty, a period that coincided with their passage from *adolescenza* into *giovinezza*. Homosexual relationships in fifteenth-century Florence were structured in a hierarchical manner that echoed the phases of life: the active role was identified with 'manly' behaviour appropriate to adult men, while the passive role was considered 'feminine' and was not to extend past the biological period of adolescence.[34] Adolescence, which is characterized by the acquisition of sexual maturity, was therefore perceived as a liminal stage that marked the passage from childhood (*puerizia*) to youth (*giovinezza*).

The image of youth, as presented in the works of fifteenth-century merchant-writers, humanists, and preachers, is also primarily negative. Leon Battista Alberti described this period of life in words that highlight the changeable character of youths, their lack of restraint, and their

---

[31] Palmieri, *Vita Civile*, p. 32.

[32] Palmieri, *Vita Civile*, p. 34.

[33] Bernardine of Siena, *Le prediche volgari*, p. 44.

[34] Rocke, *Forbidden Friendships*, especially pp. 96, 106, 114, 117.

frivolity: 'Changeable youth always follows its desires. The lusts of youth are infinite, most unstable, and I believe it is nearly impossible to establish anything permanent in the spirit of a youth.'[35] According to the medical theory of the humours, heat was the prevalent quality in the blood of *giovani* and this, in turn, determined not only their positive aspects, such as their magnanimity, generosity, and courage, but also their negative ones, such as their intemperance, concupiscence, and volubility.[36] The contrast between youth as a period of sensual dissoluteness and adulthood as a period of mature wisdom developed during the Middle Ages in parallel with the concept of youth as expressed in courtly literature where its value was emphasized and its violent behaviour somehow justified.[37]

According to the pragmatic mentality of Florentine merchant-writers, even those qualities specific to youth that courtly culture praised, for example prodigality, were considered to be really defects, failings that could undermine a family's wealth and compromise its patrimony.[38] For Florentine merchants the ideal behavioural model for youths was not to be found in the chivalric virtues of daring, strength, and display, but, instead, in the mercantile virtues of moderation, modesty, and discretion. Fathers, therefore, had to control the activities, the entertainments, and the personal friendships of their sons. Without a father's guidance, Alberti maintained, young men 'full of vice, full of license, burdened with needs, give themselves to filthy activities, dangerous, disgraceful for them and for their family.'[39] The Franciscan Bernardino da Feltre held similar views; urging fathers to look after their son's education, he affirmed that 'youth leans towards evil' ('etas juvenilis procliva est ad malum').[40]

In conclusion, we can easily see how Renaissance Florentine society had a clear perception of the various phases of life. The time that preceded adulthood was not nebulous and undifferentiated, as Ariès has claimed, but clearly subdivided into several stages and vividly characterized. Infancy and childhood were associated not only with physical and intellectual incompleteness, but also with innocence. Adolescence was associated with sexual growth. Youth was the age of full physical potential, ardour, and excesses.

---

35 Alberti, *I libri della famiglia*, p. 79.

36 Sears, *The ages of man*, p. 16.

37 See Crouzet-Pavan, 'A Flower of Evil.'

38 See Alberti, *I libri della famiglia*, p. 79.

39 Alberti, *I libri della famiglia*, p. 96.

40 Monaco, 'Aspetti di vita privata e pubblica,' p. 126.

Throughout the fifteenth century, awareness of these age differences became progressively greater in Florentine society. Humanist culture emphasized the value of time as it related to human action, work, and the ages of life. As Christiane Klapisch-Zuber has indicated, the cultural needs of the humanists dovetailed with the new requirements of a modernizing Florentine civic administration.[41] The establishment in 1427 of an universal tax system, the Catasto, and, two years later, the introduction of the 'Libro delle età,' the register that kept track of citizens' birth dates so as to determine eligibility for office, led Florentines to develop a chronological memory. In fifteenth-century Florence, age became an ever more precise criterion for the assigning of public office and for the fulfilment of institutional obligations. Florentine law, often in accordance with Roman and canon law, established age limits that marked the passage from childhood to adulthood. Minimum age requirements for the conferring of important juridical duties were debated, a minimum age for fiscal, civil, and penal responsibilities was established, the appropriate ages of emancipation from paternal authority, for bearing arms, for access to public office, for political rights, for wearing luxurious garments were fixed. Even if these age limits were not rigidly respected, the organization of public life along criteria of age implied a profound recognition of age differentiation in the roles an individual was called upon to play in pre-modern society.

*Université de Pierre Mendès France, Grenoble II*

*(Translated by Konrad Eisenbichler)*

# Cited Works
## Manuscript Sources

ASF. Firenze, Archivio di Stato.
> Carte di Corredo 52
> Carte Strozziane, serie III, 178
> Compagnia poi magistrato del Bigallo, 1459, 76
> Compagnie religiose soppresse da Pietro Leopoldo,
>> 160 (Arcangelo Raffaello, detta la Scala)
>> 1579 (San Paolo)
> Diplomatico, Patrimonio Ecclesiastico, 24 giugno 1442,

---

[41] Klapisch-Zuber, 'Il bambino,' pp. 156–59.

Manoscritti, 127 and 129, Francesco Settimanni, 'Memorie fiorentine
dall'anno 1532 all'anno 1737'
Provvisioni. Registri, 185, 187, 189, 206, 208

## Published Sources

Alberti, Leon Battista. *I libri della famiglia*, ed. Ruggiero Romano and Alberto Tenenti. Torino: Einaudi, 1969, rpt 1994.

Ariès, Philippe. *L'Enfant et la vie familiale sous l'Ancien Régime*. Paris: Editions du Seuil, 1973.

Aristotle, *Parts of Animals*. The Loeb Classical Library. Cambridge, MA: Harvard University Press / London: William Heinemann, 1983.

Bernardine of Siena, St. *Le prediche volgari*, ed. Ciro Cannarozzi. 5 vols. Firenze: Libreria Editrice Fiorentina, 1934–40.

Bernardine of Siena, St. *Prediche volgari sul Campo di Siena, 1427*, ed. Carlo Delcarno. 2 vols. Milano: Rusconi, 1989.

Burdese, Alberto. 'Età. Diritto Romano' 16:79–80 in *Enciclopedia del diritto*. Milano: Giuffrè, 1967.

Cambi, Giovanni. *Istorie*, ed. Ildefonso di San Luigi. 4 vols. Delizie degli eruditi toscani, 20–23. Firenze: Gaetano Cambiagi 1785–86.

Capponi, Filippo. *Libro intitolato Facile est inuentis addere, nel quale si trattano molte cose utili agli uomini nelle lor operationi e moti*. Venezia: Domenico de' Farri, 1556.

Crouzet-Pavan, Elisabeth. 'A Flower of Evil: Young Men in Medieval Italy' 1:173–221 in *A History of Young People in the West*, ed. Giovanni Levi and Jean-Claude Schmitt, trans. Camille Naish. 2 vols. Cambridge, MA and London: The Belknap Press of Harvard University Press, 1997.

Eisenbichler, Konrad. *The Boys of the Archangel Raphael. A Youth Confraternity in Florence, 1411–1785*. Toronto: University of Toronto Press, 1998.

Fontaine, Jacques. *Isidore de Seville et la culture classique dans l'Espagne wisighotique*. Paris: Études Augustiniennes, 1959.

Foscari, Marco. *Discorsi tratti dalla relatione del clarissimo Mess. Marco Foscari, ambasciatore a Fiorenza nel MDXXVII*. Delizie degli eruditi toscani, 23. Firenze: Gaetano Cambiagi, 1788.

Goodich, Michael. *From Birth to Old Age. The Human Life Cycle in Medieval Thought, 1250–1350*. Lanham, MD: University Press of America, 1989.

Grottanelli, Cristiano. 'Bambini e divinazione' pp. 23–72 in *Infanzie: Funzioni di un gruppo liminale dal mondo classico all'età moderna*, ed. Ottavia Niccoli. Florence: Ponte alle Grazie, 1993.

Isidore of Seville. *Etymologiarum sive originum libri XX*, ed. W.M. Lindsay. 2 vols. Oxford: Typographeo clarendoniano, 1911.

Klapisch-Zuber, Christiane. 'Il bambino, la memoria e la morte' pp. 155–81 in *Storia dell'infanzia*, vol. 1, *Dall'Antichità al Seicento*, ed. E. Becchi and D. Julia. Roma-Bari: Laterza, 1996.

Landucci, Luca. *Diario fiorentino dal 1450 al 1516, continuato da un anonimo fino al 1542*, intro. Antonio Lanza. Firenze: Sansoni, 1985.

Monaco, Michele. 'Aspetti di vita privata e pubblica nelle città italiane centro-settentrionali durante il XV secolo nelle prediche del beato Bernardino da Feltre francescano dell'osservanza' 1:77–196 in *L'uomo e la storia. Studi storici in onore di Massimo Petrocchi*. 2 vols. Roma: Edizioni di Storia e Letteratura, 1983.

Nagel, Silvia and Silvana Vecchio. 'Il bambino, la parola, il silenzio nella cultura medievale' Quaderni storici 57 (1984): 719–63.

Naz, R. 'Isidore de Séville' 6:66–74 in *Dictionnaire de droit canonique contenant tous les termes du droit canonique avec un sommaire de l'histoire et des institutions et de l'état actuel de la discipline*, publié sous la direction de R. Naz. 7 vols. Paris: Letouzey et Ané, 1935–65.

Néraudau, Jean-Pierre. 'Il bambino nella cultura romana' pp. 30–60 in *Storia dell'infanzia*, vol. 1, *Dall'Antichità al Seicento*, ed. Egle Becchi and Dominique Julia. Roma-Bari: Laterza, 1996.

Niccoli, Ottavia. *Il seme della violenza. Putti, fanciulli e mammoli nell'Italia tra Cinque e Seicento*. Roma-Bari: Laterza, 1995.

Palmieri, Matteo. *Vita Civile*, ed. Gino Belloni. Firenze: Sansoni, 1982.

Rocke, Michael. *Forbidden Friendships. Homosexuality and Male Culture in Renaissance Florence*. Oxford and New York: Oxford University Press, 1996.

Sears, Elizabeth. *The Ages of Man. Medieval Interpretation of the Life-Cycle*. Princeton: Princeton University Press, 1986.

Trexler, Richard C. *Public Life in Renaissance Florence*. New York and London: Academic Press, 1980.

# Clothes and Teenagers:
# What Young Men Wore
# in Fifteenth-Century Florence

Ludovica Sebregondi

The sumptuousness of clothing materials and ornaments, the brilliance of the accessories, and the changing styles reveal that even in fashion the Quattrocento was a time of splendour. Clothing had acquired an important role in Italian daily life because style and luxury were more than ever being used by the established nobility to affirm its dominant status, while the emerging classes used it to affirm their attainment of a higher social level.[1] Not only adults, but youths as well used clothing and fashions to emphasize their own special status and, in a sense, their youthfulness. Before we examine their specific use of dress, however, we need first to say a few words about standard male fashion in Florence in the second half of the fifteenth century.

Men wore several layers of clothes not only for protection against the weather, but also to display their family's wealth and power. This dressing 'in layers' in turn led to the distinction between *robe larghe per di sopra* (loose garments to be worn on top) and *vestiti strecti per di sotto* (tight garments to be worn underneath). This distinction, in turn, led to a clear differentiation between the two types of garments. Clothes *per di sotto* (for underneath) had to fit closely to the body so as not to impede movement once other pieces of clothing were worn on top of them. Young people, however, often wore tight fitting garments without then adding looser garments on top. This was done so as not to hinder movement in games or sports and also for reasons of sexual seduction. In fact, tight fitting clothes served very well as indicators of desired traits in both men and women. Such clothes allowed young men to display and accentuate their manly attributes and young women to reveal that they had a body and a physical constitution suitable for procreation. Loose fitting clothes 'for on top,' on the other hand, had other functions. They served, first of all, as

---

[1] See Fiorentini Capitani-Ricci, 'Considerazioni sull'abbigliamento del Quattrocento in Toscana.'

protection from inclement weather and strangers' eyes. Their complex structure also allowed the wearer to fashion an ideal body for him- or herself. Lastly, the richness of the materials could point to the economic wealth and social position of their wearer.

Tight-fitting male attire worn in private consisted of a shirt (*camicia*), a doublet (*farsetto*), and hose (*calze*), while the numerous loose-fitting garments to be worn on top of them on public occasions and at social occasions included an open robe (*giornea*), its variant with large sleeves (*cioppa*), a skirt (*gonnellino*), and a cloak (*mantello*) or mantle (*lucco*).[2]

Was this collection of male attire differentiated on the basis of age? According to Philippe Ariès, medieval males dressed in the same manner at all ages, careful only to keep in evidence through clothing the various levels of the social hierarchy. To support his claim, Ariès noted that in fifteenth-century Italy artists depicted young male children wearing the tight-fitting hose of contemporary adults, while in France and Germany everybody wore the same long gown that was in common usage there. Ilaria Taddei, on the other hand, has noted that fifteenth-century Florentine sumptuary legislation did differentiate dress by age and legislated clearly on the appropriate dress for each life stage from childhood to adulthood. If we compare these sumptuary laws and the injunctions of contemporary preachers against inappropriate fashions with the visual evidence that has come down to us in the artworks of the time, we find some differences between the clothing of children and youths and significant differences between that of young men and adults.[3]

In her examination of fifteenth-century Florentine sumptuary legislation, Ilaria Taddei has found that as a person grew from infancy into adulthood and acquired greater social status the state would echo these changes by permiting or prohibiting certain clothes and materials.[4] Furthermore, governments viewed the display of expensive cloths and materials on the part of social classes not traditionally privileged to wear them as a threat to the general social order. A constant series of sumptuary laws thus sought to keep, unchanged, the pyramid structure of contemporary society both socially and politically. For the most part, this was done under the cloak of protecting public morality, especially that of women and youths.[5]

---

[2] See Levi Pisetzky, *Storia del costume in Italia*, vol. 2, *Il Trecento e il Quattrocento*.

[3] Ariès, *Centuries of childhood*, pp. 50–57, 61.

[4] Taddei, *Fanciulli e giovani*, pp. 119–27.

[5] Muzzarelli, *Gli inganni delle apparenze*, pp. 111–15.

In January 1496/7, when Francesco Valori, a fervent disciple of
Savonarola, was *gonfaloniere* of the Republic, the government issued
sumptuary legislation for young males (only) in which, expressing the
wish that 'people live virtuously at all times and that your sons, being
virtuous in their behaviour and dress, learn virtuous and good habits
which, once acquired at a tender age, will be theirs for a long time,'
prohibited young males under the age of fourteen from wearing gold,
silver, silk, or embroidery (unless it was of 'pure silk'). It also prohibited them from wearing a *cappuccio* (see below), 'except at the funeral
of their father or mother.' Furthermore, their over-clothes could not be
either 'rose-coloured or purple,' though their under-clothes could,
except that the stockings could not be rose-coloured. Younger males
were also prohibited from wearing linings that were not locally produced.
Whoever owned such prohibited garments was required to bring them
to the Arte della Lana (the guild responsible for the wool trade) and have
them identified and noted before the end of the following month of April.
In case youths did not comply with this law, parents were deemed
responsible for them.[6]

If we take the sumptuary legislation that gives us the prescribed
theory behind dress codes and the words of moralists who launched
themselves against the fashions they saw displayed on city streets, and
compare them with the dissenting information we can gather from the
iconographic evidence available to us, we can easily understand that legal
and moral injunctions were not usually followed and that there were,
indeed, differences in dress according to age.

Such differentiations are clearly evident in a fresco from one of the
lunettes in the oratory of the confraternity of the Buonomini di San
Martino, in Florence (fig. 1). The fresco comes from the workshop of
Domenico Ghirlandaio and is dated around 1482.[7] The scene depicts
the Buonomini in the act of distributing clothes to the poor, one of
their charitable activities. On the left, behind a counter, a Buonomo
folds a piece of clothing and another makes a note of the material that
has been given out. Both men are adults over the age of thirty and they
wear over-garments—one red, the other black. A younger man assisting them in this charitable work wears a doublet (*farsetto*), a short open

---

[6] ASF, *Provvisioni. Registri*, 187, fol. 111r–v at date 18 Jan. 1496/97. See also
Taddei, *Fanciulli e giovani*, pp. 119–27.

[7] On the confraternity and its organization see, among others, Spicciani, 'The
"poveri vergognosi" in Fifteenth-Century Florence,' pp. 119–72 and Pugliese, 'Lo
statuto "riformato" dei Buonomini di S. Martino,' pp. 261–80.

robe (*giornea*), and hose with soles (*calze solate*), that is, stockings that would be worn without shoes because they came with soles.[8] A *scarsella*, or pocket-bag hangs from his belt. A young man gives a charitable donation to a boy dressed only in a shirt.[9] The young man wears hose, black shoes, and a short yellow doublet kept closed by a line of buttons; the doublet's sleeves are tied with ribbons and reveal the presence of a puffed shirt underneath. The young man is dressed like an artisan, but, probably in response to the wishes of those who commissioned the fresco and were seeking a figure that would express the appropriate quality of modesty, he wears a shirt that is longer than would have been the norm. Both the boy and the young man wear a cap (*beretta*), the most common headgear among boys and youths in fifteenth-century Italy. Usually, this cap was made of red cloth. The other men, instead, wear a *cappuccio*, that is a head covering consisting of a stuffed ring (the *mazzocchio*) from which hangs a back flap (*foggia*) and a front scarf (*becchetto*). This fresco's differentiation in head coverings reflects the 1497 sumptuary law mentioned above that prohibited youths under the age of fourteen from wearing a *cappuccio* 'except at their father's or mother's funeral.' Lastly, the older man on the right wears a red gown with large folds and the black cloak (*lucco*) that were reserved for the higher social classes.

The clothes worn by these figures can therefore serve as an indicator of their wearers' age and social condition. They reveal that the fresco depicts four different age groups—childhood, youth, maturity, old age—and three different social classes—wealthy, working class, destitute.[10] The Buonomini who commissioned it clearly wanted to illustrate visually that their charity was bestowed on anyone who needed it, regardless of age or social condition: to the older man on the right, who must once have been well off because he wears a red garment with large folds and a black cloak reserved for the higher classes, as well as to the younger artisan with his shirt coming out of his doublet. There were, therefore, differences in dress not only between different social classes, but also between different age groups.

---

[8] On the *calze solate* see Merkel, *Come vestivano gli uomini del Decameron*, pp. 27–33.

[9] On men's shirts, see Birbari, *Dress in Italian Painting*, pp. 30–36.

[10] For the standard Medieval/Renaissance subdivision of human life into six or seven 'ages,' see Taddei, *Fanciulli e giovani*, pp. 18–40 and its bibliography, not to mention her article in this volume.

Our choice of clothes has always been determined, at least in part, by our desire to attract attention, often of a sexual nature. Older persons tend to remain faithful to the styles that were in vogue in their youth, while younger persons are attracted to novelty. As a result, the way young people dress often draws to them the fury of older, more conservative persons.[11] Saint Bernardino of Siena did not hold himself back when he launched his attacks against the new styles of male attire coming into fashion in fifteenth-century Italy. He spoke directly to the young men in his audience and scolded them saying:

> You, young man, I want to start with you. When you go about wearing tight hose on your legs, with laces all around it, with your leg exposed, and your hose undone and broken, and your little doublet riding up to your belly, with this behaviour you clearly show what you are. In the same way when you return home, you take your doublet off in front of sisters and sisters-in-law and your female relatives, and they see all sorts of filth, and with this sometimes one goes on to other things. . . . You, young man, don't you care about anything? Know that God does not like it when you wear hose, or the way you wear it, with the leg open or cut up, and with your little doublet so short that it nearly shows . . .'[12]

Young men, in fact, usually wore a doublet, a tight-fitting vest that elegantly outlined the chest and reached a little under the belt. Together with a pair of hose with soles it was often sufficient not only for common people (*popolani*), but also for younger youths and for men engaged in sport. A doublet lay open at the front, much like today's jackets, and was padded. In the entire fifteenth century, it was worn both in private and in public contexts, both in formal and in informal situations.[13]

A drawing attributed to Maso Finiguerra shows how Florentine youths dressed around the year 1450 (fig. 2). Under their cloak they wore a very short doublet, tied at the front; the doublet came with eyelets and

---

[11] Levi Pisetzky, *Il costume e la moda nella società italiana*, pp. 36–37.

[12] 'O giovano, io mi voglio un poco cominciare a te. Quando tu vai co la gamba tirata, stringato intorno, a gamba rotta, e a calza sbarlata e fessa, e 'l farsettino al bellico; per certo che a questi portamenti tu dimostri d'essare quello che tu se'. Così quando tu torni in casa, tu ti trai la giornea fra suore e cognate e parenti, dove si possono spechiare in ogni ribaldaria; e per questo si viene talvolta a altro. . . . O giovinozzo, che non ti curi di nulla, sappi che a Dio non piace che tu porti la calza, come tu la porti, a gamba rotta o fessa, con salsa verde, e col farsettino tanto corto, che presso che si mostra . . .' Bernardino, *Le prediche volgari*, vol. 3, Sermon 37, 'Come ogni cosa di questo mondo è vanità,' p. 189.

[13] Morelli, 'Fogge, ornamenti e tecniche,' pp. 77–96.

ribbons used to hold up the two stockings or hose which, in fact, were not joined together at the groin. The shortness of the doublet had the inconvenience of exposing, between one stocking and the other, the puff of the shirt in a way that was not considered proper.[14]

A detail from a panel painting by Giovanni di Ser Giovanni depicting the game of the *civettino* ('the little owl') shows what young men wore when playing games or sports (fig. 3).[15] The aim of the game was to avoid the opponent's slaps while holding down his feet. In this image there are three contenders and the young man in the middle has successfully immobilized his two opponents. The young men wear doublets and hose, the most comfortable and suitable outfit for such activities. The painting also reveals quite nicely how the stockings were attached to the doubled by way of strings with metal tips (*agugelli*) that would be threaded through the eyelets in the doublet; here, they are fashioned in a colour contrasting with the hose and hang from the doublet.[16] Lastly, the panel illustrates how such garments and such games could easily let intimate apparel come into public view.

The game of *civettino* must generally have been played in doublet and hose. In a woodcut depicting *Activities in the Sun*, from the *Series of the Planets* attributed either to Baccio Baldini or to Maso Finiguerra,[17] the two contestants and the other youths 'children of the planet' practising their sports are, in fact, wearing outfits identical to those in the panel by Giovanni di Ser Giovanni.

The aesthetic inconvenience (not to mention the moral one for preachers of the time) caused by the two separate stockings and the short doublet is even more evident in Giovanni di Ser Giovanni's fresco of The Martyrdom of Saint Sebastian for the church of San Lorenzo in San Giovanni Valdarno (fig. 4).[18] The adult knave arming his bow leans forward and reveals how the two separate stockings are fixed to the doublet; at the same time, he also reveals his naked thigh, his shirt, and his underwear.

---

[14] Muzzarelli, *Guardaroba medievale*, p. 268. On the drawing, see *Gabinetto disegni e stampe degli Uffizi. Inventario Disegni di figura*, 1:21–22.

[15] c. 1450 (Museo di Palazzo Davanzati, Florence). The panel was once part of a *desco da parto*; see *Il fratello di Masaccio*, pp. 73–74.

[16] Baldi/Peri, 'Dal "farsetto" al "giustacuore,"' p. 86.

[17] The work is datable to c. 1460. See Hind, Early Italian Engravings, 1:77–82; vol. 3, figs. 120–21; and Zucker, *The Illustrated Bartsch*, XXIV, *Commentary*, Part 1, pp. 89–102, 111–12.

[18] The work is signed and dated 1457. See *Il fratello di Masaccio*, p. 76.

From these various images we can conclude that, generally, upper class males wore their hose tightly tied to their doublet while lower class males kept it more loosely tied or even let it fall untied, possibly to allow greater freedom of movement.

The short doublet used by young men was also worn by very small children, but without the added benefit of underwear, as can be seen in a cassone frontal by Giovanni di Ser Giovanni depicting the *Stories of Chaste Susanna* (fig. 5).[19] The two boys playing with the dog are wearing a doublet and a pair of hose, but not any underwear, thus leaving their genitals and rear end exposed to view. This reminds us that in an age before diapers nudity was the most convenient and practical way of dealing with the scatological need of children.

A detail from Luca Signorelli's *The End of the World* (Cappella di San Brizio, Duomo, Orvieto), a 1499 fresco depicting the end of the world, illustrates the codpiece (*braghetta*) very well (fig. 6). This was a sack which, sewn at the groin, was originally meant to solve the problem of the shirt puff protruding below the belt and between the upper parts of the two stockings. It was a solution, however, that quickly became worse than the problem, for wearers quickly took to decorating and padding their codpiece—the organ was thus concealed, but at the same time it was brought to the attention of the viewer with unabashed suggestions as to its size and consequent allusions as to its owner's sexual prowess and virility. Rosita Levi Pisetzky holds that such allusions were too crude to be viewed as courtship allurements and suggests, instead that the codpiece was symbolic of male superiority.[20] Others, instead, have seen the codpiece as a symbol of malehood, procreative ability, and so forth.[21]

The erotic implications of the codpiece are evident in a painting for the underside of a wedding chest lid now at the Museo Horne in Florence (fig. 7). Images of naked or elegantly dressed young men were often painted in such locations as an alluring and auspicious message of fertility for the newlyweds whose wedding had prompted the commission for the *cassone*.[22] Because such chests usually came in matching pairs, the figures under the two lids would often complement one another. In the panel from

---

[19] c. 1450 (Museo di Palazzo Davanzati, Firenze); *Il fratello di Masaccio*, pp. 66–67.

[20] Levi Pisetzky, *Il costume e la moda nella società italiana*, p. 40.

[21] Eisenbichler, 'Agnolo Bronzino's Portrait of Guidobaldo II della Rovere'; Persels, 'Bragueta Humanistica'; Simons, 'Alert and Erect.'

[22] For the use of alluring images on the underside of wedding chest lids, see Paolini, 'La camera da letto tra Quattro e Cinquecento,' pp. 39–40.

the Museo Horne the languidly stretched figure of Paris by an unknown Florentine artist (c. 1470) sports a codpiece that might well be a phallic symbol. The matching *cassone* probably had a reclining figure of Helen on the underside of its lid.

Formal, loose-fitting clothes 'for above' were worn on top of these informal tight-fitting clothes 'for underneath.' In Giovanni di Ser Giovanni's *Stories of Chaste Susanna*, the setting has been changed from ancient Israel to contemporary Florence (fig. 8). Susanna steps into the scene with dignified bearing and attracts the admiration of several young men dressed in formal robes—*cioppe* and *giornee*. The *giornea* was an elegant overgarment not limited to youths, but certainly considered 'youthful' attire. It was open at the sides and held in by a belt so as to form tight regular folds. Saint Bernardino, addressing himself to young men once again, firmly censored this garment saying:

> Have you considered how the *giornea* is made? It's made like a small blanket for horses, with fringes at its sides and at its feet, and so you wear clothes just like an animal. This means that on the outside you are a dressed up animal. Judging from the fact that you dress like an animal on the outside, one can assume that you must be an animal on the inside as well.[23]

The young Tobias in a painting from the workshop of Verrocchio is depicted as a youth advancing with sure step, so much so that his short cape turned back over his shoulder reveals a very elegant example of the short skirt worn with the doublet.[24] The artist has taken special care in depicting the youth's long, well groomed blonde hair. At the beginning of the fifteenth century youths had worn their hair half-way down their ear, a style that was exclusively theirs. Later in the century, youths wore

---

[23] 'Hai tu posto mente come la giornea è fatta? Ella è fatta come una covertina di cavallo co le frappe da lato e da piè, sicché tu porti il vestire a modo che la bestia. Viene a dire che tu sei una bestia vestita da la parte di fuore: puossi giudicare a vederti vestito come la bestia, che tu debbi essare dentro come una bestia.' Bernardino, *Le prediche volgari*, vol. 3, Sermon 37, 'Come ogni cosa di questo mondo è vanità,' p. 189.

[24] c. 1470–75 (National Gallery, London); see Baker/Henry, *The National Gallery*, p. 707. We find a large number of depictions of the young Tobias (or Tobiolo) with the Archangel Raphael in Tuscany, possibly because he or the archangel were seen as suitable protectors for the sons of merchant families who were sent on long and occasionally dangerous business trips north of the Alps. Such paintings thus became devotional commissions. In the Florentine iconology, the young Tobias is usually depicted as a teen-aged youth. Schaeffer, *Das Florentiner Bildnis*, pp. 80–84.

their hair longer and, as this painting reveals, carefully curled the tips. Preachers immediately attacked this fashion and urged youths to 'keep your hair a proper length.'[25]

Although normally young men wore clothes peculiar to them, on official occasions, upper class males did not wear garments that differentiated them by age from their older or younger kin. Thus, in a painting attributed to Giovanni di Ser Giovanni depicting a *Dancing Scene* (fig. 9), both the young men dancing and the young boy in the background are shown wearing open robes (*giornee*).[26] Even the figure that, according to local tradition, embodies the idealized portrait of Lorenzo de' Medici in Benozzo Gozzoli's *Procession of the Magi* wears a *cioppa*, as do other, and older, males in the same procession (fig. 10).[27] The same is true in Benozzo Gozzoli's frescoes on the life of Saint Augustine.[28] The scene where Augustine is brought by his parents to Tagaste's school (fig. 11) shows older males such as the father and the teachers dressed in thick garments with long furs down to their ankles while the children are shown dressed in wide, sober, knee-long robes (both *cioppe* and *giornee*). These garments were thus clearly tied not only to specific age groups, but also to specific circumstances and activities. In this case, sober garments are worn by both adults and youths to reflect the dignity and solemnity appropriate to the first day of school.

As these sample images have shown, there was a precise distinction in fashion and dress between adolescent and adult males in fifteenth-century Florence. Informal garments were worn only by youths, while formal garments were worn by all age groups. In the case of formal garments, differentiation by age was to be found in the type of materials used, not in the style of the garment itself. Sumptuary legislation, which sought to regulate public morality and reduce wasteful spending,

---

[25] 'mantenere e capelli a misura.' The phrase is from Friar Domenico da Pescia, Savonarola's appointee to oversee the reformation of Florentine youths; see his 'Epistola' fol. 3r (also cited in Schnitzer, *Savonarolas Erzieher*, p. 137).

[26] The detail is from the so-called Cassone Adimari, c. 1440–50, now at the Galleria dell'Accademia, Florence. Laura Cavazzini has shown that this panel was not the front of a wedding chest, as had been believed till now, but a panel for a bed's headboard; see *Il fratello di Masaccio*, pp. 58–61.

[27] Dated to 1459–63 (Palazzo Medici-Riccardi, Florence). On the persons actually portrayed in this fresco see Acidini Luchinat, 'Medici e cittadini,' pp. 363–70.

[28] Dated to 1464–65 (Duomo, San Gimignano). On this fresco cycle, see *Benozzo Gozzoli in Toscana*, pp. 59–68.

restricted the use of expensive materials or of certain colours (rose or purple) to older men. The sumptuary legislation of 1504 thus forbade men under the age of eighteen from wearing garments made of satin (*drappo*), silk, or goat or camel chamois (*ciambellotto*), but allowed youths aged eighteen to thirty to use silk or satin for their jackets and chamois for any type of head covering.[29]

While fifteenth-century youths drew furious reprimands from contemporary moralists because of their revealing doublets and hose, a century later, however, they were seen as models of purity and simplicity. The sixteenth-century historian of costume Cesare Vecellio praised them in his own *laudatio temporis acti* saying: 'the young men of that time were so upright and so alien from any malice that they kept their distance from any carnal pleasure until the age of thirty, pure and uncorrupted.' He had come to this view 'because, from the garments they wore, one cannot reach any other conclusion,' but he then qualified it with the phrase 'as one might believe.' Vecellio illustrated his words with a drawing of a youth dressed in hose and doublet, but with two rectangular pieces of cloth hanging in front of him to cover and hide his codpiece or his sexual attributes (fig. 12).[30] A century after the appearance of tight-fitting clothes that characterized the dress style of dashing young men in fifteenth-century Florence, local moralists had clearly forgotten the scandals and censures such a style had raised among their predecessors.

*Università degli Studi di Firenze*

*(Translated by Konrad Eisenbichler)*

---

[29] 'Item che a giovani insino alla età d'anni XVIII forniti sia prohibito portare veste e ornamento d'alcuna sorte di drappo, ne ciambellotti o stete [sic, for 'sete'] et da anni 18 insino in XXX forniti sia loro prohibito portare dette veste o ornamento di drappo et stete [sic] salvo che possino portare giubboni di steta [sic] o raso o dommascho non prohibito et salvo che e' possino portare qualunque veste di ciambellotto alloro piacimento. Possino ancora tutti detti giovani di qualunque età portare uno lucho soppannato di taffettà non prohibito.' ASF, *Provvisioni. Registri*, 206, fol. 15r.

[30] Vecellio, *Habiti antichi et moderni di tutto il mondo*, n. 53. 'De gli habiti della gioventù antica.' At n. 54 the figure is shown from the back.

Fig. 1.   Workshop of Domenico Ghirlandaio. *The Buonomini Distribute Clothes to the Poor*, fresco, c. 1482. Florence, Oratorio dei Buonomini di San Martino.

Fig. 2.   Maso Finiguerra (attr.). *David*, pen, watercolour, pencil,
c. 1450. Florence, Gabinetto Disegni e Stampe degli
Uffizi 42F.

Fig. 3.    Giovanni di Ser Giovanni, called lo Scheggia. *The Game of Civettino*, desco da parto, c. 1450. Florence, Museo di Palazzo Davanzati.

Fig. 4.    Giovanni di Ser Giovanni, called lo Scheggia. *The Martyrdom of St Sebastian*, fresco, signed and dated 1457. San Giovanni Valdarno, Chiesa di San Lorenzo.

Fig. 5.    Giovanni di Ser Giovanni, called lo Scheggia. *Stories of Chaste Susanna*, cassone front, c. 1450, detail. Florence, Museo di Palazzo Davanzati.

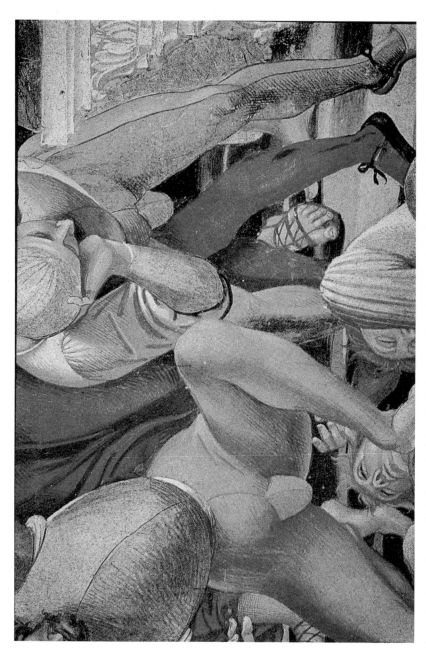

Fig. 6.   Luca Signorelli, *The End of the World*, fresco, 1499. Orvieto, Cattedrale, Cappella di San Brizio.

Fig. 7.    Unknown Florentine artist. *Paris*, inside panel of a cassone lid, c. 1470. Florence, Museo della Fondazione Horne.

Fig. 8.    Giovanni di Ser Giovanni, called lo Scheggia. *Stories of Chaste Susanna*, cassone front, c. 1450. Florence, Museo di Palazzo Davanzati.

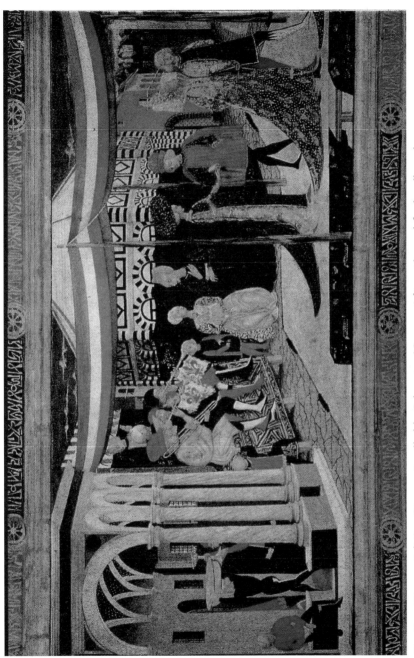

Fig. 9.    Giovanni di Ser Giovanni, called lo Scheggia. 'Cassone Adimari', panel for headboard, c. 1440–1450. Florence, Galleria dell'Accademia.

Fig. 10. Benozzo Gozzoli, *Idealized Portrait of Lorenzo the Magnificent*, fresco, 1459–1463. Florence, Palazzo Medici Riccardi, Cappella.

Fig. 11. Benozzo Gozzoli, *Augustine Brought by his Parents to Tagaste's School*, fresco, 1464–1465. San Gimignano, Chiesa di Sant'Agostino, Choir.

Giouentù antica.

Fig. 12. '*On the Dress of Youths of Olden Times,*' woodcut in Cesare
    Vecellio, *Habiti antichi et moderni di tutto il mondo,*
    Venezia: Appresso i Sessa, 1589, n. 53.

# Cited Works
## Manuscript Sources

ASF. Firenze, Archivio di Stato. *Provvisioni. Registri*, 187, 206

## Published Sources

Acidini Luchinat, Cristina. 'Medici e cittadini nei cortei dei Re Magi: ritratti di una società' pp. 363–70 in *Benozzo Gozzoli. La Cappella dei Magi*, ed. Cristina Acidini Luchinat. Milano: Electa 1993.

Ariès, Philippe. *Centuries of Childhood: A Social History of Family Life*, trans. Robert Baldick. New York: Vintage Books, 1962.

Baker, Cristopher and Tom Henry. *The National Gallery. Complete Illustrated Catalogue*. London: National Gallery Publications, 1995.

Baldi, Patrizia and Paolo Peri. 'Dal "farsetto" al "giustacuore"' pp. 83–93 in *Il costume nell'età del Rinascimento*, ed. Dora Liscia Bemporad. Firenze: Edifir, 1988.

*Benozzo Gozzoli in Toscana*, ed. Anna Padoa Rizzo. Firenze: Octavo, 1997.

Bernardino of Siena, St. *Le prediche volgari di San Bernardino da Siena dette nella piazza del Campo l'anno MCCCCXXVII*, ed. Luciano Banchi. 3 vols. Siena: Tip. Edit. all'inseg. di S. Bernardino, 1880–88.

Birbari, Elizabeth. *Dress in Italian Painting, 1460–1500*. London: John Murray, 1975.

Domenico da Pescia. *Epistola di Frate Domenico da Pescia mandata ai fanciulli fiorentini*. Florentiae: In sancto Marco, 1497.

Eisenbichler, Konrad. 'Agnolo Bronzino's Portrait of Guidobaldo II della Rovere' *Renaissance and Reformation* 24:1 (1988): 21–33.

Fiorentini Capitani, Aurora and Stefania Ricci. 'Considerazioni sull' abbigliamento del Quattrocento in Toscana' pp. 51–75 in *Il costume al tempo di Pico e di Lorenzo il Magnifico*. Exhibition catalogue, ed. Aurora Fiorentini Capitani, Vittorio Erlindo, and Stefania Ricci. (Mirandola, 27 febbraio–1 maggio 1994) Milano: Charta, 1994.

*Gabinetto disegni e stampe degli Uffizi. Inventario Disegni di figura*, ed. Anna Maria Petrioli Tofani. 3 vols. Firenze: Olschki, 1886–91.

Hind, Arthur Mayger. *Early Italian Engravings*. 2 vols. London: M. Knoedler & Company / New York: Bernard Quaritch Ltd, 1938.

*Il fratello di Masaccio. Giovanni di Ser Giovanni detto lo Scheggia*. Exhibition catalogue, ed. Laura Cavazzini (San Giovanni Valdarno, 14 febbraio–16 maggio 1999). Firenze: Maschietto & Musolino, 1999.

Levi Pisetzky, Rosita. *Storia del costume in Italia*, vol. 2, *Il Trecento e il Quattrocento*. Milano: Istituto Editoriale Italiano / Fondazione G. Treccani, 1964.

Levi Pisetzky, Rosita. *Il costume e la moda nella società italiana*. Torino: Einaudi, 1978.

Merkel, Carlo. *Come vestivano gli uomini del Decameron*. Roma: n.p., 1898.

Morelli, Ornella. 'Fogge, ornamenti e tecniche. Qualche appunto sulla storia materiale dell'abito nel Quattrocento' pp. 77–96 in *Il costume al tempo di Pico e di Lorenzo il Magnifico*. Exhibition catalogue, ed. Aurora Fiorentini Capitani, Vittorio Erlindo, Stefania Ricci. (Mirandola, 27 febbraio–1 maggio 1994) Milano: Charta, 1994.

Muzzarelli, Maria Giuseppina, *Gli inganni delle apparenze. Disciplina di vesti e ornamenti alla fine del Medioevo*. Torino: Scriptorium, 1996.

Muzzarelli, Maria Giuseppina, *Guardaroba medievale. Vesti e società dal XIII al XVI secolo*. Bologna: Il Mulino, 1999.

Paolini, Claudio. 'La camera da letto tra Quattro e Cinquecento: arredi e vita privata' pp. 27–45 in *Itinerari nella casa fiorentina del Rinascimento*, ed. Elisabetta Nardinocchi. Firenze: Fondazione Herbert Percy Horne, 1994.

Persels, Jeffery C. 'Bragueta Humanistica, or, Humanism's Codpiece' *Sixteenth Century Journal* 28:1 (1997) 79–99.

Pugliese, Olga Zorzi. 'Lo statuto "riformato" dei Buonomini di S. Martino. Riflessioni del pensiero rinascimentale in un documento confraternale' *Rinascimento* 31 (1991): 261–80.

Schaeffer, Emil. *Das Florentiner Bildnis*. München: F. Bruckman, 1904.

Schnitzer, Joseph. *Savonarolas Erzieher und Savonarola als Erzieher*. Berlin: Protestantischer Schriftenvertrieb, 1913.

Simons, Patricia. 'Alert and Erect: Masculinity in Some Italian Renaissance Portraits of Fathers and Sons' pp. 163–86 in *Gender Rhetorics. Postures of Dominance and Submission in History*, ed. Richard C. Trexler. Binghamton, NY: Medieval & Renaissance Texts & Studies, 1994.

Spicciani, Amleto, 'The "poveri vergognosi" in Fifteenth-Century Florence: The First 30 Years' Activity of the Buonomini di San Martino' pp. 119–72 in *Aspects of Poverty in Early Modern Europe*, ed. by Thomas Riis. Publications of the European University Institute, 10. Stuttgart: Klett-Cotta, 1981.

Taddei, Ilaria. *Fanciulli e giovani. Crescere a Firenze nel Rinascimento*. Doctoral dissertation, Istituto Universitario Europeo, 1998; forthcoming, Firenze: Olschki, 2001.

Vecellio, Cesare. *Habiti antichi et moderni di tutto il mondo*, Venetia: appresso i Sessa, 1598.

Zucker, Mark J. *The Illustrated Bartsch*, XXIV, *Commentary*, Part 1, Pleasantville New York: Abaris Books, 1993.

# 'Thus *Will* Giovani *Do.*'
# *Jewish Youth Sub-Culture in Early Modern Italy*

## Roni Weinstein

How did Jewish young men and women respond to the patterns of community life in early modern Italy? Did they cross the inter-religious lines, so marked and emphasized in other circumstances? Was there an adaptation, or 'Jewish' version, of the long liminal phase that men, in particular, underwent prior to marriage? The Jewish-Italian case in the sixteenth and seventeenth centuries can serve well to resolve these queries thanks, in part, to the surprisingly impressive amount of documentation at our disposal. Juridic sources form the bulk of this resource, either as Responsa literature (*Sifrut She'elot u-Tshuvot*) or as court decisions. Responsa were written by an authoritative rabbi whenever cases could not be resolved on a local basis and needed the intervention of learned and respected personalities. In most of the cases the 'question', or the event giving rise to the legal doubt, is more interesting than the response or legal commentary on it, for it unintentionally reveals fascinating practices common among Jewish youths. The legal commentary can also be of interest, however, reflecting the reaction of educated adults to the questionable behaviour of the young. Other kinds of sources such as Cabalistic tracts and 'moral literature' point to the cultural and social stereotypes of contemporary Jewish communities. The thousands of surviving letters, mostly composed in Hebrew rather than in Italian, written either as real letters or as literary exercises, reveal intimate details about daily practices and, what is most uncommon in the contemporary Jewish context, they discuss personal feelings. Other types of literary sources—stories, novelle, plays, dialogues, poetry—also reveal the hidden tensions of private life. Finally, commentaries on sacred canonical texts and in particular on the comportment of young biblical heros could be seen as another illustration of how *giovani* acted in general, for past and present blended easily and allowed for the attribution of contemporary motives even to ancient persons. This impressive amount of documentation is thus our starting point.

Jewish communities in Renaissance Italy had acquired a typically urban character. Because of their involvement in money lending, in the fifteenth and sixteenth centuries Jews lived in hundreds of small cities as well as in the large urban centres of northern Italy. Growing criticism of their economic occupation and the establishment of *Monti di pietà* led in many cases to the cancellation of the *condotta*, that is, of the contract regulating the conditions of their presence in Italian cities. This, in turn, led to their expulsion. Jews living in small towns thus emigrated into the larger communities in the major urban centres of Italy.[1] Here, the enforced closure into ghettos in the sixteenth and seventeenth centuries unexpectedly provided Jews with a distinct urban space of their own, similar in some ways to the other *quartieri*, or neighbourhoods, of the city, and this enabled them to conduct a relatively independent life.[2]

The presence of young unmarried men within these separate spaces could not be ignored. Many had left home at a young age to pursue several years of religious studies in Jewish institutions of higher education (*Yeshivot*). Others, less gifted for arduous study, had already started working as apprentices under the supervision of Jewish craftsmen and businessmen or in families.[3] Whether studying or working, young men and women left their parental home at about thirteen, an age considered in Jewish legal tradition as starting point of adulthood.

During the long years of their youth men would spent most of their free time together in peer-groups. A letter from 10 July 1560 talks of the pastimes of such a group:

> My dearest son, may God protect him, has undoubtedly written to you from Rome about what happened to him in the previous month, while going to the *borgo* with his group of companions to see the wonders of nature shown in Castel Sant'Angelo—fireworks, lightening, burning flames—as is the custom every year on the celebrations of St. Peter's. And it happened that a firework passed near his face with great and enormous speed and the fire almost burned his eyes, God forbid. And the young man was shocked and frightened, and instantly two of his companions held him up under his arms [and helped him] enter the house, for he was like an infant with no sight for two days and nights, and his eyes could not see. And many medications were used . . . and his eyes gained their sight, praised be the Lord . . . Blessed

---

[1] Bonfil, 'The Settlement in Italy of Immigrating Jews,' passim.

[2] Weinstein, '*Segregatos non autem eiectos*,' pp. 93–100 and 'The Jewish Ghetto in Relation to Urban Quarters in Italian Cities,' pp. 12–14 and 19–21.

[3] *The Jews of Rome*, vol. 2, n. 1025; Horowitz, 'Masters and Women Servants in Jewish Society,' pp. 204–11.

be He that has granted us a miracle, I shall always praise God, for he has benefited us greatly.[4]

From this concerned father's letter we learn that a group of young Jewish men had left their neighbourhood to go see the religious festivities for St. Peter's. Given Jewish religious law, we cannot consider this an innocent visit, for it is strictly forbidden for Jews to participate or witness idolatrous rituals. Since the early Middle Ages, Christian rites were considered by Jews to be idolatrous, primarily because of the use of icons and the Eucharist. To attend the celebrations of the city's patron saint (who was, furthermore, a central figure in the Christian tradition) and to go so near the Vatican was a daring act that crossed religious boundaries and infringed Jewish prohibitions. However, neither the letter writer nor the 'group of companions' thought for a moment that they needed to justify the visit. It must have seemed a normal event to them. Were it not for the accident and the miraculous recovery, the event would not have been documented. We can only wonder how many such visits, more peaceful and less dangerous, went unnoticed.

As we can infer from this letter, young men spending their bachelor years together were not always law abiding. Not only did they break laws, but occasionally also became involved in violent actions. Although the urge to express their virility and physical strength could at times be turned against the community,[5] their occasional acts of violence were more generally directed against their own peers. Ritual battles with stones and other handy weapons, well documented among the Italian Christian population, can also be found among Jewish youths.[6] In his autobiography, Rabbi Yehudah Arie de Modena (Leone Modena, 1571–1648) described the death of his son as the result of an act of violence among youths. The young man, who lived with his family in the Venetian ghetto, had had a disagreement with a gang of Jewish youths. When they chased him with swords, he managed to injure one of them slightly and escape the rest. Some time later the group sent another young man to

---

[4] *Letters of Jews in Italy*, n. 136, pp. 182–83. This letter, like the others, is written in Hebrew. The various allusion to canonic sources, mainly biblical, were not translated literally, but according to the context. Here and elsewhere (unless indicated otherwise), all translations are mine.

[5] For a possible allusion of juvenile violence against the local synagogue, see Sonne, 'Some Contributions for the History of the Jews in Verona,' p. 132.

[6] *The Jews in Piedmont*, vol. 2, n. 2151. For violence among the young, see Niccoli, *Il seme della violenza* and also the collection *Infanzie* that she edited.

lure him out of his home and come downstairs where the entire group, waiting for him with knives in their hands, proceeded to stab him. At the youth's death bed, the father could only cry out for revenge (*vendetta*).[7]

Participation in peer groups of *giovani* could last many years, but eventually such participation and *gioventù* itself came to an end with marriage. The approaching marriage ceremony was thus a suitable time for a young man to begin the process of separation from his friends.

> I heard the voices of celebrating people in your holy camp, voices of matrimonial joy, for a beloved stands at your right. You have set a date for your joyous day a few days away . . . And now, by brother,[8] turn your grace to your acquaintances, my brothers and my people, all faithful allies of yours: before your marriage ride here to Siena for ten days and you shall have daily enjoyments and benefit from the glory of our love, and in your light we—your servants—shall see light as well. Do remember, that after entering the tent of the Gazelle you are about to take, you will always fall for her love, and you will not be able to go out, but will follow her, *for thus will giovani do.* And therefore my brother and superior, only this time may your carriage lead you to celebrate the coming feast of Passover with us, and you will remain some days. Maybe you and I will decide to return together to Bologna as brothers, wherever you stay I shall stay . . . Please my brother, bear with me this time and come, in the grace of God.[9]

The writer knows well that marriage is the liminal moment after which the addressee would not be the same legally or socially and, consequently, will not behave the same towards his ex-peers. The letter is replete with erotic allusions ('we shall have daily enjoyments and benefit from the glory of our love . . . wherever you stay I shall stay'), suggesting that the intimate relations with the new wife will replace masculine comradeship and friendship. Indeed the prophecy would fulfil itself, for after marriage the new husband was rebuked for neglecting his former friends:

---

[7] Modena, *The Autobiography of A Seventeenth-Century Venetian Rabbi*, pp. 118–22. For other cases of physical violence among the young in the Jewish quarter, see *The Jews of Rome*, vol. 1, nos. 40, 165 and vol. 2, n. 1599.

[8] 'Brother' in this context is an appellation of friendship, not kinship proximity.

[9] *Letters of Rieti Family*, n. 171, pp. 198–99 (emphasis added). I translate the Hebrew term *bachurim* (unmarried young men) as *giovani* (youths). Other terms in Hebrew describing juvenile years, such as *tze'irim* or *ne'arim*, do not carry the same semantic meaning.

for this reason my eyes are sour, being afraid that you would let your pencil fall asleep . . . so that we would no longer see your handwriting, not even two letters combined together. The courtship of your companion and beloved carries you away, keeping you far from your previous thoughts, for you have become a new creature . . . the earth of your joy has opened its mouth to swallow your previous intentions, and as you cast the memory of your [previous] teachers and friends into the abyss of oblivion, moss eats them.[10]

Not only young persons found it difficult to separate from their friends, but parents as well refused at times to let go of their children. Some continued their tutorship over their sons until they reached the age of twenty five, well beyond marriage age in Jewish-Italian society.[11] It seems that the passage to adulthood was not as straightforward as suggested by contemporaries and entailed several phases of socialization in community life and family responsibilities.

The marriage process itself consisted of three major phases: matchmaking (*shiduchin*), engagement (*kidushin*), and matrimony (*nisu'in*). The first entailed finding a proper partner that suited family requirements. Then, financial and status conditions were negotiated, agreed and signed in a legal contract. Unlike Jewish communities elsewhere in Europe, Italian communities separated engagement from marriage day. Engagement was a simple legal act binding the couple into a state similar to marriage that could be annulled only by formal divorce. The ritual was performed in the presence of ten adult men, including at least two of the bride's family members. Because this phase was at the core of the Italian ritual, it remained an independent phase on the road to marriage. Matrimony was the official day to celebrate and present the couple's new status in front of guests and the day for their first sexual encounter.[12] Until the mid seventeenth century marriage remained a private event, held under the supervision and direction of the family, with no rabbis or community officials necessarily present.

---

10 *Letters of Rieti Family*, n. 172, pp. 199–200.

11 Oxford, C. Roth Collection, MS 210, fols. 43r–44v. The same tendency to limit young men's independence until the age of twenty five can be detected in other communities; see *The Jews in the Duchy of Milan*, vol. 3, nos. 3427–28, 3520, 3662, 3724, 3811, and *The Jews of Umbria*, vol. 3, nos. 1939, 2162.

12 For a more detailed discussion of these three stages, see Weinstein, 'Rituel du mariage et culture des jeunes', pp. 458–459.

The Jewish *giovani* had their own version of this process. Instead of letting their parents and families chose their future partner, they engaged in independent courtship activity that included secret meetings, love letters, and different types of erotic activity. In order to confirm their commitment they would not hesitate to recur to 'secret engagements' (*kidushei seter*), as the adults called them. The story of Salomé could be viewed as emblematic of this type of independent courting and commitment:

> Shlomit [= Salomé] acted against the Jewish religion,[13] speaking with every person in the market, showing her arms to everybody; even men have come to her gates . . . so much so that some persons have come to the rabbi complaining that she winks with her eyes and hints with her lips to bachelors around her window. And the rabbi saw her playing with them from one window to the other, especially playing love-games [*hitalsa be-ahavim*] with Zimri. According to the people, they had sworn to marry each other. Since her father did not know of the vow she had made, he matched her to Naftali. Still, Zimri keeps coming to her door day and night and she fearlessly converses with him, so much so that jealousy gripped Naftali and he was angry with her three times and more. Now there is no peace between him and her because of ugly things said to him [about her], and because of her passion for her lover.[14]

Salomé is described in a manner intended to vilify her. Because women, especially those of marriageable age, were not allowed to stroll in the streets, she was kept well guarded at home. However, because she did not want to miss the opportunity to meet young men, Salomé set herself in a liminal place, at a window or a balcony, between the street with its temptations and the house with its restrictions. Here she conversed with different suitors. With one she became so intimate and trustful that they formed an engagement ('According to the people, they had sworn to marry each other'). Confrontation with the father and his chosen husband for her was inevitable. The prospective groom confronted Salomé because he felt his masculine honour had been infringed. Since there was no room for more than one man in this situation, Naftali eventually abandoned Salomé.

The story reflects customary aspects of Jewish youth sub-culture, including active female participation. Young women were not passive

---

[13] 'Acted against Jewish religion' is a Talmudic expression, meaning behaved immodestly.

[14] Ferrara, Comunità Israelitica, MS 24, unpaginated. The protagonists' names in this responsum, as in most of the cases, are fictional.

persons in the encounter between the sexes, but used their power as best they could to attract suitors or oppose unwanted candidates advanced by their parents. Even after the match-making stage was over they could refuse to fulfil family commitments or to proceed to the marriage stage with an unwanted candidate.[15] The fact that marriage was unacceptable and uncommon in Jewish-Italian communities for young girls who were still minors enhanced the position of those young women, who, like Salomé, preferred to choose their husbands on their own.

However, in both Jewish and Christian communities a young woman's independent behaviour could be problematic. If her reputation was tarnished in any way, her value on the 'marriage market' dropped significantly and the collective honour of her entire family was affected. Jewish men responded to such fears not by confining young women completely, but by setting conditions on outdoor female sociability. The father of a young bride, for example, could ask his new son-in-law to allow the bride to stroll in the streets with her female friends.[16] This, however, does not indicate a continued presence of marriageable young women in public spaces first because women left their house less often than adolescent males and second because their movement in public space was subject to stricter controls. In Verona, for example, women were not allowed to stroll in groups larger than four.[17] Presence of adolescent males, on the other hand, was unavoidable in public spaces. One could hardly ignore them as they strolled in groups in the narrow streets of the ghetto or in its central piazza. While they set their eyes on available young women, their young male servants sought out the company of women servants, alluring them to join their company.[18] The vitality of the *giovani* and their behaviour can be

---

[15] New York, Columbia University, MS X893T67, n. 131: 'I was asked about Reuven who matched his son to Rachel, daughter of the late Simon, and she was an adult [= older than twelve years of age, and therefore of marriageable age and with legal responsibility]. She was betrothed and remained thus for several years. And now Reuven asks to continue with the marriage and she refuses, has a rebellious spirit, and does not want to marry.' In another case, the father supported his daughter in her wish not to accept an unbeloved partner; see Los Angeles, University Library, MS 779 bx.4.7, fol. 2v. For further discussion of this pattern, see Stow, 'Innovation by Conservatism,' pp. 131–33.

[16] *Letters of Jews in Italy*, n. 205, p. 260; *Letters of Jewish Teachers*, n. 162, p. 302.

[17] *Minute Book of the Jewish Community of Verona*, n. 446, 2:393.

[18] A fascinating description of courtship among Jewish servants can be found in

gleaned from a play composed for *Purim*, the Jewish equivalent of Carnival, by Yehuda Sommo (Leone de' Sommi, c.1525–c.1590) entitled *Zachut Bedichutah deKidushin*, (*A Comedy of Betrothal*).[19] The work provides a glimpse into the social life of an Italian Jewish community in the late sixteenth century. In a manner reminiscent of contemporary Italian comedy, it exposes the social mechanisms at work in the creation of a new couple. Its main protagonists are young men and women usually excluded from positions of influence. They disrespect their parents' will and arrange secret meetings, exchange love letters, and even indulge in pre-marital sex. Parents have only partial control over their children and both sides wage a battle of schemes and counter-schemes to bring their own plans to fruition.

Indeed, adults could not avoid meeting the Jewish *giovani* in public spaces. What was their interaction? Was this juvenile sub-culture considered a legitimate part of Jewish local heritage? In what sense? The attitude of older persons towards their younger folk was clearly ambivalent. In their commentaries on sacred canonical texts alluding to adolescents (biblical stories or the tract *Pirkei Avot*) contemporary Jewish scholars and rabbis reiterated the negative stereotype of youth as frivolous, sinful, violent, and inclined to unbridled behaviour. In the Responsa literature or in legal cases dealing with 'secret marriages' young men in general were described as lacking reason and even a minimal sense of responsibility.[20] In practice young men were denied any positions of influence in community life or in religious rituals conducted in the synagogue. The Christian-Italian view of youths was, on the other hand, far from such univocal denigration. There, the young were seen as regenerative of society and as a link to the world beyond. In the case of children, especially, their behaviour was used as a portent of future political events and their innocence exalted alongside the growing cult of the Child Jesus. In contrast to this, the Jewish cultural stereotype of youth was completely negative.

*Letters of Rieti Family*, nos. 296–99, pp. 314–19.

[19] Sommi, *Zachut Bedichutah deKidushin*; for the English translation, see Sommi, *A Comedy of Betrothal*.

[20] For Responsa testimonies regarding 'secret' marriage, see Modena, [*Responsa*], n. 85, pp. 131–134 and n. 108, pp. 154–56; Me'ir, *Responsa*, n. 32, fols. 67r–68r; Strasbourg, Bibliothèque Nationale et Universitaire, MS 4087, pp. 193–95; Jerusalem, Ben-Zvi Institute, MS 4001, fol. 63v; Copenhagen, Royal Library, MS Cod. Hebr. 115/4, unpaginated.

This negative stereotyping was a product of the Jewish literary and religious canon and of the harsh judgments of Hebrew moral ethics of the Middle Ages. Young men would encounter them in synagogue preaching or when rebuked by their elders. However, although the moral, or moralistic, judgment was harsh, the interaction of adults and young people should not be seen solely from this perspective. In practice the balance of opinion was more favourable to the *giovani* and sought somehow to legitimize various aspects of their life and to include them in local cultural traditions. A clear illustration of this can be found in the *ars letteras scribendi* composed by Rabbi Samuel Archevolti (active in the first half of the sixteenth centry), *The Fountain of Gardens* (*Ma'ayan Ganim*). One of the volume's sections covers letter exchanges between young lovers.[21] These sample letters are important for a variety of reasons. First, they form part of the local rhetorical tradition. Second, as sample letters that could be read by adults as well as youths, they include various 'adult' themes such as internal Jewish politics and business matters. They are also indicative of a continued renegotiating of the male/female dialectic in which the male writer presents himself as the weak side and asks his female beloved for mercy. Love letters were considered important enough to be included in a semi-official text such as *The Fountain of Gardens* because they provided a crucial medium for the personal and erotic encounter of young people prior to marriage.

These courtship rituals, though not always strictly conforming to formal religious requirements, were partially incorporated in the cultural canon, as can be seen in Italian-Jewish interpretations of the biblical *Song of Songs*. This great love-poem was traditionally interpreted in the Midrash and later in medieval Jewish culture as an allegory of the love between God and the Jews. According to mystic traditions, the canticle was also seen as a description of the godly inner world whose human sensual ingredients have gradually faded away. The Jewish-Italian exegetes of the sixteenth and seventeenth century re-endowed the *Song of Songs* with its earthly, sensual aspects and turned it into a love narrative between young lovers searching their way to intimacy and erotic closeness in the face of social barriers and hindering norms. The eroticised *Song of Songs* was spoken in the present tense, describing the erotic atmosphere of youth sub-culture in Italy.[22]

---

21 Archevolti, *The Fountain of Gardens*, section 5.
22 Weinstein, 'Rituel du mariage et culture des jeunes', pp. 468–70.

The mystic tradition was mobilized to justify not only erotic biblical texts, but even the Jewish version of *mattinata*, the Italian version of the French charivari. An anonymous Italian rabbi of the late sixteenth century used *The Book of Splendour* (*Sefer Ha-Zohar*) to claim not only that the *Mattinata* was legitimate, but that it was originally a Jewish custom and should be practised more intensely.[23] Rabbis and scholars of mystical inclinations thus became agents of change in local Jewish communities as religious rituals were re-shaped and re-interpreted.[24] As we shall later see, Cabalists had an impact on the education of the young, especially on matters touching on their sexual habits.

Even when dealing with legal matters Italian Jews insisted on defending local traditions, those of the *giovani* included. The debate about gift exchange between the unmarried young is emblematic because legal heritage (*Halakhah*) and formal religious commandments (*Mitzvot*) were the principal reference points in Jewish daily life and signs of a collective identity. No wonder that legal discourse became a basic element in defining the cultural and collective differences between the various Jewish 'ethnic groups' (*Edot*)—Sephardic, Ashkenazi, Levantine, Italiani, or Sicilian. Since, according to Jewish law, marital status was determined by the transference of even a minimal amount of property from the man to the woman, the tradition among Italian-Jewish young men and women of exchanging small gifts during courtship could be extremely problematic in the wider Jewish context. As early as the fourteenth century Jews arriving in Italy from elsewhere rightly claimed that by these gifts the Italian-Jewish *giovani* unknowingly and unwillingly created a state of marriage between donor and recipient. A long and bitter rabbinic polemic ensued in the late fifteenth and through the sixteenth centuries between Italian rabbis supporting the custom and 'foreign' commentators pointing to its problems. Italian communities, however, insisted on maintaining the aged-old tradition and defended the right of their young sons and daughters to have an independent, personal erotic space.

While there might have been significant differences between Italian and non-Italian Jews, the similarity in the way Jewish and Christian youth in premodern Italy spent their pre-marital years is undeniable. Although the majority Christian society influenced the Jewish minority directly in various aspects of its way of life, it would be a grave mistake to speak of 'direct imitation' or 'transference' from the 'Christian' to the

---

[23] Weinstein, 'Rituel du mariage et culture des jeunes', pp. 473–76.
[24] Bonfil, 'Cultura e mistica a Venezia nel Cinquecento,' pp. 480–90.

'Jewish' context. A better way of seeing this relationship would be to view it within an 'Italian' context shared by both groups and in their living in close proximity along densely populated streets and neighbourhoods, both of which led them to evolve similar solutions for similar problems. In both communities the conduct of young men and women during their adolescent years was firmly tied to basic aspects of economic, demographic, religious, and family issues pressing on the Italian population as a whole. The question, however, is not why there were similarities, but how could these similarities exist alongside intensifying religious and political hostility between adherents to the two faiths that eventually led to actual physical separation.

Separation by religion began early in an Italian's life. Nowhere in the rich documentation available to us is there any reference to youth groups consisting of both Jews and Christians. Because of this social separation, encounters with the other side would be either short lived or antagonistic. In his encomium to his son murdered in the Venetian ghetto by other Jewish *giovani*, Rabbi Yehudah de Modena underlined the fact that his son had always used his physical strength to protect his co-religionists from harassment by Gentiles.[25] The implication is that the youth did not engage in physical violence against Jews, but channelled his energy to confront young Gentiles whose curiosity towards the different styles and rituals of the ghetto and its population frequently lead to violence against Jews. Perceived as enemies of Christ and, presumably, of the city, Jews were subject to lynching, carnivalesque shaming-acts, or stone throwing. Although such action was primarily the result of inter-religious hostility, it also fit well with traditional urban hostility between different city quarters. The Christian *giovani* living in a near-by neighbourhood would confront their Jewish counterparts in the ghetto. The rival groups understood the message, for it was based on a shared cultural language of honour, virility, territoriality, and ritual combat, though re-enforced in this case with unbridgeable ethno-religious divisions.

In spite of these similarities, the basic differences could not be ignored. In the Jewish context the level of violence was definitely lower than in the Christian city. Cases of collective rape are not to be

---

[25] Modena, *The Autobiography of a Seventeenth-Century Venetian Rabbi*, p. 121: 'He was brave in battle, and none had a heart as courageous as his . . . His courage and weapons he only used in zeal for his God and to hallow his name, for he could not endure the debasement of any Jew (*hillul shem yehudi*).' See also p. 115.

found in the documents and the occasional men who forced them-selves on defenceless women were clearly adults, not youths.

A young Jewish man enjoyed certain advantages over his female counterpart. He was generally better educated, less limited in his move-ments in public space, and enjoyed the support of his peers. Yet, when courting a young woman he tended to present himself as weak and vulnerable to the arrows of Venus no less than to her. This distinctly literary topos points to the penchant of Jewish *giovani*, both male and female, for setting up a sphere of action where the use of direct physical force was unwelcome and disapproved. This might explain why Jewish communities did not hurry to suppress local courtship habits—they saw no need to do so because here the encounter between the young was always carried out within the standards and limits established by the community. Even youths who entered into 'secret marriages' remained in the community and did not elope to another town. When a young woman fell victim to an unwanted marriage, this was the result of a trick devised by the man who courted her. Again, there was no use of physical force, but subtle manipulating of both young and adult persons, men and women, Jews and Christian, who became part of this event.

The term usually used to describe these unclear situations that needed to be resolved in a court of law or discussed in the *Responsa* literature was 'play' (*mis'chak*). In medieval Hebrew the word carried a distinct negative connotation relating to sexual promiscuity, lack of seriousness, deceit, or idleness. It could very well be the equivalent of the Italian *gioco* or *burla*. The game and its ensuing pleasure demanded a separate sym-bolic space, devoid of violence. The only cases where direct violence was used relate to inter-faith clandestine marriages, when young Jewish women left their families, their people, and their religion. In such cases the Christian partner might go with armed companions or soldiers to take them by force of arms. The Jewish-Italian case seems to be unique among Jewish communities, where in cases of secret marriages we find first that women were indeed exposed to physical force and, second, that the tricksters deceiving a young woman into marriage were the father or other adults, not the young lovers themselves.[26]

While there were similarities with the neighbouring Christian commu-nity, there were also strong differences. One cannot but wonder, for example, about the lack of documentation on juvenile homoerotic

---

[26] See for example a story of romantic escape of two Jewish *giovani* in late seven-teenth-century Provence; St Petersbourg, Oriental Institution, MS B382, ff. 43v–48r.

activity among young male Jews in Italy. The silence is all the more surprising since Italian cities in the late Renaissance had a supposedly active homosexual sub-culture that was viewed either as a transitional phase leading to a 'normal' adult heterosexual life or as a permanent choice that elicited outright condemnation and severe punishment.[27]

Jewish youth culture also lacked the civic-cultural substratum of its Christian counterpart. Jewish *giovani* did not serve in communal militias drawn from the various *quartieri* of the city nor did they take part in religious processions or civic parades that reaffirmed a corporate religious or civic identity. The magical aspect of such ceremonial roles, with roots in pre-Christian times, is hardly present for Jewish youths. Even within the Jewish community they were viewed too critically by their elders to be able serve as bearers of prophecy or emblems of innocence, as their Christian counterparts did.

Sexual activity between Jews and Christians was casual rather than long lasting. Some young Jewish men, like their Christian counterparts, did frequent prostitutes as part of their socialization to adult heterosexual life. The fact that such activity was prohibited and abhorred by both the Jewish Halakha and Christian Canon Law did not deter them from it, as an uncle's complaint about his nephew clearly reveals:

> You should know, my dear brother-in-law, that all the days your son lived with me . . . I did not cease to function as his shepherd and guide him along the right way . . . and I chastised this man with punishments for his sins, like a man should chastise his own son. Indeed he hardened his spirit and his heart, his ear is deaf to rebuke, his heart has become more passionate the more he has grown up, and he thinks that none in the Jewish nation is as fair and handsome a *giovane* as he is, of fair eyes and good looking, and with a mannerly conduct, but actually he is an ignorant boy . . . lately he sinned gravely, for on Wednesday, the fourth of the month, this reckless youth went with another good-for-nothing, and they gathered in a prostitute's house and committed things not to be done . . . and when they satisfied their desire they declined to give the woman the money she was due, so that she was infuriated and went angrily to town to speak to my older brother Judah: 'men of your household named such and such committed such and such a treacherous deed. Now if I shall have my money and my fee will be paid I shall hold my tongue, otherwise my voice will be heard in the streets in front of policemen and city officials.' When my brother Judah heard this his face was saddened, but graciously he calmed the fornicating woman, then returned home infuriated and chased them away [= the addressee's son and

---

[27] See Rocke, *Forbidden Friendships*, passim.

his friend]. And had your son Josef not committed a sin as well as a crime, going to the prostitute's house and speaking to her harshly, the event would not have been known. But his acts caused the whole *quartiere* to gather, so that had he not escaped from here, he surely would have been put in prison.[28]

As in the letter describing the Jewish youths' visit to the celebrations for St. Peter's, had there been no scandal we would not have heard of this event. Unlike the previous writer, however, this letter writer strongly condemns the young Jews for going to a Christian prostitute. The fact that the prostitute recognized her clients by name and easily found their home reveals that the two youths' visit was a rather routine matter. The scandal they created, however, was not routine and it drastically altered the situation. The fact that a Jewish male—be he young—had intercourse with a Christian woman—be she a prostitute—became known throughout the *quartiere* and made it very likely that the young Jew would be arrested and prosecuted. He had no choice but to flee.

Jewish sources did not hesitate to criticize certain cultural practices as 'following the ways of Gentiles.' However, no such criticism was ever levelled at the behaviour of the young. On the contrary, some of the more daring behaviour of youths was cloaked in canonical terminology. Similar social and urban needs led Christians and Jews in Italy to behave in a similar way, but they did so in two quite different contexts governed by different symbols, institutions, and attitudes.

The non-Italian Jewish context provided other incentives and elements. The wider diaspora was a crucial background of emotional, religious, political, and economic solidarity for Jews. The shared beliefs and expectations, the ransoming of Jewish prisoners, and the prestige of non-Italian religious scholars and rabbis all contributed to the wider Jewish discourse that crossed political and religious boundaries. A person living in a Jewish community in Rome or Modena felt part of the *Oecomenium Judaicum* no less than of local city life. It would only be natural that modes of growing up and socializing to adult life in the wider Jewish diaspora would attract attention. Unfortunately, however, short of the illuminating work of Elliott Horowitz, no comparative research has been conducted on Jewish youth sub-culture during the late Middle Ages and the early modern period.[29]

---

[28] *Letters of Jews in Italy*, n. 185, pp. 239–40.

[29] Horowitz, 'Mondi giovanili ebraici in Europa, 1300–1800' and 'Educational Control and Confraternal Organization.' For further comparative research see Ha-Kohen/Hophni, [*The Book of Maturity of Rabbi Shemu'el ben Hofni Ga'on and*

Italy hosted ceaseless immigration from almost all over the Jewish world bringing with it indigenous habits from distant lands and distinct mentalities from other cultures. One would like to know more, for example, about Sephardic traditions and their spread into Europe and Ottoman Turkey. What were their reasons for prohibiting the young from strolling in the streets during the Sabbath? Were the youths frequenting brothels? There is evidence of homoerotic encounter among Sephardic Jewish adolescents as well as among Jews and Muslims, but it is unclear whether this was a temporary stage on the way to heterosexual patterns and family life or a permanent homosexual sub-culture. Were there any legitimate ways in that community for young men and women to meet?

The Ashkenazi world, with its prestigious place in the study of sacred texts, also left a great mark on Italian culture. In Eastern Europe one can find varied sources describing the habits and attitudes of young scholars in Ashkenazi advanced schools (*Yeshivot*), surprisingly similar to medieval and early modern university students. To acquire greater learning some of these young scholars would wander from one place to another, following the reputations of rabbis and institutions. Their relative independence endowed them with a distinct social position. Their masters had to provide them with food or money for their feasts. As was the case with young servants and apprentices, they also demanded that during marriage celebrations some of the dowry be payed out to them, lest they should disturb the celebrations with Charivari acts. Courtship among equals does not seem to have been practised in this community. Burlesque marriage between young scholars and female servants did occur, but both sides knew that such marriages could never be consummated because of class differences. This was not a game between two equal sides, but a vicious encounter where one side, male and well established, ridiculed the other, female and poor.

Jewish communities around the Mediterranean also kept close economic and cultural relations with Italian cities. Some had lively and active youth sub-cultures, as was the case in Alexandria, where groups of youths met on Sabbaths and feast-days near the synagogue and their violence could lead to brawls and drunkenness, or to direct interfer-

---

the Book of Years of Rabbi Yehudah Ha-Kohen] *Sefer ha-bagrut le-Rav Shemu'el ben Hofni Ga'on ve-Sefer ha-shanim le-Rev Yehudah ha-Kohen Rosh ha-seder* and Lamdan, *A Separate People.*

ence in community management. Music and dancing played a central role in their life and kept them away from work. Community regulations tried to prevent the encounter of young men and women during matrimony festivities, a time when men would cross-dress for the amusement of the audience.

In spite of the wealth of sources discussed so far, it must be noted that there is very little documentation about Jewish youths prior to the mid sixteenth century.[30] What are we to infer from this? Was youth sub-culture a phenomenon of the sixteenth century, or was interest in it the new thing of the time? In other words, did social reality change, or did collective sensibilities change? The two need not be mutually exclusive.

Although an *argumentum ex silentio* is problematic, the silence of the documents before the mid sixteenth century is actually strong evidence in favour of a sudden appearance of a youth sub-culture. There are, admittedly, a variety of places in the canonical sources before the mid sixteenth century where Jewish commentators are 'invited' to present their views on the activities of the young, mostly in order to criticize the young and not in order to come to terms with a tangible social force. The fact that in none of these sources there is any response or information is also, in itself, evidence of a forceful and all too comprehensive silence. When, on the other hand, so many different aspects of the youth sub-culture are suddenly and synchronously revealed in the mid sixteenth century, we cannot help but assume that we are facing a predominantly new aspect of Jewish communal life.

Yet, a closer look at the sources suggests that the second possibility, the development of a new sensibility towards an already existing youth culture, is also valid. Interest in the raucous behaviour of young men was not neutral; it existed in order to enforce social discipline and collective control. The vitality of such behaviour on the one hand and attempts to control it on the other, were merely contrasting elements of the same historical dynamics that, unfortunately for us, was described primarily through an adult perspective that sought to find an acceptable balance between community authority and the wishes of the *giovani*. So the documents at our disposal need a second reading not only as providers of basic information (demography, marriage pat-

---

[30] The few existing documents refer mainly to youths aged about thirteen, the Jewish age for the *Bar Mitzvah* rite of passage. See, Weinstein, 'Childhood, Adolescence, and Growing-up in Jewish Communities in Italy,' pp. 83–92.

terns, courtship and sexual habits, educational institutions, literary genres), but also as indicators of developing biases and prejudices, of a change, that is, in sensibilities.

When Jewish young men and women left their parental home in their teens, they entered into contexts that provided them with surrogates of fatherly authority that had similar, if not equal, rights over them. A craftsman, for example, could punish his apprentice as he saw fit and a teacher could scold his young disciples. A father wrote to his son's teacher:

> I have decided to send my son to draw water from your well, as I have spoken to you for some time ago . . . I know that you are wise and clever and there is no need to instruct you on the right way. Still—as if reminding and not warning—I will say that it is better not to show him a warm welcome, so that he will learn always to fear you, because at this moment he is like an untamed calf . . . I regard it as essential that you guide the boy in the art of writing, both in the holy language and the Christian one [= in Hebrew and Italian], and in good virtues, since I know well that he is not talented enough to become a rabbi or a scholar, neither do I wish it. I pray you to watch this boy, and constantly follow his comings and goings, so that he will not go astray as his heart inclines.[31]

Not pretending to follow the social stereotype of wishing that every boy would turn to be a scholar in holy tradition (*Talmid Chaham*), this father had no illusions about his son's talents. When sending the youth to the master, he formed an implicit alliance of adults. The youth was not to be received warmly, but from the very first moment he was to accommodate himself to the hierarchy and discipline of his new home.

One of the ways to socialize the disciple into the adult perspective was through letter writing. In learning epistolary rhetoric students were strictly supervised by their teachers even in their private correspondence. Some were expected to write daily to their parents. If there was nothing new to tell, the teacher would dictate to them or have them copy from sample letters. Most of the letters repeated standard literary and linguistic topoi that led the young writers to adopt, willingly or not, the adult perspective. Once received, such letters were often read aloud by the recipient to family and friends, thus bringing the young writer's words (and epistolary skills) to the attention of the community back home.

---

[31] *Letters of Jews in Italy*, n. 187, pp. 241–42.

Another way of controlling the young was through confraternities, a well known element of the Christian urban context. In the wider European context, confraternities for Jewish youths were practically unknown, except in Italy. Here, youth confraternities (*Chavurot Tze'irim*) were established in the second half of the sixteenth century in several Jewish communities.[32] Like their Christian counterparts, they were increasingly supervised by adults and the original intention to set strict age limits (to include only youths aged approximately from 13 to 24) was not always respected. Spending some of their time together in confraternal companionship kept, or was supposed to keep, youths away from the temptations of the street and to provide them with an alternative to uncontrolled youth groups.

The tacit permission to allow young men to establish their own youth confraternities was granted on the assumption that the youths would be guided by peer group pressure and would operate under adult supervision. Such organizations, in fact, were never completely independent; their meetings were either attended by adult supervisors or brought to their knowledge. Confraternity youths were also encouraged to participate in synagogal life and needs.[33] It seemed that the confraternal model pleased community members to such an extent that they described new educational institutions along confraternal lines—students spending long hours in schools were supposedly forming a confraternity headed by their master-teacher and were held together by ties of affection that bound them into a distinct 'family' unit.

The changes that affected educational institutions in the early modern period were agents of wider changes in the community. As was the case in Italian communes, most pedagogical activity in Jewish communities until the mid sixteenth century had been in the hands of private masters and the community as a whole had interfered very little in questions of curriculum, choice of space, discipline, or financial arrangements.[34] In mid-century, the growing involvement of the com-

[32] Horowitz, 'Jewish Confraternal Piety in Sixteenth-Century Ferrara' and 'A Jewish Youth Confraternity in Seventeenth Century Italy'. There is a vast and growing literature in English on Italian confraternities; for a comprehensive historical context of early modern Italian youth confraternities, see Eisenbichler, *The Boys of the Archangel Raphael*; for confraternities in general see Terpstra, *The Politics of Ritual Kinship*.

[33] See *Minute Book of the Jewish Community of Verona*, vol. 3, n. 123, for a confraternity of young men donating a candelabrum to the synagogue.

[34] For a thorough study of educational institutions in Italy from the Middle Ages

munity was accompanied by a radical change in attitudes towards education. Schools were at times separated from 'external' life and students were strictly forbidden to leave them unless escorted by their teacher. These new institutions were called *Hessgher*, that is, 'Closure.' Students were never to be left alone, but were always to be under the watchful eye of their master. Whenever he was gone, they were instructed to meditate on his imagined presence and to continue to be obedient to their superiors.

Not only was the mind to be exercised, but the body also became an object of growing interest and attention. The medieval idea of the body as the mirror of the soul acquired new dimensions in the Italian context, be that Jewish or Christian. The civilizing process, brilliantly described by Norbert Elias, had clear medieval roots in monastic life and chivalrous courts, but in the Italian urban context it developed new and different dimensions that eventually crossed the Alps and influenced the rest of Europe.[35] Some segments of Jewish society adopted the Italian 'civilizing' model and had their young instructed in it from an early age, learning not only how to think and talk in the new fashion, but also how to walk, sit, and move their body gracefully.[36] This exercise in self discipline was a reflection of the new social discipline. Paraphrasing Christian conduct literature, one could say that for a good Jewish youth it was no longer enough simply to follow religious precepts, but he had to obey his superiors and show them external signs of respect, refrain from wild behaviour, and carry himself with grace and elegance.

Once the body became an object to be manipulated, it was inevitable that sexual activity would also be controlled to fit the new ideals of behaviour for youths. Records of local courtship practices among the young that allowed for different levels of erotic and sexual proximity and even pre-marital encounters were kept primarily in order to express indignation at such practices and in an attempt to eradicate them, or at least to attenuate their more unacceptable aspects. Typical to this new restrictive atmosphere was *The Glory of Youth* (*Tif'eret Bahurim*), an edited booklet by Rabbi Pinchas Baruch ben Platya Monselice (Ferrara, 1675) intended as a guide for young men approach-

---

to the sixteenth century see Grendler, *Schooling in Renaissance Italy.*

[35] Niccoli, 'Éducation et discipline,' pp. 185–90; Elias, *The Civilizing Process,* passim.

[36] Weinstein, 'Jewish Education in Italy during the Catholic Reformation Period,' pp. 142–48 and 156–60.

ing marriage. The volume contains discussions on local courtship habits, on the prohibition against pre-marital sex, on the sin of masturbation, on the first sexual act during matrimony (as well as religious instructions to follow *in actu*), and, finally, on the intimate life of married couples. Such rules and prohibitions were certainly not unknown; the Jewish legal tradition of Halakha provided clear instructions in these and other areas pertaining to daily life. Putting them together in a single compendium wholly devoted to sexuality, however, was new. A young Jewish man reading *The Glory of Youth* was not only expected to follow these well known rules of comportment, but to be in a pious mood and have a pure mind during sexual activity, both of which were described using Cabalistic terminology.

Jewish medieval Cabala granted sexuality a unique place. God was described as having a bisexual identity. *The Book of Splendour*, a reference book for most mystics composed primarily by the thirteenth-century Spanish Rabbi Moses di Leon, did not hesitate to discuss in detail the copulation of different divine emanations (*Sefirot*).[37] The religious commandments on sex suddenly gained major importance as reflections or interactions between the earthly and heavenly spheres, between the human and the divine. Until the mid sixteenth century, however, mystics jealously guarded their books and knowledge within their privileged, esoteric circles. Italian communities were the first in Europe to preach publicly or study more meticulously in devotional groups these Cabalistic ideas. Not only did Cabala revolutionize Italian religious practices and daily rituals, but it also deeply affected various aspects of community life, among them the growing insistence on enforcing sexual regulations and restrictions on the young. Centuries-old Italian-Jewish courtship patterns were now described as licentiousness and as 'not befitting the holy nation.'

Social control over the young became part of a more general and comprehensive collective discipline. The establishment of the ghetto, in the late sixteenth and in the seventeenth century, as a separate and distinct living space for Jews encouraged similar cultural-social dynamics in both the Jewish and the Christian quarters. Officials in the Jewish communities, as well as parish priests in the Christian areas, began to seek greater knowledge of their inhabitants' private lives. In both cases,

---

[37] The work was first printed in Italy in the mid-sixteenth century amid clamorous debates. See Tishbi, 'The Poltemics about *The Book of the Splendour.*' For an extensive introduction to this work, see *The Wisdom of the Zohar*, vol. 1.

the confession ritual provided intimate detailed information on family life and sexual behaviour. Inevitably, the young bore much of the pressure to reform, since no real social change was deemed to be possible without their obedience and adherence.

Were the adults successful in imposing their will on the young? Acts of adolescent violence continued, as did vagabondage and casual sexual relations between Christians and Jews, so the answer might appear to be a negative. The change in educational institutions and the spread of stricter discipline, however, favour a more positive answer. In the end, it seems, a balance of power between adults and youths was achieved. The passage to the ghetto favoured a dynamic already active in contemporary city quarters where the young already had their rightful place in the community. The attempt of the Counter-Reformation Church and city governors to eradicate violent behaviour among the young met with only partial success. The same was true in the Jewish ghettos. Here, however, adults and elders did not seem annoyed by their limited success in taming the young or curtailing their sub-culture; the apparent deviancy of the young served the Jewish community well in exerting non-formal social control and in protecting the Jewish quarter's honour and security from external threat. Finally, it also served to blend Italian-Jewish behavioural patterns with ultramontane and ultramarine ones from the Ashkenazi, Sephardi, or Mediterranean traditions.

*Harvard University Center for Italian Renaissance Studies,*
*Villa I Tatti, Florence*

*Hebrew University, Jerusalem*

# Cited Works
## Manuscript Sources

Copenhagen, Royal Library, MS Cod. Hebr. 115/4
Ferrara, Comunità Israelitica, MS 24
Jerusalem, Ben-Zvi Institute, MS 4001
Los Angeles, University Library MS 779
New York, Columbia University, MS X893T67
Oxford, C. Roth Collection, MS 210
St Petersbourg, Oriental Institution, MS B382
Strasbourg, Bibliothèque Nationale et Universitaire, MS 4087

## Published Sources

Archivolti, Samuel ben Elchanan. [*The Fountain of Gardens*] *Ma'ayan Ganim*. Venice, 1551.

Bonfil, Roberto. 'The Settlement in Italy of Immigrating Jews during Late Middle Ages' [in Hebrew] pp. 139–53 in *Emigration and Settlement in Jewish and General History / Hagirah ve-hityashvut be-Yisra'el va-'amin: kovets ma'amarim*, ed. Avigdor Shina'n. Jerusalem: Merkaz Z. Shazar, 1982.

Bonfil, Roberto. 'Cultura e mistica a Venezia nel Cinquecento' pp. 469–506 in *Gli Ebrei e Venezia. Secoli XIV–XVIII*, ed. Gaetano Cozzi. Milano: Edizioni Comunità, 1987.

Eisenbichler, Konrad. *The Boys of the Archangel Raphael: A Youth Confraternity in Florence, 1411–1785*. Toronto: University of Toronto Press, 1998.

Elias, Norbert. *The Civilizing Process*, trans. Edmund Jephcott. 2 vols. New York: Urizen Books/Pantheon Books, 1978, 1982.

Grendler, Paul F. *Schooling in Renaissance Italy. Literacy and Learning, 1300–1600*. Baltimore and London: Johns Hopkins University Press, 1989.

Ha-Kohen, Yehuda and Samuel ben Hophni. [*The Book of Maturity of Rabbi Shemu'el ben Hofni Ga'on and the Book of Years of Rabbi Yehudah Ha-Kohen*] *Sefer ha-bagrut le-Rav Shemu'el ben Hofni Ga'on ve-Sefer ha-shanim le-Rev Yehudah ha-Kohen Rosh ha-seder*, ed. Tirtsah Yoreh Mitchum, trans. Miryam Frankel. Jerusalem: Yad ha-Rav Misim, 1999.

Horowitz, Elliott. "A Jewish Youth Confraternity in Seventeenth-Century Italy," Italia. Studi e ricerche sulla storia, la cultura e la letteratura degli Ebrei d'Italia 5:1–2 (Jerusalem, 1985): 36–74.

Horowitz, Elliott. 'Yeshiva and Hevra: Educational Control and Confraternal Organization in Sixteenth-Century Italy' pp. 123–47 in *Shlomo Simonsohn Jubilee Volume. Studies on the History of the Jews in the Middle Ages and Renaissance Period*, ed. Daniel Carpi et al. Tel Aviv: Tel Aviv University, 1993.

Horowitz, Elliott. S. 'Mondi giovanili ebraici in Europa, 1300–1800' 1:101–57 in *Storia dei giovani*, eds. Giovanni Levi and Jean-Claude Schmitt. 2 vols. Rome and Bari: Laterza, 1994.

Horowitz, Elliott. 'Masters and Women Servants in Jewish Society in Europe during Late Middle Ages and Early Modern Periods' pp. 193–211 in *Sexuality and the Family in History / Eros erusin ve-isurim: miniyut u-mishpahah ba-historyah*, eds. Yisra'el Bartal and Yesha'yahu Gafni. Jerusalem: Merkaz Zalman Shazar, 1998.

Horowitz, Elliott. 'Jewish Confraternal Piety in Sixteenth-Century Ferrara; Continuity and Change' pp. 150–71 in *The Politics of Ritual Kinship: Confraternities and Social Order in Early Modern Italy*, ed. Nicholas Terpstra. Cambridge: Cambridge University Press, 2000.

*Infanzie. Funzioni di un gruppo liminale dal mondo classico all'età moderna*, ed. Ottavia Niccoli. Firenze: Ponte alle Grazie, 1993.

Letters of Rieti Family, Siena 1537–1564 / *Ingrot Bet Ri'eti: Syenah, 297–329*, ed. Ya'akov Boksenboim. Tel-Aviv: Universitat Tel Aviv, 1987.

*Letters of Jews in Italy / Igrot Yehude Italya*, ed. Ya'akov Boksenboim. Tel Aviv: Universitat Tel Aviv, 1994.

*Letters of Jewish Teachers in Renaissance Italy (1555–1591) / Ingrot melamdim: Italyah, 315–351 (1555–1590)*, ed. Ya'akov Boksenboim. Tel-Aviv: Hayim Rozenberg / Universitat Tel Aviv, 1986.

Me'ir ben Izchak Katzenellenbeugen. *Responsa of Rabbi Me'ir of Padova*. Cracow, 1882.

*Minutes Book of the Jewish Community of Verona / Pinkas kehal Veronah*, ed. Ya'akov Boksenboim. 3 vols. Tel Aviv: Universitat Tel Aviv, 1989, 1990

Modena, Leone.[*Responsa*] *She'elot u-teshuvot Zikne Yehudah*, ed. Shlomo Simonsohn. Jerusalem: Mosad ha-rav Kuk, 1956.

Modena, Leone. *The Autobiography of A Seventeenth-Century Venetian Rabbi: Leon Modena's Life of Judah*, trans. Mark R. Cohen. Princeton, NJ: Princeton University Press, 1988.

Niccoli, Ottavia. 'Éducation et discipline: les bonnes manières des enfants dans l'Italie de la Contre-Réforme' pp. 185–218 in *La ville et la cour. Des bonnes et des mauvaises manières*, ed. Daniela Romagnoli. Paris: Fayard, 1995.

Niccoli, Ottavia. *Il seme della violenza. Putti, fanciulli e mammoli nell'Italia tra Cinque e Seicento*. Rome and Bari: Laterza, 1995.

Rocke, Michael. *Forbidden Friendships. Homosexuality and Male Culture in Renaissance Florence*. New York: Oxford University Press, 1996.

Sommi, Leone de' (Sommo, Yehudah). *Zachut Bedichutah deKidushin*, ed. J. Shirmann. Tel Aviv 1965.

Sommi, Leone de' (Sommo, Yehudah). *A Comedy of Betrothal*, trans. Alfred S. Golding. Ottawa: Dovehouse Editions, 1988.

Sonne, Isaiah. 'Some Contributions for the History of the Jews in Verona' *Zion* N.S. 3(1938), pp. 128–45.

Stow, Kenneth. 'Innovation by Conservatism. 'Refusal of Marriage' in the Roman Ghetto during the Sixteenth and Seventeenth Centuries' pp. 131–43 in [*Sexuality and the Family in History*] *Eros erusin ve-isurim: miniyut u-mishpahah ba-historyah*, eds. Israel Bartal and I. Gafni. Jerusalem: Merkaz Zalman Shazar, 1998.

*The Jews in Piedmont*, ed. Renata Segre. 3 vols. Jerusalem: Israel Academy of Sciences and Humanities and Tel Aviv University, 1986–1988.

*The Jews in the Duchy of Milan*, ed. Shlomo Simonsohn. 4 vols. Jerusalem: Israel Academy of Sciences and Humanities, 1982–1986.

*The Jews of Rome*, ed. Kenneth Stow. 2 vols. Documentary history of the Jews of Italy, 11, 12. Leiden and New York: E.J. Brill, 1995, 1997.

*The Jews of Umbria*, ed. Ariel Toaff. 3 vols. Leiden and New York: E.J. Brill, 1993–1994.

*The Politics of Ritual Kinship: Confraternities and Social Order in Early Modern Italy*, ed. Nicholas Terpstra. Cambridge, UK: Cambridge University Press, 2000.

*The Wisdom of the Zohar: An Anthology of Texts*, ed.. Fischel Lachower and Isaiah Tishby. 3 vols. Oxford: Littman Library and Oxford University Press, 1989.

Tishbi, Isaiah. 'The Polemics about *The Book of the Splendour* in Sixteenth Century Italy' *Perakim* 1 (1967–68): 131–82.

Weinsten, Roni. 'Childhood, Adolescence, and Growing Up in Jewish Communities in Italy During the Late Middle Ages' [in Hebrew] *Italia. Studi e ricerca sulla storia, la cultura e la letteratura degli Ebrei d'Italia* 11 (1995): 77–98.

Weinstein, Roni. 'Rituel du mariage et culture des jeunes dans la société Judéo-Italienne 16e–17e siècles' *Annales. Histoire Sciences Sociales* 53:3 (1998): 455–79.

Weinstein, Roni. 'The Jewish Ghetto in Relation to Urban Quarters in Italian Cities during the Early Modern Time – Similarity and Differences' [in Hebrew] *Zemanim* 67 (Summer 1999): 12–21.

Weinstein, Roni. '*Segregatos non autem eiectos* (Segregated yet not Ejected): Jews and Christians in Italian Cities during the Catholic Reformation' [in Hebrew], pp. 93–132 in *Being Different: Minorities, Aliens and Outsiders in History / Mi'utim, zarim ve-shonim: kevutsot shulayim ba-historyah*, ed. Shulamit Volkov. Jerusalem: Merkaz Zalman Shazar le-toldot Yisra'el, 2000.

# Rituals of Youth:
# Love, Play, and Violence in Tridentine Bologna

## Ottavia Niccoli

At the dawn of the modern age, the daily behaviour of youths aged roughly twelve to twenty exhibits stereotypical rituals that can be identified and analyzed thanks to the records of criminal court proceedings. Here one can unearth behavioural patterns that help establish sociological models in which the rituals of love, play, and violence illustrate a way of life within a well defined age bracket. In examining them, we see how, at this time, a number of rituals and practices were deemed to be unacceptable to the new spiritual world of Tridentine Catholicism. Ironically, it is precisely because such rituals were reproved and condemned that we are now able to identify and examine them.

In Italy, the second half of the sixteenth century and the first decades of the seventeenth was, in relation to the previous era, a period of profound changes at the political, social, cultural and religious level. Often qualified as 'Tridentine,' this period bears the stamp of the Council of Trent (1545–63) and of the ideology that sustained and promoted it. It embodies that vast Tridentine project of codification and correction that goes well beyond the immediate fight against heresy and seeks not only to eliminate all heterodox opinion, but also to correct social practices that were seen as unacceptable in the context of a society that was to be integrally re-established.[1]

First and foremost, it was the behaviour of the young that needed to be regulated and disciplined. 'One must believe that the best way of reforming the world and the Church is to give to the youth a good and holy education, by chastising the children and raising them in the fear of God'—such was the exhortation in an anonymous text entitled *Avertimenti e brievi ricordi circa il vivere christiano* (Warnings and short memoirs on Christian Life), published in Bologna in 1563 with the approval of the vicar-general of the diocese.[2]

---

[1] On the historiographical category of 'disciplining' (*disziplinierung, disciplinamento, disciplinement*) see *Disciplina dell'anima*, esp. pp. 9–160.

[2] This is a broadside at the Archivio Arcivescovile di Bologna, Misc. Vecc. 798,

A number of court cases, both civil and ecclesiastical, reveal the existence of, as well as the attempt to suppress, ritual practices tied to a variety of local customs. At the end of the sixteenth and beginning of the seventeenth century, for example, just as the battle against heresy was being brought successfully to an end,[3] one notices a marked intensification of inquisitorial trials against magical practices. Similarly, after 1560, there is a growing number of trials in episcopal counts against irregularities in the celebration of marriages and against undisciplined priests. Criminal courts bear witness of this difficult battle, as well as to the habits and rituals of young persons against which the campaign was being mounted. In this article, the examples of this attempt to control the ritual behaviour of the young are all connected with the city of Bologna and the territory in its immediate vicinity, but can be seen to reflect the situation in the entire Papal States and even Italy.

Bologna was, by order of importance, the second city of the Papal States. After having been governed for some decades by the Bentivoglio family, in 1506 it returned to direct papal control when Pope Julius II della Rovere, putting into effect his program of regaining direct jurisdiction over his territory, ousted the Bentivoglio and made a solemn entry into the city. In the years that followed a system of mixed government was set in place consisting of a Senate of forty citizens drawn from the aristocracy of the city and a Legate named by the pope who served as the direct representative of papal power in the city and its territory.[4] Since the different offices in the city depended from one or the other of these powers, frequent tension was inevitable.

One of the city's offices was the criminal court of the Torrone, so called because of the great tower where it met (*torrone*). The court depended directly from the Papal Legate who named its judge or *Auditore*.[5] Fully functional since 1540, the Torrone would remain in operation until 1796 when the arrival of the Napoleonic army brought an end to a large number of institutions in the Papal States. Its archives contain about ten thousand folio volumes of criminal court proceed-

---

2. See Niccoli, *Il seme della violenza*, pp. 113–39.

3 On the work of the tribunals of the Inquisition in Italy see Prosperi, *Tribunali della coscienza*. On Bologna in particular see Dall'Olio, *Eretici e inquisitori nella Bologna del Cinquecento*.

4 On Bologna and its government see at least De Benedictis, *Repubblica per contratto* and Gardi, *Lo stato in provincia*.

5 On the court of the Torrone see Di Zio, 'Il tribunale criminale di Bologna nel sec. XVI' and Fornasari, *Il 'Thesoro' della città*, pp. 192–207.

ings; each volume consists of about 300–1000 sheets, or more. The sheer number of records reveals how the court worked steadily throughout the years, recording even the smallest conflictual situations in the city and the territory.

In this study we will focus on about sixty volumes covering the years 1590 to 1630, approximately. This is a mere fraction of a collection too rich to be studied completely by a single individual, but it does offer a vivid picture of society at the time. The various communities in the territory delegated to their bailiffs (*massari*) variety of responsibilities, in particular the responsibility of referring back to the Torrone all criminal activity that came to their attention. These *massari* carried out their duties zealously, sometime going so far as to refer to the Torrone disputes between children who, according to the regulations of the court, should not have been considered. Though the scribes recorded in good Italian the denunciations and the testimony uttered in Bolognese dialect, they retained the original terminology touching on work utensils or other objects whose names were untranslatable. The depositions were transcribed if not integrally at least with so much minute detail that they now constitute a rich source of information about the economic and social life of the region at any given point in time.

In the years under our scrutiny, 1590–1630, Bologna and its territory had suffered from the same famines that had struck most of north-central Italy and Europe. Those of 1591–92, 1622–23, and 1629 had been particularly severe. Then, in 1630, the plague struck and wiped out entire communities.[6] While the cases we will examine do not mention these enormous calamities directly, they do nonetheless deal with events that took place at this time of severe crisis. Furthermore, the incidents described in these court cases are often set in mountainous territories or in isolated and impoverished hamlets where old customs survived longer and where the local clergy, whose level of instruction and competence were mediocre at best and whose drive for pastoral work was minimal, was not often inclined to fight against a culture which, in many ways, it shared with the mass of the population. The events we will examine will thus speak of the ritual and violent behaviour of youths, of the efforts of the political and ecclesiastical

---

[6] On the famines and the plague that struck Italy in the first decades of the seventeenth century see Malanima, *La fine del primato*; Pastore, *Crimine e giustizia in tempo di peste nell'Europa moderna*; Romano, *L'Europa tra due crisi.*

authorities to contain them, and of the difficulties that ensued from this—in short, they will speak of order and disorder.

Youths aged twelve to twenty often appear in the proceedings of the Torrone not only as victims, but also as witnesses and as accused. Because the municipal statutes of Bologna did not provide for immunity on account of age, there are many cases brought against adolescents and even against children.[7] In the case of young boys under the age of fourteen, who were considered not to have reached puberty yet, the documents often give their exact age (or, as exact as possible, since even the parents were sometime unsure of their children's exact age); otherwise, the documents speak of *putti* (children), *giovani* (youths), *tosi* (youths), *tosotti* (younger youths) *tosacci* (bad youths).

These youths are sometime accused of theft. They enter into houses and steal foodstuffs (bread, cheese), clothes (shirts), and occasionally coins or jewelry.[8] The culprits are, for the most part, young beggars or vagabonds with no family who eke out a living by any means possible. The manner of the crime betrays the poverty of the society in which they operate: children and youths are marked from the beginning of their lives by the scarcity of resources that afflicts a large part of Europe at the end of the sixteenth and beginning of the seventeenth centuries. These young beggars and vagabonds are so numerous as to constitute one of the favourite subjects of the art of this period, as we can see in the works of Caravaggio (1571–1610) and of many others.[9]

It is not theft, however, but violence that characterizes the behaviour of the young, a violence that at this time was endemic in the cities as well as in the countryside and which expressed itself particularly in the relationships between young people. In rural communities, the youths in these trials are often young shepherds or stable boys of fourteen or fifteen years of age who graze their animals together and fight with sticks or with the wooden ladles they carry for drawing water.[10] The reasons for their differences may be tied to their work (for example, animals that wander over into someone else's lands) or to frequent play altercations. They amuse themselves with nuts, balls,

---

[7] Niccoli, *Il seme della violenza*, pp. 141–93; on the general question of punishing minors, see pp. 10–14. The pre-modern statutes of Bologna have been published as *Statuta civilia et criminalia civitatis Bononiae*.

[8] ASB, Torrone, 5472, fols. 145r–147r and 220r; 5718, fols. 96r and 115r; 5737, fol. 14r; 5738, fol. 297r; 5761, fol. 289r.

[9] See the exhibition catalogue *Da Caravaggio a Ceruti*.

[10] ASB, Torrone, 5748, fol. 116r; 5752, fol. 20r; 5762, fol. 14r.

hard-boiled eggs (trying to crack their adversary's egg), they play 'a gamed called the stick,' at rolling cheese rounds or rolls of wood down the road; in brief, they play at all sorts of games, any of which could provide reason enough for disputes, blows, or injury. In 1579 Orazio Lombardelli wrote that on feast days the youths 'besiege the streets with their playing ball, *pallone, palla al maglio,* 'cheese' and *a la druzzola,* they have fist fights or throw rocks.'[11] In fact, the court scribes constantly register complaints against the aggressive and violent behaviour of the young in their games.[12]

## Stone-throwing

The most dangerous game, whether in the city or in the countryside, was, without a doubt, the stone fight. These rock-throwing battles had a long and ancient pedigree: Suetonius mentions them in his *Lives of the Caesars* and Saint Augustine in his *On Christian Doctrine.*[13] In the Middle Ages they acquired deeper meanings: the outcome of these battles between gangs of children or youths had, for the adult population of the time, divinatory properties. At the end of the fifteenth century and beginning of the sixteenth, these dangerous games were observed with great attention in the hope of predicting from them the outcome of the wars that were ravaging Italy at the time. When the wars in Italy ended in the middle of the sixteenth century, so did the inclination to seek prophetic meaning from the outcome of the rock-throwing battles among children. The battles themselves, however, did not cease and remained a favourite pastime for bands of youths in spite of the fact that they were forbidden by civic and ecclesiastical authorities. The Church, for one, feared these games would waylay the youth from attending the schools of Christian Doctrine.[14] As Teofilo Folengo pointed out in his peculiar macaronic Latin, 'est quasi communis totas

---

[11] Lombardelli, *Degli uffizi e costumi de' giovani,* p. 11. *Pallone* is a form of soccer, *palla al maglio* 'mallet ball,' a game played with a wooden ball and a mallet, 'cheese' and *a la druzzola* were games that involved rolling a large cheese round or a roll of wood down the street.

[12] ASB, Torrone, 2259, fols. 245r–247v, 262r–v; 5712, fols. 30r, 231r; 5737, fols. 92r, 156r; 5638, fol. 301r; 5742, fol. 105r; 5746, fol. 260r; 5752, fol. 81r; 5755, fol. 170r; 5867, fol. 164r; 5907, fol. 120r.

[13] Suetonius, *The Lives of the Caesars,* II, 45, p. 68; Augustine, *De Doctrina christiana,* IV, 24, 53, in PL 34, col. 115; Augustine, *Teaching Christianity,* p. 234.

[14] Niccoli, *Il seme della violenza,* pp. 41–59, 126–29.

usanza per urbes / ut contrari agitent saxorum bella citelli' (it is nearly the common custom in cities for boys to divide into teams and do battle with stones).[15]

At times the young also threw stones at buildings that carried some sort of symbolic meaning. The houses of Jews were the target of such activities especially during Holy Week or in the wake of the election of a new pontiff. Carlo Ginzburg, Laurie Nussdorfer, Sergio Bertelli, and Agostino Paravicini Bagliani have illustrated in various ways the violence and ritual pillaging that accompanied these occasions.[16] In Bologna on 16 September 1590, on the occasion of the election of Pope Urban VII, a crowd of children and adolescents nearly destroyed the city's synagogue and pillaged an oven named in honour of Saint Stephen. Following a complaint lodged by the leaders of the Jewish community, a trial took place where witnesses testified to having seen 'about two hundred *tosi*,' or even three hundred, throw rocks into the shop; others mentioned 'a great number of *tosatti* and *gioveni*' (children and young people) in the area.[17] The number of youths implicated in this event was so large it was impossible to bring them to justice.

Testimony on all types of stone-throwing battles are numerous in the documents of the court of the Torrone, demonstrating that, although city authorities deemed them to be intolerable, such events were in fact quite frequent. Stones were thrown against the windows of a young girl and she responded by complaining she was being treated 'like a prostitute'; pebbles were thrown at a merchant with cries of 'spione becco fottuto' (fucking cuckolded spy) and he responded asking for justice 'against these insults'; stones were thrown 'for fun' behind the church in Roffeno, a town in the Apennines, or also near the market in Bologna.[18] While cases at the Torrone often ended without a sentence being pronounced, this last case ended with nine young men being found guilty; all nine were condemned to suffer the strappado in public and seven among them were further condemned to be whipped. The court clearly wanted to draw as much attention as possible to this punishment so as to make it exemplary. The court felt

---

[15] Folengo, *Opere*, p. 141.

[16] Ginzburg, 'Saccheggi rituali'; Nussdorfer, 'The Vacant See'; Bertelli, *Il corpo del re*, pp. 39–57; Paravicini Bagliani, *The Pope's Body*, pp. 99–107; *Cérémonial et rituel à Rome*, pp. 11, 35, 49.

[17] ASB, Torrone, 2338, fol. 207 and following.

[18] ASB, Torrone, 2263, fol. 179r; 5783, fol. 199r; 1939, fol. 171r; 2270, fols. 217r–225v.

that it was no longer acceptable to throw stones at each other and everyone needed to know this.

## Honour offended

Other types of ritual behaviour also reveal a very marked aggressiveness that manifests itself in strongly stereotyped forms. These are specifically urban behaviours tied to concepts of honour evident in all seventeenth-century Italy.

Among them are displays of violence from university students against shop-keepers and land-lords who, it seems, did not show sufficient consideration for the young gentlemen whom they served or lodged. On 13 April 1590 a land-lord requested rental payments from five students from Mantua; they answered him with a series of insults, among which 'becco fottuto' (fucking cuckold). The man, offended, responded by pointing out that this kind of behaviour was not worthy of gentlemen; at this point one of the students punched the land-lord in the eye and called him a 'forfante insolente' (insolent rogue). The following day, the court scribe registered a similar episode. A certain Elisabetta Rossi denounced Sandro, a student to whom she had rented a room, for having broken a chair, for refusing to pay for it, and for having threatened her; apparently, when she had reproved him saying his conduct 'was not worthy of a gentleman,' the young man, deeming himself to have been offended, had punched her in the face and had given her a nose bleed.[19] In many other episodes we see students insult, threaten with swords, break doors, all the while claiming proudly their status as gentlemen and not allowing it to be placed in doubt.[20]

Honour and the violence committed for its sake are not the prerogative of young gentlemen. Many complaints reveal just how often the town people considered themselves offended by glances, touches, eavesdropping, each of which they consider an infringement of their privacy and therefore an injury. On three occasions in January 1590 and again in April 1630 the court scribes register dialogues that can be reduced to the following pattern: 'I ran into a certain person and looked at him because he was in front of me and he said to me "Why are you looking at me?" and I said "Why, am I not allowed to look at you?" and he drew his sword and came towards me, and I drew my

---

[19] ASB, Torrone, 2277, fols. 170r, 173r–v.

[20] Niccoli, *Storie di ogni giorno*, pp. 104–8.

dagger to defend myself and he wounded me'; or else: 'I ran into a certain person and looked at him involuntarily (or, I looked at him without malice), and he said to me "Why are you looking at me?" and I said "Can't I look at you?" and he then said to me "You think I don't know you, you fucking cuckholded spy?" and then I said to him "I am an honest man" and having heard that he began to punch me.'[21] A third case is slightly different (the victim looked at the aggressor's girlfriend),[22] but the elements of the dialogue remain the same: 'Why are you looking?' 'Why, can't I look?' On another occasion a youth is embroiled in a fight because he has touched (without any intention to steal) some money that did not belong to him. In this case the dialogue unfolds between two blacksmiths using terminology we have already encountered among students: 'This is not the way an honest man conducts himself'; 'I am an honest man, it's you who is the rascal'; 'You are a fucking cuckold'; 'You are a liar.'[23] The blacksmiths' insults follow the usual scenario. As Robert Muchembled has already noted for the French countryside and Peter Burke for Genoa and Rome, in the seventeenth century artisans as well as nobles play their part in the comedy of honour.[24]

## Love and honour

Love stories are also marked by violence, by a sense of honour, and by rituals. Each pregnant young girl denouncing the father of her child who now refuses to marry her tells the same story: while she was working all alone in the house or in the countryside she was joined by a young man whom she knew (often a work companion or the son of the master); he takes her by surprise, violates her and thus steals her honour (the girl always claims to have been a virgin). The description of the initial rape is very detailed so as to leave no doubt on the matter that might mitigate the point. Following the act, the young man promised to marry her; they had had further sexual relations, always with the promise of marriage, and finally the young girl had become pregnant; now she asked either for the young man to marry her or at least for him to give her a dowry that might allow her to secure a husband of some sort. Under interrogation the accused most often

---

[21] ASB, Torrone, 5729, fols. 141r, 157r.

[22] ASB, Torrone, 2263, fol. 203r–v.

[23] ASB, Torrone, 2277, fols. 234v–235r; 2304, fols. 72r–74v.

[24] Burke, *The Historical Anthropology of Early Modern Italy*, pp. 9–14; Muchembled, *Popular Culture*. See also Cohen, 'The Lay Liturgy of Affront.'

denies having had the affair or else claims that the girl was not a virgin to start with; he is tortured but, if he manages to stick to his side of the story, he is generally acquitted. Occasionally he admits his error and the trial comes to an end when he or his family bestow a certain sum of money on the girl.[25] There are many love stories, especially in the countryside, that begin with an act of violence but then proceed with the consent of the young woman. At least, that is the way in which the young women tell their stories, believing that this pattern makes them more credible. What we notice is that in the collective consciousness initial violence does not exclude the continuation of sexual relations.

When the young man courts the young woman he does so according to a standard ritual. He pays homage to his beloved 'not only by greeting her, but by looking at her at the window.'[26] Above all he makes it clear, if necessary by a show of force, that he will not tolerate other young men paying homage to his beloved. At least five trials follow this pattern. In December 1629 a young man from Crevalcore, near Bologna, tells how his rival 'drew a dagger from his knapsack and came towards [him] swearing "Damn God" and saying "If you go once more to the house of Andrea Malagodi to see his daughter, I'll kill you with this dagger.' At these words the young man responded by punching him out.[27] Another time, in August 1630, a young man sought to kiss Maria, a sixteen-year-old village girl, against her will and in the presence of one of her aunts; then, armed with a long stick, he went to see the girl's father declaring that he objected 'that anyone should make love to Maria.'[28] To court a girl, then, entailed rituals, threats, forced kisses, and demonstrations of force, all of which had the purpose of declaring the young man's rights over the young woman.

## Public kissing

The proceedings of the court of the Torrone reveal that in the space of a few months there were several cases such as Maria's of young women who had been kissed against their will. These are interesting cases for

---

[25] See, for example, ASB, Torrone, 5736/1, fols. 505r–527r. See also Niccoli, *Storie di ogni giorno*, pp. 123–27.

[26] Ferrari, *Fido conseglieri*, p. 2.

[27] ASB, Torrone, 5713, fol. 499v. Blasphemy, it should be noted, is included as an aggravating circumstance; for blasphemy and insults see Burke, *The Historical Anthropology*, pp. 95–109.

[28] ASB, Torrone, 5752, fol. 283r–v.

us because their meaning is not what they might at first appear to be. Such kisses are not necessarily expressions of love or preludes of violence. In fact, a sixteenth-century jurist observed that 'if a lay man kisses a woman in public, I find it difficult to believe he does so for erotic reasons' ('si laicus mulierem oscularetur in publico non praesumerem quod animo venereo ita faciliter').[29] His opinion is understandable, for such kisses are always public kisses, given in front of witnesses for the sake of publicity.

On Palm Sunday evening, 13 April 1631, in the village of Casalecchio de' Conti, a certain Pietro Giacomo Tosarelli, armed with an arquebus and a pistol and accompanied by three comrades, approached Domenica Balbani, a young woman of twenty years of age, who was just coming out of church in the company of some other women; he placed his arm around her neck and, pulling her towards him, kissed her on the left cheek and cried out 'I call you all to witness that I have kissed Domenica here present.' What had led Pietro Giacomo to kiss her, Domenica explained to the judge some time later, 'was without a doubt the fact that he loved me and wanted to marry me, but my father and mother did not want to give me to him and had promised me to another man.' In other words, as the young woman's mother clearly put it, 'he expected with this kiss to take her as his wife.'[30]

The two women's explanation sheds light on another unusual case from September 1630. A man had entered under some pretext into the house of an eleven-year-old orphan girl who lived alone with a servant; he dragged her into the street and kissed her in front of everyone. Proceedings against him were initiated but, some time later, the young girl's grandfather and sole guardian withdrew the charges against him.[31] It seems that by kissing the young girl by force and in public the young man had sought to ensure a good marriage for himself: the orphaned girl was, apparently, the sole heir of her grandfather's wealth. We can assume that the grandfather withdrew his charges against the man because the latter, in turn, had withdrawn his pretensions on the young girl.

According to popular opinion, then, kissing a young woman in front of witnesses gave a man marriage rights over her. The same act could also be used to block an unwanted marriage. Jurists, however, con-

---

[29] Gambiglioni. *De maleficiis*, p. 345.
[30] ASB, Torrone, 5762, fols. 560r–571r.
[31] ASB, Torrone, 5748, fols. 282r–283r.

demned this practice quite severely. As the Roman jurist Giovan
Battista De Luca claimed at the end of the seventeenth century, 'when
a violent kiss is placed on an honest woman in order to force a marriage
or to impede by this means that she marry another man, this action is
punishable by death.'[32]

Another complaint lodged on 1 June 1630 tells us that in Barbarolo,
a small hamlet in the Apennines over Bologna, the young Maddalena
della Castellina had been kissed by force and in public by a certain
Domenico Magnani just as she came out of church. At first this act
seemed incomprehensible, for Magnani showed no interest, either
personal or economic, in the young woman, whom he barely knew
and who was already betrothed to another man. The truth, however,
quickly came out: the kiss had been commissioned by the nephews of
the prospective groom, a much older man whose wealth the nephews
had hoped to inherit. The trial ended with a sentence that dealt harshly
with Domenico Magnani but exonerated the nephews. The episode
itself also ended in favour of the nephews, for the uncle did, in fact,
cancel his engagement to the young woman.[33]

## Kissing and the marriage ceremony

In order to understand better this ritual of publicly kissing a woman in
order either to marry her oneself or to block her marriage to another
man, we need to introduce a parenthesis that will review the marriage
rituals current in Italy from the Middle Ages to the sixteenth century.
Until the Council of Trent, Italian marriage rituals were marked by their
complexity and diversity. Many were the result of a mixture of Roman
and German legal systems that varied from region to region across the
peninsula. Whatever the local situation might be, and regardless of the
many steps and the amount of time the process entailed, the crucial
moment that gave immediate factual and legal validity to a marriage
took place when the couple gave their oral consent, in front of a notary
who drew up the marriage contract, to enter at that moment into
marriage ('per verba de praesenti'). The consent was then confirmed
by a series of gestures that the notary conscientiously recorded because
they were considered juridically significant: the placing of the wedding
ring on the finger, the *toccamano* (that is, the couple's joining of

---

[32] De Luca, *Il dottor volgare*, 4:372.
[33] ASB, Torrone, 5746, fols. 414r–451v.

hands), and the kiss. The latter was, in fact, seen as the mimetic symbol of the consummation of the marriage and, consequently, of the act of union of the couple.[34]

Before the Council of Trent, therefore, the kiss was an act with legal and ritual validity. It is mentioned in the statutes of several Italian towns for it granted the bride the right to a marriage gift that, because of this kiss, came to be known as the *osculum* (in Latin), or *basiatico* or *basiatura* (in Italian).[35] All this explains to a large extent the behaviour of the young villagers who, in the countryside around Bologna or any other Italian city, suddenly kissed a young woman in order to marry her themselves or to prevent her from marrying someone else.

In its attempt to reorganize and discipline everything that pertained to the ecclesiastical realm, the Council of Trent placed the marriage ritual under the strict control of the Church. Until that time, and in spite of the fact that marriage was viewed as a sacrament, the presence of a priest at a marriage ceremony had been supplemental and occasional. In the wake of a very animated debate, on 11 November 1563 the Council of Trent decreed that marriage ceremonies were to take place inside a church, after the obligatory publication of bans, and in the presence of two witnesses and the parish priest. The latter was to ascertain the consent of the bride and groom and to register the marriage. The marriage was not valid unless these directives were strictly respected.[36]

Although previous expressions of consent, including the kiss and the joining of the hands, lost their legal validity, they remained firmly anchored in the popular imagination as rituals that 'made' the marriage and marked a liminal point after which it was not possible to return on one's intentions.[37] Numerous diocesan synods reiterated (vainly, it seems) that promises and oaths did not constitute a valid marriage, not even when confirmed by a kiss. Other synods—in Liguria, Piedmont, and Campania, for example—legislated even against the retention of the ritual kiss in church marriages.[38] The ritual kiss was forbidden not

---

[34] Niccoli, 'Baci rubati,' pp. 225–34.

[35] Tamassia, '*Osculum interveniens,*' pp. 262–63.

[36] *Conciliorum oecumenicorum decreta*, pp. 755–59.

[37] Bonvini Mazzanti, *L'opera pastorale*, p. 147.

[38] Brandileone, *Saggi di storia della celebrazione del matrimonio*, pp. 494–96; Jemolo, 'Le disposizioni sul matrimonio,' p. 12; Jemolo, *Il matrimonio nel diritto canonico*, p. 33.

only because it was deemed inappropriate, but because it was seen as ambiguous, in the sense that someone could believe it contributed to the validity of the marriage ritual. The fact that we find directives against the ritual marriage kiss in synods throughout the century testifies to the survival of ancient marriage rituals in the imagination of the people and in general practice.

The forced kiss could also be viewed as an offence and as such was punishable by civil law. Contemporary legal codes in fact listed the crime of 'violent kissing.' Several edicts issued by the papal legates in Bologna and elsewhere in the Papal States threatened to severe punishments. In 1608 Cardinal Benedetto Giustiniani, papal legate in Bologna, proposed as an appropriate punishment for those guilty of 'forced kissing' a fine of three hundred *scudi* and five years of forced labour in the galleys (which was, in fact, the punishment inflicted *in absentia* on Domenico Magnani, whom we met above).[39]

We can thus understand the specific social practice of the public kiss and, at the same time, the two major reasons for its suppression: the marriage kiss was forbidden by the papal legates as an act of violence and by the bishops as a remnant of a non-ecclesiastical ritual. In spite of legal and ecclesiastical directives, however, the public kiss remained in practice in isolated and mountainous regions.

## May-trees[40]

It was not the public kiss, however, but the *maggio*, or May-tree, that was the most common love and disdain ritual to be brought in front of the Torrone.[41] From France to England, from Germany to the Baltic countries, all of Europe in the Ancient Regime planted May poles. This was a fertility ritual celebrated the night of the first of May by young people who set up branches, bunches of flowers, or young trees in the village square or in front of houses, and in particular at the door or at the window of the young women they sought to honour. This custom was well known in Renaissance Rome. Young Roman men planted laurel or some other young trees in front of the door of their beloved,

---

[39] *Bando generale*, p. 55.

[40] I am using this neologysm, rather than the standard English term 'Maypole,' in order to indicate that the Bolognese version generally used a young tree, not a pole for its May-day festivities (translator's note).

[41] I will not discuss the *charivari*, which is already well known, for we find very few cases of it in these records.

coloured its trunk gold, and filled its branches with presents. 'There were quails, partridges, pieces of damask cloth, satin, velvet, family crests, and a thousand other fantasies attached to the branches,' writes the Venetian gentleman Marcantonio Michiel in a letter from Rome dated 4 May 1519.[42]

In the Apennines below Bologna the custom was quite wide spread and universally appreciated. As the judge for a 1599 trial noted, 'by simply planting a May-tree in front of someone's door, one does not do that person any offence, but rather a pleasure, for this is done everywhere in the world.'[43] In another trial in September 1630 a young man from Budrio, in the plains around Bologna, tells the judge that he had planted a May-tree for a young woman some months before and for that he had exchanged blows with one of her suitors, and then added: 'The first day of May, it is the custom in Budrio for everyone to plant May-trees for young women.'[44] In fact, this practice was a lively source of conflict. Other trial records speak of veritable brawls around this practice: bands of young men planted May-trees at night while other bands of armed young men tried to prevent them from doing so and reduced the May-trees to bits.[45]

## Defaming rituals

The youth could use the May-tree ritual not only to court, but also to defame a young woman, especially if she had refused their attention. This is evident in a long trial of May 1630 in which two fourteen-year-old girls describe the May-trees they had received in their little hamlet in the mountains. The first, Maria, found quince tree flowers in front of her window; the other, Laura, expected some branches of pomegranate, but found instead various objects and some wild rose flowers tied to a post.[46] In Italian wild roses are called *rose canine* (dog roses) or *spini* (thorns), names that immediately suggest that the purpose of the May-tree Laura had received was not to pay her homage, but rather to show her disdain or to offend her. Her May-tree also held a donkey's bell, a pair of slippers, and a rag doll. The donkey's bell is fairly obvious in its meaning, the

---

[42] Sanuto, *I Diarii*, vol. 27, col. 273.

[43] 'per puram et simplicem plantationem maii ante portam alterius non fit ei aliqua iniuria, stante quod ita fit fere per totum mundum.' ASB, Torrone, 3123, fol. 31r.

[44] ASB, Torrone, 5737, fol. 239r.

[45] ASB, Torrone, 2277, fols. 261r–262v.

[46] ASB, Torrone, 5761, unnumbered folios.

slippers were an allusion to exposed female genitalia, while the rag doll suggested a play on the words *putta* (young girl, doll) and *puttana* (prostitute). Laura herself expounded some of these meanings when she said 'There was a *putta* made of rags lying in a paper cradle by which those who set up the May-tree wanted to indicate, I believe, that I was a *puttana.*' Laura's mother, a widow who lived alone with her daughter, thought she knew who the culprit was: a certain Domenico Righi, who had asked to marry Laura and had been refused.

At the time, legislation in Bologna and in the Papal States pursued anyone who attached defamatory objects to someone's door, for such behaviour was deemed to reflect seriously on the honour of the offended party. Thirty years before, the Roman jurist Prospero Farinacci had defined the topic and gathered under the heading of 'public libel' ('libello famoso') an array of such defamatory behaviour including written insults, defamatory songs, the posting of horns or some other object on someone's house, and the like.[47] As early as 1454 the statutes of Bologna had mentioned these actions, without however giving them a legal definition.[48] Giovan Battista De Luca's extensive treatise on these crimes points to the growing importance of the ideology of honour during the course of the seventeenth century.[49] Not surprisingly, the process of change outlined in this article sought to suppress May-trees because they could be potentially defamatory and harmful to the culture of honour.

A 1599 case deals with a young couple from Sasso, on the hills above Bologna, that became the victims of a veritable libel persecution: defamatory pamphlets were posted, cow horns were hung at their door, and finally a May-tree decorated with yellow flowers (the colour of prostitutes and Jews) and with tree roots reminiscent of horns was planted in front of their house—in short, all the possible variants of public offence and anonymity, all interchangeable among themselves, were used.[50]

The May-tree could be a complex symbolic system, as a case from May 1630 shows. In a mountain village very near to the one where Laura lived, a post was planted bearing objects whose meaning unequivocally insulted the woman of the house. There was a fig branch full of fruits, a paper penis tied with a red string, a bunch of nettle, and an oven broom.[51] In

---

[47] Farinacci, *Praxis et theorica criminalis*, pp. 420–27.
[48] *Statuta civilia et criminalia*, 1:485.
[49] De Luca, *Il dottor volgare*, 4:414–17.
[50] ASB, Torrone, 3123, fols. 4r–35v.
[51] ASB, Torrone, 5472, unnumbered folios.

this case, as well, it was the sexual honour of the woman that was being assailed. The paper penis was self-evident, the figs alluded to female genitalia (*fico/fica*), the oven broom to the penis (as implied in the vulgar term *scopare*), and the nettle, like the wild roses before, suggested that the culprits wanted to pester the woman.

In their structure, these May-trees remind us of the emblems that formed such an important part of seventeenth-century culture. Not without reason the jurist Giovan Battista De Luca observed that one can wound and injure someone with the use of a hieroglyph.[52] If an emblem was a metaphor expressed by an image (sometime accompanied by a caption), the May-tree was an emblem (and therefore a metaphor) constructed with real objects, not with representations, and it, too, was to be interpreted 'as a hieroglyph.'

## The end of May rituals

In the seventeenth century in the Apennines above Bologna, then, the May-tree was a wide-ranging social custom practiced by young persons and universally appreciated by the community as a way of offering some of its members public tokens of love or, vice versa, infamy.

In Bologna itself, as in the rest of Italy and in other countries of Europe, ecclesiastical authorities sought to Christianize the May rituals by turning their expressions of homage for a woman into a tribute for the Virgin Mary, inviting the faithful to bestow on her the flowers that would normally be laid at the windows of young women. Already in a provincial council of 1579 in Milan Cardinal Charles Borromeo had spoken out strongly against the May-tree, pointing out that the first of May was already consecrated to saints Philip and James and that one should not celebrate anything else on that day. He harshly condemned the custom of planting 'profane, leafy trees' ('profanas eas arbores frondescentes') and suggested that the holy tree of the cross should, instead, be raised on this day.[53] This condemnation was taken up with insistence and in nearly the same terms by many diocesan synods, especially in northern Italy.[54]

Since the Middle Ages in Bologna, as in other Italian cities, custom demanded that on the first of May a young woman be designated the Queen of the May. Decked out with flowering branches, she was

---

[52] De Luca, *Il dottor volgare*, 4:414.

[53] *Acta Ecclesiae Mediolanensis*, p. 212.

[54] Corrain and Zampini, *Documenti etnografici*, pp. 45, 69, 88–89.

accompanied under the arcades and to the city gates by a happy retinue that demanded a coin from all passerbys. By the middle of the sixteenth century this custom had changed; we are told that 'now one decks out altars with images of saints' and the faithful are invited to offer flowers and alms to them, instead.[55]

In Bologna the first of May held not only religious, but also civic significance for it coincided with the installation of the new *Gonfaloniere* and the *Anziani* (Elders), all of whom were fundamentally opposed to the papal power in the city. On this day they also formally received the homage of the light cavalry of the city's garrison. This civic May Day celebration, therefore, countered papal power at both the spiritual and the political level. It comes as no surprise, therefore, that on 28 April 1687, using as an excuse the incidents that had occurred the previous year at the installation of the *Gonfaloniere*, the papal legate Antonio Pignatelli (who would later be elected Pope Innocent XII) officially and finally forbade 'the popular and profane erection of May-trees' in Bologna and in all of its territory 'so as to avoid the scandals that might arise from it.'[56] The Bolognese ambassador in Rome signalled the unhappiness of the city with this decision, but to no effect.[57] With this decree the courting and profane customs that had been tied to May-tree celebrations disappeared, at least in the city; in the villages they survived underground, at times transformed in songs one sang with the accompaniment of violins and other instruments.[58]

## Conclusion

A variety of ritual practices among Italian youths in Tridentine Italy can be identified in Bolognese archival sources. These are practices firmly rooted in an ancient and complex tradition. While they were fairly wide ranging in their time, they generally do not appear in the literature and art of the time. Ironically, today we can identify and examine them only in so far as they appear in court proceedings that reveal how contemporary authorities sought to eradicate them. Ecclesiastical leaders sought to gain firmer control over the souls of the faithful, while secular leaders sought to maintain civic order—two lines of action that were

---

[55] Masini, *Bologna perlustrata*, p. 299.

[56] *Notificatione sopra la prohibitione della Festa populare del Maggio.*

[57] Mazzone, '"Con esatta e cieca obbedienza,"' p. 80.

[58] Prosperi, 'La religione della Controriforma,' pp. 202–22 and *America e Apocalisse*, pp. 307–18.

different but converged in a unified programme of Tridentine social control. Urban youth proved to be easier to control and bring into line with the changing attitudes to social practices, while youth in the isolated world of the countryside or in the mountain hamlets along the Apennines were more difficult to rein in. It was they who were able to retain for a much longer time the traditional rituals of love, play, and violence we uncovered in the court records.

*Università degli Studi di Trento, Italy*

*(Translated by Konrad Eisenbichler)*

## Cited Works
## Manuscript Sources

ASB. Archivio di Stato di Bologna. Torrone, 1939, 2259, 2263, 2270, 2277, 2338, 3123, 5472, 5638, 5712, 5713, 5718, 5729, 5736/1, 5737, 5738, 5742, 5746, 5748, 5752, 5755, 5761, 5762, 5783, 5867, 5907.

## Published Sources

*Acta Ecclesiae Mediolanensis.* Mediolani [Milan]: Ex officina typographica quon. Pacifici Pontii, 1599.

Augustine. *De Doctrina christiana.* Patrologiae cursus completus, series latina, 34. Ed. J.P. Migne. Paris, 1845. Coll. 15–122.

Augustine. *Teaching Christianity*, ed. John E. Rotelle, trans. Edmund Hill. New York: New City Press, 1996.

*Avertimenti e brievi ricordi circa il vivere christiano.* Broadside at the Archivio Arcivescovile di Bologna, Misc. Vecc. 798, 2.

*Bando generale dell'Illustrissimo e Reverendissimo sig. Benedetto Card. Giustiniano Legato di Bologna.* Bologna: V. Benacci, 1608.

Bertelli, Sergio. *Il corpo del re. Sacralità e potere nell'Europa medievale e moderna.* Firenze: Ponte alle Grazie, 1990.

Bonvini Mazzanti, Marinella. 'L'opera pastorale di frate Piero Ridolfi da Tossignano, vescovo di Senigallia dal 1591 al 1601' *Picenum Seraphicum*, 17 (1984–87): 131–67.

Brandileone, Francesco. *Saggi di storia della celebrazione del matrimonio in Italia.* Milano: U. Hoepli, 1906.

Burke, Peter. *The Historical Anthropology of Early Modern Italy. Essays on Perception and Communication.* Cambridge and New York: Cambridge University Press, 1987.

*Da Caravaggio a Ceruti. La scena di genere e l'immagine dei pitocchi nella pittura italiana*, ed. Francesco Porzio. Milano and Brescia: Skira, 1998.

*Cérémonial et rituel à Rome (XVI–XIX siècle)*, ed. Maria Antonietta Visceglia, Cathérine Brice. Roma: Ecole Française de Rome, 1997.

Cohen, Thomas V. 'The Lay Liturgy of Affront in Sixteenth-Century Italy' *Journal of Social History*, 25 (1992): 857–77.

*Conciliorum oecumenicorum decreta*, ed. Giuseppe Alberigo et al.. Bologna: Istituto per le scienze religiose, 1973.

Corrain, Cleto and Pierluigi Zampini. *Documenti etnografici e folkloristici nei sinodi diocesani italiani*. Bologna: Forni, 1970.

Dall'Olio, Guido. *Eretici e inquisitori nella Bologna del Cinquecento*, Bologna: Istituto per la storia di Bologna, 1999.

De Benedictis, Angela. *Repubblica per contratto. Bologna, una città europea nello Stato della Chiesa*. Bologna: Il Mulino, 1995.

De Luca, Giovan Battista. *Il dottor volgare, ovvero il compendio di tutta la legge civile, canonica, feudale e municipale nelle cose più ricevute in pratica.* 4 vols. Firenze: V. Batelli e compagnia, 1839–43.

*Disciplina dell'anima, disciplina del corpo e disciplina della società tra medioevo ed età moderna*, ed. Paolo Prodi and Carla Penuti. Bologna: Il Mulino, 1994.

Di Zio, Tiziana. 'Il tribunale criminale di Bologna nel sec. XVI' *Archivi per la storia*, 4 (1991): 126–34.

Farinacci, Prospero. *Praxis et theorica criminalis amplissima quatuor titulis partita*. Parma: Erasmo Vioth, 1605.

[Ferrari, O.], *Fido conseglieri ne gli sposalitii libri tre. Avanti le nozze, nelle nozze, doppo le nozze. Opra utilissima e curiosissima per le persone vergini, maritate, vedove.* Modena: Per Giulian Cassiani, 1628.

Folengo, Teofilo. *Opere*, ed. Carlo Cordié. Milano and Napoli: R. Ricciardi, 1977.

Fornasari, Massimo. *Il 'Thesoro' della città. Il Monte di Pietà e l'economia bolognese nei secoli XV e XVI*. Bologna: Il Mulino, 1993.

Gambiglioni da Arezzo, Angelo [Angelus Aretinus]. *De maleficiis. Cum additionibus D. Augustini Ariminensis, D. Hieronimi Chucalon, et D. Bernardini de Landriano*. Venetiis: D. Lilius, 1558.

Gardi, Andrea. *Lo stato in provincia. L'amministrazione della Legazione di Bologna durante il regno di Sisto V*. Bologna: Istituto per la storia di Bologna, 1994.

Ginzburg, Carlo. 'Saccheggi rituali. Premesse di una ricerca in corso' *Quaderni storici*, 65 (1987): 615–36.

Jemolo, Arturo Carlo. 'Le disposizioni sul matrimonio in alcuni sinodi italiani post-tridentini' *Archivio di diritto ecclesiastico*, 1 (1939): 6–32.

Jemolo, Arturo Carlo. *Il matrimonio nel diritto canonico*. Milano: F. Vallardi, 1941.

Lombardelli, Orazio. *De gli ufizii e costumi de' giovani libri IIII*. In Fiorenza: Appresso Giorgio G. Marescotti, 1579.

Malanima, Paolo. *La fine del primato. Crisi e riconversione nell'Italia del Seicento*. Milano: Mondadori, 1998.

Masini, Antonio. *Bologna perlustrata*. 3 vols. Bologna: Erede di V. Benacci, 1666–90; rpt. Sala Bolognese: A. Forni, 1986.

Mazzone, Umberto. '"Con esatta e cieca obbedienza": Antonio Pignatelli cardinal legato di Bologna (1684–1687)' pp. 45–94 in *Riforme, religione e politica durante il pontificato di Innocenzo XII (1691–1700)*, ed. Bruno Pellegrino. Galatina: Congedo, 1994.

Muchembled, Robert. *Popular Culture and Elite Culture in France, 1400–1750*, trans. Lydia Cochrane. Baton Rouge: Louisiana State Univerity Press, 1985.

Niccoli, Ottavia. 'Baci rubati. Gesti e riti nuziali in Italia prima e dopo il Concilio di Trento' pp. 224–47 in *Il gesto nel rito e nel cerimoniale dal mondo antico ad oggi*, ed. Sergio Bertelli and Monica Centanni. Firenze: Ponte alle Grazie, 1995.

Niccoli, Ottavia. *Il seme della violenza. Putti, fanciulli, mammoli nell'Italia tra Cinque e Seicento*, Bari and Roma: Laterza, 1995.

Niccoli, Ottavia. *Storie di ogni giorno in una città del Seicento*. Bari and Roma: Laterza, 2000.

*Notificatione sopra la prohibitione della Festa populare del Maggio*. In Bologna: dall'erede del Benacci per la Stamperia camerale [28 aprile 1687].

Nussdorfer, Laurie. 'The Vacant See: Ritual and Protest in Early Modern Rome' *Sixteenth Century Journal* 18 (1987): 173–89.

Paravicini Bagliani, Agostino. *The Pope's Body*, trans. David S. Peterson. Chicago and London: University of Chicago Press, 2000.

Pastore, Alessandro. *Crimine e giustizia in tempo di peste nell'Europa moderna*. Bari and Roma: Laterza, 1991.

Prosperi, Adriano. *America e Apocalisse e altri saggi*. Pisa and Roma: Istituti editoriali e poligrafici internazionali, 1999.

Prosperi, Adriano. 'La religione della Controriforma e le feste del Maggio nell'Appennino tosco-emiliano' *Critica storica*, 18 (1981): 202–22.

Prosperi, Adriano. *Tribunali della coscienza. Inquisitori, confessori, missionari*. Torino: Einaudi, 1996.

Romano, Ruggiero. *L'Europa tra due crisi (XIV e XVII secolo)*. Torino: G. Einaudi, 1980.

Sanuto, Marino. *I Diarii*. 58 vols. Venezia: Visentini, 1879–1903.

*Statuta civilia et criminalia civitatis Bononiae*, ed. Filippo Carlo Sacchi. 2 vols. Bononiae: Ex typ. C. Pisarri, 1735.

Suetonius. *The Lives of the Caesars*, trans. Catharine Edwards. Oxford: Oxford University Press, 2000.

Tamassia, Nino. '*Osculum interveniens*. Contributo alla storia dei riti nuziali' *Rivista storica italiana*, 2 (1885): 241–64.

# Ritual, Religion, and the Royal Teenager: The Case of Edward II of England

Virginia A. Cole

As the long-awaited heir to the English throne, from the moment he was born in 1284, Edward II was in a spotlight that intensified through his teen years. Though some medieval theorists posited twenty-four as the end of adolescence, in England, the age of twenty-one served as an official age of majority for aristocratic males who were allowed at that age to take formal possession of their inheritance. Edward was twenty-three when he became king in 1307, putting an end at one stroke to his status of adolescent and heir. This study will first set the royal adolescence of Edward II in context by comparing it to that of his father and grandfather, and then will turn to Edward's navigation of the difficult years between teenager and adult, heir and king.

Edward II's adolescence is one of the most well-documented of the medieval period because the prince's large, complex, expensive household, like the king's household, generated a number of official documents—household and wardrobe accounts as well as correspondence.[1] This rich collection of sources, supplemented with chronicles, can be used to explore Edward's teenage years, particularly his public ritual moments. Most of these public occasions were clearly orchestrated by his forceful father, King Edward I, to fit his own political and military agendas, so much so that it is tempting to see Edward II as an object, a political pawn completely manipulated by his father attempting to shape a political and personal identity for his son. Following the lead of Paul Griffiths in his recent book *Youth and Authority: Formative Experience in England*, in which he discusses the agency of early

---

[1] For documents produced by the Household and Wardrobe, classed as Exchequer documents, see *List of Documents Relating to the Household and Wardrobe, John to Edward I, Public Record Office Handbooks*, no. 7. Material can also be found in the Close, Patent, and Pipe Rolls. Prince Edward's correspondence has been published in *Letters of Edward Prince of Wales, 1302–1305*. Useful bibliographies to the documents produced by the prince's household can be found in Johnstone, 'Wardrobe and Household Accounts' and her *Edward of Carnarvon, 1284–1307*.

modern teenagers, in this paper I will explore the agency of a medieval teenager, albeit a royal one. Removed from parental influence and nominal head of his own household from the age of four, Edward may have had in some ways far more scope for independent action than 'ordinary' medieval teenagers, but his unique position as Prince of Wales also entailed significant constraint. Rather than looking to the events and incidents of daily life for evidence of agency, I will focus instead on royal ritual. In fact, the records show how Edward II used ritual as a tool to assert his own sense of identity by signalling stages of personal and political transformation for himself against the backdrop of his father's manipulation of the royal rituals of adolescence for his own ends.

## The Rituals of Edward's Youth

Royal ritual was a forum for the intersection of the personal and political in the ritual-rich culture of the Middle Ages. In the twelfth and thirteenth centuries, a European-wide trend was set in motion in which kings and their ministers took advantage of any opportunity to create new royal ceremony and display or to remould traditional royal ritual. Occasions for royal ceremonial such as births and birthdays, coronations, knightings, betrothals, marriages, deaths, and funerals, underwent renovation. Coronation steadily became more elaborate with more pre- and post-ceremony activities and participants. So too did royal funerals, especially as partitioning of the corpse became common practice, allowing a number of different ceremonies at multiple places of internment as the heart went to one foundation and the entrails to another. Royal babies and children who had previously received little attention now were provided with expensive tombs upon their early demise. In addition, completely new royal rituals were created during this period: the ritual touching for the king's evil, the royal maundy, and, in the fourteenth century by Edward II himself after he had become king, the distribution of cramp rings on Good Friday.[2]

As part of the trend in royal ritual, it was becoming typical practice for royal adolescence to proceed in small stages which were made public through coming of age rituals. In England, King Henry III

---

[2] See Richardson, 'The Coronation in Medieval England,' pp. 111–202; Schramm, *A History of the English Coronation*, pp. 27–73; Hallam, 'Royal Burial and the Cult of Kingship,' pp. 364–67; Binski, *Medieval Death*, pp. 63–65; Tanner, 'Tombs of Royal Babies,' pp. 26–34; Bloch, *The Royal Touch*, pp. 28–51, 92–107; Barlow, 'The King's Evil,' pp. 3–27; Kellett, 'King John's Maundy,' pp. 34–39.

(1214–72), Edward II's grandfather, whose influence on royal ritual has been underrated, was largely responsible for creating the public displays of royal adolescence. Henry III's interest in ritual was shaped by his personal circumstances. His own adolescence had been fraught with personal and political difficulty. His father, the notorious King John, had died when Henry was nine and his mother had returned to France leaving the boy-king to rule a troubled kingdom under the supervision of the pope and a council of regents. The result was a muddy adolescence both personally and politically. Henry was knighted and crowned at nine; then crowned again at sixteen. At some point there had been provisions for ending the regency at the age of fourteen at which point the pope officially withdrew, but the regency dragged on, lightening at sixteen, but never officially coming to an end.[3]

Henry III made sure the childhood and adolescence of his own children passed quite differently. He was an affectionate, involved parent who incorporated his family, including all his often young children, into royal ritual. Edward I (1239–1307), Edward II's father, was his eldest son and heir. Edward I's early adolescence progressed through carefully constructed public stages: at ten, he was given lands in Gascony; at fifteen in 1254 he was married, knighted and given the duchy of Aquitaine. However important and defining these ritual moments were, they did not signify a complete leap from adolescence into adulthood since Henry III still remained in authority over his son. Edward's public participation in tournaments and enjoyment of military pursuits during this period can be seen as a socially acceptable expression of identity in distinct contrast to his father's pacific, religious interests. The king's supervision may have caused some friction between father and son in the later teen years, possibly contributing to Edward's flirtation with the rebels in the revolt of the barons and in his later departure on crusade.[4]

Despite the differences and friction, when Edward I became king, he followed the tradition of royal ritual that he had learned from his father. He himself was neither a completely absent parent nor a completely indulgent parent. He had at least fourteen children, but lost

---

[3] Carpenter, *The Minority of Henry the Third*, pp. 13, 19–20, 123–24, 162, 188, 241–43, 301–2, 389.

[4] Michael Prestwich calls the period 1263–72, beginning when Edward I turned twenty-four and continuing until he inherited the throne at thirty-four, a period of apprentice kingship; see Prestwich, *Edward I*, pp. 9–11, 15, 16–24, 35–37, 45–46, 694 and Johnstone, *Edward*, p. 109.

a series of sons and heirs to illness at a young age.[5] When his son Edward II was born, Edward I was deeply involved in various ambitious projects including wars in Scotland and France. The prince's younger years seem to have been fairly isolated from direct parental influence and it was not until adolescence that there was more direct contact between father and son, after the youth's mother, Eleanor of Castile, had already passed away.

King Edward not only followed the emerging trend of carefully controlling the progression of the heir's childhood and adolescence, but amplified it by creating additional coming of age rituals. From the age of four the prince had his own household, though its finances were controlled by his father until his death. At the age of six, after the death of his mother, the prince was given the counties of Ponthieu and Montreuil. Typically, the heir-apparent was instructed by a *magister* who provided experience in the ways of court and war. Prince Edward was eleven years old when he received a *magister*, perhaps a little older than usual when compared to Henry VI, for example, who was only seven.[6] The arrival of the prince's *magister* signals the official dawn of adolescence when Prince Edward began to take an active, if ceremonial role in the affairs of the kingdom. Many aristocratic males began their participation in tournaments in these early years of adolescence as did Edward's teenage cousins.[7] Edward never participated in tournaments, but gained military experience in his father's wars. At the age of twelve, when invasion by the French seemed imminent, plans were made for Prince Edward to take part in the defence of the country by assuming military command, a precaution that turned out to be unnecessary.[8]

Several significant ritual moments in this progression of teenage coming of age rituals can be identified, moments which had become part of the standard repertoire for apprentice kings, and which could include such public ceremonies as investiture with lands and titles, knighthood, military command, being proclaimed heir, and being inducted as regent. The moments were arranged by the king when he

---

[5] Parsons, 'The Year of Eleanor of Castile's Birth,' pp. 249–65.

[6] Edward's *magister* was Guy Ferre, former steward of the prince's grandmother Eleanor of Provence. Ferre retained the post until Edward was nineteen. Johnstone, *Edward*, pp. 65, 15–17; Griffiths, R. *The Reign of King Henry VI*, p. 52.

[7] Two of Edward's cousins, Thomas and Henry of Lancaster, began to participate in tournaments when they were about twelve. Johnstone, *Edward*, p. 17.

[8] Johnstone, *Edward*, p. 33.

deemed them appropriate. Edward I was particularly adept at timing his son's significant moments to coincide with his own agenda.

Thus the first significant moment for the prince came on 11 July 1297 when the king publicly proclaimed Prince Edward, then thirteen years old, his heir and future king. In an artfully staged assembly, the barons were required to swear public fealty to the prince, and the other attending nobles to acclaim him by holding up their right hands.[9] It was an unusual, unprecedented ceremony elicited by an unusually dire political crisis. It served the king's need to resolve an on-going dispute with the Church over taxation and to drum up political, military, and financial enthusiasm from the resistant nobility for the proposed war in France.[10] At the same time, the king's staging of a grand ceremony was also a proclamation of his son's graduation to a new level of personal and political responsibility.

A month after the ceremony the king departed for France. Young and inexperienced as he was, Prince Edward then served as regent, a not uncommon responsibility for boy-heirs in medieval England.[11] The brief regency, from August 1297 to January 1298, was an opportunity for the young Edward to see and be seen, and to dabble publicly in the craft of kingship, though guided by a council of barons and churchmen. The prince was undoubtedly a figurehead, but the records show his presence, token as it might have been, at meetings and in the daily routine of business.[12]

Another significant ritual moment came just before Prince Edward turned seventeen, when in February 1301 he was awarded the title of Prince of Wales. King Edward used the award of the title to make his recent conquest of the Welsh concrete, to inspire the English, and to

---

[9] Walter of Guisborough, *The Chronicle*, p. 291.

[10] Prestwich, *Edward I*, pp. 420, 414–35.

[11] Johnstone, *Edward*, pp. 35–39. Henry II had already set precedents by having his son and heir Henry serve as regent at a young age; see Warren, *Henry II*, p. 580. Edward III left his seven year old son Edward, the Black Prince, as regent when he departed for France in 1338; see Chaplais, *Piers Gaveston*, p. 35; Harvey, *The Black Prince*, p. 57.

[12] Johnstone, *Edward*, pp. 35–36. The Close and Patent Rolls of official correspondence from the period of the regency contain many instances of orders issued 'at the instance of' or 'at the request of Edward, the king's son,' but those formalized phrases should be viewed with some scepticism since the first time the phrase was used in the records was in August 1290 when Edward was a mere six years old; *Calendar of the Patent Roll, Edward I*, 2:383.

threaten symbolically the Scots who were his next target for conquest. On this occasion, the king promoted his son, but then allowed him only a narrow scope for independent action. After his investiture as Prince of Wales, 'by ordinance of the king,' Edward II was allowed to travel to Wales without the king in order to survey his land and receive homage. On his return to England after a tour of five weeks, Edward then received the homage of English barons who held land in Wales.[13] Next, the prince was deemed old enough to accompany his father on campaign and to lead, under the guidance of more experienced officers, one prong of the attack. Edward's half of the army did not see much action, but he seems to have made a good impression on contemporaries and to have met his father's expectations well enough.[14]

Thus the earlier years of Edward's adolescence passed fairly tension-free. As a child, there had been little lengthy contact between father and son. During early adolescence that pattern shifted as father and son spent significant amounts of time in closer proximity.[15] Spending time together continued into the later years of the prince's adolescence when he was beginning to assert tentatively a sense of his own identity and independence.

The construction of identity is of course as complex for teenagers as it is for adults; in part it is a matter of preferences, something that fathers cannot usually control. From all accounts, the prince and his father had entirely opposite tastes: the king as a young man had enjoyed such chivalric pastimes as tournaments and grew up to be a warrior-king; his son was athletic, a good swimmer and horseman, but never participated in tournaments as a young man and seemed to feel no inclination for things military; he seemed to have enjoyed, instead, practical pastimes such as building, or recreational activities such as music, feasts, display, merry-making and good company.[16]

---

[13] British Museum Add. MS. 7966A, fol. 155 as quoted by Johnstone, *Edward*, pp. 61 and 63.

[14] A poet wrote of the prince, 'A youth of seventeen years of age and newly bearing arms, he was of well proportioned and handsome person, of a courteous disposition.' *The Roll of Arms, of the Princes, Barons, and Knights who attended King Edward I to the siege of Caerlaverock in 1300*, trans. Thomas Wright (London: J. C. Hotten, 1864) as quoted in Saaler, *Edward II*, p. 18.

[15] For instance, when Edward was fourteen-fifteen years old in 1298–99, father and son were together for a total of 292 days. Johnstone, *Edward*, p. 44.

[16] Hutchison, *Edward II*, pp. 10–12.

Rebellion is another age-old method for teens to express identity, but there is little of that in the evidence of Edward's teenage years. Only a few instances of misbehaviour can be interpreted as rebelliousness. The most famous comes from 1305 when Edward was twenty-one. The details are not clear, but apparently Edward stole deer from Bishop Langton's park and then was obnoxious about it in public. It was his rudeness that caused the king to explode. As punishment Edward was banished from his father's presence and pocketbook for six months. The prince reacted by strict obedience, by asking his sisters and step-mother to intervene, and by carefully courting his father's favour for several months.[17]

Another instance which might problematically be termed rebelliousness comes from 1306–7, the last year of Edward I's reign when the king apparently decided that his son and his closest friend, Piers Gaveston, had formed an inappropriate attachment. As a result, Piers was sent back to his homeland with an annuity. Edward had no choice but to obey. Since Piers' recall was one of the prince's first acts as king, it is clear that he had viewed his father's action as punishment, though it is likely that the king had intended his action to be preventative and precautionary, as much as punitive.[18]

The Langton disagreement in 1305 may have delayed the prince's knighthood, another of the significant ritual moments of medieval male teenagers.[19] Edward was almost twenty-two when he was knighted in May 1306. Quite probably the delay was political. It allowed the king to time the dubbing with a call for political, military, and financial support for yet another campaign in Scotland. The ceremony took place not long after Robert the Bruce had himself crowned and served as a symbolic response.[20] Edward's was a grand statement. Because it was one of the largest dubbings en masse ever seen in England, the ceremony was also a recruitment tool for the war, a way for the king to increase the number of knights (an ever diminishing resource by this point).[21] Three hundred young men answered the

---

[17] 'Annales Londoniensis' in *Chronicles of Edward I and Edward II*, 1:138; Johnstone, *Edward*, pp. 97–99.

[18] Hamilton, *Piers Gaveston*, pp. 34–35.

[19] Knighting usually took place between the ages of thirteen and twenty-two. Marchello-Nixia, 'Courtly Chivalry,' p. 138.

[20] Walter of Guisborough, *Chronicle*, p. 367.

[21] Denholm-Young, 'Feudal Society,' p. 119; Walter of Guisborough, *Chronicle*, pp. 367–68; *Flores Historiarum*, 3:131.

invitation to be knighted, so many that they could barely be housed for the overnight vigil. Each of the teenage boys received clothes from the king and, after the ceremony, was feted at a banquet called 'the feast of the swans' at which oaths of vengeance on the Scots were sworn. Again, though the ceremony was contrived by the king, Edward was given some opportunity for independent action. He was the first to be made a knight and it was he, rather than his father, who then knighted the others. Accompanying the elevation to knighthood, the king made an effort to establish a tradition when he gave Edward the county of Aquitaine, the same land he had received when he was knighted (and married) at the age of fifteen.[22]

## Edward's Agency

Prince Edward's own agency in the significant ritual moments of his adolescence can be determined from the official records—the financial records produced by the exchequer and the accounts of household expenses produced by the wardrobe. These documents were by and large concerned with property, fines, payments, wages and other such administrative detail. Aspects of adolescence that involved no financial transactions have mostly escaped notice in these records, but some activities have been captured. Not surprisingly they tend to be religious ones, especially the charitable activities evidenced in almsgiving, recorded in the documents because they incurred a cost to the household.

In her excellent biography of Prince Edward, Hilda Johnstone described the prince's almsgiving as 'entirely routine and unremarkable,' because she believed that it occurred at the direction of the prince's personal almoner and/or his two Dominican confessors.[23] I would agree that there is a large amount of routine, but within that routine there are glimpses of individual action as evidenced by the frequent phrase in the alms rolls 'per preceptum ejuisdem.'[24] Johnstone was partly correct in seeing this almsgiving as unremarkable, for in the thirteenth and fourteenth centuries these activities had crystallized into routines, but they were also rituals that were infinitely capable of political, religious, and perhaps even personal self-expression in the same way that royal baptism, knighting, marriage, coronations, and funerals were capable of nuanced self-expression.

---

[22] Johnstone, *Edward*, pp. 106–9.

[23] Johnstone, *Edward*, p. 86.

[24] See, for example, *Liber quotidianus*, p. 39.

Although according to Matthew 6:3 almsgiving should be private, 'the left hand should not know what the right hand does,' European kings had made it public ritual for centuries. By the thirteenth century they were increasingly manipulating almsgiving for political ends as part of a package of royal rituals projecting an image of good Christian kingship. In that package, kings discovered that almsgiving ritual was particularly malleable because of its political neutrality—it offended no one that mattered since it did not infringe on the rights, privileges, or authority of the Church or the nobility. Royal almsgiving projected a powerful image of the king as protector and 'father of the poor' and, by extension, as protector and father of all his subjects. Besides, royal almsgiving was easily administered and arranged through the small staff of the royal almonry, and inexpensive since distributions of a single small coin or a meal amounted to little even when thousands of paupers presented themselves for help. In the twelfth and thirteenth centuries, almsgiving, like other royal rituals, underwent constant experimentation by individual kings.

As prince, Edward II used the same tools of royal ritual as his father to express his own sense of progress in the transformation into adulthood and kingship. The extant documentation for Edward's adolescence suggests that Edward's use of ritual became most pronounced in his later teen years, at the point when his father staged important coming of age rituals for him.

The first clear instance of this use of ritual by the prince occurred when in May 1300, at the age of sixteen, he accompanied his father to wage war against Scotland. Father and son made a stop at Bury St Edmunds, an abbey that was a centre for the important royal cults of Saints Edward and Edmund. This particular visit was partly a peace-making visit (the king and the monks had been at odds over clerical taxation and related issues) and partly to seek St Edmund's special blessing against the Scots. This accomplished, the king departed. The abbey's anonymous chronicler at the time reported:

> The king's son, who had stayed for a longer time, sought a more secluded place in the monastery for his visit. He had been made in chapter one of our brethren, for the regal dignity of the abbey and the monks' abundance of spiritual comforts pleased him. Every day he asked for a monk's allowance, just as the brethren ate in the refectory, to be given to him. It is said certainly that he alleged that the grandeur of the place and the agreeable companionship of the monks always pleased him. On the twelfth day, however, he said goodbye to the brethren and hastened to join his father.[25]

---

[25] 'Filius regis diucius perhendinans loca peciit in eodem monasterio ad

Outsiders such as the prince who were made members of the 'brethren,' the monastic confraternity, were guaranteed special prayers and masses by the monks in return for favours and a bequest.[26] It is not clear whether King Edward I had joined the confraternity earlier, but I suspect that it might have become common practice in the twelfth century for all kings to be enroled in it. By the late thirteenth century, it may have been standard practice to enrol as a teenager; this would have allowed yet another opportunity for a coming of age ritual for royal teenagers.

The father-son joint visit and the enrolment in the Bury confraternity were undoubtedly initiated by the king, as was most likely the prince's stay as well, but the prince's satisfactory behaviour must have been his own. The tone of the passage is obviously self-congratulatory on the part of the monks and could be dismissed out of hand were it not for the fact that the comments mesh with other indications about the prince's love of theatricality and enjoyment of regal display. The records hint at this already in his teenage years when, for instance, he adopted the fashion of keeping exotic animals symbolic of royalty, in this case by travelling with a lion.[27] Edward was also not adverse to the traditional royal cults; as a teenager, he purchased an illuminated life of Edward the Confessor and later, as king, he showed great interest in the relics of St Albans at Ely. After spending Palm Sunday at St Albans, Edward went to Ely for Easter where the monks showed him around the monastery. According to the chronicler Walshingham, writing at St Albans in 1377–92, Edward asked to see if they also had St Alban's body. The casket was opened and indeed the cloak which Alban had received from Amphibous had fresh blood on it. Everyone fell to the ground in awe and Edward alone managed to close the tomb, though he was obviously impressed since he talked of St Albans enthusiastically for the rest of his visit.[28]

---

immorandum secreciora frater enim noster factus est in capitulo. Multum enim sibi placuit loci regalitas et crebra fratrum solacia. Singulis eciam diebus peciit liberacionem monachilem, uidelicte sicut in refectorio reficiuntur fratres sibi exhiberi. Ferunt utique eum dixisse numquam [non] sibi loci magnalia dulciaque fratrum complacuisse consorcia. Duodecimo tamen die ualefaciens fratribus ad patrem suum regem properauit.' *Chronicle of Bury St Edmunds*, pp. 157.

[26] Knowles, *The Monastic Order in England*, pp. 475–79.

[27] Johnstone, *Edward*, p. 86.

[28] Johnstone, *Edward*, pp. 30–31.

About a year after the Bury visit, Edward celebrated his seventeenth birthday which came shortly after he had been awarded the title of the Prince of Wales and while he was on his first father-son campaign against the Scots. When the prince was born, the king had marked the occasion and every birthday thereafter with a larger than usual distribution of alms to the poor. On his seventeenth birthday, the prince himself took over the custom when he had his almoner give a penny to each of three hundred paupers, a far greater distribution than usual for him, clearly intended to mark a particularly special occasion.[29]

This does not mean that the prince went 'completely independent' in his practice of royal religious ritual by the time he was seventeen years old. King Edward I, like his father before him, believed that the family that prayed together, made oblations together, and gave alms together stayed together and would be saved together. In the records, the prince can clearly be seen participating in the normal family activities just as he had when he was a boy, visiting shrines and making oblations with his father and new stepmother. For instance, at the end of February, the family visited Canterbury where the prince and his parents made offerings at the shrines of St Adrian, St Augustine, and St Mildred in the church of St Augustine, and in the cathedral at the statue of the Virgin, and at Becket's crown.[30]

The same can be said of much of Edward's almsgiving. By the time of the prince's middle adolescence around 1300–1, the number of paupers to which King Edward's personal almoner routinely distributed alms had escalated to more than six hundred per week. The prince's almoner also distributed alms on the prince's behalf, but they were far fewer, usually to about 30–50 paupers every week, and that figure remained constant from the time the prince was about nine until he was twenty-one years old.[31] The modesty of the number reflects the prince's fewer financial resources and dependency on the king for

---

[29] Johnstone, *Edward*, p. 86; PRO E101/363/18 fol. 2v.

[30] Johnstone, *Edward*, p. 45; *Liber Quotidianus*, pp. 29, 30.

[31] *Liber Quotidianus*, 16–25; PRO E101/353/18; E101/355/28; E101/370/22/2; E101/365/13; E101/365/12; E101/368/4. Edward had had requiem masses said, at which alms were distributed, in November 1302 in his presence for his mother Eleanor of Castile; in December for his grandmother Eleanor of Provence; in 1303 in January for one of his clerk's; in February for Walter of Beauchamp, formerly the king's squire, and for William Comyn the prince's yeoman; in April for Guy Ferre. Johnstone, *Edward*, 86.

funds, as well as the prince's respect and caution not to upstage the king.

Another almsgiving ritual which had achieved prominence by the thirteenth century was the royal maundy, as it is known in England. The term seems to be a popular corruption of the Latin, 'mandatum novum,' Jesus' new commandment to love one another. The maundy was a ritual reenactment of the Last Supper in which Jesus washes the feet of the disciples. Beginning in the fourth century, high ranking churchmen routinely reenacted the scene assuming the role of Christ, who in John 12 is described as master and lord (*magister et dominus*), while a group of paupers or lower clergy assumed the role of the disciples described in the same text as servants (*servus*). When paupers rather than monks or lower clergy participated in the maundy, as they did in the royal version, then the ritual was combined with a distribution of food, money, or clothing. The maundy thus became a form of almsgiving as well as a ritual of power and humility. By the thirteenth century, the French and English monarchies had coopted the ritual from the Church. Edward II's grandfather, Henry III had made it normal practice to draft his young children into his performances of the maundy. Edward I had grown up performing it and, as an adult, continued the practice of family participation by having his queen and young children perform it with him.

Prince Edward had already performed a maundy with the rest of the family by the time he was six.[32] It was not until 1303, however, when he was nineteen, that he 'went solo' with the royal maundy. At the time, both king and prince were stationed with their respective households in opposite suburbs of Nottingham, about five miles apart. For the prince's maundy, his almoner distributed a penny and a pair of shoes to thirty paupers, exactly as he had when the Prince was nine.[33]

The prince's taste for ritual, already evident in the maundy, blossomed the moment he was allowed greater scope. This happened at his coronation in 1307. Edward was almost twenty-four, the end of his youth by some medieval standards, so the coronation was a perfectly timed opportunity for the ritual expression of personal and political transformation from youth and prince into adult and king. Edward took full advantage of the opportunity. He carefully planned the ceremony himself and the result was an intriguing combination of

---

[32] Johnstone, *Edward,* p. 89; PRO E101/363/18 fols. 1, 5.

[33] Johnstone, *Edward,* p. 89; PRO E101/363/18 fols. 1, 5; C47/4/4/ fol. 40.

masterfulness and ill-judgement. The event is notable for its numerous innovations (some of which became traditional when they were adopted in later coronations): special prominence was given to his friend Piers Gaveston, who carried the crown and sword of St Edward and fastened on the royal spur; two statues of Edward the Confessor were offered at the altar; the ceremony was lengthened; the oath was rewritten; changes to the liturgy and accompanying music were made; etc.[34] Collectively, the innovations were intended to promote ritually the authority and sacral nature of the king. In the context of Edward's previous teenage use of royal ritual, the combination can be seen not only as a conscious political statement of independence, but also as a personal, brazen declaration of adulthood.

Although coloured at times by his own personality, Edward II's adolescence is representative of a medieval English royal heir's 'coming of age.' As his grandfather and father had determined it, royal adolescence was given form in a series of rituals. Edward I was especially adept at timing his son's ritual graduations with his own political needs. The prince's adolescence was atypical in that the ritual moments were somewhat delayed, ostensibly to coincide with the king's agenda, but also to allow the king careful control, even caution and protectiveness, as can be seen in the king's frequent arrangement for the prince to enjoy a narrow opportunity for action after each ritual promotion. In that arena, the prince seemed to have performed unremarkably, receiving no comment from chroniclers or royal accountants. A teenage medieval English heir-apparent was allowed, and probably even expected, some scope to announce his own transformation and identity. For Edward I that declaration took the form of military pursuits—tournaments, crusades, and the like. Edward II, on the other hand, rejected the small opportunities for action and self-identity arranged by his father. Instead, he preferred royal religious ritual, in its milder forms while a teenager and a prince, in more explosive forms once he became an adult and a king.

*Binghamton University*
*Binghamton, New York*

---

[34] Richardson, 'The Coronation of Edward II,' pp. 1–10; Wilkinson, 'The Coronation Oath of Edward II,' pp. 445–69; Hughes, 'Antiphons and Acclamations,' pp. 150–68; Chaplais, *Piers Gaveston*, pp. 42–43. Prominent nobles had participated in previous coronations to a similar degree, but it was controversial for Edward II to highlight Gaveston in such a way given the rumours that were circulating.

# Cited Works
## Manuscripts

Public Record Office, Kew, U.K. E101 Exchequer, King's Remembrancer, Accounts Various.

## Published sources

Barlow, Frank. 'The King's Evil' *The English Historical Review* 95:374 (Jan. 1980): 3–27.

Binski, Paul. *Medieval Death: Ritual and Representation*. Ithaca, NY: Cornell University Press, 1996.

Bloch, Marc. *The Royal Touch: Monarchy and Miracles in France and England*, trans. J. E. Anderson. New York: Dorset Press, 1989.

*Calendar of the Patent Rolls preserved in the Public Record Office: Edward I*. 5 vols. 1893; rpt. Nedeln, Leichtenstin: Kraus Reprint, 1971.

Carpenter, D. A. *The Minority of Henry the Third*. Berkeley: University of California Press, 1990.

Chaplais, Pierre. *Piers Gaveston: Edward II's Adoptive Brother*. Oxford: Clarendon Press, 1994.

*The Chronicle of Bury St Edmunds, 1212–1301*, ed. with intro. and trans. Antonia Gransden. London: Nelson, 1964.

*Chronicles of the Reigns of Edward I and Edward II*, ed. by William Stubbs. 2 vols. London: Longman, 1882–83.

Denholm-Young, N. 'Feudal Society in the Thirteenth Century: The Knights' *History* 29 (Sept. 1944): 107–19.

Edward II, King of England. *Letters of Edward Prince of Wales, 1302–1305*, ed. Hilda Johnstone. Cambridge: Cambridge University Press, 1931.

*Flores Historiarum*, ed. Henry Richards Luard. 3 vols. London: Eyre and Spottiswoode, 1890.

Griffiths, Paul. *Youth and Authority: Formative Experience in England, 1560–1640*. Oxford: Clarendon Press, 1996.

Griffiths, Ralph Alan. *The Reign of King Henry VI: The Exercise of Royal Authority, 1422–1461*. Berkeley: University of California Press, 1981.

Hallam, Elizabeth M. 'Royal Burial and the Cult of Kingship in France and England, 1060–1330' *Journal of Medieval History* 8 (1982): 359–80.

Hamilton, J. S. *Piers Gaveston, Earl of Cornwall, 1307–1312: Politics and Patronage in the Reign of Edward II*. Detroit: Wayne State University Press, 1988.

Harvey, John. *The Black Prince and His Age*. Totowa, NJ: Rowman and Littlefield, 1976.

Hughes, Andrew. 'Antiphons and Acclamations: The Politics of Music in the Coronation Service of Edward II, 1308' *The Journal of Musicology* 6:2 (Spring 1988): 150–68.

Hutchison, Harold F. *Edward II*. New York: Stein and Day, 1972.

Johnstone, Hilda. 'The Wardrobe and Household Accounts of the Sons of Edward I' *Bulletin of the Institute of Historical Research* 2 (1924): 37–45.

Johnstone, Hilda. *Edward of Carnarvon, 1284–1307.* Manchester: Manchester University Press, 1946.

Kellett, Andrew. 'King John's Maundy' *History Today* 40 (Apr. 1990): 34–39.

Knowles, David. *The Monastic Order in England: A History of its Development from the Times of St Dunstan to the Fourth Lateran Council, 940–1216.* Cambridge: Cambridge University Press, 1963.

*Liber quotidianus contrarotulatoris garderobae: anno regni regis Edwardi primi vicesimo octavo A.D. MCCXCIX & MCCC.* London: J. Nichols, 1787.

*List of Documents Relating to the Household and Wardrobe, John to Edward I,* Public Record Office Handbooks, 7. London: Her Majesty's Stationer, 1964.

Marchello-Nixia, Christiane. 'Courtly Chivalry' 1:120–72 in *A History of Young People in the West,* ed. by Giovanni Levi and Jean-Claude Schmitt, trans. by Camille Naish. 2 vols. Cambridge, MA: Belknap Press of Harvard University Press, 1997.

Parsons, John Carmi. 'The Year of Eleanor of Castile's Birth and her Children by Edward I' *Medieval Studies* 46 (1984): 245–65.

Prestwich, Michael. *Edward I.* Berkeley: University of California Press, 1988.

Richardson, H.G. 'Early Coronation Records: The Coronation of Edward II' *Bulletin of the Institute of Historical Research* 16:46 (June 1938): 1–11.

Richardson, H. G. 'The Coronation in Medieval England: The Evolution of the Office and Oath' *Traditio* 16 (1960): 111–202.

Saaler, Mary. *Edward II: 1307–1327.* London: Rubicon Press, 1997.

Schramm, Percy Ernst. *A History of the English Coronation,* trans. Leopold G. Wickham Legg. Oxford: Clarendon Press, 1937.

Tanner, Joan D. 'Tombs of Royal Babies in Westminster Abbey' *Journal of the British Archaeological Association,* 3rd Series 16 (1953): 25–46.

Walter of Guisborough, *The Chronicle of Walter of Guisborough Previously Edited as the Chronicle of Walter of Hemingford or Hemingburgh,* ed. by Harry Rothwell. London: Offices of the Society, 1957.

Warren, W. L. *Henry II.* Berkeley: University of California Press, 1983.

Wilkinson, B. 'The Coronation Oath of Edward II and the Statue of York' *Speculum* 19:4 (Oct. 1944): 445–69.

# Henry VI: The Ritual Education of an Adolescent Prince

## Robert Zajkowski

The pageantry surrounding the entry of the adolescent Henry VI into London in 1432 must be analyzed within the context of some of the momentous events occurring during the early reign of this monarch. When discussing the royal entry, it is important to emphasize a salient aspect of ritual practice. Ritual, according to definition, is repetitive and fixed, but it is also quite historically specific. Although entry spectacles and civic rituals associated with Richard II, Henry V, and Henry VI share geography (London) as well as some elements of metaphor and pageantry, the uses to which this geography and these elements were put varied with contemporary social, economic, and political circumstances. Civic rituals tend to divulge a community's sense of identity, especially in relation to the monarch; they also reveal a conception of social values.[1]

The central political circumstance surrounding the royal entry of Henry VI in 1432 concerned the young king's father, Henry V, military conqueror and defender of the Church who unexpectedly and inconveniently died in 1422 soon after becoming regent of France and heir to the French throne, the potential ruler of a dual monarchy. The subsequent inheritor of this patrimony, with a minority government in England and a disputed throne in France, was the infant Henry VI. The reign of young Henry began as a protectorate led by a council composed of ambitious and often restless magnates, in particular his uncles, the dukes of Bedford and Gloucester, and his great uncle, Cardinal Beaufort. Political turmoil was inevitable.

The ten years following the change in monarchs witnessed considerable internal fighting among the ruling council. While in England a growing disenchantment with the continuing war effort in France, primarily an aristocratic affair, was becoming evident, on the continent there was a deterioration of the English position marked by the coronation of the hitherto excluded dauphin, Charles VII. In England itself

---

[1] *The Invention of Tradition*, pp. 1–14; and Muir, *Civic Ritual*, pp. 3–8.

there was growing lawlessness and continued fear of Lollardy, a fear
which became fully realized in 1431 when, during the king's absence
in France, there was a rising in London and southern England. This
rebellion, through its violence, written propaganda, anticlericalism,
and threat of social revolution, aroused terror among ecclesiastics,
magnates, and merchants and culminated in a swift and violent repression. It was also clear to many observers that the rule of law and justice
was being severely compromised. These were some of the concerns
oppressing the citizens of London when their young monarch arrived
in England on the wake of his previous participation in an entry
spectacle in Paris.[2]

There are two sources for this spectacle: a Latin letter written by the
town clerk, John Carpenter, describing the pageants and addressed as
a commission to his friend, the poet John Lydgate, and the resulting
vernacular poem of 537 verses, closely following the description by
Carpenter. The commemorative composition, entitled, 'King Henry
VI's Triumphant Entry into London, 21 February 1432,' reprises the
particulars of the royal progress, thus bringing its message to the
attention of a wider audience.[3]

As represented by the verse of Lydgate, the approach of the king,
analogous to the advent of David to Jerusalem, is a cause of rejoicing
for the citizens of London. The young monarch is greeted by a procession led by the mayor and aldermen dressed in scarlet together with
the craftsmen who are clad in white. After a welcoming speech by the
mayor celebrates Henry's status as ruler of both England and France
and refers to London in the traditional way as being the king's chamber, the progress of the young monarch and his entourage consists of
a sequence of seven pageants arranged between the London Bridge

---

[2] Good general treatments of the reign are in Ralph Griffiths, *The Reign of Henry
VI* and Wolffe, *Henry VI*. A standard account of conflict between England and
France during this period is Perroy, *The Hundred Years War*, esp., parts vii and
viii. Magnate dominance of the affair and the disillusion of the middle class may
be seen in M. R. Powicke, 'Lancastrian Captains,' esp., p. 379. The real and
perceived threat of Lollardy is discussed in Aston, *Lollards and Reformers* (see in
particular the chapter 'Lollardy and Sedition, 1381–1431,' which is a revised edition
of the original article published in *Past and Present* 17 (1960): pp. 1–44). For law
and justice see Carpenter, 'Law, Justice and Landowners,' esp., p. 209; and Powell,
'Law and Justice.'

[3] The letter is most readily accessible in *Munimenta Gildhallae Londoniensis*,
3:451–464; the poem in Lydgate, *The Minor Poems*, pp. 630–648.

and St Paul's Cathedral. At St Paul's the king is met by an ecclesiastical procession. Along with the mayor and citizens, the king and churchmen proceed to Westminster, where the *Te Deum* is sung. The king and his entourage then repair to his palace, while the citizens of London return home. On the following Saturday the mayor and aldermen provide Henry with a gift of £. 1,000 and the mayor addresses him, referring a second time to the city of London as the king's chamber.

Spectacles such as the London entry have a function apart from the mere celebration of a royal visit and there are a number of elements at play among these pageants. One cannot ignore the ideological aspects of this affair. The dual lineage from the Confessor and St Louis, that is, the Lancastrian justification for the dual monarchy is central, as is the representation of the divine sanction for this dynastic ambition. There is also a strong liturgical and messianic element running through these pageants. Not only does the advent of the king become a similitude of the entry of David into Jerusalem, but the lineage of the young Henry is associated with psalmic prophecy and with the Tree of Jesse, and therefore to Jesus, whose champion the monarch is to become. These themes represent civic expectations, although much of the content also reflects and is probably directly inspired by Lancastrian propaganda.[4]

Another central motif of the spectacle concerns the community of London itself and its relationship to the monarch, a relationship of intimacy explicitly defined in the mayor's reference to the chamber. The city and monarch are joined together into a family and household.

This idea of intimacy is traditional, as earlier spectacles evoke the metaphor of the chamber. The metaphor, however, is a complicated one. For Richard II it becomes a bridal chamber.[5] For Henry VI, the intimacy of the chamber is associated with a dominant theme of this royal entry, that of an eleven-year-old monarch who is expected to mature into an effective and just ruler. It is evident that the pageant sequence reflects on the part of the London elite an awareness of, and sensitivity to the implications of royal adolescence. Despite the Lydgatian title, this is not a triumphant entry in the spirit of Henry V's *adventus* in the aftermath of Agincourt.[6] Rather, the royal entry of 1432 is a

---

[4] For a discussion of these and other aspects of this pageant sequence see Bryant, 'Configurations of the Community in Late Medieval Spectacles'; Kipling, *Enter the King*, pp. 143–169; McKenna, 'Henry VI of England and the Dual Monarchy'; and Osberg, 'The Jesse Tree.'

[5] Kipling, *Enter the King*, pp. 16–17.

[6] For a detailed description of Henry V's Royal Entry of 1415 see *Gesta Henrici*

spectacle of anticipation; it is a spectacle that allows the civic chamber to become both the setting and the inspiration for the ritual education of an adolescent prince.

The conceptual background of the London pageant sequence is informed by the central place accorded by both authors and their public to the role played by advice, instruction, and edification, and by the practical literature providing these in the intellectual life of the early fifteenth century. There were numerous works produced at this time, many on commission from the intended audience, whether poems, histories, political tracts, Mirrors for Princes, ethical treatises, tractates on the virtues and vices, even courtesy books, which were felt to provide moral and political lessons and rules of action.[7]

The literature of advice was, according to Richard Firth Green, a reflection of the widespread belief among fifteenth-century readers that it was possible to modify one's actions according to the lessons learned from the successes and failures of one's predecessors.[8] It is also possible to discern a popularization of the traditional ideas concerning the prince and his role in society previously expressed in Latin or French through the many English compositions and translations made available to a public eager for this commonplace wisdom.[9]

Much of the general expectation underlying these works was reflected in the attitude of a poet such as John Lydgate, the author of the vernacular rendition of the royal entry, who was convinced of the power of the poet and of poetry to lead readers to virtue and the community to social order.[10] More specifically, the popularity of such works as the *Secretum Secretorum*, the fictionalized account of Aristotle tutoring his pupil Alexander, and their widespread use in the education of the youthful aristocrat has long been known.[11]

Another factor that must be taken into consideration when analyzing the royal entry of Henry VI is the role that education played in the lives of the youthful citizens of London. On the most fundamental level, the final goal in the education of the medieval youth was the development of a virtuous Christian. It is important to remember that

---

Quinti, pp. 101–113.

[7] An excellent introduction to this literature as it pertains to the reign of Henry VI may be found in Watts, *Henry VI and the Politics of Kingship*, esp., chaps. 1–2.

[8] Richard Green, *Poets and Princepleasers*, p. 138.

[9] *Four English Political Tracts*, pp. ix–xix.

[10] Ebin, *Illuminator, Makar, Vates*, pp. 19–48.

[11] Orme, *From Childhood to Chivalry*, pp. 81–111.

in this development learning was not compartmentalized. Socialization, intellectual attainments, practical vocational skills, and religious and moral formation were not considered to be discrete spheres in the educational growth of the child.[12]

Thus, although didactic writers argued that the moral education of a Christian was to be the goal of both contemplatives and active laymen, the need to develop the intellect and prepare the youth to assume his responsibilities in society were hardly ignored, nor was the inculcation of a conception of the goodness and immutability of the existing social order.[13] Whether he was a young urban adolescent aspiring to mastership in a guild, or a young member of the nobility or gentry seeking education for government in the household of a magnate, the focus was on apprenticeship: 'apprenticeship in service.' For both groups this apprenticeship included the inculcation of morals (and manners) along the development of professional expertise.[14] A familiarity with hierarchy and social structure as well as the expectation of supervised instruction for a specific occupation became ingrained.

Youth itself was regarded as 'contested territory,'[15] a period during which the individual served as a focal point for the battle between the virtues and vices.[16] It was considered to be a period of great danger but also of enormous promise during which the young person, at a time when he is most flexible and apt to learn, might be channelled toward the proper attitudes and sense of obligations owed to his estate. He was to be prepared for adult life.[17]

An analysis of the spectacle provided by the city of London for the royal entry of Henry VI reveals an acquaintance on the part of the organizers with the expectations of a young aristocrat for edification, as well as a familiarity with a number of ideas to be discovered in the contemporary literature of advice. The educative function of the pageants appears to represent the growing concern of Londoners for learning, both practical and spiritual, while also reflecting some of the intellectual and religious sources from which an interested laymen might draw.

---

[12] Denley, 'Elementary Teaching Techniques,' p. 224.

[13] Shahar, *Childhood in the Middle Ages*, pp. 166–177.

[14] Simon, *Education and Society in Tudor England*, pp. 7–8.

[15] Paul Griffiths, *Youth and Authority*, pp. 18–19.

[16] Hanawalt, *Growing Up in Medieval London*, p. 109.

[17] Paul Griffiths, *Youth and Authority*, pp. 27, 47–54.

Of considerable importance in the pageant sequence is the emphasis placed upon virtue. Henry's initial exposure to this theme occurs at the tower erected on London Bridge. Here a giant, 'a sturdy champeoun' (verse 74), appears, a champion and mentor who promises to make the young monarch, 'myhty with vertuous levyng' (verse 87). He is accompanied by two antelopes bearing the arms of England and France. The use of the giant is a familiar device in the royal entry. Nevertheless, for the young Henry VI this traditional figure is given a significance that departs considerably from previous spectacles.

When, during the triumphant entry provided by the city in the aftermath of Agincourt, Henry V approached the entrance to the bridge, the gigantic champion represented on the tower acted merely as an agent presenting the keys of the city to the king. Together with an accompanying gargantuan figure of a woman, he served to welcome the king with praise. A legend on the wall proclaimed London as the city of the king of justice.[18] If the giant couple were representative of the citizens of London, and the *Gesta Henrici Quinti* implies this exegesis, then their reception was symbolic of the passive stance of a community celebrating the triumph of a royal champion.

Conversely, the giant champion of the 1432 spectacle is a far more active and powerful figure: looking as stern as a lion and brandishing his sword, he promises, 'Alle fforeyn enmyes ffrom the Kyng to enchace' (verse 77), and to defend the royal estate. He also pledges in psalmic terms to clothe the king's enemies in confusion. Thus, the giant in this spectacle is presented not only as an agent stimulating the growth of virtue in the adolescent monarch and in this way 'hem to encresen as Cristis champioun' (verse 89), but also as providing defence of person and realm. This protective mentoring on the part of this representative of the city sets the tone for the subsequent royal progress.

Proceeding along the bridge the entourage encounters a tower from which issue three empresses: Nature, Grace and Fortune, who provide the king with gifts. This second pageant begins the process by which the king acquires, as gifts received within the chamber, the virtues necessary to become an effective ruler. It appears that the gifts of the three empresses, strength, fierceness, knowledge (*sciens*), wisdom or understanding (*kunnyng*), and prosperity, are derived from one of the most popular works for late medieval readers: Frere Lorens's *Somme*

---

[18] *Gesta Henrici Quinti*, p. 103.

*le Roi*, translated into English as *The Book of Virtues and Vices*.[19] However, Lorens speaks of these goods in a negative fashion as being ephemeral or of little account and, further, discusses how the gifts of fortune, nature (*kynde*), and grace are especially subject to the development of vainglory.[20] Lorens's treatment of these gifts appears to be considerably more negative than the presentation found in the second pageant. This is especially brought out by Lydgate's poem which, in an embellishment of the Carpenter letter, represents Empress Fortune presenting the crowns of England and France to the young monarch. In the context of a royal entry, it is unlikely that these signs of rulership would be designated as either ephemeral or of little account.

Rather than concentrating on Lorens, one should consider the role that Fortune plays in the work of other writers. Roman moralists and historians such as Cicero and Livy saw fortune, the Goddess *Fortuna*, in a more favourable light than the blind power depicted by the Christian heirs of this tradition. Specifically, it was possible to attract the favourable attention of this mutable entity by exhibiting *virtus*, which from Cicero's *Moral Obligation* came in the first instance to be associated with the 'cardinal virtues' of prudence, justice, fortitude, and temperance.[21]

It is this conception of Fortune and the qualities that a ruler needs to attract it that stand behind the giving of gifts by the three empresses. And it is this connection with the cardinal virtues that ennobles the gifts of Nature, Grace, and Fortune preventing them in this pageant from being placed, as Lorens would have it, in a completely negative opposition to the gifts of the Spirit. Grace's final gift, 'Vertuously lange in thy ryall citee, / with septre and crovne to regne in equyte' (verses 153–54), reinforces this tendency and makes it more immediately applicable to the political context of the spectacle.

Thus, the gifts of the three empresses, the first series of gifts in the second pageant, are the practical gifts of the earthly world. What would be considered the more spiritual gifts are presented by seven maidens who stand at the right of the three empresses: these are the seven gifts of the Holy Ghost: wisdom, understanding, knowledge, fortitude, the spirit of counsel, and fear of the Lord. Despite similarities to the earthly gifts of the empresses, these gifts possess an otherworldly tone.

---

[19] Kipling, *Enter the King*, p. 148; and Osberg, 'The Jesse Tree,' pp. 222–23.

[20] *The Book of Vices and Virtues*, pp. 75–78, 19–21.

[21] Skinner, *Machiavelli*, pp. 27–36.

The spiritual Gifts of wisdom and understanding detach the Christian from the world, direct his attention toward heaven and the way to salvation, and enable him to understand religious truths. The gifts of the Holy Ghost are inner qualities that make one attentive to the promptings of God and more susceptible to the workings of grace. Thomas Aquinas adds that the gifts are superior to the virtues, specifically they are 'divine virtues' that serve to perfect the virtues and sanctify the individual.[22] That the gifts of the seven maidens are bestowed at the same pageant as the more worldly gifts of the three goddesses is no accident, for here the mundane and the spiritual are conjoined. The gifts of the seven virgins standing to the left of the three empresses protect the young monarch with the shield of faith, while fitting him with the helmet of salvation. They also include the equipage of a ruler: the sword of justice and the sceptre of clemency. Thus, once again, the spiritual and the earthly are combined.

The allusion to Ephesians is expected to conjure up the image of battle in which the follower of Christ encased in the 'whole armour of God' may withstand the 'spiritual forces of evil' (Eph. 6:11–17). It also reverberates with echoes of the *conflictus* genre, developed from Ephesians, which together with the *Psychomachia* of Prudentius were major authorities for composers of treatises on the virtues and vices, treatises which were often, in the manner of Prudentius, structured in the form of a battle.[23] In this case, nevertheless, the Pauline 'sword of the spirit' (Eph. 6:17) is transformed into the 'swerde off myht and victorie' (verse 199).

These same virgins sing a roundel of welcome to Henry in which the king is described as the contentment, joy, source of satisfaction, abundance and wealth of the city, thereby conflating the gifts offered to the young monarch with the needs and expectations of the mayor, aldermen, and citizens of London. This is one of the keys to the interpretation of both this particular pageant and the spectacle as a whole. The virtues with which the adolescent king is imbued in this pageant, whether spiritual or earthly, personal or public, are associated in their utility to the royal city.

Inextricably linked to this motif of virtuous utility is the theme of education. The production of *Summae* on the virtues and vices derived

---

[22] *Catholic Encyclopedia*, s.v. 'Holy Ghost VI: Gifts of the Holy Ghost,' 7:413–14; *New Catholic Encyclopedia*, s.v. 'Holy Spirit, Gifts Of,' 7:98–99; Burgess, *The Holy Spirit*, pp. 79–80; and Aquinas, *Summa Theologica*, Part 1 of 2, Question 68.

[23] Newhauser, *The Treatise On Vices and Virtues*, pp. 161–62.

great impetus from the Church's crusade, that emerged in the wake of the Fourth Lateran Council, to instruct the laity in the truths of the faith. The famous *Somme le Roi* itself was composed at the command of a layman, King Philip III of France (1270–85). The genre was also represented in English. By the fourteenth and fifteenth centuries vernacular works of this kind became, along with other types of religious and mystical tracts, extremely popular in England.[24] So popular and pervasive was this literature that one fifteenth-century writer was moved to exclaim: 'There are so many books and treatises on the vices and virtues . . . that any man's life, which is so short, would end before he could either study or read them.'[25] So compelling was this impulse for the moral formation of the untutored youth that even courtesy books which were popular among burghers associated the acquisition of manners with the excellence of the individual's spiritual life.[26] Clearly this was analogous to the conflation of the personal and the public virtues in the personality of the ruler.

A wide and diverse audience was intended for this literature, and along with this a diversity of function developed. Peraldus's *Summa Vitiorum*, together with his corresponding work on the virtues, could be found in many libraries, whether monastic or lay, in the fourteenth and fifteenth centuries. Originally created to provide for the examination of conscience in preparation for confession, the literature of virtues and vices came to provide materials for personal lay meditation in the household as well as subject matter for princes' mirrors.[27] In terms of instruction, the same diversity applies. In the aftermath of Fourth Lateran demands, even parents were enjoined to instruct their children in the vices and virtues.[28]

All this gives the impression of wide familiarity with these works among both the pageant creators and the audience of the spectacle, whether that be the king and his entourage or the citizens of London. Thus, the will of John Carpenter, the London clerk, lists as bequests such works as *Prosperus de vita contempliva*, *Speculum morale regium*,

---

[24] Newhauser, *The Treatise On Vices and Virtues*, pp. 135–42.

[25] Wenzel, 'The Continuing Life,' p. 135.

[26] Denley, 'Elementary Teaching Techniques,' p. 225; J.R. Green, *Town Life in the Fifteenth Century*, 2:3; and Nicholls, *The Matter of Courtesy*, pp. 1–74.

[27] Newhauser, *The Treatise On Vices and Virtues*, pp. 65, 149–50; and Wenzel, 'The Continuing Life,' p. 136.

[28] Newhauser, *The Treatise On Vices and Virtues*, p. 135; and Denley, 'Elementary Teaching Techniques,' p. 221.

*De remediis utriusque fortunae*, and *De quatuor virtutibus cardinalibus*.[29] The numerous vernacular religious tracts in circulation have provided a pervasive ethical vocabulary and ideology, a moral ambience that is reflected in the presentation of gifts in pageant two.

From the pageant of the empresses and the virgins the king proceeds to the tabernacle of Dame Sapience, who is surrounded by the seven liberal arts. The tabernacle is adorned with royal trappings, an evident reference to the close relationship of wisdom to proper rule, an idea made explicit by an accompanying legend: *Per me reges regnant. Et gloriam sapiencie possidebunt* (Kings rule through me. And will possess the glory of wisdom). This reflects the popular Ciceronian idea that *Sapientia* and *Iustitia* serve to unify society.[30] A second legend devised by Sapience,

> To yonge kynges seyynge in this wyse,
> 'Vnderstondith and lernyth off the wyse,
> On riht remembryng the hyh lorde to queme,
> Syth ye be iuges other ffolke to deme.'
> (verses 268–71)

This is one of the fundamental lessons of the entire pageant sequence, reflecting both the pedagogical emphasis of the literary advisors of princes and the expectations of a citizenry similarly imbued with the value of authoritative mentoring.

The seven liberal arts who accompany Dame Sapience represent human wisdom, which is therefore associated with divine wisdom in the same way that man is made in God's image and likeness.[31] It is possible to discern this attitude toward the arts in Robert Grosseteste's late twelfth-century *Introitus* to the arts. Grosseteste refers to the arts as being *ministrae* or attendants to the study of ethics (as well as to the study of the philosophy of nature) and serve as remedies for human error and imperfection. In this one moves beyond practical education to a sense of that moral interiority that was an important element of the second pageant.[32]

Also important to the fundamental themes of the pageant sequence is the role that the seven liberal arts play as a body of knowledge propaedeutic to the study of the law. Once again it is possible to see

[29] Brewer, *Memoir of the Life and Times of John Carpenter*, pp. 131–44.
[30] Tuve, 'Notes on the Virtues and Vices,' p. 294.
[31] Schiller, *Iconography of Christian Art*, 1:31–32.
[32] Callus, 'Robert Grosseteste as Scholar,' p. 17.

that the personal and spiritual gifts of wisdom and understanding are included in the royal sphere of effective rule, the rule of justice.

This rule is the central theme of the following pageant, which displays a beautiful child arrayed like a king on a rich throne, a throne of justice. Three ladies surround him: Mercy, Truth, and Clemency, who preserve and strengthen the throne and provide the king with lasting prosperity. The two judges and the eight sergeants standing before the throne represent 'doom' and 'rihtwysnesse,' Lydgate's translation of the accompanying legend (*iudicium & iusticiam*). According to the poet, this judgement and justice is exercised for the 'comvne profyte' (verse 296). An accompanying legend expresses the love of the king for justice, while a second points to its divine origin. Lydgate interprets these psalmic references as an exhortation for the king to surround himself with those expert in the law.

This pageant represents a scene of an anticipated rule of justice, a central component of a reign of peace and prosperity. It also represents for the benefit of the young monarch some of the deepest beliefs held by fifteenth-century thinkers concerning law and justice. Among the most important of these was the divine origin of the law, the close association of the king with the rule of law, and the further close connection of law and justice with the preservation of God-ordained social hierarchy, the estates, and the peace and harmony of society.[33] When Hoccleve informs his princely audience that, 'Justice is of the kynde and the nature of God,' that 'A kyng is made to kepen and maynteene justice,' and that, 'a kyng in fulfillinge of 'at, is to god lik,' he is articulating one of the central conceptions of the literature of advice.[34] It is this reign of law and justice that will, according to Lydgate, prevent 'His myhty throne ffrom myschieff and ffallyng' (verse 289), that will, 'A kyng preserve in lange prosperytee' (verse 292).

Another important *topos* conveyed by the pageant is the relationship of the proper working of the law to the 'comvne profyte,' the common good of society. Ultimately derived from the Aristotelian notion of the human community, an entity having as its ultimate objective the life of virtue rather than merely the life of material prosperity, the idea of the common good became an important area of scholastic debate in the thirteenth and fourteenth century.[35]

---

[33] Powell, 'Law and Justice,' p. 30.

[34] Hoccleve, *Regement of Princes*, lines 2507–8, 2514–15, 2521–22.

[35] Kempshall, *The Common Good*, p. 6.

As interpreted by Aquinas, 'legal justice orders the actions of all virtues towards the common good.'[36] This identification of justice with all the virtues makes this pageant the culmination of the gifts presented previously. Aquinas goes on to draw a distinction between theory and practice, providing a strong conceptual background for the enthroned child pageant and a further insight into the aims of the spectacle as a whole. He claims that, while in theory the common good depends upon the presence of the virtues in individual members of the community, in practice the common good is contingent upon the presence of all the virtues in the person of the ruler.[37] This is an explicit claim for the role of the monarch as the representative of the community as a whole, a concept that is also implicit in the ideology of the royal entry. What the young Henry VI is expected to derive from this pageant is an idea characteristic of late medieval advice literature: the role of the virtuous and just king is to act for the common good.

The final lesson to be extracted from the throne of justice is revealed by the inclusion of the two judges and eight sergeants standing before the child king. As has been noted, the mastery of the seven liberal arts serves as a preparation for the study of the law, making the fourth pageant a logical continuation of the third. However, the course of arts precedes the study of civil law at the universities. In a significant departure from this sequence, the presentation of the eight sergeants, sergeants-at-law, graduates of the inns of court, signals that the focus in this pageant is on the common law, the subject matter of the inns. The two judges, appointed from the ranks of the sergeants, would administer the common law at Westminster.[38] Of course, it is most likely that the only legal experience of the pageant originators is with the common law. Further, there is evidence that at least by the late fifteenth century a number of London lawyers are providing their sons with university training in the arts as a preparation for the inns. Perhaps it might be possible that the same course of action is beginning to occur at this earlier period.[39] However, at the most fundamental level, this is an attempt by Londoners to associate themselves and their city more closely with the young monarch. Although the nobility manifested an interest in the inns of court, the common law was the sphere of the ambitious

---

[36] Kempshall, *The Common Good*, p. 118.

[37] Kempshall, *The Common Good*, pp. 123–24.

[38] Powell, 'Law and Justice,' p. 32.

[39] O'Day, *Education and Society*, p. 87.

younger sons of wealthy merchants and tradesmen, that is, the class of the pageant originators.[40] The inns of court were in London; they were associated with the city rather than with the university towns. Therefore, if the close identification of the monarch with the law becomes in this case the close association of Henry VI with the common law and its practitioners, then in the fourth pageant the young monarch becomes one with his royal city and its burghers.

From this point, having been defended and mentored by the giant champion, strengthened in virtue by the three goddesses and by the gifts of the Holy Ghost; having become associated with Dame Sapience, divine wisdom, broadened by the seven liberal arts and prepared by them for the study of law; having been exhorted to a reign of justice and identified with the common law and by extension the royal city, the king now enters, at the great conduit at Cheapside, the earthly paradise that can be the issue of the just and enlightened reign of a virtuous king.

Here, wine, the token of joy, flows from fountains meant to represent the rivers of paradise, and a more serious and significant note is sounded as, in an embellishment of Carpenter by Lydgate, three virgins, Mercy, Grace, and Pity, offer the wine of temperance, good government, comfort, and consolation. The *topos* of law and order associated with pageant four is continued. These offerings are meant primarily to prevent overhasty or overly severe judgement and punishment based upon the desire for vengeance. In other words they represent the triumph of reason over passion, a triumph that would be expected in a monarch in close association with Dame Sapience, a monarch who is ruled by virtue.

Along with the fountains, the king and his entourage are entertained by the sight of fruit and flowers of all types. The young monarch is congratulated by the two inhabitants of the terrestrial paradise, Enoch and Elijah, who also pray for the prosperity of his realm and the prevention of harm from enemies. The portrayal of the efforts on the part of the two biblical figures reinforces the idea that the promise of this celestial paradise, this garden of London, is yet to be fulfilled. This pageant represents the expectation that Henry VI will become the recipient of God's grace. Specifically, he will be the recipient of the gifts of the Holy Ghost. According to Aquinas these gifts, perfecting the virtues in various intense actions, inspire the fruits of the Holy Ghost.[41] And it appears that the Holy Ghost, acting upon and intensi-

---

[40] Simon, *Education and Society*, pp. 9, 14.

[41] Francis, *Book of Vices and Virtues*, pp. 95–97; *New Catholic Encyclopedia*, s.v.

fying the virtue of justice, will yield the fruits of the fountains of Cheapside. Specifically, it is anticipated that Henry VI, united as one with London through an enlightened rule inspired by his perfected state of virtue, will allow his city to share in blessedness.

From the earthly paradise the entourage approaches a castle of green jasper. Two trees growing before the castle are arrayed with leopards and fleurs-de-lis, symbols of the twin lineages of Edward the Confessor and St Louis, in recognition of the young king's descent from the ruling families of England and France. On the other side of the castle is a Jesse Tree, in its representation of the Davidic descent of Jesus, a messianic parallel to the royal trees, a reminder of the divine origin of royal power and a clear representation of that important theme of the pageant cycle: the kingly responsibility to realize fully, though the cultivation of knowledge and virtue, the implications and possibilities of his illustrious genealogy.

The concluding pageant appearing in front of St Paul's displays the throne of the Trinity surrounded by an angelic court. Each person of the Trinity bestows a blessing upon the young king: promising angelic protection, peace and unity, the love and faithful obedience of his subjects, joy, long life, and salvation, the rewards of a virtuous reign. The king is also promised heavenly aid in ending the war in France. It is a promise also associated with the special blessedness and beatitude acquired by the soul through the intense action of the gifts of the Holy Ghost on the virtues.[42] The young king is linked in this final pageant to one of the ultimate fruits of the Holy Ghost, 'Blessed are the peacemakers for they will be called children of God' (Matt. 5:9). In this promise of peace he is also linked to one of deepest concerns of the population of his city.

The pageants arranged for the royal entry of 1432 were dominated by the idea of an adolescent monarch ruling during a period of internal and external anxiety. In the face of these perceived threats to peace, to prosperity, and to the continued existence of the social order, the city designed a royal progress that had clear associations to a pattern of education. It was an education in the moral qualities and behaviour proper to a prince, the elements of which were found in the popular literature of advice, the large number of treatises on the vices and virtues, histories, poems, courtesy books, ethical treatises, and mirrors for princes

---

'Holy Spirit, Fruits of'; and Aquinas *Summa Theologica*, Part 1 of 2, Question 70.

[42] *New Catholic Encyclopedia*, s.v. 'Holy Spirit, Fruits of'; and Aquinas *Summa Theologica*, Part 1 of 2, Question 69.

in circulation in England at this time. Their moral and political common-places were intended to instruct and edify their lay audience. The pageant sequence of the London entry appears to represent, ceremonially and pictorially, these written efforts.

Lying behind the contemporary literature of advice is a recognition of the desirability of directing, rather than limiting royal authority.[43] This is especially apt when the monarch is an adolescent. The efforts of both authors and pageant organizers may also be seen as an acknowledgement that in certain circumstances kingship is contested territory. The pageants of the 1432 entry provide the young king with an apprenticeship in service where royal authority is channelled toward the promotion of the commonweal.

Much of the thinking of political moralists was informed by an organic conception of the king and community of the realm: that of the body politic. Kanterowicz has traced the development of the concept of the king and realm comprising one body, with the king identified as the head.[44] It was important that the head worked harmoniously with the other members. The head, according to the poet Lydgate in his rendition of the St Edmund legend, does not disdain the foot, nor do the members disobey the head: they are united as one in love.[45] Central to this thinking is the conception of each member of an estate fulfilling his proper role. A further important aspect of what Lydgate refers to as the moral image of society is that the king in his own person represents the realm as a whole. Consequently, the inner inclinations of the king are of consequence to the disposition of the kingdom.[46]

With these considerations in mind it should not be surprising that an extraordinary amount of energy on the part of advice writers was expended on the virtues of the monarch. Fortune was attracted by the social virtues of prudence, justice, fortitude, and temperance. It was also a staunchly held opinion, central to the pageant sequence of the royal entry, that the moral and the social were conflated and that even the most personal of virtues were to be used for the common profit, for the peace and prosperity of the realm, as is stated in a contemporary poem, *Publique and privathe is alle one.*[47]

---

[43] Watts, *Henry VI*, p. 21.

[44] Kantorowicz, *The King's Two Bodies*, chap. 5.

[45] Lydgate, 'The Lives of St Edmund and St Fremund,' verses 970–76.

[46] Watts, *Henry VI*, p. 18.

[47] *Political Poems and Songs*, 2:226; see also Watts, *Henry VI*, p. 23.

For kingship, justice was paramount. It was the proper working out of Lydgate's moral image of society, each member of the body politic, including the head, maintaining its proper place, performing its proper function. But it was also a justice associated with temperance, in that a truly just ruler was expected to control his anger and his thirst for vengeance, ideas that were also prominent in the London entry. Justice and mercy as discussed in the mid-fifteenth-century tract, 'The III Considerations Right Necesserye To The Good Governaunce Of A Prince,' includes both the idea of the firm and unwavering fulfilment of promised action and of the diligent embrace of truth. A prince must love truth and hate falsehood. This tract echoing the royal entry also notes that the virtues of 'Science' and 'Kunnyng' are necessary for proper governing of the realm, but that the wellspring of wisdom is fear of the Lord.[48]

'The III Consideraciouns' argues further that the wiser a king is, the greater effort he should make to surround himself with able advisors.[49] This idea of good counsel assumed importance in both the literature of advice and in the sequence of pageants. Thus we may understand the wide popularity of the proverb, 'werk al by conseil and thou shalt nat rewe.'[50] The king who possessed the greatest authority, who was burdened with the responsibility for the fortunes of his subjects, was in the greatest need for advice in the difficult task of correctly identifying the common good. That this advice was not solely the province of the king's council was born out by the widely held belief that, 'what affected all should be advised by all.'[51] The wide net cast by the ruler's need for good counsel was demonstrated by Hoccleve's praise for Edward III's alleged proclivity for going out in disguise to hear the opinions of his more humble subjects.[52] For Gower *vox populi* was often *vox dei.*

In the pageant sequence of the royal entry of 1432, the city of London itself assumes the proper identity and function of the counsellor. In the polysemous metaphor of the chamber, London in 1432

---

[48] 'The III Consideracions Right Necesserye To The Good Governaunce Of A Prince,' in *Four English Political Tracts of the Later Middle Ages,* pp. 200–1, 191.

[49] *Four English Political Tracts,* p. 194.

[50] Richard Green, *Poets and Princepleasers,* p. 162. Green notes that this saying, appearing in the Miller's Tale (verse 3530), 'was one of the most frequently quoted proverbs in the middle ages.'

[51] Watts, *Henry VI,* p. 2.

[52] Hoccleve, *Regement of Princes,* verses 2556-62.

becomes a council chamber: the council chamber of an adolescent prince whose royal entry becomes the occasion of a ritual education in the virtue that will flourish in maturity.

*Binghamton University*
*Binghamton, New York*

## Cited Works

Aquinas, Thomas. *The 'Summa Theologica' of St Thomas Aquinas*, trans. Father of the English Dominican Province. London: Burns, Oates and Washbourne, 1927. 2nd ed. 7 vols.

Aston, Margaret. *Lollards and Reformers: Images and Literacy in Late Medieval Religion.* London: Hambledon Press, 1984.

*The Book of Vices and Virtues: A Fourteenth Century English Translation of the Somme Le Roi of Lorens D'Orlean*, ed. W. Nelson Francis. Early English Texts Society, Original Series, No. 217. London: Oxford University Press, 1942.

Brewer, Thomas. *Memoir of the Life and Times of John Carpenter, Town Clerk of London in the Reigns of Henry V and Henry VI, and Founder of the City of London School.* London: Arthur Taylor, 1856.

Bryant, Lawrence M. 'Configurations of the Community in Late Medieval Spectacles: Paris and London During the Dual Monarchy' pp. 3-33 in *City and Spectacle in Medieval Europe*, eds. Barbara A. Hanawalt and Kathryn L. Reyerson. Minneapolis: University of Minnesota Press, 1994.

Burgess, Stanley M. *The Holy Spirit: Medieval Roman Catholic and Reformation Traditions, Sixth-Sixteenth Centuries.* Peabody, MA: Hendrickson, 1997.

Callus, D.A. 'Robert Grosseteste as Scholar' pp. 1-69 in *Robert Grosseteste, Scholar and Bishop. Essays in Commemoration of the Seventh Centenary of his Death*, ed. D. A. Callus, intro. Maurice Powicke. Oxford: Clarendon Press, 1969.

Carpenter, Christine. 'Law, Justice and Landowners, *Law and History Review* 1:1 (1983): 205–37.

*Catholic Encyclopedia.* New York: The Universal Knowldege Foundation, 1913.

Denley, Marie. 'Elementary Teaching Techniques and Middle English Religious Didactic Writing' pp. 223–41 in *Langland, the Mystics and the Medieval English Religious Tradition: Essays in Honor of S.S. Hussey*, ed. Helen Phillips. Cambridge: D.S. Brewer, 1990.

Ebin, Lois A. *Illuminator, Makar, Vates: Visions of Poetry in the Fifteenth Century.* Lincoln: University of Nebraska Press, 1988.

*Four English Political Tracts of the Later Middle Ages*, ed. Jean-Phillipe Genet. Camden Fourth Series, vol. 18. London: Royal Historical Society, 1977.

*Gesta Henrici Quinti. The Deeds of Henry the Fifth*, eds. and trans. Frank Taylor and John S. Roskell. Oxford: Clarendon Press, 1975.

Green, Richard Firth. *Poets and Princepleasers: Literature and the English Court in the Late Middle Ages*. Toronto: University of Toronto Press, 1980.

Green, J.R. (i.e., Alice Stopford Green). *Town Life in the Fifteenth Century*. 2 vols. London: Macmillan, 1907.

Griffiths, Paul. *Youth and Authority: Formative Experiences in England 1560–1640*. Oxford: Clarendon Press, 1996.

Griffiths, Ralph Alan. *The Reign of Henry VI: The Exercise of Royal Authority 1422–1461*. London: Ernest Benn, 1981.

Hanawalt, Barbara. *Growing Up in Medieval London: The Experience of Childhood in History*. Oxford and New York: Oxford University Press, 1993.

Hoccleve, Thomas. *Hoccleves's Works. The Regement of Princes and Fourteen Minor Poems*, ed. Frederick J. Furnivall. Early English Texts Society, Extra Series, No. 72. London: Kegan Paul, Trench, Trubner, 1897; rpt. Millwood, NY: Kraus Reprint, 1975.

Kantorowicz, Ernst H. *The King's Two Bodies: A Study in Mediaeval Political Theology*. Princeton: Princeton University Press, 1957.

Kempshall, M.S. *The Common Good in Late Medieval Political Thought*. Oxford: Clarendon Press, 1999.

Kipling, Gordon. *Enter the King: Theatre, Liturgy, and Ritual in the Medieval Civic Triumph*. Oxford: Clarendon Press, 1998.

*The Invention of Tradition*, eds. Eric Hobsbawm and Terence Ranger. Cambridge: Cambridge University Press, 1983.

Lydgate, John. *The Minor Poems of John Lydgate*, ed. Henry Noble MacCracken. Early English Texts Society, Original Series, No. 192. 2 vols. London: Oxford University Press, 1934, rpt. 1961.

Lydgate, John. 'The Lives of St Edmund and St Fremund' pp. 376–445 in *Altenglische Legenden. Neue Folge*, ed. Carl Horstmann. Heilbronn: Gevr. Henninger, 1881.

McKenna, J.W. 'Henry VI of England and the Dual Monarchy: Aspects of Royal Political Propaganda, 1422–1432' *Journal of the Warburg and Courtauld Institutes* 28 (1965): 145–62.

Muir, Edward. *Civic Ritual in Renaissance Venice*. Princeton: Princeton University Press, 1981.

*Munimenta Gildhallae Londoniensis. Liber Albus, Liber Custumarum, et Liber Horn*, ed. Henry Thomas Riley. 3 vols. Rolls Series, No. 12. London: Longman, Green, Longman, and Roberts, 1862.

*New Catholic Encyclopedia*. New York: McGraw-Hill, 1967.

Newhauser, Richard. *The Treatise On Vices and Virtues in Latin and the Vernacular*. Turnhout: Brepols, 1993.

Nicholls, Jonathan. *The Matter of Courtesy: Medieval Courtesy Books and the Gawain-Poet*. Woodbridge, Suffolk: D.S. Brewer, 1985.

O'Day, Rosemary. *Education and Society 1500–1800: The Social Foundations of Education in Early Modern Britain*. New York: Longmans, 1982.

Orme, Nicholas. *From Childhood to Chivalry: The Education of the English Kings and Aristocracy 1066–1530*. London: Methuen, 1984.

Osberg, Richard. 'The Jesse Tree in the 1432 London Entry of Henry VI: Messianic Kingship and the Rule Of Justice' *Journal of Medieval and Renaissance Studies* 16:2 (1986): 213–31.

Perroy, Edouard. *The Hundred Years War*, intro. David C. Douglas, trans. W. B. Wells. New York: Oxford University Press, 1951.

*Political Poems and Songs, Relating to English History, Composed During the Period From the Accession of EDW. III to that of RIC. III*, ed. Thomas Wright. Rolls Series, No. 14. 2 vols. London: Longman, Green, Longman, and Roberts, 1859–61; rpt. London: Kraus Reprint, 1965.

Powell, Edward. 'Law and Justice' pp. 29–41 in *Fifteenth-Century Attitudes: Perceptions of Society in Late Medieval England*, ed. Rosemary Horrox. Cambridge: Cambridge University Press, 1994.

Powicke, M.R. 'Lancastrian Captains' pp. 371–82 in *Essays in Medieval History Presented to Bertie Wilkinson*, eds. T.A. Sandquist and M.R. Powicke. Toronto, University of Toronto Press, 1969.

Schiller, Gertrud. *Iconography of Christian Art*, trans. Janet Seligman. 2 vols. Greenwich: New York Graphic Society, 1971–72.

Shahar, Shulamith. *Childhood in the Middle Ages*. London and New York: Routledge, 1990.

Simon, Joan. *Education and Society in Tudor England*. Cambridge: Cambridge University Press, 1966.

Skinner, Quentin. *Machiavelli*. New York: Hill and Wang, 1981.

Tuve, Rosemund. 'Part 1: Notes on the Virtues and Vices' *Journal Of The Warburg And Courtauld Institutes* 26 (1963): 264–303.

Watts, John. *Henry VI and the Politics of Kingship*. Cambridge: Cambridge University Press, 1996.

Wenzel, Siegfried. 'The Continuing Life of William Peraldus's *Summa Vitiorum*' pp. 135–163 in *Ad Litteram: Authoritative Texts and Their Medieval Readers*, eds. Mark D. Jordan and Kent Emery, Jr. Notre Dame: University of Notre Dame Press, 1992.

Wolffe, Bertram. *Henry VI*. London: Methuen, 1981.

# Taking Pains for the Prince:
## Age, Patronage, and Penal Surrogacy in Samuel Rowley's When You See Me, You Know Me

### Mark H. Lawhorn

The first staging of Samuel Rowley's *When You See Me, You Know Me* in 1604 would have been a unique theatrical event. The acting company responsible for this production was the first such commercial theatrical organization sponsored by a young prince of England and had recently undergone an appropriate name change from The Admiral's Men to Prince Henry's Men. Court performances by Prince Henry's Men 'in the next few years were mainly presented in front of the royal children who were not even teenagers yet.'[1] In their first two seasons (1604–6), the company played before the prince sixteen times, as compared with a mere three performances before the king during the same period.[2] There is a distinct possibility that Prince Henry saw Rowley's play more than once. The play itself is rare for its substantial roles depicting a young English prince of an earlier generation, Prince Edward, and his royal whipping boy, Edward Browne. Rowley seems to have written the play with his newly acquired patron in mind. The role of Prince Edward in particular seems calculated to capture the eye and ear of his Jacobean counterpart.

The historical and stage lives of Prince Henry and Prince Edward, respectively, intersect not only on the plane of social rank, but also on a liminal plane of age, where each of them hovers between childhood and youth. In the following pages I will explore how, within the context of the play's initial performance, political and cultural hopes and expectations shaped the princely character as 'coming of age' in a political sense that transcends the 'historical' ages of the characters represented dramatically. In addition to the renowned historical personage of Prince Edward, Rowley's play also depicts figures about whom comparably little has been written, such as those young individuals whose duty it

---

[1] Gurr, *The Shakespearian Playing Companies*, pp. 246–47.

[2] Gurr, *The Shakespearian Playing Companies*, p. 247.

was to serve as lordly whipping boys, members of the chapel royal, or pages in service to a noble household. Did the young actors and choristers who came together to perform Rowley's play have any sensitivity to the social and political contexts by which their stage work was shaped and bound? Although the dramatic energies, for example, that sometimes infused boys' performances were often derived from erotic and aesthetic social dynamics about which many modern audience members may be unfamiliar or to which their own sensibilities may not be attuned, the young actors themselves were surely savvy in many ways about the politics of their own playing. Perhaps Rowley's play itself, in the way it focuses attention on the young body as a valued and serviceable commodity within the royal domestic sphere, suggests an awareness of the precursory development in early modern English theatre of a youthful labour force that was subject to economic and sexual exploitation.

The play forces literal age to take a back seat to political and cultural concerns of maturation that shape a dramatic figure's formation. While the main characters in the play are, for the most part, at the low end of the 'youth' spectrum, one might keep in mind Paul Griffiths' discussion of the early modern period's 'vocabulary of age' suggesting that ten seems to have been, in some contexts, a transitional age for marking the movement from 'child' to a more mature stage of life.[3] The wish expressed by Shakespeare's Shepherd in *The Winter's Tale* that 'there were no age between ten and three-and-twenty, or that youth would sleep out the rest' (3.3.59, 60) further suggests that ten may not be too young an age to consider as transitional from child to youth.

Prince Henry, born on 19 February 1594, was ten when Rowley's play was first staged in early April 1604 by the company that acted in his name. The figure of Prince Edward depicted at the end of Rowley's play would have been, historically, between nine and ten. No one who has read historical drama of the early modern period has any illusions about the frequent lack of literal and detailed correlation between dramatic figures or events and historical ones. Cardinal Wolsey is still kicking around at the end of Rowley's play, for example, and he ought to have been dead and buried for sixteen years by the time Bishop Gardiner brought charges of heresy against Catherine Parr. There is some indication that a whipping boy was appointed for the young Edward *after* he became king, not before as in Rowley's play.[4] Thus, one should not be surprised

---

[3] Griffiths, *Youth and Authority*, p. 25.
[4] Weir, *The Children of Henry VIII*, p. 15.

to find characters who are presented dramatically as being either older or younger than historically drawn contexts might lead one to infer. It is unusual in the drama of the period for a character to announce his or her age in order to illustrate membership in an age-marked social class. Definite ages are not mentioned in *When You See Me, You Know Me*. What is most often important dramatically is whether a character is portrayed as ready or ill-prepared to assume a social responsibility such as a form of service or to face a natural consequence such as death.

Rowley culminates the stage development of his Prince Edward with a scene that illustrates the boy's diplomatic skills in welcoming the Emperor Charles, a scene that echoes the historical Edward's conduct at age eleven of welcoming ceremonies for a formal envoy led by the Admiral of France. Although Edward was King of England at age eleven, this historical fact has little to do with Rowley's effort to illustrate for Prince Henry's benefit the manner in which the stage Edward moves from childhood to adolescence by asserting himself in ways that earn the approbation of Henry VIII. The play addresses the issue of a prince's 'coming of age' with some care, however, since the subject may have been a politically sensitive one, considering the way Prince Henry's popularity soared and the cult surrounding him began to grow almost the moment he set foot in London. In a few years the Prince's court would rival, in some respects, that of the king. Although the virtues of 'youthful' maturity are promoted by Prince Henry's playwright for political reasons, not the least of which was the young Prince Henry's association by militant Protestants with chivalric models such as Sidney and Essex,[5] Rowley must have been careful not to depict the young Edward as being so preternaturally mature that he was prepared to assume his father's mantle of power. The associations between the stage Edward and the young Prince Henry were obvious and must have been tantalizing to the minds of Henry's supporters. Though Henry was ostensibly Rowley's patron, James was Rowley's king. Prince Henry's name, however, virtually assured that a powerful mythology would spring up around him.

There has never been a Henry IX of England, but his near presence hovers so insistently over Tudor and Jacobean history as to be almost palpable. This absent presence is revealed at a crucial moment in *When You See Me, You Know Me*. Looking forward to the day that the English crown would come to his family, James had named his first child Henry

---

[5] Strong, *Henry, Prince of Wales*, p. 4.

as a reminder of the boy's Tudor lineage extending from Henry VII.[6]
*When You See Me, You Know Me* offers at one point the time-bending
fantasy that the playwright's young patron has been legitimized by Henry
VIII himself. To Queen Jane, dramatically 'bigge with Child' and experiencing labour pains, the character of King Henry urges, 'Now Jane God
bring me but a chopping boy, / Be but the Mother to a Prince of Wales
/ Ad a ninth Henrie to the English Crowne, / And thou mak'st full my
hopes' (ll. 265–68). Upon Jane's death from childbirth complications,
however, King Henry has his son named for the day's patron saint,
Edward. The scene, with its forceful expression of desire for an heir and
with the tragic cost of that desire's realization, would have resonated
powerfully with the play's young patron who sat poised to fulfil the hope
for a ninth Henry.

It is crucial to remember the difficult balancing act that Rowley had
to perform in writing this play. He must insult neither the prince his
patron nor the king his sovereign. He must be careful to present the
figure of a prince growing into 'kingly' stature and supply ample opportunity for the prince to show the proper deference to his royal father.
Maintaining the balance in performance must have been tricky because
the play is filled with foolery, wordplay, and ribald wit. As his heavily
edited script, now in London's Theatre Museum, reflects, Poel's production of 1927 cut much of the humour and used the platform stage to keep
the 'political' action going simultaneously in 'competing' spheres. On
occasion, for example, King Henry appeared in his pavilion on the
forestage as Prince Henry maintained a scene on a raised back stage.[7]
Restraining the comic elements a little is especially important to the
scene involving the prince and the breeching boy. In a scene that
establishes the play's attention to the maturation of the prince, the
humour could easily slide into farce that would undermine the seriousness of the issues at stake. The presence and antics of a clown need not
necessarily negate the effective realization of weightier themes. *King
Lear*'s fool provides ample support for this view. Because Will Somers'
jokes about breeching might suggest that the scene is designed to
produce a comic effect that prevails over the concerns of the two boys
and over the serious strength of their relationship, I will comment on the
institution of the breeching boy and on the relationship between Edward
and his whipping boy. I want to establish that mockery of the stage

---

[6] Parry, *The Golden Age Restor'd*, p. 64.

[7] Somerset, *When You See Me, You Know Me*, p. 120.

Prince would in all likelihood not have been well received by the play's young patron for whom the knighting of Ned Browne might not seem a clearly risible form of childish play. Apprentices in the audience at the Fortune who may have identified with Ned's servile role might also have had reason to temper their laughter.

The disciplinary policy of influencing the prince via the punishments of others is strikingly depicted in *When You See Me, You Know Me*. While Edward received some physical chastisement from his early tutor, the clergyman Richard Cox, in the form of 'a sharp slap or spank,'[8] Rowley's play affirms that at some point the practice of using a breeching or whipping boy was instituted. In Rowley's play, his boy, whose real-life counterpart was Barnaby Fitzpatrick, bore the name Edward Browne. Prince Edward was educated among his noble peers, just as his illegitimate half-brother Richmond (Henry Fitzroy), who died before Edward's birth, had received his education in the company of 'several young noblemen . . . brought together to be his schoolfellows, to set him an example of diligence, to excite him to emulation, and further by the punishments they received, to let him see what he deserved, that he might in some measure dread the like discipline, even if he did not sustain it in his own person.'[9] Although it had been a royal tradition since at least Edward II's reign for the monarchs of England to provide at court for a number of young male wards referred to as 'henchmen,' during Elizabeth's rule this practice was discontinued to the great wonderment of some of the nobility.[10]

Rowley's description of Ed Browne as a 'fearfull boy' who 'haunts' the prince underscores the seriousness of the beatings to which young scholars were subjected and alludes to an educational commonplace of the period that is reflected in the Latin motto *Initium sapientiae timor domini* (The beginning of wisdom is the fear of the master). The focus of the poem 'The Birched Schoolboy' (*c.* 1500) is the experience of corporal punishment in school:

> I would fain be a clerk
> but yet it is a strange work.
> The birching twigs be so sharp
> it makes me have a faint heart.
> What avails me though I say nay?
> My master looks as he were mad:

---

[8] Erickson, *The First Elizabeth*, p. 55.
[9] Nichols, 'Inventories of the Wardrobe,' p. xxxvii.
[10] Chambers, *The Elizabethan Stage*, 1:45.

'Where have you been, you sorry lad?'
'Milking ducks, my mother bade.'
It were no marvel though I were sad.
What avails me though I say nay?

My master peppered my arse with well good speed:
It was worse than finkle seed.                    [fennel seed]
He would not leave till it did bleed . . .[11]

In an essay on flagellation and the fine arts, William Ober offers the following description of a 1526 French Book of Hours' illustration for the motto: 'The elaborately robed schoolmaster is in his *sedia* and his victim is ensconced over a flogging block, his hands held by two ushers while three of his schoolmates witness his punishment from the background.'[12] Witnessing a punishment seems clearly designed to be a deterrent, although Ober's linking of flagellation with sexual gratification colours the picture with a tinge of voyeurism. The classical link between pederasty, corporal punishment, and educational institutions can be observed in a work that greatly influenced later humanist educators such as Erasmus and Ascham, Quintilian's *De Institutione*, which expresses disapproval of both pederasty (although 'common and acceptable in certain circles') and flogging.[13] 'Alert to the sexual and professional exploitation of children,' as Richmond Barbour has noted,[14] Ben Jonson labelled the 'rival epigrammist' John Owen 'a pure pedantic schoolmaster, sweeping his living from the posteriors of little children,'[15] a description echoed by Samuel Butler in this way:

The Pedant in the Schoolboyes breeches,
Does claw and curry his own itches.[16]

---

[11] Quoted in Davies, *Teaching Reading*, pp. 81–82.

[12] Ober, 'Bottoms Up!' p. 17.

[13] Monroe, *A Textbook*, p. 199.

[14] Barbour, '"When I Acted Young Antinous",' p. 1013.

[15] Jonson, *Ben Jonson*, ed. Donaldson, p. 600.

[16] Quoted in *The Children's Petition*, p. 17. Laments over the abuse of children reach a high pitch in *The Children's Petition* of 1669, which includes the following: 'But when our sufferings are of that nature as makes our schools to be / not meerly houses of Correction, but of Prostitution, in this vile way of / castigation in use, wherein our secret parts, which are by nature shameful, / and not to be uncovered, must be the Anvil exposed to the immodest eyes, / and filthy blows of the smiter . . .' p. 7.

In Rowley's play, the fool Will Somers jests lewdly on the flogging experience that Ned Browne endured, 'Marry ithe last action, I can assure you, there was hot service, and some on um came so neere him, they had like to smelt ont: but when all was done, the poore gentleman was pittifuly wounded in the back partes, as may appeare by the scarrc, if his knightship would but untrusse there' (ll. 1888–92).

The Tudor stage itself, which was at times a conduit for the moral and scholastic edification of the young, could resonate powerfully with the imagery of 'corrective' flagellation. It is not surprising that the imagery recurs in Rowley's Jacobean play since his efforts are designed with a very particular youthful audience in mind. Furthermore, while the commercial theatre that had blossomed in London played to the pocketbooks of a largely adult audience that wanted more than didacticism and moralism, there were also some quite young theatre-goers. It would be a mistake to think of a Jacobean theatre audience as devoid of children and youth. Among the crowd described as turning out to watch Anne Boleyn's coronation procession in Shakespeare and Fletcher's *Henry VIII* are a group of pebble-flinging boys, whom the porter identifies as 'the youths that thunder at a playhouse, and fight for bitten apples' (5.3.58–59). An account of the Globe's burning on 29 June 1613 written only a few days after the event by Henry Bluett mentions that 'the people escaped all without hurt except one man who was scalded with the fire by adventuring in to save a child which otherwise had been burnt.'[17] Andrew Gurr has asserted that apprentices 'were much in evidence at the playhouses.'[18] Why would a commercial enterprise want to exclude a large base of future patrons? Dramatic characters depicting some form of service, such as the whipping boy in Rowley's play, evoked the concerns and interest of playgoing members of the servant ranks.

Historically, commercial theatre in England sprang from theatrical labours directed at youthful audiences. Nicholas Udall, who wrote *Ralph Roister Doister* (c. 1550) as an entertainment blending the sight of vanity reproofed and folly punished, was sometimes called 'the flogging master of Eton' and was known for his harshness with students.[19] Writing of Eton in his poetic autobiography, Thomas Tusser commented,

---

[17] Quoted in Shakespeare, *King Henry VIII*, ed. Margeson, pp. 2–3.

[18] Gurr, *Playgoing*, p. 53.

[19] Byrne, *Elizabethan Life*, p. 1961.

> From Paul's I went, to Eton sent,
> To learn straightways the Latin phrase.
> Where fifty-three stripes given to me
>       At once I had
> For fault but small or none at all.[20]

In his *Scholemaster*, Ascham observes that many boys run away from Eton because they fear flogging and asserts that 'yonge children are sooner allured by love than driven by beating to atain good learning.'[21] Some didactic morality plays such as Thomas Ingelend's *The Disobedient Child* and *The Nice Wanton*, which focused on the difficulties of guiding youth through the maturation process that led them to fit successfully into the existing social order, often illustrated the necessity of using the chastening rod. In *The Disobedient Child*, a youth who wants to leave school describes one of his reasons, the treatment of pupils, to his father in the following way:

> Their tender bodies both night and day
> Are whipped and scourged, and beat like a stone
> That from top to toe the skin is away
> . . .
> Diseases among them do grow apace;
> For out of their back and side doth flow
> Of very gore-blood marvelous abundance;[22]

When his father declares that the account is a gross embellishment, the son goes on to recount even more horrific corporal penalties, including this description of a dead student:

> Men say of this man, his bloody master
> Who like a lion most commonly frowned,
> Being hanged up by the heels together,
> Was belly and buttocks grievously whipped;
> And last of all (which to speak I tremble),
> That his head to the wall he had often crushed.[23]

Whether the above tortures were dramatic exaggerations, one certainly has the sense that physical correctives administered to children and youth in early modern England could be quite severe and were part of a long tradition. One bizarre part of that heritage involved

---

[20] Tusser, *The Last Will and Testament*, verse 8.

[21] Ascham, *The Scholemaster*, p. 183.

[22] Ingelend, *The Disobedient Child*, pp. 48–49.

[23] Ingelend, *The Disobedient Child*, p. 50.

whipping children on Holy Innocents' Day, a non-punitive medieval tradition that St. Francis termed a 'reenactment of the Slaughter of the Innocents.'[24] The tone of the flogging accounts that strive in some fashion to capture the child's experience varies markedly from an earlier work such the *Colloquy* of Aelfric (d. 1020), where a student gives the following brave response when the teacher asks whether pupils are ready to accept beatings to further their education: 'We'd rather be flogged so that we can learn than remain ignorant. Of course we know that you are a kind person and you'll not beat us unless you really have to.'[25]

The 'spare the rod' theme of early didactic drama ran directly counter to the feelings of the noted Dutch scholar and theologian Desiderius Erasmus, whose own early educational experiences, which included arbitrary beatings he endured as a fourteen-year-old at the hands of his master,[26] caused him to describe his training at St. Leubin's in Deventer as 'in the age of barbarism.'[27] The extensive and largely affectionate expressions of concern for children by Erasmus sought to place them at the centre of the early sixteenth-century household.[28] Love and respect for the child were the foremost elements of the method promoted by Erasmus, who wrote unequivocally, 'I am, at heart, one with Quintilian in deprecating flogging under any conditions.'[29] Corporal punishment was to be eschewed in favour of a mixture of just reproach and praise, accompanied in the classroom by a sympathetic and stimulating teaching style. 'Wholly wrong,' wrote Erasmus, 'are those masters who expect their little pupils to act as though they were but diminutive adults, who forget the meaning of youth, who have no standard of what can be done or be understood except that of their own minds.'[30] Erasmus, who preferred that students be taught at home or in public school, directly attacked the cruel techniques used in sixteenth-century schools such as those maintained by ecclesiastical authorities where 'blows and shouts, sobs and howls fill the air.'[31]

---

[24] Marcus, *Childhood and Cultural Despair*, p. 15.

[25] Quoted in Davies, *Teaching Reading*, p. 81.

[26] Stewart, *Close Readings*, p. 95.

[27] Erasmus, *De Pueris*, ed. Woodward, p. 3.

[28] De Molen, 'Erasmus on Childhood,' p. 25.

[29] Erasmus, *De Pueris*, ed. Woodward, p. 208.

[30] Erasmus, *De Pueris*, ed. Woodward, p. 211.

[31] Erasmus, *De Pueris*, ed. Woodward, p. 204.

While we can assume that it was not unusual for blood to have been shed, as Rowley's Prince Edward implies that the blood of Ned Browne was shed for him (ll. 1858–59), it is by no means possible to assume that all adults held attitudes in favour of corporal punishment of the young. Still, even an exemplary humanist like Thomas More, whose upper class family was highly esteemed by Erasmus, resorted to corporal punishment when Christian duty seemed to call for particularly forceful correction. According to Susan Brigden,

> When one child in More's household, taught 'ungracyouse heresye' by George Joye, began to instruct another child in error, More had him whipped, for his first aim was always to prevent the corruption of youth, and to 'make almost euery boy able to perceuyue the false folly' of the new doctrine.[32]

In the particular instance cited by Brigden, punishment arises from a concern about the influence on a child by one of his fellows. The harsh penalty is evidence of adult anxieties about the particular power of formative exchanges between the young.

Behaviour could be cast as a form of theatre in which a poor performance by a young person could have powerfully negative effects on his or her companions and in which performing one's social role properly in front of one's peers could operate as a kind of formative guide to shape and modify behaviour in a positive way. The value of performing corporal punishment, however, is not unquestioned in Rowley's play. When Prince Edward offers proof of his proficiency in logic by propounding a syllogism in defence of the punishment Browne has received, his theoretical position is undermined by the practical humour of Will Somers, the court fool, who counters the Prince's rational argument with the sceptical remark, 'since hee can proue a rodde to bee so good, let him tak't himselfe next time' (ll. 1848–50). Whatever the historical Prince Edward learned from the practice of penal surrogacy at court—be that responsibility for his own actions or a willingness to let another suffer in his stead—he formed a lifelong attachment to the boy who dutifully took the prince's punishments.

Barnaby Fitzpatrick, 'the poorest and most agreeable' of the prince's youthful henchmen, was the only member of that elite group with whom Edward became a bosom companion and 'with whom to the

---

[32] Brigden, 'Youth and the English Reformation,' pp. 58, 59.

very end of his life the King spoke with an ease and informality suggesting a strong personal affection.'[33] Apparently, Edward felt there was no one else with whom he could lower his guard in youthful pleasure and relax briefly what Jordan calls 'the steel of self-discipline.'[34] Among the most intimate pieces of evidence that reveal something of Edward's personality are the nine letters he composed to Fitzpatrick. Although the young king wrote to his best friend in 'a strange admixture of boyish enthusiasm and spontaneity,' he would also abruptly revert to a kind of official sovereign veneer that reflected the formal and serious side which was the demeanour fostered by the rigours of his training to assume the throne.[35] Edward's tutors are to be credited with a great deal, yet one is hard pressed to argue with Jordan's assessment that while '[t]he tutors selected with such shrewd care by Henry VIII had made a king; they had also destroyed a boy.'[36] In a period that saw forms of dress and discipline that seemed to reflect a desire to bring a child quickly to adulthood, the case of Edward's upbringing was certainly not an isolated one in its focus on speeding up the maturation process. As Erasmus observed, 'there are not a few parents who can make no allowance for childhood and wish their children to be grown up.'[37] The pressures on the young prince to grow up quickly must have been incremented by his particular royal stature; as a result, Edward's relationship with Barnaby Fitzpatrick seems to have been the young king's only link to his lost boyhood. Perhaps it is not so odd that the two seemingly mismatched boys became close. Barnaby Fitzpatrick was, in a sense, an exile from his home and country, having been 'sent to the English court really as a hostage' to insure the loyalty of his father, 'an Irish chieftain who after the rebellion of 1537 made his subscription to the English authorities.'[38] Prince Edward was a hostage of a different sort, confined and restricted by all manner of cultural expectations and demands.

Whatever was at the basis for their relationship, Prince Edward and his 'proxy for correction,' as Barnaby Fitzpatrick is called in Fuller's *Church History* (bk. vii, par. 47), shared an important personal connection that must have been charged with emotion for both of them.

---

[33] Jordan, *Edward VI: The Young King*, p. 44.

[34] Jordan's introduction to *Chronicle*, p. xxiii.

[35] Jordan, *Edward VI: The Threshold of Power*, p. 404.

[36] Jordan's introduction to *Chronicle*, pp. xxiii, xxiv.

[37] Quoted in Krupski, *Shakespeare's Children*, p. 38.

[38] Jordan, *Edward VI: The Threshold*, p. 404 n. 4.

In the long scene in which Rowley presents the subject of the whipping boy's unique service to the realm, the principal characters besides the prince are Cranmer, as Edward's chief tutor, Doctor Christopher Tye, lecturer in music, Will Somers, the court fool, and Browne, one of the children of the chapel royal. I include enough of the scene to capture its lively contrasting of youth and age.

*Enter Cranmer, doctor Tye, and young Browne meets them with the Prince's cloake and hat.*

| | |
|---|---|
| *Cranmer.* | How now yong Browne, what have you there? |
| *Browne.* | The Prince's cloake and hat, my Lord. |
| *Cranmer.* | Where is his Grace? |
| *Browne.* | At Tennis, with the marquesse Dorset. |
| *Cranmer.* | You and the marquesse draw the prince's mind |
| | To follow pleasure and neglect his booke: |
| | For which the king blames us. But, credite me, |
| | You shall be soundly paid immediately. |
| *Browne.* | I pray ye, good my Lord! Ile goe call the Prince away. |
| *Cranmer.* | Nay, now ye shall not. Who's within there, ho? |
| *Servant.* | My Lord. |
| *Cranmer.* | Goe bear this youngster to the Chapel straite, |
| | And bid the Maister of the Children whippe him well: |
| | The Prince will not learne, sir, and you shall smart for it. |
| *Browne.* | Oh, good my Lord! Ile make him ply his booke tomorrow. |
| *Cranmer.* | That shall not serve your turne. Away, I say! |
| | So, sir, this pollicie was well-devised: |
| | Since he was whipt thus for the Prince's faults, |
| | His Grace has got more knowledge in a month, |
| | Than he attained in a yeere before; |
| | For still the fearefull boy to save his breech, |
| | Dothe hourely haunte him whereso ere he goes. |
| *Tye.* | 'Tis true, my Lord, and now the Prince perceives it, |
| | As loath to see him punisht for his faultes, |
| | Plays it of purpose to redeem the boy (1771–99) |

Part of what makes this conversation remarkable is its recognition of the growth between the two young Edwards of a mutually caring relationship whose dignity the adult smugness of the Tye and Cranmer figures does little to diminish. Their report and assessment of the 'well-devised' disciplinary method may emphasize their own satisfaction with the happy achievement of their goal of improved scholarly habits, but it is clear that Rowley has also put these characters in a position to give evidence regarding the compassion of the young prince for his fellow. Thus, the focus modulates between the adult manipulations of the well-designed policy and the more intimate social negotiations between young friends. After the whipping takes place offstage and Browne returns weeping in the company of the king's fool, Cranmer and Tye hide to overhear an exchange between Browne and the prince, who enters with his tennis partner and others.

| | |
|---|---|
| *Prince.* | Why how now, Browne, what's the matter? |
| *Browne.* | Your grace loyters, and will not ply your book, and your Tutors has whipt me for it. |
| *Prince.* | Alas, poore Ned, I am sorrie for it. I'le take the more paines and intreat my Tutors for thee; yet in troth the lectors they read me last night out of Virgill and Ovid, I am perfect in: onlie I confesse I am something behinde in my Greeke authors. |
| *Will.* | And for that speech, they have declynde it upon his breech.          (ll. 1826–35) |

A few lines later the Prince offers a reward to Browne for his two years of noble service as whipping boy.

| | |
|---|---|
| *Prince.* | In truth, I pittie thee, and inwardly I feele the stripes thou barest, and for thy sake, Ned, Ile plie my book the faster. In the meane time, thou shalt not say, but the Prince of Wales will honourably reward thy service: come, Browne, kneele downe! |
| *Will.* | What wilt thou knight him, Ned? |
| *Prince.* | I will; my father has knighted many a one that never shedde drop of blood for him; but hee has often for mee. |
| | (ll. 1851–59) |

The king subsequently enters and, after supporting Browne's knighthood, bestows a thousand marks annually upon the elated Browne, who exclaims, 'I hope my Lord, they dare not whip me now' (l. 1929).

Besides urging Henry, the play's young patron, to pursue his studies with the devotion which Edward pledges, the scene depicts the young heir beginning to take royal initiative in a way that prompts the character of his father Henry VIII to declare, 'nowe by my Crowne young Ned thou hast honord me. / I like thy kingly spirit that loves to see / Thy friends advanc't to types of dignitie' (ll. 1901–3). Before granting Browne a generous income, the king asks Prince Edward what living he will give the new knight and the prince replies, 'from mine owne allowance Ile maintaine him (ll. 1915–16). The 'kingly spirit' which the princely program is designed to instill includes generosity and pity, noble action and sentiment associated with the royal father whom the prince emulates in this instance. In a later scene, however, we see the prince evincing a 'kingly spirit' in a way that requires him to confront the wrath of the king on behalf of another, Edward's stepmother Catherine Parr, who is accused of heresy.

In this scene Edward insistently defies the king's commands to be silent and shows instead his princely aptitude as domestic peacemaker. To the distraught Catherine young Edward promises to pacify the king and 'move his majestie, / That you may answer your accusers presently' (ll. 2499–2500). At first the king sternly admonishes the prince, 'Go too Ned, I charge ye speake not for her, / shes a dangerous traytor' (ll. 2580–81). After sinking to his knees in rebuffed supplication, the prince summons the king's attention with a vow based on royal honour that the king cannot ignore: 'Ile pawne my princely word, right royall father, / She shall not speake a word to anger ye' (ll. 2619–20). At this the king relents, confessing, 'The Prince of Wales his word is warrant for a king, / and we will take it Ned, go call her in' (ll. 2622–23). It is not the age of the prince that gives power to his actions but the character's steadfast willingness to invoke the power of his princely stature in the face of the rather imposing royal opposition represented by his father the king.

The young patron for whose benefit Rowley's play was first mounted eventually became the sort of domestic go-between presented by Edward in Rowley's play. Anne appears to have maintained Prince Henry's devotion despite her reputation for pettiness and religious differences over which one might expect that she and her son would diverge. After all, Anne's adherence to Catholicism, even if lukewarm as some have suggested, was not something that her young son Henry, in whose strongly Protestant household 'attendance at sermons was obligatory,'[39] could easily have overlooked. In the 1590s Anne, who had been a Lutheran in Denmark, adopted the Catholic faith rather than embrace Scottish Presbyterianism. While Willson asserts that Anne's 'conversion did not make her serious or devout,'[40] Strong points out how Anne's Catholic sympathies came to the fore when she came to consider possible matrimonial matches for her children.[41]

---

39 Strong, *Henry, Prince of Wales*, p. 54.

40 Willson, *King James VI and I*, p. 95.

41 Strong, *Henry, Prince of Wales*, p. 25.

Remarkably, however, the young prince seems to have remained devoted to his mother and, mirroring the domestic peacemaker role assigned to Edward in Rowley's play, Henry often played the difficult role of go-between in his parents' disputes.[42] While the official stance regarding a child's duty to mother and father may be summed up in Henry VIII's declaration that 'although sons and daughters were bound to some obedience toward their mothers, their chief duty was to their fathers,'[43] domestic practice seems to have allowed some space for children to exercise a kind of power over the father on behalf of the mother. At least Rowley's play establishes such a balance of power as a dramatic possibility, and the record of Prince Henry's position of parental go-between suggests a measure of domestic leverage that a mother had through the medium of a child who was also heir to the throne and whose word as 'Prince of Wales' carried significant weight even with the king. One important by-product of the princely training and treatment that promoted what Rowley's King Henry calls a 'kingly spirit' is the creation of a child heir capable of exercising a powerful influence on the monarch within the domestic sphere. Because both Edward and Henry died before having the opportunity to prove themselves as monarchs, we cannot guess what the long term result of their unique upbringing might have been. Yet it is possible to observe the degree to which James's jealousy and concern over the cult encircling Henry grew as Henry himself did.

As the hope of militant Protestants, Prince Henry is witnessing in Rowley's play his princely counterpart defend a Queen with decidedly Protestant sympathies. At the domestic level, Henry is observing a child's defence of the mother figure who has brought a stronger sense of family to the royal household. This is not to imply that Catherine Parr completely rearranged the domestic order. Henry VIII's children continued to have their own households and to follow the cycle of moving from one house to another. But even in her role as an overseer often somewhat removed from the children, Queen Catherine exerted considerable influence as mother figure to Edward and Elizabeth and advisor to Mary, and as a woman who made education a priority among her household concerns.[44] She is considered to have been responsible soon after her wedding to the king for prompting the unusual congre-

---

[42] Strong, *Henry, Prince of Wales*, p. 16.
[43] Cited in Erickson, *The First Elizabeth*, p. 44.
[44] Erickson, *The First Elizabeth*, p. 55.

gation of all three children within the same house as their father.[45] Although Rowley's play provides no appearances of Mary and Elizabeth, at one point we are alerted to their presence at court by the king's query, 'God a mercie, but where are our children? / Prince Edward, Mary, and Elizabeth, / The royal Issue of three famous Queens, / How haps we have not seene them here today?' (ll. 1538–41).

How haps indeed? We can answer the question in part by considering how the play's focus on the character of Edward is being shaped for the benefit of Prince Henry. The nearest Elizabeth and Mary come to having a presence on stage is through letters from each addressed to Edward that touch on religious matters. Edward's character, who is depicted as being clearly sympathetic to Elizabeth, reads the whole of Elizabeth's letter but abbreviates his reading of Mary's in obvious disgust with her papal admonishments. In an earlier exchange with Cranmer concerning the existence of purgatory, the young prince, who noted how the country stood 'wavering in her Faith, / Betwixt the Papists and the Protestants' (ll. 1991–92), had alluded to the epistolary efforts of his 'Sister *Marie* and her Tutors' (l. 1998) to persuade him to embrace their Catholic beliefs. The strong association between Edward and Elizabeth is borne out historically in letters and in the exchange of gifts between them. In Rowley's play Edward suggests also a kind of nostalgia for Elizabethan heroes such as Philip Sidney and Robert Devereux, 2nd Earl of Essex, models of militant Protestant chivalry for Rowley's young Protestant patron. Thus Edward's strength in speaking on behalf of his stepmother is reflective of cultural expectations revolving around the figure of Prince Henry. Edward's readiness to defend (symbolically) the Protestant faith and to negotiate effectively with a king are not constructed as functions of his age but as dramatic evidence of his movement toward the kind of political and spiritual maturity that can be characterized as 'kingly.'

Edward's growth is emphasized again near the end of Rowley's play as the young prince is presented welcoming Emperor Charles V and his entourage to England. The emperor expresses his own astonishment at the prince's sophisticated diplomatic abilities, flattering the prince by suggesting that the king himself could not surpass his son's statesmanship in this instance, so well has the prince delivered his royal welcome. This dramatic moment is one which requires some special care on Rowley's part. Although he seeks to elevate the prince

---

45 Fraser, *The Wives of Henry VIII*, p. 371.

to a pinnacle of regal achievement and honour, he must be careful not to allow the prince to overshadow dramatically the figure of the king. Thus, the prince modestly responds to the emperor's praise by asserting that in the king 'theres Majesty, / In me theres love with tender infancie' (ll. 2907–8). The prince's next and final action in the play, however, is one that evidences his own stature. When Woolsie comments upon the sound of the trumpet that 'the King is comming' (l. 2910), the prince issues the command, 'Go all of you attend his royall person, / Whilst we observe the Emperors Majesty' (ll. 2911–12). The balance of majesty that is created in this scene is remarkable. While the prince directs attention to the approaching monarch, he is able to maintain a powerful regal position of his own by separating himself from all the others whom he controls both by commanding them and by using the royal 'we' to indicate what his next action will be—to observe majesty while continuing to reflect it himself. The adults may have the dialogue that brings the play to a rather lighthearted close, but the young prince, who has amazed the emperor and impressed his father with his 'kingly' spirit, remains silently on stage so that all may continue to observe his majesty and his maturity.

As I have suggested, the splendid princely bearing of Prince Edward enacted upon the stage in the first performances of *When You See Me, You Know Me* mirrored cultural hopes and expectations for Henry, Prince of Wales. Since the birth of Edward, sixty years earlier, England had not experienced the security of having a monarch with a male heir. The apotheosis of the desire for, and celebration of such security is mirrored for the play's young patron in the role of Rowley's Prince Edward. The developmental correspondence between the stage prince and the play's princely auditor is emphasized not by any direct reference to age, but by situations that depict the intellectual and spiritual evolution desired in a royal male heir. While estimations of Henry quickly rose in the popular eye, his lack of devotion to his studies was a frequent source of dissention between him and his father the king.[46] The play's scenes involving educational and corrective themes must have struck a directly personal and political chord with its audience when the play was staged at court before the royal chidren. In the venue of a public theatre such as the Fortune, however, the service provided by the whipping boy and royal chorister may have resonated especially among the young spectators who were themselves in service

---

[46] Strong, *Henry, Prince of Wales*, p. 15.

of some sort. The bawdy jests of Will Somers reminded the audience of other possible costs to the bodies of the young in service and to those subject to correction at the hands of teachers and other masters. Just as the play enacts a cultural fantasy of precocious princely virtue, the compassion and reward bestowed on Ned Browne by the prince in Rowley's play evoke a dream of freedom from service and focus attention on the young who painstakingly served economic, political, and sexual interests more powerful than themselves.

*University of Hawai'i at Kapiolani*
*Honolulu, Hawai'i*

## Cited Works

Ascham, Roger. *The Scholemaster.* London, Iohn Day, 1571; rpt New York: Da Capo Press, 1968.

Barbour, Richmond. ''When I Acted Young Antinous': Boy Actors and the Erotics of Jonsonian Theater' *PMLA* 110:5 (Oct. 1995): 1006–22.

Brigden, Susan. 'Youth and the English Reformation' *Past and Present* 95 (May 1982): 37–67.

Byrne, Muriel St. Clare. *Elizabethan Life in Town and Country.* 6th ed. rev. London: Methuen, 1950.

Chambers, E. K. *The Elizabethan Stage.* 4 vols. Oxford: Clarendon Press, 1923.

*The Children's Petition: OR, A Modest Remonstrance of that intolerable grievance our Youth lie under, in the accustomed Severities of the School-discipline of this Nation.* London, Printed for Richard Chiswell at the two Angels and Crown in Little-Britain, 1669.

*The Chronicle and Political Papers of King Edward VI,* ed. and intro. W. K. Jordan. Folger Shakespeare Library. Ithaca, NY: Cornell University Press, 1966.

Davies, Frank. *Teaching Reading in Early England.* London: Pitman, 1973.

De Molen, Richard L. 'Erasmus on Childhood' *Erasmus of Rotterdam Society Yearbook* 2 (1982): 25–46.

Erasmus, Desiderius. *De Pueris,* pp. 180–222 in *Desiderius Erasmus: Concerning the Aim and Method of Education,* ed. William Harrison Woodward. Cambridge: Cambridge University Press, 1904.

Erickson, Carolly. *The First Elizabeth.* New York: St. Martin's Press, 1983.

Fraser, Antonia. *The Wives of Henry VIII.* New York: Random House, 1992.

Fuller, Thomas. *The Church-History of Britain.* London: Printed for Iohn Williams, 1655.

Griffiths, Paul. *Youth and Authority: Formative Experiences in England, 1560–1640.* Oxford: Clarendon Press, 1996.

Gurr, Andrew. *Playgoing in Shakespeare's London.* Cambridge: Cambridge University Press, 1987.

Gurr, Andrew. *The Shakespearian Playing Companies*. Oxford: Clarendon Press, 1996.

Ingelend, Thomas. *The Disobedient Child* and *Nice Wanton* in *The Dramatic Writings of Richard Wever and Thomas Ingelend*, ed. John S. Farmer. London: Early English Drama Society, 1905; rpt. Guilford, England: Charles W. Traylen, 1966.

Jonson, Ben. *Ben Jonson*. ed. Ian Donaldson. Oxford: Oxford University Press, 1985.

Jordan, W.K. *Edward VI: The Threshold of Power: The Dominance of the Duke of Northumberland*. London: George Allen & Unwin, 1970.

Jordan, W.K. *Edward VI: The Young King*. Cambridge, MA: Harvard University Press, 1968.

Kay, Dennis. *Shakespeare: His Life, Work, and Era*. New York: William Morrow, 1992.

Krupski, Jadwiga. *Shakespeare's Children*. Dissertation. McGill University, 1992.

Marcus, Leah S. *Childhood and Cultural Despair: A Theme and Variations in Seventeenth-Century Literature*. Pittsburgh: Pittsburgh University Press, 1978.

Monroe, Paul. *A Text-book in the History of Education*. London: Macmillan, 1905.

Nichols, John Gough. 'Inventories of the Wardrobe, Plate, Chapel Stuff, Etc. of Henry Fitzroy, Duke of Richmond, and The Wardrobe Stuff at Baynard's Castle of Katherine, Princess Dowager. Edited with a Memoir and Letters of the Duke of Richmond' *Camden Miscellany*, III, vol. 61. London, 1855.

Ober, William B. *Bottoms Up!: A Pathologist's Essays on Medicine and the Humanities*. New York: Harper & Row, 1987.

Parry, Graham. *The Golden Age Restor'd: The Culture of the Stuart Court, 1603–42*. New York: St. Martin's Press, 1981.

Poel, William. Programme for *When You See Me, You Know Me*. Holborn Empire, London. 10 July 1927. Copies in London's Theatre Museum.

Rowley, Samuel. *When You See Me, You Know Me*, (1605 quarto) ed. F.P. Wilson. Oxford: Malone Society/Oxford University Press, 1952.

Shakespeare, William. *The Winter's Tale*, ed. Stanley Wells and Gary Taylor, in *The Complete Works*. Oxford: Clarendon Press, 1988.

Shakespeare, William. *King Henry VIII*, ed. John Margeson. Cambridge: Cambridge University Press, 1990.

Somerset, J. A. B. *When You See Me, You Know Me*. M.A. Thesis. Shakespeare Institute, 1965.

Stewart, Alan. *Close Readers: Humanism and Sodomy in Early Modern England*. Princeton: Princeton University Press, 1997.

Strong, Roy. *Henry, Prince of Wales and England's Last Renaissance*. New York: Thames and Hudson, 1986.

Tusser, Thomas. *The Last Will and Testament and Autobiography*. Great Totham, Essex: Charles Clark, 1846.

Weir, Alison. *The Children of Henry VIII: The Heirs of King Henry VII, 1547–1558*. New York: Ballantine, 1996.

Willson, David Harris. *King James VI & I*. New York: Oxford University Press, 1956.

# Troublesome Teens:
## Approaches to Educating and Disciplining Youth in Early Modern Italy

### Christopher Carlsmith

In the fall of 1541, eighteen year-old Lattanzio Marchese, of Bergamo, joined dozens of other young men at the University of Padua to pursue a degree in arts and medicine. He received free housing and a generous annual stipend of 100 lire from a lay confraternity in Bergamo known as the Misericordia Maggiore (commonly abbreviated as MIA). Lattanzio, however, was not a model scholarship student. Less than a year after his arrival the MIA suspended his stipend for two months owing to an unspecified but 'very serious scandal.' Within six months of that infraction Lattanzio became involved in a brawl with several foreign students enroled at the university. In punishment for having wounded one of these students, city authorities banished Lattanzio from Padua and threatened him with a fine of 300 lire. Lattanzio immediately asked the MIA for special permission to complete his studies at the University of Bologna. Despite Lattanzio's misbehaviour and a Venetian decree that all citizens of the *Serenissima* had to study within the confines of the Republic, the MIA voted 7–5 to grant him 25 gold scudi so that he might finish his studies there, as he wished. Three years later, and apparently without further incident, Lattanzio received his degree from the University of Bologna.[1]

The example of Lattanzio Marchese occurred at a critical moment in the history of education and social discipline when Renaissance humanism and Tridentine Catholicism were reshaping the theory and practice of instruction. Fuelled by the dissemination of printed books, the rise of courtly societies, and dramatic shifts in the economy, schooling assumed an ever-increasing importance in early modern Europe. Although schools had always served as a means to socialize and educate the children of the elite, the wider diffusion of instruction after 1550 significantly increased the opportunity to train youngsters of all backgrounds in what to believe and how to behave. The popularity of

---

[1] Carlsmith, 'Il *Collegio Patavino*,' pp. 89–90.

behavioural handbooks such as Castiglione's *Il Cortegiano* and Giovanni della Casa's *Galateo*, underscores the importance of 'buoni costumi' (proper comportment) during this era. During the fifteenth and sixteenth centuries, seminaries and clerical academies sought to instill a rigorous sense of obedience to the precepts of the Catholic Church, while humanist schools emphasized allegiance to civic institutions and/or monarchs. If studied in conjunction with other examples from sixteenth-century Bergamo, the case of Lattanzio Marchese not only suggests the increasing importance of an adolescent's education, but also illustrates a new emphasis on obedience and conformity.

This article explores the twin issues of educating and disciplining adolescent males in the northern Italian city of Bergamo between 1500 and 1650. Many examples are drawn from the archives of the Misericordia Maggiore, the wealthiest and most powerful confraternity in Bergamo. In size, membership, and function, the MIA resembles the *scuole grandi* of Venice studied by Brian Pullan thirty years ago.[2] Subsequent examples are taken from other confraternities, the diocesan seminary, and independent academies. An analysis of student misbehaviour in Bergamo's schools can illustrate important societal norms regarding instruction and social discipline on the eve of the Counter-Reformation. Because it possessed neither an internationally known schoolmaster nor a world-famous educational institution, Bergamo's ordinariness may allow the city to serve as a benchmark for the 'typical' types of schooling available in small and medium-sized provincial Italian cities.

Disciplinary problems were a recurring issue in nearly all of Bergamo's schools. From petty theft and blasphemy to physical assault and accusations of heresy, it seems that students presented a wide variety of disciplinary problems. And although all members of Italian society were subject to the increasingly austere and rigid guidelines set by the Tridentine Church, it also seems that the standards of behaviour for students, at least in the prescriptive literature of the sixteenth century, stiffened significantly as the Counter-Reformation proceeded. Schools thus provide a convenient entry point for a more detailed study of social discipline among the young and the various ways in which society enforced its expectations regarding public (and occasionally private) behaviour.

---

[2] Pullan, *Rich and Poor in Renaissance Venice* and, more recently, 'Town Poor, Country Poor.'

*    *    *

Before examining cases of student misconduct, it is important to note the absence of any such examples in the archives of commune-sponsored schools. Bergamo's city council generally upheld its self-proclaimed responsibility to hire a qualified teacher of grammar and the humanities to provide public instruction at no charge, but it specifically enjoined the teacher(s) to handle all disciplinary issues. Doubtless these schoolmasters faced naughty and disobedient students, but the records of such infractions have not been preserved. Unlike the members of a confraternal executive council or the Father General of a religious order, who demanded to be informed about all disciplinary matters and often prohibited teachers from deciding upon punishment, Bergamo's city council willingly renounced this obligation. The issue of discipline was only one of several that the city council expected the teacher to handle independently; for example, Bergamo's city council never suggested a particular textbook, nor did it mandate a specific curriculum. The public school teacher was viewed by the city council as an autonomous sub-contractor with the liberty to make his own decisions.[3]

In vivid contrast, the records of the Misericordia Maggiore confraternity frequently document instances of student misbehaviour and the MIA's close interest in such matters. It seems unlikely that the MIA schools attracted naughtier students or that their curriculum promoted a greater degree of misbehaviour. More realistically, the abundance of documentation on the misbehaviour of students is a result of the MIA's effort, particularly after 1550, to enforce its rules with a heavy hand. Other confraternities displayed a similar concern with the morality and regular attendance of their students. The visitation records of church-affiliated institutions, such as the diocesan seminary or the Schools of Christian Doctrine, also bring to light many unruly students. Thus a significant body of documentary evidence exists concerning student discipline in sixteenth-century Bergamo.

---

[3] The example of Andrea Cato, and his relationship with the Caspi Academy and Bergamo's city council, is instructive here. Hired by the private Caspi Academy in 1547 to teach grammar and rhetoric, Cato corresponded frequently with the Academy fathers regarding pedagogy, curriculum, and choice of texts. Cato had a significant amount of autonomy in organizing the Caspi Academy; when he was hired to teach in the communal school in 1548, his contract with the city council suggests that he enjoyed similar freedom of choice. See Carlsmith, "Una scuola dei putti."

Anticipating possible problems with student behaviour, the MIA had appointed three deputies annually to monitor the Paduan college and to conduct visitations as necessary.[4] These deputies intervened in disciplinary affairs, assisted students in renting a house, and recorded the names of those who had obtained a degree. The MIA also instituted the position of 'prior' or 'prefect,' an advanced student charged with supervising other students and reporting misbehaviour. Correspondence between the confraternity and the students in Padua reveals the MIA's close interest in students' academic progress and its concern that they conduct themselves in a disciplined and appropriate manner.[5]

Selected by the MIA in 1531 to be among the first group of Paduan scholars, Maffeo Guarneri received 300 lire plus free housing in the college. In the spring of 1534, however, the MIA demanded that he return the money because 'this Maffeus is not devoted to his studies as he is required to be.' Two years later, after Guarneri had obtained a benefice from Luigi Vianova, a canon of the church of Santa Maria Maggiore in Bergamo, the MIA again demanded that he renounce his scholarship and repay his debts.[6] Ten years after that, on 15 April 1547, his father Jacopo Guarneri drew up a will that disinherited Maffeo on account of the extravagant expenses he had incurred in the previous two decades. Jacopo's will provides a detailed accounting of the 3,620 lire he had squandered on his son's sumptuous and dissolute lifestyle. Prior to Maffeo's departure for Padua, Jacopo Guarneri claimed, he had spent 250 lire to send his son to various mountain valleys with a tutor and plenty of spending money. Then he spent 100 lire to hire a grammar teacher named Maestro Fedrigino [Taluino] to teach Maffeo in Bergamo, but his son sold all of his books and clothes in order to escape to Brescia. Despite the place that Maffeo had won in the MIA's college at Padua, Maffeo's father twice found him a furnished room there at a cost of 200 lire. He paid additional sums to have Maffeo transported in style from Bergamo to Padua, and another 1,000 lire on

---

4 Bergamo, Biblioteca Comunale, Archivio MIA n. 1260, *Terminazioni*, fol. 171r (21 Aug. 1531); n. 1261, *Terminazioni*, fol. 75r (15 Feb. 1535), fol. 105r (4 Mar. 1536).

5 Bergamo, Biblioteca Comunale, Arch. MIA n. 1260, *Terminazioni*, fols. 173r–175r (14 Sept. 1531); n. 1261, *Terminazioni*, fol. 75r–v (15 Feb. 1535).

6 Bergamo, Biblioteca Comunale, Arch. MIA n. 1644, 'Processo consortij contra Rev. D. Mapheum De Guarneris Canonicum Bergomensem' (1551), fols. 1–8; n. 1261, *Terminazioni*, fol. 54v (30 Mar. 1534); fol. 105r–v (4 Mar. 1536); n. 1262, fols. 117v–118r (4 Mar. 1536).

books. The list of expenses continues for several pages: illicit expenses and sumptuous banquets ('spesa illicite et banchetti sumptuose' [sic]), living expenses for Maffeo and a friend of his, food and medicine during a fever, horses and a velvet cloak for a trip to Marseilles, legal fees, and 'other expenses which for the sake of decency cannot be named here.' It need hardly be added that Maffeo Guarneri's name does not appear among the list of graduates from the University of Padua.[7]

In 1539, in response to Maffeo Guarneri's misadventures, the MIA appointed three new deputies to review the rules of the college and to suggest appropriate changes.[8] A year later (5 June 1540), it declared that henceforth any student expelled from the college for poor behaviour would have to repay all expenses incurred at Padua. Furthermore, warned the MIA, the student's family shared responsibility for such a debt.[9] As we will see, the MIA did not always enforce its own rule, but perhaps it wished to serve notice to candidates and their families not to expect a free ride. Its response underscores its determination to spend its money in a 'profitable' manner, one that would bestow honour upon the confraternity, its students, and God.

In the same meeting of 4 June 1540, Ludovico dei Conti di Calepio was elected to the MIA's *Collegio Patavino*. Two years later the MIA suspended his stipend for a minimum of two months because he had invited certain foreign students to sleep inside the college. Even worse, these students had organized a party where dancing had occurred, and all this during the first week of Lent. The MIA lamented that the college had suffered a 'very serious scandal' as a result of these escapades. One month later, in an act of charity, the MIA revoked Calepio's suspension on account of the penitence that he had demonstrated for his errors. In 1545 the MIA awarded seven ducats to Calepio so that he might pay his rent. Still identified as a scholar of the confraternity's *Collegio Patavino*, he was encouraged to continue his studies as he

---

[7] Bergamo, Archivio di Stato, *Atti Notarili* di Giuseppe Gritti, busta 2254 (15 Apr. 1547). I am grateful to Father Giovanni Bonacina for the reference. I have not even been able to find Maffeo Guarneri listed as a witness at the graduation of other Bergamasque students, which suggests that he was rarely at university.

[8] Bergamo, Biblioteca Comunale, Arch. MIA n. 1263, *Terminazioni*, fol. 2r (29 May 1539). The three deputies were the MIA's president (Archdeacon Marc'Antonio Bolis), the minister Ezekiel Solza, and Francesco Alzano.

[9] Bergamo, Biblioteca Comunale, Arch. MIA n. 1263, *Terminazioni*, fol. 32r (4 Jun. 1540).

had been elected to do.[10] This suggests that the MIA continued to look after the Bergamasque students in Padua even if it no longer provided housing for them. It also implies a willingness to forgive past indiscretions that was noticeably absent later in the century.

Alessandro Roncalli, elected in 1539, was expelled in 1542 for unspecified violations of the rules of the MIA's Paduan college (perhaps he, too, had participated in the dance party). He appealed to the MIA to be readmitted, confessing that he had made mistakes and promising to reimburse the confraternity for all of his expenses in the event of another expulsion, and had his two brothers and father appear before the council to provide surety. The MIA accepted his appeal. In spite of such promises and assurances, just a few months later Roncalli was involved in another scandal in Padua. This time the confraternity suspended his stipend and warned him that, under pain of forfeiting all his benefits, he was not permitted to re-enter the college while the MIA was deliberating his fate. When he nevertheless dared to move back in, the MIA did not hesitate to expel him. A few months later, Gian Giacomo Roncalli successfully petitioned the confraternity to excuse him from the debt incurred by his brother. Indeed, the MIA even went so far as to grant Gian Giacomo 50 lire 'for the love of God and so that his studies might be completed.' In 1544 both Alessandro and Gian Giacomo Roncalli were identified as law students at the University of Padua.[11] Despite the MIA's previous threat to demand repayment of all expenses, the two boys apparently were able to continue their studies.

The most intriguing case may be that of Guglielmo Gratarolo, the famous medical doctor who converted to Protestantism and fled to Basel in the 1550s, where he corresponded with Calvin and wrote influential religious and medical treatises.[12] Twenty years earlier, as a student at the

---

[10] Bergamo, Biblioteca Comunale, Arch. MIA n. 1263, *Terminazioni*, fol. 32r–v (4 Jun. 1540); 64v (20 Mar. 1542); 66r (17 Apr. 1542); 124r (13 Apr. 1545). At the Studio Ludovico replaced Pietro Zanchi, who had graduated.

[11] Bergamo, Biblioteca Comunale, Arch. MIA n. 1263, *Terminazioni*, fol. 7v (29 May 1539); 64r (16 Mar. 1542); 66r (17 Apr. 1542); 71r (1 Sept. 1542); 84v (27 May 1543); 89r (19 Nov. 1543); 89r (19 Nov. 1543); 102r (19 May 1544).

[12] For a brief history and more bibliography on Gratarolo (also Gratarolus, Grataroli), see Church, *The Italian Reformers 1534–64*, 194–201; Thorndike, *History of Magic and Experimental Science*, 5:600–16; Gallizoli, *Della vita, degli studi, e degli scritti di Guglielmo Grataroli*; and Belotti, *Storia di Bergamo e dei Bergamaschi*, 4:260–66.

MIA's Paduan college, Gratarolo was involved in a scandal concerning 'particular behaviour, speeches, and letters of his.' The confraternity immediately investigated and Gratarolo's fellow students wrote a letter asking that he be pardoned and allowed to remain at the university.[13] Perhaps intentionally, the students' letter does not specify Gratarolo's misbehaviour; however, Orazio Bravi, who has studied Protestantism in Bergamo at considerable length, is convinced that Gratarolo must have been experimenting with new religious ideas.[14] Gratarolo apparently received his doctorate in 1537 and within two years was a member of the College of Physicians in Bergamo.[15] In 1544 he was required to abjure 'certain articles concerning which he was held suspect' by the Milanese inquisitor. Soon after, the bishop of Bergamo, Vittore Soranzo, warned him to be more careful about his public statements. By 1549 Gratarolo had headed north and in 1551 the Congregation of the Holy Office declared him to be an obstinate and relapsed heretic.[16]

It seems unlikely that these five students represent a typical cohort of young men selected for Bergamo's Paduan college. Between 1531 and 1541 nearly a dozen other students, none of whom engaged in the kind of misbehaviour cited above, were members of the college. Gian Anselmo Maffei, for example, not only received an additional award of 25 gold scudi to study law as a reward for his diligent efforts, but was praised as a model student.[17] Pietro Zanchi, too, was lauded for his virtue, his honour, and his 'wise and studious' ways.'[18] Girolamo di Olmo (also known as Hieronymo Lulmi) graduated with a medical degree in October 1539 and pursued a successful medical career in Bergamo.[19] Julio Agosti corresponded regularly with the MIA about events in the

---

[13] Bergamo, Biblioteca Comunale, Arch. MIA n. 2306, 'Lettere varie del sec. XVI' (3 May 1538).

[14] Personal communication, June 1997. See also Bravi, 'Note e documenti.'

[15] Church, *The Italian Reformers*, pp. 195–96.

[16] Church, *The Italian Reformers*, pp. 196–99.

[17] Bergamo, Biblioteca Comunale, Arch. MIA n. 1261, *Terminazioni*, fol. 64v (17 Sept. 1534). Julio Agosti praised Maffei in a letter asking for additional financial support for an eighth year of study: Bergamo, Biblioteca Comunale, Arch. MIA n. 2306, 'Lettere varie del sec. XVI,' fol. 4 (25 Nov. 1540). Maffei graduated in law on 3 Oct. 1534. For this and other records of graduation from the University of Padua, see *Acta Graduum*, no. 2062.

[18] Bergamo, Biblioteca Comunale, Arch. MIA n. 2328, [no title] fol. 1r (9 Apr. 1536). Zanchi graduated in medicine on 5 May 1540; *Acta Graduum*, no. 2710.

[19] Di Olmo graduated in medicine on 23 Oct. 1539; *Acta Graduum*, no. 2640.

college and penned an oration in Latin giving thanks to the confraternity for its financial support. After earning a degree in law, he was elected to the College of Jurists and appointed to teach civil law in Bergamo in 1542.[20]

Nevertheless, the MIA eventually decided that the bad behaviour of its students at the Collegio Patavino outweighed the college's positive benefits. In a decree of 17 April 1542, the confraternity decided to close the college and reallocate the money to a more profitable purpose. In a rather aggrieved tone, it explained:

> Whereas on 14 September 1531 a college for five poor scholars from Bergamo was founded and erected in the city of Padua by the magnificent ministers of this confraternity of the Misericordia for the purpose of studying the liberal arts, as explained in greater detail in the rules and regulations announced on that day. Whereas they created this pious and holy institution hoping that students would acquire the greatest virtue and glory for themselves, their fatherland, their family, and their friends, from their daytime study and their nighttime reading. Whereas Pietro Andrea Zonca, the distinguished president of the aforementioned confraternity, considering the way that this pious organization has been cheated [of its hope], and that not all of the students have taken advantage of the benefits offered to them, as it was hoped, but have done very little; nor did they behave as they should have, nor are they behaving as they ought to, in an exemplary manner, [but] many of them have caused diverse complaints to reach the ears of the magnificent ministers of the confraternity, bringing scandal and displeasure to all of them, in contrast to the godly motives for which this institution was created. Considering the modest accomplishments of these students, and the scarcity of funds available to this confraternity owing to the many debts by which it is already oppressed and which can be paid off only with difficulty, [therefore] they judge that it would be better if the money allocated to this fruitless enterprise of the scholars were to be distributed in other works more beneficial to God and to the world.[21]

---

[20] A draft copy of the oration is in Bergamo, Biblioteca Comunale, Arch. MIA n. 2306, 'Lettere varie del sec. XVI,' n.d. This same file contains several other letters from Julio Agosti, who appears to have served as prefect or prior in the *Collegio Patavino*. See also Bergamo, Biblioteca Comunale, Arch. Storico del Comune, *Azioni*, vol. 21, fol. 34r (19 Dec. 1541). Agosti graduated (after ten years) on 19 Jan. 1541; *Acta Graduum*, no. 2769.

[21] Bergamo, Biblioteca Comunale, Arch. MIA n. 1263, *Terminazioni*, fols. 66v–67r (17 Apr. 1542).

Henceforth, announced the MIA, no new scholars would be elected to the college in Padua, although those already in residence would be allowed to remain till the completion of their degree. The motion passed by a vote of 10–2.

What do these examples from the MIA's Paduan college reveal about the education and discipline of young males in sixteenth-century Bergamo? For one thing, the confraternity's demand that each student complete his degree within seven years indicates that the MIA was concerned about the academic progress (and financial outlay) of its students. Maffeo Guarneri, for example, was chastised by the confraternity for having failed to attend to his studies. Students at the college were expected to behave properly and the confraternity did not hesitate to hand down punishments when those rules were broken. Because the founding charter of the college had promised that the students would be 'cared for in both body and soul,' the brothers of the confraternity took this responsibility seriously.[22]

Yet the most surprising aspect may be the MIA's willingness to forgive repeated transgressions by its students. The misbehaviour cited above—assault, heresy, and flagrant disregard for the rules of the confraternity—would have been frowned upon by nearly any institution in the sixteenth century.[23] Yet the MIA repeatedly forgave its troublesome students by readmitting them to the college, granting them special permission to study elsewhere, and failing to follow through on its threats to demand reimbursement from expelled students. Even the extravagant lifestyle of Maffeo Guarneri, which was perhaps more a question of economic profligacy than of social discipline, reveals that the MIA was willing to give him a second chance.

The MIA's soft-hearted policy of the 1530s and 1540s changed, however, during the second half of the sixteenth century. Although the confraternity continued to suffer from disciplinary problems, intervention by Church officials and ecclesiastical institutions combined with a stricter moral climate to produce less tolerance for students who behaved poorly. This growing concern with discipline and orthodoxy is clearly evident in other schools run by the MIA. In addition to sponsoring the Paduan college, the Misericordia Maggiore had pre-

---

[22] Bergamo, Biblioteca Comunale, Arch. MIA n. 1260, *Terminazioni*, fols. 173r–175r (14 Sept. 1531).

[23] For more on sixteenth-century expulsions from the university, see Seneca, 'Antonio Rosato.'

viously founded a day school for clerics in Bergamo. Only scattered instances of disciplinary problems surface in the first fifty years of the day school's existence. One such case occurred in 1510 when one-third of the students were dismissed for lack of effort and were replaced by a new group of clerics 'eager to be more diligent in their studies.'[24] For the most part, however, the confraternal records do not speak of concerns with discipline or punishment until after 1550.

By 1557 the mindset and the institutions of the Catholic Reformation were becoming more influential. In that year the MIA hired Reverend Michele Millio of Valcamonica to teach sixty-three students for a salary of 450 lire per year and a house where he could lodge ten of his students.[25] In the spring of 1559, four of Millio's adolescent students lodged with the Holy Office of the Inquisition accusations of heresy against their teacher.[26] After Millio had been incarcerated in the inquisitor's prison in the episcopal palace, the students—Lorenzo Rota, Christoforo Betarolo, Simone Terzo, and Hieronimo Federico—confessed to the MIA's council that the accusations were false. Condemned by the confraternity for participating in a 'diabolical conspiracy' against their master and for bearing false witness with wicked, criminal, and evil intentions, the students were immediately expelled and ordered to pay back their stipends. Unlike the students in the MIA's Paduan college, these students were in fact required to reimburse the MIA. A fifth youth, Camillo de Licini, was also expelled for lying about this incident. Despite this unpleasant experience, Millio continued to teach and to receive praise from the confraternity for his superior instruction.[27]

The students' decision to involve the Holy Office reflected heightened religious tension and fear of Protestantism in northern Italy. Bergamo's proximity to Switzerland, and the repeated investigations of its own bishop, Vittore Soranzo, on charges of heresy, made its religious climate particularly sensitive. Similar false accusations would probably have been censored just as strongly in the 1530s and 1540s,

---

[24] Bergamo, Biblioteca Comunale, Arch. MIA n. 1256, *Terminazioni*, fol. 102v (14 Jan. 1510), fol. 104v (28 Jan. 1510), fol. 106v (11 Feb. 1510).

[25] Bergamo, Biblioteca Comunale, Arch. MIA n. 1265, *Terminazioni*, fols. 113v–114r (10 May 1557) and 120v–121r (bis) (14 Jun. 1557).

[26] Bergamo, Biblioteca Comunale, Arch. MIA n. 1265, *Terminazioni*, fols. 202v–203r (20 Mar. 1559). See also del Col, *L'Inquisizione*, p. cxxx.

[27] Bergamo, Biblioteca Comunale, Arch. MIA n. 1260, *Terminazioni*, fol. 71r (11 Nov. 1560); Arch. MIA n. 1267, *Terminazioni*, fol. 34r (19 Apr. 1563); fol. 52v (12 Aug. 1563); fol. 103v (5 Jan 1564).

however, it is telling that such accusations sprouted just as the Catholic Reformation was gaining momentum.

In 1564, when Michele Millio eventually resigned, the MIA closed its day school and then, two years later, opened a new, residential academy for clerics (*Accademia dei Chierici*). In many ways this new academy resembled the school founded by the MIA in 1506: both were designed for the education of adolescent *chierici*, both taught Latin grammar and catechism, both gave preference to youths who served in the church of Santa Maria Maggiore, and both were funded entirely by the MIA. However, the new academy reflected a half-century of further experience and a heightened commitment to religious orthodoxy. In the second half of the sixteenth century the rigorous and austere vision of the Catholic Church led to stricter control over lay confraternities, schools, texts, and teachers. The MIA's Academy of Clerics embodies this more rigid vision of a school. For example, the new academy was a boarding school, with much stricter rules and increased supervision.[28] Students were required to confess regularly and attend Mass, and they were prohibited from wandering around the town or to engage in idle conversation with city residents. In short, the MIA's Academy of Clerics reflected not only the religious fervour of the later sixteenth century and the demand for more rigorous preparation of churchmen, but also the desirability of strict discipline among the young and the prestige of a good education.

The students within the Academy of Clerks lived a regimented lifestyle under the close supervision of their teachers. The day began and ended with bedside prayer and a solemn trip to the chapel in Santa Maria Maggiore. Detailed instructions specified the order and number of prayers to be recited on each occasion, even explaining how low a student must kneel when visited by his teachers, the ministers of the MIA, or the bishop of Bergamo. Students were allowed to exit the academy only in the company of a teacher and were expected to walk two by two according to age. Licentious books were forbidden, all meals were eaten in common, and recreation inside the academy was carefully regulated. In an effort to reduce distractions and promote cohesiveness among the *chierici*, friendships with youths outside the academy were discouraged. With the exception of mothers and sisters, the presence of women was of course prohibited.[29] As we will see shortly, despite (or perhaps

---

[28] Locatelli, 'L'istruzione a Bergamo,' p. 134. Barachetti, 'La *Domus Magna*,' esp. pp. 71–72.

[29] Bergamo, Biblioteca Comunale, Arch. MIA n. 1519, *Liber Capitulorum,* fols.

because of) these rigid guidelines, the MIA's academy suffered from recurrent disciplinary problems.

On 15 February 1574 the MIA angrily denounced several of its students as disobedient and poor learners and voted to expel them immediately. Considerable soul-searching followed, as the confraternity considered whether to continue investing its resources in the academy.[30] Ultimately it decided to continue with the academy but agreed to share the expense of hiring a new teacher with Bergamo's city council. In September 1575 Archbishop Carlo Borromeo arrived for an apostolic visitation of the diocese.[31] On 24 September he visited the Academy of Clerics and subsequently issued a harsh evaluation of the students. Rather than noting any disciplinary problem, Borromeo's report condemns the students' lack of intellect and low motivation. His visit, however, foreshadowed darker days ahead for the academy. Despite the presence of a renowned teacher (Nicolò Cologno) and financial assistance from the commune, the confraternity continued to question whether the academy was worth the effort.

The principal complaint against the academy was that the students were disrespectful and mocked the rules. In February of 1577, for example, the MIA complained bitterly that 'after great effort, exertion, and expense on the part of this consortium,' the students 'with a series of cunning and deceitful tricks have avoided the discipline of the teachers and have repeatedly skipped classes.'[32] In response, the MIA reorganized and expanded the academy, both to increase competition among students and to ensure a sufficient number of students to serve in the cathedral.[33] Only three years later, however, the confraternity denounced the 'disorder and difficulties that occur every day as a result

---

48r–52r (31 Apr. 1566). See also fols. 107v–108v for the 1590 redaction of the students' *capitoli* and a list of punishments for various infractions such as tardiness, swearing, skipping mass or meals, punching another student, or failure to complete homework.

[30] Bergamo, Biblioteca Comunale, Archivio MIA n. 1270, *Terminazioni*, fols. 91v–92r (15 Feb. 1574); see also Bergamo, Biblioteca Comunale, Archivio MIA n. 1385, *Spese*, fol. 145r–v (n.d., but clearly post-1575).

[31] This is briefly discussed in Carlsmith, 'Schooling and Society in Bergamo,' chap. 2; Angelo G. Roncalli (later Pope John XXIII) published many of the documents in *Gli Atti della Visita Apostolica di San Carlo Borromeo a Bergamo, 1575.*

[32] Bergamo, Biblioteca Comunale, Arch. MIA n. 1271, *Terminazioni*, fols. 82v–83v (24 Feb. 1577).

[33] Roncalli, *La MIA di Bergamo*, p. 66.

of the poor behaviour of the academy students. . . . since many of these ungrateful wretches have profited from their study of grammar or music which should have benefited both the Academy and the Church.'[34] A letter from the music teacher Giovanni Florio in 1588 confirms the persistent lapses in student discipline: Florio found one of his students lounging on a dormitory bed instead of attending his class, but upon scolding him he was 'seriously threatened by the student's brother with vile and slanderous words.'[35] On the other hand, letters from Valeriano Guarguanti suggest that the school's difficulties were not caused by students alone. Guarguanti had been a student at the academy in 1585, but his teacher, Paolo Cordaro, had tormented him to such a degree that his mother sent him to Venice and then to Rome with the Bergamasque nobleman Giovanni Girolamo Grumelli until the teacher was replaced. Guarguanti cited instances of verbal abuse, argument, and insult on the part of Cordaro.[36] In 1590 the MIA's deputies issued a new set of *capitoli* stipulating the responsibilities of everyone from the head teacher to the cook and to the *chierici*, but such action did little to improve the situation.[37]

Faced with the prospect of increasing unrest, the MIA reacted by hiring back a familiar and trusted face, just as it had done when faced with a similar crisis in its day school a half century before. Nicolò Cologno was asked to return for six months, for in his absence the academy 'had gone from bad to worse.' Cologno agreed, but would come only on his own terms: 'After much discussion, I responded [that] I would be happy to do this job again, but that I would not set foot there unless I were given absolute authority to run the school.'[38] Ensconced in the school by 1 November 1590, he exercised great effort in rousing the youths, teaching them grammar and rhetoric, and supervising the assistant teachers. However, his unlimited authority apparently rankled some members of the MIA's Council, whereupon Cologno

---

[34] Bergamo, Biblioteca Comunale, Arch. MIA n. 1272, *Terminazioni*, fols. 9v–10r (30 Apr. 1580).

[35] Bergamo, Biblioteca Comunale, Arch. MIA n. 1447, *Scritture/Suppliche*, fol. 64r (ca. 1588).

[36] Bergamo, Biblioteca Comunale, Arch. MIA n. 1447, *Scritture/Suppliche*, fol. 373r–v (ca. 1591).

[37] Bergamo, Biblioteca Comunale, Arch. MIA n. 1519, *Liber Capitulorum*, fols. 104r–113r (various dates).

[38] Bergamo, Biblioteca Comunale, Arch. MIA n. 1447, *Scritture/Suppliche*, fols. 226r–227r (31 Aug. 1590).

angrily declared his intention to step down. By the beginning of the next academic year Cologno had been appointed reader of moral philosophy at the University of Padua, where he finished his career.[39]

The MIA's academy survived for another two decades, beset by continuing problems with the students. In 1590, for example, the MIA investigated the alleged beating of the academy's cook by two *chierici*, Francesco Muzio and Cristoforo Romanello.[40] In 1595 the academy was rocked by the theft of 20 lire from the servants' quarters; the MIA was forced to investigate and interrogate each of the students in turn.[41] Despite the successful example of colleges and seminaries organized by the Jesuits, the Somaschans, and Archbishop Borromeo, the MIA's Academy continued to founder until it was finally closed in 1610.[42]

In fewer than three decades, then, the MIA's Academy of Clerics suffered from a significant number of disciplinary problems. Clearly frustrated by its inability to keep students out of trouble, the confraternity repeatedly examined its performance, but to little avail.

Why did the MIA encounter so many problems with disciplining its students? Perhaps it enforced unusually high standards, or was more meticulous in recording disciplinary infractions. Perhaps increased competition made students more willing to take chances and operate beyond the pale in an effort to gain an advantage. The exaggerated number of incidents, however, suggests that the root causes of increased disciplinary issues existed outside the school(s). It seems probable that the new rules of the Tridentine Church were imposed upon educational institutions that had either direct or indirect affiliations with the Catholic Church. If this were true, a corresponding

---

39 Venezia, Archivio di Stato, Fondo *Riformatori dello Studio di Padova* [vol. 348], 'Lettori nello Studio di Padova,' *s.v.* Cologno, Nicolò [p. 13]. Cologno is listed as a *lettore di filosofia morale in Padova* (6 May 1591).

40 Bergamo, Biblioteca Comunale, Arch. MIA n. 2045, 'Accademia', fols. 1–8 (17–23 Jan. 1590).

41 Bergamo, Biblioteca Comunale, Archivio MIA n. 1148, 'Furto nell'Accademia,' fol. 37 (4 Nov. 1595 – 13 Feb. 1596). The file includes interviews, summaries of fact, and other documents, but most are illegible, and therefore I do not know the outcome of the investigation.

42 Locatelli, 'L'istruzione a Bergamo,' p. 78, cites Bergamo, Biblioteca Comunale, Arch. MIA n. 1334, *Relazioni*, fald. 20, fol. 3r (22 Jul. 1795), which explains that the confraternity closed the academy for the following reasons: the number of priests had increased substantially; the Tridentine Seminary was providing too much competition; the financial burden on the MIA was too great.

increase of disciplinary cases in other schools of the era should be evident.

Although other institutions in Bergamo lack the vast documentation of the MIA, even a cursory glance at other schools and academies confirms the trend visible in the MIA's schools. In 1561, for example, the confraternity of Sant'Alessandro in Colonna, expelled Paolo Stabello because he had refused to attend the lessons of master Antonio Villa, but permitted Paolo's brother to attend in his place.[43] In 1565 the confraternity insisted that henceforth all teachers must bring their students to a special meeting once a month to demonstrate what had been learned. Lay students who had reached the required level of competency in reading, writing, and mathematics were to be excused so that others might take their places; students who demonstrated a lack of ability and little promise were to be dismissed immediately.[44] A *Regola* (Rule) published in 1589 specifically assigned members to conduct monthly visitations of the schools in order to determine 'if the students are lazy and might be occupying places better filled by more eager students.'[45] The deputies were to report immediately any student who was disobedient, distracting, or obstinate, for which behaviour the ministers of the confraternity promised immediate expulsion from the school. The confraternity of Sant'Alessandro della Croce displayed a similar attitude toward its schools, expelling Zo (Giovanni) Maria Chiodi in 1596 after he failed to show up for church services and classes four days in a row.[46] The confraternity's council also insisted upon the importance of 'buoni costumi' for all students, emphasizing that those who could not discipline themselves would be subject to expulsion. These examples mirror the concerns of the MIA and reflect the increasingly common tendency to expel troublesome students rather than rehabilitate them.

Another parallel exists in the desire of confraternal executive councils to handle disciplinary matters themselves rather than delegate such responsibility to the teacher. As we have seen, the MIA's Council of Presidents usually decided upon punishment of students. The one exception to this tradition came with the appointment of Nicolò Colo-

[43] Bergamo, Archivio Parrocchiale di Sant'Alessandro in Colonna, *Libro delli Parti (1549–1567),* fol. 193v (10 Mar. 1560), and fol. 205r (24 Jan. 1561).

[44] Bergamo, Archivio Parrocchiale di Sant'Alessandro in Colonna, *Libro delli Parti (1549-1567),* fol. 274r–v (28 Dec. 1565).

[45] *Regola del Ven. Consortio di Santo Alessandro in Colonna,* p. 35.

[46] Bergamo, Archivio Parrocchiale di Sant'Alessandro della Croce, n. 1050, *Libro delli Parti,* fol. 46r (11 Feb. 1596).

gno in 1590, an experiment that ended soon after in recrimination and regret. In 1574 the brothers of Sant'Alessandro in Colonna issued a list of requirements (*capitoli*) for the grammar master whom they intended to hire for a local school. Although the teacher was encouraged to teach Greek and Latin as he saw fit, he was specifically prohibited from dismissing students without the express permission of the confraternity.[47] An additional parallel is evident in the subtle shift in preference for the instruction of aspiring priests rather than lay youths. Despite the fact that a confraternity typically educated ten times as many lay youths as their ecclesiastical counterparts, the confraternity of Sant' Alessandro in Colonna declared in 1589 that schooling for *chierici* was of much greater importance than schooling for poor youths.[48] This declaration reflected the Catholic Church's strong push to promote the training and religious education of clergy in the later sixteenth century.

In the sixteenth and seventeenth centuries Bergamo possessed a number of independent academies that educated young men. With the singular exception of the Caspi Academy,[49] we know little about the other institutions that provided instruction and housing to students. However, one document from the very beginning of the seventeenth century suggests that the disciplinary issues raised by Tridentine reform efforts were also evident here. In the Academy of Borgo Pignolo, Nicolo Benaglio served as an assistant teacher to the *maestro,* Bartolomeo di Grigno. In July 1603 Benaglio's sixteen-year-old son, Vincenzo, grossly insulted an elderly man in via Pignolo Vecchio, across the street from the academy. According to the statement of seventy-year-old Francesco di Gozzi, he had come outside on a Sunday afternoon at the request of young Vincenzo Benaglio, whom he recognized as one of the local clerics. Di Gozzi said that, without any warning, Vincenzo 'began to provoke him with injurious words and then to make many, many villainous remarks insulting and dishonouring him and his family, and not content with that, the said Benaglio reached underneath his tunic to pull out a hidden club [*uno bastone*]

---

[47] Bergamo, Archivio Parrocchiale di Sant'Alessandro in Colonna, *Libro delle Terminationi (1574–1584)*, fols. 32v–33r (2 Apr. 1574).

[48] *Regola del Ven. Consortio di S. Alessandro in Colonna*, p. 35.

[49] Carlsmith, 'Una scuola dei putti,' passim. Despite the fortuitous survival of a number of documents about the Caspi Academy—a small, residential, elementary-level school for the children of the elite founded in Bergamo in 1547—no mention of disciplinary issues appears in other extant sources. For an overview of academies in Bergamo, see Torri, *Dalle antiche Accademie all'Ateneo.*

with which to offend him, and he did offend him.'[50] Vincenzo Benaglio was subsequently brought before the bishop's court and threatened with corporal punishment, a stiff fine, and the possibility of incarceration or exile. The bishop's vicar, Bernardino Costa, further instructed Benaglio that neither he nor any of his friends were to approach Gozzi's house or disturb him in any way. Costa made it quite clear that the episcopal court was prepared to reopen the case immediately if any similar incidents occurred. The incident may have been nothing more than a teenage prank, but the response of the episcopal court was in keeping with the strict new interpretation favoured at this time.

The diocesan seminary, founded by Bishop Federico Cornaro in 1567, also reveals a concern with the private morality and public behaviour of students. The seminary closely resembled the MIA's Academy of Clerics in terms of curriculum, adolescent student body, and residential living. Both institutions sought to restrict contact between their impressionable young men and the outside world; for example, a redaction of the seminary's rules in 1575 specified that 'the house must be arranged in a proper manner: specifically, the second [inner?] door must be locked with a key so that outsiders cannot enter.'[51] Both institutions initially accepted lay youths as day students, but by 1575 had forbidden their presence. The desire to separate and define education for the laity as distinct from education for future religious was typical of the post-Tridentine program.

Also similar was Archbishop Carlo Borromeo's report on the seminary, in which he criticized the students as mediocre and unmotivated, pointing in particular to the lack of discipline. Borromeo legislated a list of changes to be instituted immediately and then installed a new rector, Massimo Bonello, to ensure that his reforms would be observed.[52] These changes largely reiterated the Tridentine decrees of session XXIII. They were accompanied by a new set of rules in the same year that offer a revealing glimpse into seminary life and the strict philosophy promulgated by Borromeo.[53]

---

[50] Bergamo, Archivio della Curia Vescovile, Mensa Vescovile, *1547 e seguenti, Accademia dei [Caspi]*, fald. 68/1, fol. 73r–v (21 July 1603).

[51] *Atti della visita apostolica*, 1:290–91; also cited in Roncalli, *Gli inizi del Seminario di Bergamo*, pp. 56–58.

[52] Carlsmith, 'Schooling and Society in Bergamo,' pp. 158–61.

[53] *Atti della Visita Apostolica*, 1:290–93; Roncalli, *Gli inizi del Seminario di Bergamo*, pp. 63–64.

Bonello resigned after only four months, sending an angry letter of resignation to Borromeo:

> Most Illustrious and Reverend Monsignor,
>     It pains me greatly to inform your Reverence of new unpleasantness and more insupportable behaviour on the part of those men of the seminary, from whom I would have hoped to be aided, but everything has happened in such a contrary fashion that I cannot and should not be expected to tolerate any more. . . . At the present moment I am not able to describe the malice and hatred that they demonstrated [toward me] in so many ways. . . . And then the very scornful and arrogant responses of the clerics. . . . but in truth I finally realized that some of them are a long ways from wanting the reform and that they still wish to preserve their ingrained habits; understanding that I am not equal to the task, I hereby resign.
>     Your most humble servant, Massimo Bonello.[54]

Bonello's letter clearly emphasizes the lack of discipline that he perceived in the seminary. However, other sources collected by Borromeo paint quite a different picture of the seminary as a place where study, discipline, and confession were paramount. For example, each Sunday one of the seminarians was required to prepare a reflection on the Gospels, and every year the students organized a sacred play to counterbalance the excesses of Carnival. Furthermore, expulsions and disciplinary matters do not appear in any of the extant records, and the seminary continued to grow slowly until around 1630 it reached an enrolment high of fifty students. It appears that its youths were subject to similar expectations regarding orthodoxy and 'godly discipline' as were those in other academic institutions in post-Tridentine Bergamo. Indeed, the standards at the seminary were almost certainly higher, especially under pressure from a determined reformer such as Carlo Borromeo.

\* \* \*

In conclusion, what do these examples of Bergamasque students reveal about education, discipline, and adolescents? Scholars have repeatedly shown that student misbehaviour was not uncommon in early modern Europe. With its prestigious universities and dense urbanization, Italy had a plethora of adolescent students living in close proximity to each other and to the townspeople. The annals of Padua and Bologna are full of incidents where students contravened the town

---

[54] Roncalli, *Gli inizi del Seminario di Bergamo*, p. 68.

laws, university regulations, and sexual mores of the era. I suggest that in the middle of the sixteenth century a decisive shift took place regarding how adults and institutions responded to the misbehaviour of youths. A convergence of several historical trends thus resulted in students after 1550 receiving different treatment for similar misconduct than they had earlier in the century.

The first important change was that education, at both the secondary and the university level, became more desirable and more accessible. The number of options for schooling in Bergamo grew significantly in the sixteenth century as the city council, the Church, and the confraternities competed to attract and train youths in various fields. A similar growth is evident in Bergamo's neighbouring cities to the east: Brescia, Vicenza, and Verona all witnessed an expansion of educational opportunities in the sixteenth century. The MIA's Paduan college was one of many colleges founded to provide greater opportunity for youths to continue their education. Compared to the population as a whole, Lattanzio Marchese and his classmates were still among the educational elite, but more and more students were seeking instruction.

The increased role of the Catholic Church evident in the developments discussed in this article is critical in explaining the second change: the greater emphasis upon imposing obedience, orthodoxy, and 'godly discipline' among adolescents evident after 1550. The examples from Bergamo show that the severity of responses to student misbehaviour increased markedly in the second half of the sixteenth century. Students were viewed more carefully, for suddenly the stakes were higher. The advent of Protestantism and fear of its implications were sufficient to galvanize many institutions to examine education more carefully. Thus what had formerly been simple questions of discipline now became a question of orthodoxy. The fear of 'contamination' in schoolrooms was seen as adequate justification for the harsher responses. Trouble in the classroom, it was feared, could lead to trouble everywhere. The greater willingness to expel a student probably also reflects the increased demand for education in the sixteenth century, for schools could be certain of replacing expelled students quickly.

Concern over disciplining youths was part of a larger effort whereby secular and religious authorities sought to impose greater control upon the population and enforce greater discipline over education, the distribution of poor relief, the organization of popular festivals, and so forth. Students were merely caught up in this larger reform movement.

As a greater number of youths entered the schools, and as the goals and authority of the State and the Church developed throughout the sixteenth century, it was inevitable that public behaviour and private discipline would affect adolescents to an unprecedented degree.

*University of Massachusetts*
*Lowell, Massachusetts*

## Cited Works
## Manuscript Sources

Bergamo, Biblioteca Civica 'A. Mai'
    Archivio MIA n. 1148, 'Furto nell'Accademia'
        nn. 1256, 1260–1263, 1265, 1267, 1270–1272, *Terminazioni*
        n. 1385, *Spese*
        n. 1447, *Scritture/Suppliche*
        n. 1519, *Liber Capitulorum*
        n. 1644, 'Processo consortij contra Rev. D. Mapheum
            De Guarneris Canonicum Bergomensem'
        n. 2045, 'Accademia'
        n. 2306, 'Lettere varie del sec. XVI'
        n. 2328, [no title]
    Archivio Storico del Comune, *Azioni del Consiglio*
Bergamo, Archivio della Curia Vescovile, Mensa Vescovile, *1547 e seguenti, Accademia dei [Caspi]*, ff. 1–84.
Bergamo, Archivio di Stato, *Atti Notarili* di Giuseppe Gritti, busta 2254
Bergamo, Archivio Parrocchiale di Sant'Alessandro della Croce n. 1050, *Libro delli Parti*
Bergamo, Archivio Parrocchiale di Sant'Alessandro in Colonna, *Libro delli Parti (1549–1567) Libro delle Terminationi (1574–1584)*
Venezia, Archivio di Stato, Fondo *Riformatori dello Studio di Padova* [vol. 348], 'Lettori nello Studio di Padova'

## Published Sources

*Acta Graduum Academicorum Universitatis Patavinae.* 5 vols. Padova: Antenore, 1970–.
*Atti della Visita Apostolica di San Carlo Borromeo a Bergamo, 1575,* ed. Angelo G. Roncalli. 5 vols. Florence: Olschki, 1936–1957.
Barachetti, Gianni. 'La *Domus Magna* della MIA' *Bergomum* 59:1 (1965): 63–86.
Belotti, Bartolo. *Storia di Bergamo e dei Bergamaschi.* 9 vols. Bergamo: Bolis, 1989.
Bravi, Giulio Orazio. 'Note e documenti per la storia della Riforma a Bergamo (1536–44)' *Archivio Storico Bergamasco* 11 (1987): 185–228.

Carlsmith, Christopher. '"Una scuola dei putti": L'Accademia dei Caspi a Bergamo' *Atti del Ateneo di Scienze, Lettere, ed Arti di Bergamo* 61 (1997–98): 291–302

Carlsmith, Christopher, 'Il *Collegio Patavino* della Misericordia Maggiore di Bergamo, 1531 – ca. 1550' *Bergomum: Bollettino della civica biblioteca di Bergamo 93:1–2 (1998): 75–98.*

Carlsmith, Christopher. 'Schooling and Society in Bergamo, 1500–1650' Ph.D. dissertation, University of Virginia, 1999.

Church, Frederic C. *The Italian Reformers 1534–64.* New York: Columbia University Press, 1932.

del Col, Andrea. *L'Inquisizione nel Patriarcato e Diocesi di Aquileia, 1557 –1559.* Trieste: Edizioni Università di Trieste, 1998.

Gallizoli, Giovanni Battista. *Della vita, degli studi, e degli scritti di Guglielmo Grataroli, filosofo e medico.* Bergamo, 1788.

Locatelli, Giuseppe. 'L'istruzione a Bergamo e la Misericordia Maggiore' *Bergomum* 4:4 (1910): 57–169, and 5:1 (1911): 21–99.

Pullan, Brian S. *Rich and Poor in Renaissance Venice: The Social Institutions of a Catholic State to 1620.* Cambridge, MA: Harvard University Press, 1971.

Pullan, Brian S. 'Town Poor, Country Poor: The Province of Bergamo from the Sixteenth to the Eighteenth Century' pp. 213–36 in *Medieval and Renaissance Venice*, ed. Ellen E. Kittell and Thomas F. Madden. Urbana: University of Illinois Press, 1999.

*Regola del Ven. Consortio di Santo Alessandro in Colonna, ove oltre gli Ordini, si contengono anche l'Origine, l'Antichità, e i Confini suoi.* Bergamo: Comin Ventura, 1589; rpt Bergamo: Francesco Locatelli, 1767.

Roncalli, Angelo G. *La MIA di Bergamo e le altre istituzioni di beneficenza amministrate dalla Congregazione di Carità.* Bergamo: Tipografia S. Alessandro, 1912.

Roncalli, Angelo G. *Gli inizi del Seminario di Bergamo e S. Carlo Borromeo.* Bergamo: SESA, 1939.

Seneca, Federico. 'Antonio Rosato, bidello generale dello Studio Patavino, e i "disordini" del 1599' *Quaderni per la Storia dell'Università di Padova* 16 (1983): 109–118.

Thorndike, Lynn. *History of Magic and Experimental Science.* 5 vols. New York: Columbia University Press, 1941.

Torri, Tancredo. *Dalle antiche Accademie all'Ateneo.* Bergamo: Stamperia di Gorlè, 1975.

# Teen Knights:
## Interpreting Precocity in Early Modern Life-Stories

### Marian Rothstein

From the fourteenth to the sixteenth century, much recreational liter-ature in France was in the form of *romans en prose*, an expression usually rendered into English as 'prose romances' (but which I will speak of as 'novels').[1] Medieval examples, such as *Tristan* or *Lancelot*, were reprinted well into the sixteenth century. The great best-seller and style-setter of mid-sixteenth-century France, *Amadis,* had its ori-gins in late fifteenth-century Spain. Other, newer forms, such as *Gar-gantua, Pantagruel,* or *Alector,* were heavily invested in parodying earlier forms, indicating that the readers of such fiction, like its authors, could be assumed to be familiar with the genre being parodied. Many years ago, I was taken aback in a graduate seminar when the distin-guished medievalist teaching it brushed aside a question about repe-titious, formulaic romance plots saying that these things were read only by adolescents anyway. That answer may well have been constructed off the cuff largely for its shock value, but once the question of the intended audience of medieval and Renaissance romans en prose is raised, one is led to note that teen-aged youths often do have a much larger place than might be expected. The next question is why should this be so, why are the adventures of pre-adult heroes recounted?

Part of the answer lies in the audience intended by the authors of such works. Most of what we know or may conjecture about this audience is based largely on the evidence the books themselves offer, bolstered here and there by comments from contemporary readers. In 1444, Enea Silvio Piccolomini, the future Pope Pius II, prefaced his *Historia de duobus amantibus* with a letter to the Sienese jurist Mario Sozzini. As they often did with prefatory material, early modern pub-lishers treated this letter as part of the work, so that it still prefaces the

---

[1] The genre indicated by *romance* is typically associated with a closed-ended quest. Other stories are better served by the word 'novel,' which is after all the English equivalent of *roman* in most contexts and which makes no false promises about their often deliberately open-ended form.

mid-sixteenth-century French translation. Piccolomini reproves his friend saying:

> You ask that I do something unsuited to my age and most contrary and repugnant to your own. I who am now over forty, cannot properly write a love treatise, nor is it appropriate that you who are over fifty, should hear one. Such things please young spirits and delight soft hearts. Old people are as suited to speak of love as young ones of prudence, and there is nothing less fitting than that age, without potency, desire it in the flesh.[2]

Piccolomini's objection is, strangely enough, based solely on age and does not take into consideration other factors that might have been relevant, such as socio-legal status—Piccolomini was a clergyman and Sozzini a married man. Nonetheless, the prelate agrees to comply with his friend's request because, after all, Sozzini had loved all his life and still did, and because 'in all the world, nothing is more common than love, known in every city, town, and village. And I believe that there is no man nor woman who at the age of fifteen did not feel some of the fire of the power of love.'[3] Perhaps one conclusion to be drawn from Piccolomini's words is that novels, at least in the Renaissance, were written for the adolescent in all of us. Following on this observation, this article will examine what tales and lessons Renaissance novelistic practice conveys about the love-life of fifteen-year-olds.

---

2 'Vous me demandez chose non convenable à mon aage, & à la vostre fort contraire & repugnante. Car à moy qui ay ores plus de quarante ans n'est seant de faire aucun traicté d'amours, ne à vous qui en avez cinquante & plus n'est convenable d'en ouyr parler. Car telles choses appartiennent aux jeunes courages pour eux delecter & à tendres cueurs pour les requerir. Car les vieulx sont aussi propices, pour parler d'amours, comme les jeunes de prudence, & n'est au monde chose plus difforme que vieillesse qui sans puissance desire puissance charnelle.' Bouchet, *Les Angoisses et remedes d'amours*, sig. K4[r].

3 'Et pource que pour toute vostre vie avez esté amoureux et n'est encore le feu tout estaint, voulez que je compile l'hystoire des deux amans, certes c'est vostre fol et leger couraage qui ne vous souffre estre vieulx, parquoy puis qu'ainsi est, delibere d'obtemperer à vostre plaisir. Toutefoys, pour vostre descharge et la mienne, je veulx qu'on sache qu'en tout l'universel monde n'est chose plus commune qu'amours, comme ainsi soit qu'il n'ayt cité, ville ne village qui en soit excepté. Et croy qu'il n'y a homme ne femme en l'aage de quinze ans qui n'ayt sentu [sic] quelque peu du feu de la puissance d'amours.' Bouchet, *Les Angoisses et remedes d'amours*, sig. K5[v]. As the focus of this article is sixteenth-century France, the version received by Renaissance French readers is cited here.

Generally, novels claim by their very title to be the hero's life-story. Inasmuch as these stories are presented as exemplary, fictional life-stories can usefully be considered in the same category as those claiming to record events that actually did take place. Furthermore, in early modern usage, fictional and real often mingle—Jean Bouchet's *Panégyrique du Chevalier sans reproche*, the life of Louis de la Tremoille, deliberately includes allegorical episodes. Similarly, despite his claim to be writing history, Jean Lemaire's moral, political, and rhetorical aims are more important than facts in shaping the life of Pâris narrated in his *Illustrations de Gaule et Singularitez de Troye*.

Life-stories, whether fictional or real, rarely contain scenes from childhood, in part because of the scarcity of documentation, but also because few people do anything noteworthy as children.[4] When such scenes do appear, their purpose is to prepare the reader for things to come and to promote the ethical aims of the story. Bouchet starts his *Panégyrique* with a moral epistle to Louis's young grandchildren urging them to read, as soon as they are able, this life of their grandfather both for recreation and in order to learn from the actions, behaviour, and attitude of an exemplary young child (*jeune enfant*).[5] Xenophon begins his life of Cyrus by discussing the Persian educational system, source of Cyrus's early training, before turning to the child of twelve who already demonstrated his strong sense of justice, noble liberality, stern resistance to luxury and gluttony, and keen powers of observation. Moving between the courts of the Medes and of the Persians, young Cyrus was able to draw from each culture those moral and physical lessons it was best suited to teach. The wisdom he exhibited in his childhood presaged the greatness of his adult life. For the same reason Plutarch recounts how the young Alexander had tamed the horse Bucephalus.

These classical examples did not go unheeded in early modern France. Bouchet reports that the early beauty and sweetness of the young Louis de la Tremoille foreshadowed his future greatness, as did, once he was a little older, his skill at running, wrestling, and archery, and 'all things appropriate to those who wish to follow [a career in] arms and the courts of great princes.'[6] The hero's character reveals a fortunate mix of

---

[4] Another factor is that some biographies of children are no longer extant. The first two books of Quintus Curtius's life of Alexander the Great, for example, have not come down to us; the surviving account begins with Alexander at about twenty-three years of age.

[5] Bouchet, *Le Panégyrique du chevalier sans peur*, opening sig. 3$^r$.

[6] 'par son excellente beaute, doulceur, et benignité enfantine, donnoit ja ung

nature and training. His actions demonstrate that he is *bien né*, well endowed by nature (the expression refers to his individual nature, not the status of his family). Whether by strength or by cunning, Louis won all mock battles against youths his own age, yet he always gave credit to others, and led his peers to accept him as their leader. Bouchet's description may be based as much on Lemaire's account of the childhood of Pâris of Troy as on actual fact. Young Pâris, a child of exceptional beauty and great skill at hunting, grew up far from court, believing that the shepherd who had raised him was his father. Pâris's superior judgement was apparent to all the peasant children who called on him to adjudicate their disputes, which he did so well that even the gods noticed it, and we all know the rest of the story. Bouchet further tells us, although Plutarch did not, that Alexander was twelve when he tamed Bucephalus, just the age at which the king invited little Louis de la Tremoille to court.[7] Louis's father managed to keep him home, but only for another year or so.[8]

The idea that precocity is a mark of greatness is placed into relief by the real-life case of Montaigne, who spoke fluent Latin when he was six. However, as though reacting to readers' expectations when told of exceptional early achievements in novels and other life stories, Montaigne seems to be making a special effort to contrast his own experience with the expectations created by the topos of the exceptional child. He is at pains to tell his readers that he was an indifferent student. He channels all praise for his early achievement to his father, to whose care and wisdom in arranging his upbringing he attributes his precocious learning. Unlike the account of the early achievements of Louis de la Tremoille or Pâris of Troy, Montaigne makes it clear that his precocity is not meant to be taken as a harbinger of things to come.[9]

---

espoir aux cler voyans quil seroit chevallier dexcellente vertuz . . . Et des ce quil sentit ung commencement de force et astuce puerille qui suyt sans moyen limbecillite denfance, nature luy administra agillite et force correspondente a sa beaute avec ung areste vouloyr de faire toutes choses appartenans a gens qui veulent suyvir les armes et les cours de princes illustres, comme courir, saulter, luycter, gecter la pierre, tyrer de larc.' Bouchet, *Le Panégyrique*, sig. B4[r–v].

7 Rabelais also uses the story of Alexander's taming of Bucephalus as an indication of an intelligent child, comparing young Gargantua to this incident in the life of Alexander. Rabelais does not specify Alexander's age at the time of the horse-taming incident. Rabelais, *Gargantua*, chapter 13.

8 Bouchet, *Panégyrique*, sig. B2[r].

9 Montaigne, *Les Essais*, 1.26.174–75. I was led to consider Montaigne's precocity

The novel, *Perceforest*, originally written in the fourteenth century, announces in the *privilege* of its first printed edition (1528) that it will present

> chronicles and histories of England, deeds and acts of the noble King Perceforest, formerly done and compiled for the instruction and practice of arms, stories decorated and adorned with many fine expressions and authorities for the edification of those who wish to see and read them.[10]

Although anyone might expect edification as a by-product of recreational reading, the implied readers of *Perceforest* are those who need to know about arms, that is, men. In this case it may be assumed they are primarily young men, since the field experience of seasoned soldiers would have obviated their need to learn by reading. At the end of the sixteenth century, Blaise de Monluc suggests that the intended readers of his *Commentaires,* the memoirs of a long life as a soldier, are young noblemen, warriors just starting their military careers.[11]

In the preface to his translation of Plutarch's *Parallel Lives,* Jacques Amyot retells an anecdote taken from Cicero about Lucius Lucullus, the Roman statesman newly appointed to direct the army. Having no experience of war, Lucullus spent the time it took to travel to the battlefield diligently reading histories. As a result of this, when he arrived at the camp he was ready to assume his command as though it were not new to him.[12] Since reading about something was seen as a close analogue to experiencing it, François de La Noue, like Monluc a great soldier in

---

in this context by Professor Cynthia Skenazi, whom I thank warmly.

[10] The novel explains on the title page that it will recount '*Croniques et histoires Dangleterre, faitz et gestes du noble roy Perceforest,* jadis faitz et compilez pour linstruction et exercice des armes: lesdictes histoires aornees et decorees de plusieurs belles sentences et auctoritez a ledification de ceulx qui les vouldront veoir et lyre.' The final doublet, 'veoir et lyre' (see and read) is an unusual variant of the more common 'veoir et ouyr' (see or hear) commonly found in prefaces to printed French recreational texts until the end of the first third of the sixteenth century.

[11] Monluc, *Commentaires*, p. 833.

[12] Plutarch, *Les vies,* sig. *6ʳ⁻ᵛ. Although Cicero's apparent willingness to treat recalled reading as the equal of recalled experience does not seem convincing to a modern reader, today's science offers support for his position: researchers now tell us that 88% of the same neurons are involved in seeing something and in recalling having seen it; Kreiman, 'Imagery Neurons.'

his day, expressed concern that young men might mistakenly treat the scenes of combat in which Amadis single handedly defeats six knights in the same way Lucius Lucullus treated his histories—as manuals for warfare.[13] La Noue's concern was not unimaginable in a world where history and fable shared ethical goals to which they accorded a primacy that blurs the distinction between fact and fiction. Both these seasoned soldiers, Monluc and La Noue, assumed that impressionable young men were among the readers of *romans d'aventures* such as *Amadis de Gaule.*

Readers of Renaissance life-stories are further defined, albeit implicitly, by those to whom the stories were dedicated. Bouchet makes it clear his primary intended audience were the children of the La Tremoille family. Book one of Lemaire's *Illustrations,* containing the account of the childhood of Pâris of Troy, is specifically aimed at the young Charles V of Austria. Novels were often dedicated to members of the royal family, prominent nobles, churchmen, or jurists; they were rarely dedicated to women. Another group of implicit readers were poets and friends of the author who composed liminary verses to appear in the preliminary pages of such novels. Neither the dedicatees nor the poets were particularly young, attesting that novels did regularly have adult readers. The many references to novels, most especially to *Amadis de Gaule,* to be found in sixteenth-century poetry and essays also suggest that adults were familiar with them, or at least with the major best-sellers of the day. In sum, the available evidence suggests that the intended readership of novels consisted of a fairly broad range of the well-off literate public, although the inscribed reader is usually a young nobleman.[14]

Teen-aged youths do play an oddly prominent role in many of the novels themselves. The nobler and more exceptional the hero, the earlier it seems his special talents become apparent. Since the heroes of *romans d'aventures* tend to be separated from their families of origin in infancy, depriving them of the social position due them by virtue of their birth, they need to earn such a position for themselves, and they strive to do it as soon as possible. Amadis de Gaule provides an example of this. At six, Amadis champions his foster brother against

---

[13] 'Discours six: Que la Lecture des livres d'Amadis n'est moins pernicieuse aux jeunes gens que celle des livres de Machiavel aux vieux.' La Noue, *Discours politiques et militaires,* pp. 160–76.

[14] On the readership of *Amadis,* see my *Reading in the Renaissance,* and especially chapter four, 'The Reader.'

an older bully, acting like a miniature knight defending the distressed child. King Lisuart, an unseen and unintentional observer of this action, asks Amadis's foster father to send him to court as a page, a common step in the education of a young nobleman. At six, Amadis is still several years younger than the normal age for removing children from their parents—Louis de la Tremoille, for example, went to court when he was about thirteen. The reader is thus meant to understand this precocity as another indication of Amadis's excellence, much like his oft-mentioned beauty and his skill at archery or hunting. A few years later, at the age of twelve, we are told, one would have taken him for fifteen. He then falls in love with the ten-year-old princess Oriane. Suddenly learning he is a foundling, he is obliged to *make* a name for himself—having inherited none, he needs to earn his reputation as a knight in order to remain in his lady's good graces. Sometime after this, the king refuses Amadis's request to be made a knight on the grounds that he is too young for so strenuous an undertaking. However, Amadis is soon dubbed a knight by his biological father, King Perion of Gaul, although neither father nor son yet knows they are related. A few pages later, Amadis saves his father from attack by two knights, and then goes on to defeat in single combat the gigantic king of Ireland who had attempted to usurp Gaul from Perion.[15]

As in medieval fiction, so too in Renaissance novels time is relative. We are told something happens two weeks after something else, or that it will happen in a year, but it is virtually never possible to chart the passage of time as one would do in a chronicle or other historical record. Even seasonal changes are noted only exceptionally. Specific time references are sporadic, unsystematic, and fairly rare because time in these novels is primarily about sequence. In this context, literal contradictions in recording the passage of time are trivial accidents, whereas the mention of a specific age is an extraordinary indication and should be treated as meaningful. Therefore, it is noteworthy that the reader is told that when Amadis was twelve he could be taken for fifteen and of no consequence that we do not know at what age Amadis became a knight or saved his father's kingdom. In the case of Amadis's younger brother, Galaor, we read that he was kidnapped at the age of two and raised in apparent isolation by a hermit; at the age of eighteen an irresistible desire to become a knight consumes him and he soon realizes this dream. There is nothing exceptional about the age when Galaor begins his military

---

15 *Amadis de Gaule*, chapters 4, 5, and 10.

career; it coincides quite well with sixteenth-century practice—Blaise de Monluc, for example, recalls that he himself joined the army in 1520, at the age of seventeen.[16] Monluc, however, did not become a captain for another decade, whereas Galaor is ready from the start to deal with all the military demands of knighthood. Amyot and La Noue remind us of the commonplace recorded by Plutarch and treasured by humanists, that to do something well requires the joint agency of nature, nurture, and practice. Aside from having read a book of chivalry, Galaor was prepared for his new life only by his nature, his blood; he had neither practice, experience, nor observations to prepare him to become, as he does, an instantly excellent teen-knight.

These few cases are the only instances in which the first book of *Amadis* gives specific ages. They do not help the reader gauge the passage of time. There is no indication of Amadis's exact age when he was knighted, nor of how much older he is than Galaor. Amadis seems to dub his eighteen-year-old brother shortly after he himself restores Perion's kingdom, and this is only a few episodes after his own knighting, which took place when he was perhaps fifteen or sixteen years old. Arithmetic is not useful here. The purpose of the age markers is not to pin-point the passage of time, but to convey a moral message, to guide our reading of the young men's actions. The focus on Amadis's youth is essential information, something readers need to know in order to appreciate the exceptional nature of the protagonist.

What we see in *Amadis* is stock in trade for the genre: young princes separated in infancy from their family; raised under a variety of extraordinary circumstances; making their way in the world and putting their mark on it; eventually being reunited by serendipity with their family and thereby regaining the noble status that is theirs by birth, a status which, by that time, they have also earned independently by their valour. The insistence on the precocity of the hero reappears in other novels of the period. A short sampling of the topos reveals its consistent message.

In *Palmerin d'Angleterre*, infant princes are stolen and raised by the wife of a wild man, le Sauvage, who wants to use them as lion fodder. The lions, instead, come to serve as the children's hunting dogs. Again, the children are so fine (*si fort beaux*) that one would have taken them for being much older than they were.[17] The adjective *beaux* may, in this case, have the sense of big, as it often does in French, or good-

---

16 *Amadis de Gaule*, chapter 6. Monluc, *Commentaires*, p. 30.

17 *Palmerin d'Angleterre*, sig. c2ʳ.

looking, or most likely both. At the age of ten, one of the princes is discovered in the forest by a knight from his father's court who nearly mistakes the child for the father, so close is the resemblance. Taken to court, the young prince seems perfectly prepared for life there, despite his wild upbringing—as with Galaor, nature has supplied what the child's wild nurture had omitted. When he is old enough, the prince becomes a knight and pursues knightly adventures which further prove his valour.

Although little Theseus of Coulogne is raised by his parents, when he is about ten the king, his father, becomes convinced that such an ugly child cannot be his and orders him killed. Young Theseus is offended by the suggestion that he is a bastard and attacks the sergeant sent to kill him, knocking out two teeth and rendering the man unconscious.[18] In addition to strength of body, the child demonstrates fearlessness, asking only to be killed by the sword, as befits a noble-man. Awaiting death, he prays and miraculously becomes beautiful.[19] The child's inner goodness is now properly marked externally. As in *Amadis,* a curious slippage of time then follows; the text moves seamlessly from the judicial combat which concluded the question of ten-year-old Theseus's legitimacy to a time that must be four or five years later, and yet is treated as the next moment. When Theseus is fifteen, his father dubs him a knight and he departs in search of adventure. At this point in the narrative the text does not comment on his youth; perhaps the reader is supposed to recognize the topos of the exceptional individual who undertakes the life of an adult at so young an age. Theseus travels to Rome and falls in love with Flore, the emperor's daughter. Although Theseus's eloquence and courage are admired at court, the emperor does not grant him his daughter in marriage. In his pursuit of Flore, Theseus demonstrates intelligence, cunning, courage, and determination. He has a golden eagle made as a gift for her and then has himself transported to her room inside it.

---

[18] If nobility of blood and soul is marked by precocity, so too is bastardy. "Il se va bien monstrant quil est bastard: car ung bastard doist estre fier et hardy." *Theseus de Coulogne,* sig. a4$^v$. On the strength of bastards, see Rothstein, *Reading in the Renaissance,* pp. 137–38.

[19] 'Nostre seigneur y demonstra un beau miracle car tout en lheure il donna telle grace a lenfant que son corps se va changer incontinent tout entierement de ses membres en sorte que lenfant devint si bien forme de corps et de visaige que oncques nature nen forma ung plus bel ne plus advenant.' *Theseus de Coulogne,* sig. a6$^r$.

After they are secretly married and Theseus has engendered a son, Flore has the eagle sent back to the goldsmith with the excuse that the beak needs repairing, allowing Theseus to leave the heavily guarded palace same way he entered it, inside the bird. Theseus and Flore have further adventures that separate them before he learns of the birth of his son, Gadifer. When that son is seventeen, 'he was already very big and well built so that he seemed a kind of giant, considering his age, so well formed was he in body and limbs. . . . there was no knight in all Greece who was nearly as big and everyone said that never had nature made someone more beautiful nor more forthcoming in all things.'[20] At this point in his life, Gadifer, like Amadis, learns he is in fact a foundling. Following the laws of coincidence which rule in novels, he soon takes his father, Theseus, prisoner and uncovers his own true identity.

The early life of Artus de Bretagne is similar to that of Theseus. He, too, is raised at his parents' court. When he is ten, he is given a tutor. At fifteen, just the age Piccolomini warned us about, he learns fencing. Artus is remarkable for his beauty, grace, and courtesy.[21] Despite his age, the text continues to refer to him as 'the child' (l'enfant). Indeed, that is the term used even when Artus comes upon a beautiful but impoverished fourteen-year-old noble maiden, Jeannette, living with her mother in the forest. Artus spends more and more time away from court and in secret with Jeannette. For some pages the text alternates between referring to Artus as a child and as a man. His parents notice his absences and decide that he ought to be married before he gets into trouble, 'for it is appropriate that someone who is seventeen, should be married.'[22] There is a marriage ceremony, but a true marriage does not ensue, for on the wedding night Jeannette replaces Artus's intended bride. Artus thus consummates the marriage with a woman to whom he had made no vows, and has no carnal knowledge of the woman to whom he did vow himself, who dies of shame soon after when it is revealed she is not a virgin. Only

---

[20] 'Or estoit celluy damoiseau ja devenu moult grant et bel et bien fourny en sort quil sembloit proprement dung geant veu son aage tant estoit bien forme de corps et de membres . . ." *Theseus de Coulogne*, sig. o4ʳ. In this passage *bel* is rendered especially ambiguous by appearing joined to two expressions of size.

[21] 'Si creut l'enfant de jour en jour et divint beau, tant qu'en tout le monde n'avoit plus beau, plus doux, plus gracieux, plus courtois qu'il estoit.' *Artus de Bretagne*, p. 2. In this case, as well, the word *beau* might mean he was big for his age as well as handsome.

[22] *Artus de Bretagne*, p. 7.

many adventures and presumably some years later, does Artus finally marry a woman of his own rank.

*Alector*, Barthélémy Aneau's strange *histoire fabuleuse* (that is, untrue tale) is frequently parodic of *romans d'aventures* and of Rabelais's novels, which slightly earlier parodied the same sources. By the age of five, the hero, Alector, was approaching the status of a teenage youth, being 'as large powerful and dexterous in body, and as prudent and discreet in spirit as a fifteen year old. He learned to tame horses, fence, and hunt so well that at the age of six he could not be equaled by any twenty-year old.'[23] This is also the age at which he became interested in women, whereupon his mother, fearing for her own virtue, decided to send him in search of his wandering father. Aneau is playing with a familiar pattern.

Like Alector, Rabelais's giants seem advanced at birth. In *Pantagruel* the young giant's age is never discussed; the text passes rapidly from his birth to his student years. We are, however, given markers for young Gargantua. Chapter ten covers the period between three and five when he starts, like young Alector after him, to be interested in sex with his governesses as though he were a teenager. The standard insistence on a young prince's skill at archery or hunting is limited here to his collection of hobbyhorses. In a proto-humanist display of intellectual curiosity at the end of his fifth year, he invents the *torchecul*.[24]

The topos gives us a model in which an exceptional child is already exceptional by the age of five or six, as we saw with Amadis, Alector, and Gargantua. Theseus and Palmerin had come close to their adult strength or form by age ten. To the examples already cited we might add from *Gérard d'Eurphrate* the case of the equally precocious eponymous hero who at age ten could be taken for sixteen or eighteen. In the same novel, Milon d'Auverngne is fifteen when he learns his true identity and is brought to his father's court. In Jean Maugin's version of *Tristan*, Tristan feels the first stirring of love at fourteen, 'the time when the sap of love rises to men's hearts,' although the virtuous young Tristan resists the advances of a king's daughter.[25]

Very early in their lives these heroes are remarkable for their precocious maturity. By the time they reach their chronological teen-years,

23 Aneau, *Alector*, p. 111.

24 Rabelais, *Gangantua*, chapters 10–12.

25 'le temps auquel le seve d'amour comence à monter au couer des hommes.' Maugin, *Le Nouveau Tristan*, sig. M3ᵛ.

by age fifteen, they are on their own, often sexually active, competing physically and morally with grown men. Their beauty is the outward sign of their goodness, as their strength and skill mark their moral courage, and their natural tastes for martial arts denote their nobility. The age markers are clearly used deliberately and formulaically. Before turning to the purpose of these apparently systematic exaggerations of young noblemen's natural capacities, a quick look at the expectations and the vocabulary applied to that period of human life which constitutes the transition from childhood to mature manhood (or *pueritia* to *juventus*) will shed further light on the significance of the phenomenon examined here.

Since cultural assumptions are undeniably a force forming and changing language, the linguistic signs available at a given time to express a concept are a tool for understanding how that concept was conceived. In the present case, the notion under examination is what we today call teenagers. Sixteenth century French, like Latin, has definite lexical limitations for categorizing young people. Conscious that the very idea may be an anachronism, I have used the words teenager and teen-aged youths to refer to these young knights. In the Renaissance the term *adolescent* had a broad and variable range of meaning depending on the context and the user; generally it referred to a person between his mid-teens and his mid-thirties. Rabelais applies it to Gargantua between the ages of three and five and purposely entitles chapter ten 'De l'adolescence de Gargantua,' presumably for comic exaggeration of his precocity. It is attested in French since the fourteenth century. In the seventeenth century Cotgrave translates *adolescence* into English as 'youth'. In 1501, however, when he would already have been twenty-five, Jean Bouchet still refers to himself as an *adolescent*. Clément Marot uses the word in the title to his collection of poems, *L'adolescence clémentine*, first published in 1532, when he was thirty-six. There is no word in the sixteenth-century vocabulary to designate what we call the teen years or that developmental period seen as suspended between childhood and adulthood for which we use adolescence. At the same time, the early-modern use of *enfant/child* is much less closely defined with chronology than it came to be later. The expression *enfant de famille* conveys the idea of noble lineage, not age. Artus de Bretagne is called an *enfant* in his late teens, as is Jehan de Saintré after the age of twenty. *Enfant* and *homme* are both used to refer to the same character, sometimes within a single sentence. In this period *garçon* still designates a servant rather than an age. *Demoisel* and *jouvenceau* both imply youth, but are rarely used in this corpus except as an honorific.

Some light is shed on this confusion in terminology by Philip Aries' suggestion that what determined adulthood in the early modern world was marital status, not specific age.[26] Adulthood began when a man became the head of his own household. The current state of research suggests that although European noblemen married earlier than their non-noble counterparts, they were generally at least in their early twenties; women, on the other hand, were much younger.[27] Montaigne writes that he married at thirty-three, and evokes the advice of both Plato and Aristotle in favour of late marriage for men.[28]

Because there are so few clear chronological markers supplied for the heros of the life-stories considered here, it is hard to tell at what age these young men were married. Theseus was probably under twenty, Artus probably still in his twenties; for most of the rest, the evidence is insufficient. Clearly, their actual age at marriage was not considered important. However, while age at marriage may have been irrelevant in

---

[26] Ariès, *L'Enfant et la vie familiale*, pp. 8–14.

[27] François Lebrun distinguishes between high nobles, where the median age of marriage was 21 for men and 18 for women, and the members of the Parlement of Besançon, who were slightly over 30 when they married women who were on the average just under 22. Clearly there were departures from this norm, like the jurist André Tiraqueau who married a girl of twelve when he was only 24, or the scholar Guillaume Budé, who was 38 when he married a fifteen year old. See Lebrun, *La vie conjugale*, pp. 31–37. Robert Mandrou gives the median age of marriage in seventeenth and eighteenth-century France as 27–28 for me, 25–26 for women; see Mandrou, *Introduction à la France moderne*, p. 119. See also Maryanne Kowaleski, 'Singlewomen in Medieval and Early Modern Europe.' Marguerite de Navarre's *Heptameron* has several references to noble women married at a very young age. In *nouvelle* twelve, Margaret, the illegitimate daughter of Emperor Charles V, is too young to have sex; *nouvelle* fifteen *une dame fort riche* is referred to as a child (although this might merely mean not-yet-married); none of the men can be understood to have married in his teens.

[28] 'Je me mariay à trente-trois ans, et louë l'opinion de trente cinq, qu'on dit estre d'Aristote. Platon ne veut pas qu'on se marie avant les trente; mais il a raison de se moquer de ceux qui font les oeuvres de mariage après cinquante cinq.' Montaigne, *Les Essais*, 2.8.390. Lebrun (*La vie conjugale*, p. 32) reads late age of marriage for women as a social contraceptive; for both sexes the result was also that by the time children were born, the couple had often already inherited the estates of their own parents. The age of marriage was earlier in the Middle Ages and gradually became later as the population grew.

itself, the public celebration of marriage was significant. In the novels we have examined, clandestine marriages do not have any perceivable effect on the behaviour of the young men who contract them, while public marriages lead them to change their life and give up knight-errancy altogether. The unmarried Perion is originally shown in *Amadis* fearlessly killing a lion single-handedly; in battles engaged after his public marriage, he is shown instead requiring the help of his son Amadis—as if his formal, public marriage had sapped his knightly skills. In a similar vein, Amadis himself will stay home after his public marriage, leaving the limelight to his son. The reason for such 'retirement' from knightly action may be suggested by Montaigne's advice that the age difference between father and son ought to be great enough to preclude any competition between them.[29] In fact, all our fictional examples do avoid any appearance of competition. Clandestine marriages allow the hero to prove his heroic precocity by being able continue to perform valorous deeds in spite of his being married.

Under these circumstances, what are we to make of this cohort of teenaged youths for whom puberty and manhood seem to coincide, successfully joining the ranks of adult knights in the pursuit of chivalry? In its very flaunting of reality, the topos marks the heroes as exceptional individuals beyond the limits of ordinary mortals. Given that they are all young princes for whom marriage would be obligatory sooner rather than later, the topos of the teenaged hero extends the length of time when the young male can take unreasonable risks, emerging from them triumphant, his reputation for valour bravely earned and securely affirmed.

All available evidence suggests that the intended audience of life-stories of exceptional teenagers consisted above all of young noble-men, the class that defined its natural role as military, regardless of the actual career choices noble youths made. For the most part, these life-stories focus more often on single combat, war, and politics than on the hero's love interests. That is not to say that women and other readers with no desire to don armour and wield a sword were not also interested in reading them. What it does mean is that other readers

---

[29] 'Il semble que . . . il nous fache qu'ils [nos enfants] nous marchent sur les talons . . . l'ordre des choses porte qu'ils ne peuvent, à dire verité, estre ny vivre qu'aux despens de nostre estre et de nostre vie.' 'Il ne nous faudroit pas marier si jeunes que nostre aage vienne quasi à se confondre avec le leur.' Montaigne, *Les Essaies*, 2.8.387 and 389.

often read vicariously, as though they were young men, much as the young Chinua Achebe identified with Marlowe when enthusiastically reading *Heart of Darkness.*

For ordinary young men, the temptation to emulate these models too closely was limited by nature as well as by nurture and common sense. Few fifteen-year-olds seem to have been tempted to contract a clandestine marriage or rush off to seek knightly adventures. Few fifteen-year olds had the strength to manoeuvre a lance or a pike while fully clad in armour. Any who tried would soon return, chastened, knowing what they were meant to have understood from these stories in the first place: just how exceptional the literary teenaged knights were. Monluc and La Noue, both of whom worried about the dangers of young people imitating the models furnished by *Amadis*, overlooked the fact that one of the functions of an exemplum was to provide readers with an ideal that went beyond the capacities of the ordinary mortal. In the last analysis, we learn that, however glorious those adolescent years might be, even the most adventuresome and heroic knight eventually settles down to ruling his kingdom. Just as the early physical beauty and strength of these heroes were early signs of their moral virtue, so their teenaged knightly valour is a sign of the moral authority and equity with which they will conduct the rest of their lives. In sum, teen knights are the stuff of dreams, set forth as a useful model to all.

*Carthage College*
*Kenosha, Wisconsin*

## Cited Works

Amadis de Gaule. *Le premier livre d'Amadis de Gaule*, ed. Hugues Vaganay. Paris: Librairie Nizet, 1986.

Aneau, Barthélémy. *Alector*, ed. Marie-Madeleine Fontaine. Geneva: Droz, 1996.

Ariès, Philippe. *L'Enfant et la vie familiale sous l'ancien régime*. Paris: Editions du Seuil, 1973.

*Artus de Bretagne*, ed. Nicole Cazauran and Christien Ferlampin-Acher. Paris: Presses de l'École Normale Supérieure, 1996 [facsimile of Paris: Nicolas Bonfons, 1584].

Bouchet, Jean. *Les Angoisses et remedes d'amours du traverseur à son adolescence. Auquel est adjouste une plaisante histoire de Eurial & Lucrece redigée en langue Latine par Aeneas Silvius Poete excellent et depuis traduitte en vulgaire Françoys*. Paris: à lenseigne de l'Elephant, s.d..

Bouchet, Jean. *Le Panégyrique du chevalier sans reproche*. Paris: Jean de Marnef, 1527.

*Gerard d'Eurphrate*. Paris: Groulleau, 1547.

Kowaleski, Maryanne. 'Singlewomen in Medieval and Early Modern Europe: The Demographic Pespective' pp. 38–81 in *Singlewomen in the European Past, 1250–1800*, ed. Judith M. Bennett and Amy M. Froide. Philadelphia: University of Pennsylvania Press, 1999.

Kreiman, Gabriel, Christof Köch and Itzhak Fried. 'Imagery Neurons in the Human Brain' *Nature*, 408 (16 Nov. 2000): 357–61.

La Noue, François de. *Discours politiques et militaires*, ed. F.E. Sutcliffe. Geneva: Droz, 1967.

Lebrun, François. *La Vie conjugale sous l'ancien régime*. Paris: Armand Colin, 1975.

Mandrou, Robert. *Introduction à la France moderne 1500–1640*. Paris: Albin Michel, 1961.

Maugin, Jean. *Histoire du noble Tristan prince de Leonnois, chevalier de la Table ronde et d'Yseulte*. Paris: Nicolas Bonfons, 1586.

Monluc, Blaise de. *Commentaires, 1521–1576*, ed. Paul Courteault. Paris: Editions Gallimard, 1964.

Montaigne, Michel de. *Les Essais*, ed. Pierre Villey. Paris: Presses Universitaires de France, 1988.

Palmerin d'Angleterre. *Le premier [-second] livre du preux, vaillant et tres victorieux chevalier Palmerin d'Angleterre, filz du Roy Dom Edouard*. A Lyon: Par Thibauld Payen, 1553.

Perceforest. *La treselegante, delicieuse, melliflue et tresplaisante histoire du tresnoble, victorieux et excellentissime roy Perceforest, Roy de la grande Bretaigne, fundateur du Franc palais et du temple du vouverain dieu, . . .* Paris: Pour Galiot du Pré, 1528. 6 vols.

Plutarch. *Les vies des hommes illustres*, trans. Jacques Amyot. Geneva: Jacob de Stoer, 1621.

Rabelais. *Gargantua*, ed. M.A. Screech. Geneva: Droz, 1970.

Rothstein, Marian. *Reading in the Renaissance. Amadis de Gaule and the Lessons of Memory*. Newark, DE: University of Delaware Press/London: Associated University Presses, 1999.

Theseus. *Hystoire trescreative traictant des faictz et gestes du noble et gaillant chevalier Theseus de Coulongne*. Paris: Jehan Longis & Vincent Sertenas, 1534.

# Young Knights Under the Feminine Gaze

## Ruth Mazo Karras

For the young aristocrat in the later Middle Ages, establishing one's position in life most often meant proving oneself as a knight. Successful knighthood meant prowess in arms (whether in battle or, perhaps more often, in tournaments) and the successful use of violence.[1] Expertise in the use of violence, however, was not the only important feature of knighthood. The achievement of manhood depended on mastering the sometimes conflicting, sometimes complementary ideals of prowess and love. Medieval texts often depict young knights or prospective knights doing great deeds for the sake of love. Love inspires the man, and the beloved lady is the judge of the man's deeds. Much of late medieval chivalric culture, so important in the mentalities of the aristocracy, was built around a myth of women's power over men through love. This system ignored or denied what real political and economic power women had and gave them an empty authority. While men were ostensibly performing for the sake of women, women were not really represented as independent agents. They functioned to mediate relations between men.

It was in the life stage of young manhood (*adolescentia* or *juventus*, depending on the classificatory scheme), before they married, that knights or prospective knights competed for the love of women. Young aristocrats were typically knighted around the age of twenty-one (although this was not a hard and fast rule), and married somewhat later. The factor that determined when they married was often the acquisition of land, so a married knight was a landowner and house-holder, although he might still attend tournaments or accompany his lord on a campaign. It was the younger knights, the *juvenes* or knights bachelor, and the young men who had not yet been knighted who were able to devote themselves full time to the practice of arms and the social world that went with it.

Learning military skills was not the only purpose of the training of a young potential knight. A future knight (for one did not actually have to be knighted to joust) was to learn aristocratic behaviour through

---

[1] See Kaeuper, *Chivalry and Violence in Medieval Europe.*

attendance at and participation in jousts, in particular how to behave towards other knights before and after a battle, how to fight them during it, and how to behave with women. A fifteenth-century version of Ramón Llull's didactic work on chivalry explained what a young man needed to learn:

> It behooves that the son of a knight, during the time that he is a squire, can take care of a horse. And it behooves him to serve, and that he be subordinated before he is a lord. Otherwise, he should not know the nobility of lordship when he is a knight. Therefore, it behooves every man who wishes to achieve knighthood learn in his youth to carve at the table, to serve, to arm and dub a knight, for in the same way as a man who wishes to learn to sew to be a tailor or a carpenter needs to have a master who can sew or hew, in the same way a noble man that loves the order of chivalry and wants to be a knight needs first to have a master who is a knight.[2]

The young knight must emulate his mentor both in military aspects and in other aspects of demeanour (for example, carving at table and manners at feasts). Llull did not mention the love of women, but emulation of the successful older knight applied in this case as well. One who had achieved knighthood could serve as a model for younger or aspiring knights.

Although in the fourteenth and fifteenth centuries young men could be educated in knightly skills and behaviour within their fathers' households, more often this occurred in the household of another man: an uncle or other relative, or a patron of the father. All great households included a number of such youths. Here they heard the romances they were to emulate, practised the military skills they would need, and learned courtly pastimes. The hero of *Petit Jehan de Saintré* became a page to the King of France and learned by observing what older men did: 'for a thirteen-year-old, he was a very skilful and hardy youth, whether for riding a very rough horse, for singing or dancing, for playing tennis, for running, for leaping, and for all the other contests and amusements which he saw the men do.'[3] Royal or other especially large households had teachers in various subjects for the youths.[4] Manuals of behaviour and morality included advice on table manners for youths in

---

2 Llull, *The Book of the Ordre of Chyvalry*, p. 21.

3 La Sale, *Le petit Jehan de Saintré*, pp. 11–12. Unless otherwise indicated, this and all other translations are mine.

4 Orme, 'The Education of the Courtier,' pp. 74, 82.

such households. From their earliest age, the youths were also expected to learn music and chess, and to play with weapons and hunt. In noble households they were given special training sessions with arms, and special tournaments were organized for them. By their mid-teens they were expected to play an actual role in fighting.[5]

Although a youth at a royal or noble court would have been highly aware of his family background, he did not live the formative years of adolescence among his kin in a familial setting, but in a military atmosphere, highly charged with knightly values. His daily companionship was with other men, with whom a young knight competed for the favour of a higher-status man. Women were by no means absent from this life, but they were present in an eroticized, rather than a familial setting. The young knight-to-be thus learned that women were objects to be won, while men were comrades in the winning of honour. Young knights had a greater or lesser opportunity to be exposed to and to internalize these ideas depending on where they stood on the social ladder. Not all families would have been able to place their sons in a noble household, for this required special connections. Still, even relatively obscure or impoverished members of the county gentry or petty nobility sought such service when they could, for knightly military activity remained an important path to social advancement.

The lives of late medieval knights, as written by biographers and chroniclers, show a strong resemblance to the lives of knights in literature. In part, this was because their biographers were steeped in courtly literature and in part because, in behaviour at court, life and art imitated each other. These biographies can show us what was expected of a young man if he was to develop into the ideal knight.

The Burgundian knight Jacques de Lalaing died young, so his entire biography may be taken as an account of the training and development of a young knight. Jacques came from a family of Burgundian petty nobility affiliated with the duke of Cleves, who took Jacques with him to the court of Burgundy 'at the end of his childhood.'[6] According to his biographer, Georges Chastellain, the youth showed great precocity in chivalric combat, as well as in hunting and chess. This attracted many women to him. In one joust he wore the tokens of two duchesses. However, although Jacques always spoke with ladies in a courtly and genteel manner, and became involved in some mild intrigues with

---

[5] Orme, *Childhood to Chivalry*, 133–41, 181–210.
[6] Chastellain, *Le Livre des faits*, 8:11.

great married ladies, he did not marry. Instead, he decided that his goal was to defeat thirty worthy opponents before he was thirty years old.[7] He travelled around Europe, challenging knights in France, Spain, Scotland and England to jousts; he then returned to Burgundy to hold a *pas d'armes*, the Fountain of Tears.[8] It took place at a pavilion with an image of the Virgin Mary on it, inhabited by a damsel in a robe covered with tears and a unicorn bearing three shields, also covered with tears. Challengers touched one of the three shields to indicate their choice of weapon. Jacques maintained this *pas* for a year against twenty-two challengers; Olivier de la Marche notes that because of this, 'you may believe that the ladies of the land made gracious mottoes in his praise and called him a good knight.'[9] This was only one of many such *pas d'armes* in the Burgundian realm in the middle of the fifteenth century. The fairy-tale aspect gave a game-like quality to the actual fighting and turned it from sheer force and violence into part of a courtly story.

For Jacques de Lalaing, however, fighting was not just a game. He also fought on behalf of the Duke of Burgundy in Luxembourg and against the rebellious citizens of Ghent. Confirming the views of historians who argue that mounted shock troops were obsolete by this time, Jacques died in a rather un-knightly way: at the age of thirty-two he was struck down by a cannonball outside the walls of the town of Pouques.[10]

The story of Jacques de Lalaing, renowned as the greatest knight of Europe, tells us something about what late medieval people admired in a knight. Primarily, they looked for military prowess. In young men, such prowess was demonstrated in single combat much more than in actual campaigns in the field. The latter may have been more practical, but the former was a more important part of the mental world of the knight. Jacques' biography also stresses his courtly manner, his treatment of those around him, including women, and his elaborate dress and accouterments that were part of an aristocratic ethos of masculine display.

The description of the mercenary Galeas of Mantua, written by Thomas of Saluzzo in 1394–95, contains similar chivalric elements. Among other adventures, Galeas jousted for the sake of his lady with

---

[7] La Marche, *Mémoires*, 2:143.

[8] Chastellain, *Livre des faits*, 8:188.

[9] Chastellain, *Livre des faits*, 8:189–97, 201–37; La Marche, *Mémoires*, 2:203.

[10] Chastellain, *Livre des faits*, 8:252–53.

a German knight who had taken a vow to fight any man who would take up his challenge. Galeas fought on the French side in the Hundred Years' War and was knighted for it; he also fought in the service of the kings of Cyprus and Hungary. Describing him at age thirty, Thomas said that 'if he lives long enough, he will be one to compare for his chivalry with the good Sir Tristam of Lyonesse or Sir Palamedes.'[11] Whether or not love really motivated Galeas to undertake his adventures, Thomas nonetheless presents him in this romantic mould. Galeas' life combined prowess and courtesy, and his biographer was very aware of the literary context in which contemporary knights operated.

Don Pero Niño, a Castilian knight of the late fourteenth to early fifteenth century, had an early life similar to Jacques de Lalaing's. His biographer recounts that the youth was taken early into a great household and describes his exploits there as more military than sporting, since Don Pero was involved more in battles, especially at sea, than in tournaments. At the same time, however, the young man was also successful at jousting and at other sports.[12] Don Pero did his greatest deeds after coming to the age of 'his manhood' (*virilidad*) that is, after his twenty-fifth year.[13] He married the widowed Doña Costanza, sister-in-law of his patron Ruy Lopez. The biographer claims that the two fell in love because they were often together. Doña Costanza 'had heard many gallant things told of this knight, young, fair, generous, bold, courageous, gentle' and therefore chose him. The biographer does not mention the obvious political advantages of this union for Don Pero.[14]

In all three biographies, then, the authors if not the subjects stress love as an important shaping force in the young man's quest for prowess. Love was important in the young knight's emergence into manhood because it was a sign of his chivalric virtues. A knight who appealed to women through his behaviour simultaneously demonstrated to other men that he knew how to behave with women.

The display that knights put on, with their elaborate clothing, armour, and coats of arms, was believed to appeal to women, who would marvel at the knights as they went by. Illuminations in René d'Anjou's *Livre des Tournois* depicting ladies watching a tournament

---

[11] Keen, *Chivalry*, pp. 18–19, from an unpublished MS, BN MS Fr 12559.

[12] Díaz de Games, *El Victorial*, p. 354.

[13] Díaz de Games, *El Victorial*, p. 375.

[14] Díaz de Games, *El Victorial*, pp. 369–78, 585, 593, 676–79.

(and showing very few male spectators) graphically illustrate the importance of the female gaze to the way medieval people understood the tournament. Jacques de Lalaing's biographer describes the women leaning out of the windows to watch him go by on the way to the joust.[15] Díaz de Games depicts ladies discussing a joust with a great deal of technical knowledge about why one knight defeated the other.

> Doña Margarita said, 'If the knight falls it's no great wonder, when his horse falls; it's not the knight's fault, it's the horse's.' Doña Beatriz answered, 'You saw, I believe, that this knight fell because he buckled under the weight of the blows, and pulled on the reins so hard that both horse and rider rolled onto the ground.'[16]

The idea that women watched the knights parade by, or attended tournaments to see who was the worthiest knight, supports the idea that knights performed valiant deeds to prove themselves worthy of a lady's love. In a Middle Dutch lyric, a high-born lady is wooed by a fashionable and well-spoken young man, but she prefers a crippled old man who has 'proven his manhood by dint of arms . . . By his arms you can tell the man, not by his dancing.'[17] Women, therefore, were judges not only of appearance, but also of knightly prowess.

Although the texts describe the women as the spectators, the knights were using this display of noble array, or of success in battle, at least as much to appeal to the male as to the female gaze. To the men present at the joust, the display might express not sexual desirability but wealth, nobility, and prowess. The fact that a knight appealed to women could in itself increase his worth in the eyes of other men. As Louise Fradenburg suggests, the tournament promoted homosocial bonding in that it 'brings men together but allows them to constitute themselves as "men," who fight for and who are watched by women. The "lady" thus enters the tournament—as spectator, as prize—in part to signify the masculinity of the knight. . . . The lady dramatizes the masculinity of the warrior by being what he is not and by watching his effort from another place.'[18] Aristocratic men thus reaffirmed their

---

[15] Pognon, *Livre des Tournois*, unpaginated [fols. 76v–77r, 97v–98r, 100v–101r]; Chastellain, *Livre des faits*, p. 83.

[16] Díaz de Games, *El Victorial*, p. 675.

[17] *Die Haager Liederhandschrift*, no. 66, 1:81–82, trans. in van Oostrom, *Court and Culture*, pp. 93–94.

[18] Fradenburg, *City, Marriage, Tournament*, p. 212.

masculinity by performing deeds before the admiring gaze of women and then displaying the rewards of such admiration before other men.[19]

The elaborate trappings of knighthood created a display that was not at all incompatible with chivalric masculinity. Attention to personal appearance, at least among the aristocracy, was not gendered feminine as it tends to be today. Medieval aristocrats considered the aesthetic virtues characteristic of women, but that did not mean that men who exhibited them were effeminate. Rather, such men were viewed as worthy of the society of women and of heterosexual fulfilment. Extravagant dress and courtly manners were condemned in the later Middle Ages as wasteful or dishonest, but the critique was quite different from that in the twelfth century when a courtier's effeminacy was connected with sodomy.[20] Now, instead, when writers complained about the extravagant dress of either men or women, they condemned it on the grounds of vanity and lust, not on the grounds that men made themselves like women. In the mid-fourteenth century Jean de Venette commented on the indecent dress of the French aristocracy, but did not call it effeminate.[21]

Geffroi de Charny, in his fourteenth-century treatise on chivalry, suggested that elaborate clothing was more appropriate for women than for men, because 'the qualities of men are more quickly known and recognized and in more ways than the qualities and reputation of women can be known.' Men demonstrated their rank as well as personal qualities through their deeds, whereas women had only their clothing to signify it. Excessive adornment might make men neglect deeds. Even he, however, allowed that it befitted a young man to be 'elegantly dressed and in good fashion,' as long as it was not done out of pride and did not lead to neglect of deeds.[22] Writers could comply with the moralists' strictures against clothing that was too elaborate by describing their subjects as well-dressed (with ample detail) while denying that they took pride in their clothing or that such clothing was 'curious.'[23] Even critiques of

---

[19] See Bousmar, 'La place des hommes et des femmes dans les fêtes de cour bourguignonnes.'

[20] Keiser, *Courtly Desire*, pp. 42–43. Effeminacy was also connected with heterosexual debauchery; medieval people did not see same-sex and opposite-sex lustfulness as mutually exclusive.

[21] De Venette, *Chronique Latine*, 2:185, 237–38.

[22] De Charny, *The Book of Chivalry*, pp. 193, 189, 191.

[23] *Le livre des faits du bon messire Jehan le Maingre*, pp. 392, 414.

extravagance in clothing from some quarters did not stop chroniclers and authors of romances from describing it (or horses' trappings) in loving detail.[24]

Medieval people often understood the display of the (clothed and even armoured) male body, especially in the context of the tournament, as an attempt to appeal to women. So, too, did they understand the adoption of courtly manners, polish, and elegance. These efforts would seem to place women in a position of relative power and to contradict the theories of the masculine gaze advanced by feminist theorists following Laura Mulvey. In their schema, the gaze is gendered masculine and active while the object of that gaze is gendered feminine and passive.

> In a world ordered by sexual imbalance, pleasure in looking has been split between active/male and passive/female. The determining male gaze projects its phantasy onto the female figure which is styled accordingly. In their traditional exhibitionist role women are simultaneously looked at and displayed, with their appearance coded for strong visual and erotic impact so that they can be said to connote *to-be-looked-at-ness*[25]

In this passage Mulvey is speaking of cinema, obviously a radically different genre from the various texts connected with medieval chivalry, and does not intend her dictum to apply to all areas of representation, but other scholars have widely generalized from her views.

Late medieval chivalric culture would seem to be an exception to this observation, but it is not. The attribution of power and of the penetrating gaze to medieval women is largely a myth or a construct. Aristocratic women were participants in a male-designed system for measuring masculine prowess. The lady functioned to support masculinity not only by standing as an opposite to it, as Fradenburg suggests, but also by serving as the prize to be won. Aristocratic men affirmed their masculinity by performing deeds before the gaze of women, but they then expected these women to respond by giving their love to the man who performed successfully—and described them as cruel if they

---

24 See, for example, La Marche, *Mémoires*, 1:309–10; La Sale, *Le petit Jehan de Saintré*, pp. 81–85.

25 Mulvey, 'Visual Pleasure and Narrative Cinema,' p. 62. For further feminist elaboration and discussion of this idea of the gaze, especially when many spectators are female, see Pribram's 'Introduction' to *Female Spectators*, pp. 1–11, as well as other articles in that volume; and also Doane, 'Film and the Masquerade.'

failed to do so. The women's own desires did not matter, for in this system, they served only to encourage male aggression against other men. In effect the chivalric ethos did not give women much of a choice. They were simply the currency in which a knight demonstrated to other men his worthiness. In short, men used the love of women to prove themselves to other men.

To prove his masculinity it was not enough for a young knight to create a display that appealed to women. In the later Middle Ages, participation in heterosexual love relationships was part of what made him a knight. Malory's Isolde can question Sir Dinadan's knightliness because he criticizes love: '"Why," said La Belle Isolde, "are you a knight, and are no lover? Truly, it is a great shame to you, for you may not be called a good knight except if you make a quarrel for a lady."'[26] In other words, no matter how skilful a knight might be at fighting, he needed a woman to be the raison-d'être of that skill and, thereby, validate it. Whether love was the motivation for prowess or its result, in the late medieval chivalric ethos prowess earned love. Jacques de Lalaing's biographer reports the advice of Jacques' father, who combined the Christian and the courtly-love aspect of chivalry using the doctrine of the seven deadly sins to encourage his son to be a good knight and thereby win his lady: 'you must flee the sin of pride, if you want to come to good and acquire the grace of your desired lady,' and so forth for the other sins as well. Even though no particular lady is mentioned at this point in the text, the father assumes that a lady will be the goal of Jacques' chivalrous efforts. In so doing, the father is not really referring to an individual woman, but to a generic incentive for good knightly behaviour.

A knight who was not interested in the game of love was mocked, as was the case with Sir Gawain in *Sir Gawain and the Green Knight*:

> As good a knight as Gawain is held to be
> With courtesy so pure in him,
> Could not have dallied so long with a lady
> Without craving a kiss, by his courtesy.[27]

Malory's Tristan says that 'a knight may never be of prowess, but if he be a lover.'[28] This attitude led young knights to seek a lady to love not

---

[26] Malory, *The Works*, 2:693. This is Malory's abbreviation of a much longer conversation about love found in the thirteenth-century prose *Tristan*: see notes in Malory, *The Works*, 3:1511–13.

[27] *Sir Gawain and the Green Knight*, p. 36, vv. 1297–1300.

[28] Malory, *The Works*, 2:689.

out of any particular desire for her or because of any emotional bond with her, but merely because of the necessity of doing love service. In *Petit Jehan de Saintré*, a lady of the court upbraids the youth for saying that he has no lady love:

> Oh, feeble gentleman! And you say that you love none? By this I know that you will never be worth anything! And, feeble heart that you are! from where come the great valour, great enterprises and knightly deeds of Lancelot [here she lists other knights] . . . if not to obtain the service of love and keep them in the graces of their most desired ladies.[29]

The need for a lady to love does not mean that knighthood excluded other types of desire. Clearly, however, a knight was expected to love women. Late medieval knightly masculinity was defined by sexual object choice, that choice being what we today would call heterosexual (though such a choice did not have to be exclusive). What might make a knight less than knightly was not a desire for men—that issue did not arise—but simply lack of desire for women.

The importance of heterosexual desire to late medieval knighthood comes less from an attempt to overcome male anxieties about same-sex desire or to promote marriage and reproduction, and more because women were one of the currencies in which a knight's success was measured. Whether a knight felt desire or not, he had to demonstrate to others that he did. Although a knight performed deeds of prowess ostensibly to earn the love of a woman, the subplot to this scheme was that he served a woman so as to advertise his deeds more effectively. Because it was the convention for women to be used in this way, the love of ladies was a necessary part of aristocratic masculinity, a sort of 'compulsory heterosexuality' that would demonstrate to other men not their particular 'sexual orientation' (which was not, in any case, a medieval concept), but their superiority to other men in the competition for women. That women were tokens in a game of masculine competition is further indicated by the adultery triangles that appear in Arthurian literature. It is women who threaten male community because men fight over them.[30] It is they who bring conflict into the chivalric world, even though it is through men's desires that they activate that conflict.

---

[29] La Sale, *Le petit Jehan de Saintré*, pp. 20–21.

[30] Ingham, *Sovereign Fantasies*, p. 154.

The idea of a knight performing valiant deeds to win the love of a woman may not seem especially noteworthy to anyone coming out of a European cultural tradition. We hear from an early age stories of young knights or princes striving to win the love of beautiful princesses. This particular medieval social arrangement seems unremarkable to us because its legacy is still with us. Yet, a look at the social world of the Japanese samurai demonstrates that the medieval European pattern is far from being the only possibility for a warrior elite. The samurai achieved honour by winning the love of young boys, whose beauty they celebrated in romantic poetry.[31] The contrast indicates that the European situation requires an explanation. The emphasis Christian culture placed on heterosexual marriage as a sacrament, and not just a means of producing heirs, may be part of the reason for such a difference. A large part may also lie with the fact that women did wield significant political power in medieval society, if not always in their own right, at least as widows and mothers. In this scenario, the language and ideology of love would reveal male efforts to shift that real power into a realm where it had less impact and then to undermine it by making love a commodity earned by the deserving male, rather than something that is bestowed on men by a woman's personal choice.

The tournament was an important place where knights or young men who sought knighthood could display their heterosexual desire and their attractiveness to women. Knights fought with favours from their ladies displayed on their helmets and the lady whose knight did well in a joust or tournament was honoured by it. A lady would give out the prize at the end of a tournament and might kiss the victor.[32] The reward, however, was not really the kiss, but the public recognition via the kiss of the knight's prowess and desirability.

The desire to win the love or approval of ladies was also the occasion for rash behaviour on the part of young knights who were posturing as much for each other as for the ladies. Froissart reports on a group of knights bachelor who went about with one eye covered because they had made a vow to some ladies not to uncover their eyes until they performed deeds of arms in France.[33] The vow was made to

---

[31] Ikegami, *The Taming of the Samurai*, pp. 209-210. I am grateful to Luke Roberts for calling this aspect of Japanese culture to my attention.

[32] Pognon, *Livre des Tournois*, no pagination [fol. 103v]; Nickel, 'The Tournament,' p. 238.

[33] Froissart, *Les Chroniques*, 1:1:63, 1:58; see also 1:1:69, 1:71.

ladies, but the men no doubt made it in competition with each other and to impress their peers. Although Christine de Pisan, using the classical example of Paris, might make the point that a man who appeals to the ladies is not always the best choice for a military endeavour, for the most part the two were equated.[34]

By the fourteenth and fifteenth centuries, the idea that love improves the lover, which had begun as a literary topos in the twelfth century, had permeated courtly society and was an important part of the rhetoric brought into play when it came time for young knights to marry.[35] It was found not only in romance and didactic literature, but also in social practice. Knights and ladies adopted speech patterns from romance literature and used the same language in their letters (and not just in their love letters!).[36] When Edward III of England became attracted to the Countess of Salisbury, for example, this was not simply another case of a king sleeping with any woman he wanted; instead, he cast his desire for the Countess in courtly love terms.[37] A sixteenth-century account of the fifteenth-century English knight Sir John Stanley depicts him and an heiress falling in love at first sight; even if more mundane factors, such as the lady's wealth, clearly played a role in Sir John's interest in her, the poet who chronicled the Stanley family attributed the knight's love for the lady to her beauty and her admiration for the knight to what she had heard of his prowess.[38] Whether or not 'courtly love' had been a reality in the twelfth century, people in the fifteenth century, who read chivalric romances as historical fact, believed it had been so, and attempted to emulate it.[39]

This type of love was not primarily an emotional relation between two people, but rather a prize to be awarded for a man's achievement and therefore primarily a measure of the latter. Women may have experienced it differently, but from a youth's perspective love was a commodity that he could earn. As Charny suggested, 'glances and desire, love, reflection and memory, gaiety of heart and liveliness of body set them off on the right road and provided a beginning for those

---

[34] Christine de Pisan, *Letter of Othea to Hector*, p. 114.

[35] In his *Ennobling Love* Jaeger argues that it began as an idea of same-sex love.

[36] Benson, *Malory's Morte Darthur*, pp. 161-162; Benson, 'Courtly Love and Chivalry,' pp. 242-245, 249-251.

[37] Stanesco, *Jeux d'errance*, pp. 103-104; Froissart, *Les Chroniques*, 1:1:165-166, 1:145-146 and 1:1:191, 1:164.

[38] *Palatine Anthology*, pp. 218-221.

[39] Keen, *Nobles, Knights, and Men-at-Arms*, pp. 21-47.

who would never have known how to perform and achieve the great and honourable deeds through which good men-at-arms can make their name.'[40] The biographer of the French Marshal Boucicaut adopted the literary topos of the love of a woman improving a man. Boucicaut impressed his beloved at the coronation of Charles VI with his good looks and rich clothing, horse, and retainers. Inspired by the sweet glances she gave him, he won his jousts. At this time, aged fourteen, he was not yet a knight, but was knighted in 1382 at the unusually young age of sixteen during an expedition against Flanders. Even though he now deserved the prize of his lady's love, Boucicaut chose, as his biographer tells us, to wait until he had done even greater deeds.[41] The implication is that she grants her love because he deserves it, not because his deeds cause loving feelings to swell up within her. Both in the literary and more historical (though heavily literary) accounts, love is a commodity.

Froissart tells of Isabella de Juliers who fell in love with Eustace d'Ambreticourt (whom she later married) because of his gallant deeds of arms. She sent him horses and love letters, and this spurred him to perform more feats of chivalry.[42] There is a practical element here, of course: a wealthy woman might be able to be of great material assistance to her chosen knight. When Jehan de Saintré names a ten-year-old girl as his love, a lady of the court says 'You, sir, should choose a lady of high and noble blood, wise, and who has the wherewithal to help you and supply your needs.'[43] When Sir John Stanley chose his lady love, it was because he

> made such search not only of her degree
> But as well of conversation and beauty
> And heard by fame to be honest and fair
> Her father old and she his undoubted heir.[44]

In Sir John's case, the romantic and the pragmatic clearly merged in his choice of lady.

The idea that Isabella fell in love with Eustace or Lord Latham's daughter with Sir John Stanley because of his deeds of arms is common; ladies were described as falling in love because of men's achievements

---

[40] Charny, *The 'Book of Chivalry'*, p. 115.

[41] *Le livre des faits du bon messire Jehan le Maingre*, pp. 27-40.

[42] Froissart, *Les Chroniques*, 1:2:91, 1:401.

[43] La Sale, *Le petit Jehan de Saintré*, p. 29.

[44] *Palatine Anthology*, p. 219.

in tournaments.[45] The idea that military success was what made a young knight erotically desirable ties together these two important aspects of masculinity. This is no more implausible than the spectacle of women today offering themselves to sports heroes. Patricia Ingham suggests that the references to women's desire for displays of knightly prowess are a means of displacing onto women men's desire for violence.[46]

In the examples of Sir John Stanley and the daughter of Lord Latham, and of Eustace d'Ambreticourt and Isabella de Juillers, love is shown to lead to marriage. Medieval authors spoke of even arranged noble marriages in courtly love terms.[47] Although the young knight might enter the game of love hoping to acquire a wealthy wife, and although marriages might be described in the terminology of romantic love, most of the love described in literature, chronicles, or didactic texts does not view marriage as its goal. Jacques de Lalaing, for example, was not seeking a wife, and when the marital status of the ladies to whom he appealed is mentioned, we find out that they were already married. His biographer notes on several occasions that women wished their husbands were like him or would like him to change places with their husbands.[48] Even if the rhetoric of love did not necessarily change the way medieval aristocrats formed their marriages, they clearly took this rhetoric seriously. Young knights, not yet of an age or a fortune to marry, were encouraged to choose a lady to love as part of their masculine life stage.

It might seem, then, that women exerted a great deal of power and control over the young knight at the time when he was learning not just the skills, but also the comportment of the chivalric class. In most of these circumstances, however, the power of the female gaze is a myth. It was not really the women who were evaluating the young man, but other men. A young knight's appeal to women was one part of that evaluation, but not the most important one. The men who were watching him may indeed have been more interested in determining whether the young knight's behaviour matched what they thought should be attractive to women, and not whether women in fact felt deeply attracted to him. In a sense, then, the women's gaze that measured the worth of the young knight did not belong to the women themselves.

---

[45] Fleckenstein, *Ordnungen und formende Kräfte des Mittelalters*, p. 410.

[46] Ingham, *Sovereign Fantasies*, p. 131.

[47] Benson, 'Courtly Love and Chivalry,' p. 250.

[48] Chastellain, *Livre des faits*, pp. 30, 105.

The women themselves may have seen things differently. They may have seen themselves as quite active participants in this game, even dominant, deciding for themselves which knights were worthy of their love. For them, however, this was a rather empty form of dominance. It did not allow them to get the men to do what they wanted—the men's service entailed winning tournaments and other things that did not do the women any good except in terms of prestige and few were the damsels in distress whom the knights actually rescued. Nor did it acquire husbands for them.

The women served a ratifying function for a youth's entry into a masculine hierarchy of knightly prestige, but they did not themselves choose the criteria by which they evaluated the men. A woman's gaze at a young knight was not a sign of her activity as opposed to his passivity, but rather the sign that she was the prize he was to win, the currency in which his worth in other men's eyes was to be measured.

*University of Minnesota*
*Minneapolis, Minnesota*

## Cited Works

Benson, Larry. 'Courtly Love and Chivalry in the Late Middle Ages' pp. 237–57 in *Fifteenth-Century Studies. Recent Essays*, ed. Robert F. Yeager. Hamden, CT: Archon Books, 1984.

Benson, Larry. *Malory's Morte Darthur*. Cambridge, MA: Harvard University Press, 1976.

Bousmar, Eric. 'La place des hommes et des femmes dans les fêtes de cour bourguignonnes (Philippe le Bon—Charles le Hardi)' pp. 123–43 in *Fêtes et cérémonies aux XIV$^e$–XVI$^e$ siècles. Actes / Rencontres de Lausanne (23 au 26 septembre 1993). Publications du Centre Européen d'Études Bourguignonnes, 34. Neuchatel: Centre Européen d'Études Bourguignonnes, 1994.

Chastellain, Georges. *Le Livre des faits du bon chevalier Messire Jacques de Lalaing*, ed. Kervyn de Lettenhove, 8:1–259 in *Oeuvres de Georges Chastellain*. Brussels: Victor Devaux, 1863–66.

Christine de Pisan. *Christine de Pisan's Letter of Othea to Hector*, trans. Jane Chance. Newburyport, MA: Focus, 1990; rpt. 1997.

De Charny, Geoffroi. *The 'Book of Chivalry' of Geoffroi de Charny. Text, Context, and Translation*, ed. Richard W. Kaeuper, trans. Elspeth Kennedy. Philadelphia: University of Pennsylvania Press, 1996.

De Venette, Jean. *Chronique Latine de Guillaume de Nangis de 1113 à 1300 avec les continuations de cette chronique de 1300 à 1368*, ed. Hercule Géraud. 2 vols. Société de l'Histoire de France, Publications 33, 35. Paris: J. Renouard, 1843.

Díaz de Games, Gutierre. *El Victorial*, ed. Rafael Beltrán Llavador. Salamanca: Ediciones Universidad, 1997.

Doane, Mary Ann. 'Film and the Masquerade: Theorizing the Female Spectator' pp. 41–57 in *Issues in Feminist Film Criticism*, ed. Patricia Erens. Bloomington: Indiana University Press, 1990.

*Female Spectators: Looking at Film and Television*, ed. E. Deidre Pribram. London and New York: Verso, 1988.

Fleckenstein, Josef. *Ordnungen und formende Kräfte des Mittelalters: Ausgewählte Beiträge*. Göttingen: Vandenhoek & Rupprecht, 1989.

Fradenburg, Louise Olga. *City, Marriage, Tournament: Arts of Rule in Late Medieval Scotland*. Madison: University of Wisconsin Press, 1991.

Froissart, Jean. *Les Chroniques de Sire Jean Froissart*, ed. Jean Alexandre C. Buchon. 3 vols. Paris: Desrez, 1837–38.

*Die Haager Liederhandschrift*, ed. E.F. Kossmann. 2 vols. Den Haag: Martinus Nijhoff, 1940.

Ikegami, Eiko. *The Taming of the Samurai. Honorific Individualism and the Making of Modern Japan*. Cambridge, MA: Harvard University Press, 1995.

Ingham, Patricia Clare. *Sovereign Fantasies: Arthurian Romance and the Making of Britain*. Philadelphia: University of Pennsylvania Press, 2001.

Jaeger, Stephen. *Ennobling Love: In Search of a Lost Sensibility*. Philadelphia: University of Pennsylvania Press, 1999.

Kaeuper, Richard. *Chivalry and Violence in Medieval Europe*. Oxford and New York: Oxford University Press, 1999.

Keen, Maurice. *Chivalry*. New Haven: Yale University Press, 1984.

Keen, Maurice Hugh. *Nobles, Knights, and Men-at-Arms in the Middle Ages*. London and Rio Grande, OH: Hambledon Press, 1996.

Keiser, Elizabeth B. *Courtly Desire and Medieval Homophobia. The Legitimation of Sexual Pleasure in Cleanness and its Contexts*. New Haven, CT: Yale University Press, 1997.

La Marche, Olivier de. *Mémoires d'Olivier de la Marche, maître d'hotel et capitaine des gardes de Charles le Téméraire*, ed. Henri Beaune and J. d'Arbaumont. 4 vols. Société de l'Histoire de France, Publications en octavo 213, 219, 220, 240. Paris: Renouard, 1883–88.

La Sale, Antoine de. *Le petit Jehan de Saintré*, ed. Pierre Champion and Fernand Desonay. Paris: Editions du Trianon, 1926.

*Le livre des faits du bon messire Jehan le Maingre, dit Bouciquaut, mareschal de France et gouverneur de Jennes*, ed. Denis Lalande. Geneva: Droz, 1985.

Llull, Ramon. *The Book of the Ordre of Chyvalry, Translated and Printed by Willliam Caxton from a French Version of Ramón Lull's 'Le libre del orde de Cauayleria'*, ed. Alfred T.P. Byles. Early English Texts Series, OS 168. London: EETS, 1926.

Malory, Thomas. *The Works of Sir Thomas Malory*, ed. Eugène Vinaver, rev. P.J.C. Field, 3rd ed. Oxford: Clarendon Press, 1990.

Mulvey, Laura. 'Visual Pleasure and Narrative Cinema' pp. 57–79 in *Feminism and Film Theory*, ed. Constance Penley. New York: Routledge/London: BFI, 1988.

Nickel, Helmut. 'The Tournament: An Historical Sketch' pp. 213–53 in *The Study of Chivalry: Resources and Approaches*, ed. Howell Chickering and Thomas H. Seiler. Kalamazoo, MI: Medieval Institute Publications, 1988.

Orme, Nicholas. *Childhood to Chivalry. The Education of the English Kings and Aristocracy, 1066–1530*. London and New York: Methuen, 1984.

Orme, Nicholas. 'The Education of the Courtier' pp. 63–85 in *English Court Culture in the Middle Ages*, eds. V.J. Scattergood and J.W. Sherborne. London: Duckworth, 1983.

*Palatine Anthology: A Collection of Ancient Poems and Ballads, Relating to Lancashire and Cheshire*, ed. James Orchard Halliwell. London: For private circulation only [printed by C. and J. Adlard]: 1850.

Pognon, Edmond. *Le Livre des Tournois du Roi René, de la Bibliothèque Nationale (MS Français 2695)*, ed. François Avril. Paris: Hersher, 1986.

*Sir Gawain and the Green Knight*, ed. J.R.R. Tolkien and E.V. Gordon, 2nd ed. rev. by Norman Davis. Oxford: Clarendon Press, 1967.

Stanesco, Michael. *Jeux d'errance du chevalier médiéval: aspects ludiques de la fonction guerrière dans la littérature du Moyen Age flamboyant*. Leiden: Brill, 1988.

Van Oostrom, Frits Pieter. *Court and Culture: Dutch Literature, 1350–1450*, trans. Arnold J. Pomerans. Berkeley: University of California Press, 1992.

# Teenagers at War During the Middle Ages

## Kelly DeVries

Early in 1212 a young man from western Germany, whose name has come down through history only as Nicholas, became the focal point of an attempted military endeavour against the Muslims in the Holy Land. Sweeping through the Rhineland, the fervour for participation grew with such vigour that more than a thousand like him joined the endeavour. They were fearless, willing to leave the comforts of their homes and families to travel thousands of miles and fight enemies whose different religion compelled them to make the journey. Because of their relative youth, this 'crusade' has become known historically as the 'Children's Crusade.'[1]

More than a century later, late in the afternoon of 26 August 1346, a young man stood firm in his position. It was important that he not show fear at what he was about to encounter. He was obviously rich, with a noble and brave demeanour the result of years of training in military arts. He was well armed and well armoured. He was also young and fear must have crossed his heart. No doubt he thought about the role he was to play in ensuing events, for he was in command of the most vulnerable spot on the battlefield, the central position of the middle of three solid defensive lines. Although only a teenager, a mere sixteen years old, Edward, Prince of Wales, later to be known as the Black Prince, was about to engage the French army at Crécy.[2]

Not one hundred years after the Black Prince fought at Crécy, early in the morning of 7 May 1429, another teenager, Joan of Arc, prepared to make military history. On this occasion, she was not waiting in a defensive formation as the Black Prince had done at Crécy, but poised

---

[1] For a good, short summary of the Children's Crusade, see Madden, *A Concise History of the Crusades*, pp. 138–40; for more in-depth studies see Raedts, 'The Children's Crusade'; Miccoli, 'La "crociata dei fanciulli"'; and Zacour, 'The Children's Crusade.'

[2] It seems that 'the Black Prince' as a nickname was not assigned to Prince Edward until the sixteenth century, and then probably at the bidding of antiquarians such as John Leland. Barber suggests this was done perhaps to differentiate this prince from Edward of Woodstock, later King Edward IV; *Edward*, pp. 242–43.

to attack an enemy-controlled position, the strongly fortified bridge-head called the Tourelles that stood opposite the besieged city of Orléans.[3] This was not her first military engagement, for she had been fighting against the besiegers of Orléans for more than a week, but it was to be her first great military effort, a direct assault on a fortification packed with the enemy armed with a large number of gunpowder weapons as well as with more traditional medieval arms. Like the 'children crusaders,' but unlike the Black Prince, Joan probably felt little fear, for she had a divine mission to fulfil, and that mission began with the relief of the English siege of Orléans.

All three of these military incidents, with their adolescent partici-pants, have given historians the impression that warfare in the Middle Ages was fought often, if not primarily, by warriors under the age of twenty: teenagers. Judging from what little age-related evidence there is, however, this may actually not have been the case. In fact, the children of the Children's Crusade may not actually have been chil-dren, or even adolescents, while the young age of the Black Prince and of Joan of Arc may have been unusual in leadership roles, but seems not to have mattered as the two youths showed military skill far beyond their teenage years.

There is no doubt that throughout history youths in their teens fought in wars. Even beyond those who were recruited in early modern armed forces as musicians (pipers, buglers, and drummers) and as logistical personnel in armies or as ensigns in navies, many teenagers chose to enlist among those actually fighting. Muster rolls in the early modern and modern periods, which sometimes contain age-related details, have confirmed this fact. For example, a statistical analysis of late eighteenth-century British soldiers found an average age of 21.6 years for 74 soldiers serving in the British army in America in 1776–82 and 24.0 years for 951 soldiers serving in the British army during the Napoleonic Wars of 1790–99. These same soldiers' ages stayed rela-tively the same during proximate years of peace: an average of 22.8 years for 35 soldiers serving in the British army in 1762–75 and 24.0 years for 56 soldiers serving in the same army in 1783–89.[4] Still,

---

[3] For a description of the Tourelles and its importance see DeVries, *Joan of Arc*, p. 60.

[4] Steegmann, 'Eighteenth Century British Military Stature.' McKern/Stewart showed that the average age of Korean War soldiers was 23.7 years; see their *Skeletal Age Changes*. The average age of American soldiers fighting in Vietnam was 19; Boylston, 'Physical Anthropology' p. 5.

because of poor and frequently dishonest recruitment information, it is almost impossible for the historian seeking statistical evidence to determine how many teenagers actually fought in any engagement.

Yet another source of evidence has facilitated the historians' search for soldiers' ages: the excavation of corpses from military conflicts. For example, excavations of graves from a 1812 battle at Snake Hill, near Fort Erie, Canada, have established that 17 of the 32 bodies were of soldiers under the age of 25, with 9 of these under the age of 20. The youngest was only 14 years old.[5] These findings are further corroborated by the excavations of 21 eighteenth-century military corpses from Fort Laurens, Ohio, whose average age was 23.5 years, with two soldiers aged between 12 and 15 years.[6] Other age-related studies of victims of war indicate a similar young age of the soldiers: five who died during the attacks on Fort William Henry in 1757 averaged 23.3 years, and thirty New York Provincials who died during engagements in 1760 averaged 25.5 years.[7] It is this evidence that has led some early modern military historians to estimate that while the largest portion of men serving in armies of the period were between 20 and 40 years of age, up to a quarter of the soldiery might have been under 20 years of age, with many only 15 or 16 years old.[8]

Can the same estimation apply to soldiers fighting during the Middle Ages? While there are several medieval muster rolls, such as that for Edward III's Crécy campaign in 1346 or the Bridport muster roll of 1457, none of these contain the ages of their listed participants.[9] Nor have prosopographical studies of medieval military endeavours aided this understanding; even James M. Powell's *Anatomy of a Crusade*, a detailed study of the Fifth Crusade that uses an extremely large number of sources, has not been able to determine how old, or young, those crusaders were.

---

[5] Pfeiffer, 'Estimation of Age at Death,' pp. 167–75. For a discussion of how age is determined in these excavations see Boylston, 'Physical Anthropology,' pp. 45-59.

[6] Sciuli/Gramly, 'Analysis of the Fort Laurens, Ohio, Skeletal Sample.'

[7] These are included with references on a table found in Knüsel/Boylston, 'How Has the Towton Project,' p. 171.

[8] Tallett, *War and Society*, pp. 85–86.

[9] Wrottesley has edited Edward III's Crécy muster roll (*Crecy and Calais from the Public Records*) while Richardson has done the same for the Bridport muster roll ('The Bridport Muster Roll of 1457'). There are others, but none contain age-related information.

What about the excavations of medieval military corpses? Despite knowing the locations of several grave mounds and cemeteries, only a few have been excavated. The unearthing by Bengt Thordeman of more than a thousand skeletons from the largest of these, the battlefield of Visby, where in 1361 the Danes defeated the Gotlanders, revealed no information on the ages of these soldiers, primarily because Thordeman was little concerned with the bodies themselves and even bagged all the bones together.[10]

However, two recent excavations are far more profitable for determining the age of medieval soldiers. The first, undertaken by the Council for British Archaeology at St. Andrew's cemetery in the Fishergate area of York, while not a military cemetery *per se*, did reveal 29 skeletons which had sustained fatal blade injuries. Their average age, however, was much older than the early modern corpses mentioned above: 28 years old.[11] Far more secure evidence of medieval soldiers' ages can be found in the second excavation, that of 32 bodies from the battle of Towton, fought in 1461 during the English Wars of the Roses. These skeletons, found only in July 1996, have received extremely close scrutiny by forensic archaeologists on all aspects, including age. Using both dental and bone data, it was discovered that the average age of these victims of this most bloody battle fought on English soil was 29.2 years of age. Moreover, of these 32 corpses, only 11 can be identified as between 16 and 25 years old, with the archaeologists unwilling to specify whether these 11 were teenagers or not. This makes the average age of the Towton warriors considerably older than their early modern and modern counterparts.[12]

And yet, what about the famous examples of medieval adolescent soldiers mentioned at the beginning of this article? How do they reconcile with the age-related detail from the excavations that showed a relatively more advanced age for medieval soldiers? The simple answer could be that all three examples—the Children's Crusade, the Black Prince, and Joan of Arc—were special and unusual cases, and that while

---

[10] *Armour from the Battle of Visby.* Dental means of identifying age among these combatants have shown that in one of the three mass graves excavated over a third of the corpses were of teenagers (the other two mass graves did not contain a large number of youths). However, as the Gotlander contingent in this battle included many civilians (or militia) from the countryside, such findings have not been seen as representative of medieval soldiers as a whole, especially in the absence of the more firm bone evidence; see Ingelmark, 'The Skeletons.'

[11] Stroud/Kemp, *Cemeteries of St. Andrew, Fishergate.*

[12] See Boylston, 'Physical Anthropology,' pp. 47–53.

they included famous teenagers in military roles, they were anomalies. That may be so, and certainly the cases of the Black Prince and Joan of Arc seem to confirm this thesis. In the case of the Children's Crusade, however, these famous young soldiers were not soldiers, or even young. For, despite a persistence among nineteenth-century writers to glorify or even romanticize this 1212 military endeavour by 'poor children,' more modern research has argued that the Children's Crusade was, to use Thomas Madden's words, 'not an army of children, and it was not a crusade.'[13]

As is well known to medieval historians, by 1212 the crusades were not going well. During the previous half century, endeavours in the Holy Land had met with ineptitude and bickering between the resident crusaders in Outremer and their reinforcements (the Second Crusade), with military failure when facing a superior enemy (the Third Crusade), or with misdirection of crusading efforts to suit more personal ambitions and greed (the Fourth Crusade). Jerusalem was no longer in the hands of Christians and the other Latin kingdoms in the Middle East stood on the brink of surrender. Only the death of Saladin, it seems, had prevented all of the gains of the First Crusade to fall back into the hands of the Saracens.

Scholars have frequently debated how much of this news from the Middle East reached the poorer 'grassroots' of Europe. Some have claimed that victory or failure in the Middle East had little effect on what was happening in Europe;[14] judging from the responses given to Gerald of Wales' crusading sermons, such an assertion may have validity.[15] Perhaps early thirteenth-century peasants in the Rhineland would never have known of the failings of these Crusades had preachers not told them about them and warned them of the disastrous future of Christianity because of them. Whether this was the case or not cannot be determined from our meagre sources, but what can be determined is that when some lower class groups heard of the plight of the Holy Land they were spurred on with an enthusiasm that knew no equal among the upper classes. Such had certainly been the case with the popular crusaders of the First Crusade who, led by preachers such as Peter the Hermit and Walter the Penniless, had met their end outside Nicea without making even so much

---

[13] Madden, *A Concise History of the Crusades*, p. 138. For a review of nineteenth- and twentieth-century writings about the crusades see Raedt, 'The Children's Crusade,' pp. 279–82.

[14] See, for example, Gilchrist, 'The Erdmann Thesis.'

[15] Giraldus Cambrensis, *Itinerarium Kambriae*, passim, in *Opera*.

as a single military foray. Since that time, most of these poorer crusaders, even if initially enthused about service in the Holy Land, would soon realize the futility of such endeavours and return to their previously militarily uneventful lives, as Gerald of Wales witnessed.

Such seems not to have been the case in 1212. Contemporary sources note that between 25 March and 13 May a popular crusading movement gained strength primarily along the border lands between France and the Holy Roman Empire.[16] They record that thousands of *pueri* accepted the call to crusade, joining with a *puer* named Nicholas who may have been the originator of the crusade—or had risen quickly to be its chief instigator. Their mission was to relieve the crusader holdings in the Holy Land, to redeem Jerusalem, and to recover the Holy Sepulchre, doing so essentially because it was not being done by the soldiers of their kings and princes.[17]

Who this Nicholas was is somewhat of a mystery. Some sources indicate he came from the region around Cologne, but there is no certainty in this, especially as the Cologne chroniclers reporting on this crusade say nothing about it.[18] Nor do any of these sources indicate his age, beyond saying that he was a *puer*. Contemporary Giovanni Codagnello suggests that Nicholas had received a vision in which he had been instructed by an angel to regain the Holy Sepulchre and remove it from Saracen control.[19] (It is uncertain here and elsewhere whether Nicholas or any of his followers had a precise understanding of who their enemy would be, beyond the simple designation 'Saracen.') Most other original sources give no such divine rationale for this crusading movement.

Starting in the Rhine region near Cologne, the Children Crusaders travelled south to Alsace, stopping along the way perhaps at Trier and definitely at Speyer. According to Alberic of Troisfontaines, a separate French Children's Crusade led by a shepherd boy named Stephen, inspired by the German one, also began around Vendôme at this time and marched south to Marseilles, but most modern historians see this as a confused figment of the writer's imagination.[20] These crusaders

---

[16] Raedt, 'The Children's Crusade,' pp. 282–89.

[17] So says Reiner of Liège, *Reineri annales*, p. 665.

[18] Raedt, 'The Children's Crusade,' p. 290.

[19] Codagnello, *Annales Placentini*, p. 426.

[20] Alberic of Troisfontaines, *Chronicon*, p. 893. Alberic claims that these children, some 30,000 in number, were either shipwrecked and drowned or were betrayed and sold into slavery. Those doubting this story include Raedt, 'The Children's Crusade,' pp. 293–94; Zacour, 'The Children's Crusade,' p. 337; and Munro, 'The

were humble, poor, and, perhaps more importantly, poorly prepared for the endeavours of European travel. Several seem to have died of hunger, thirst, and exposure along the way; others turned back at Mainz and returned home.[21] Many more travelled through the Alps and reached northern Italy, arriving in Genoa on 25 August. This in itself was an impressive undertaking—the city annalist, Ogerius Panis, expressed awe when he counted the 7,000 crusaders who had arrived there with Nicholas.[22]

In Genoa the crusade somehow began to fall apart. Perhaps some crusaders began to doubt Nicholas' divinity when no transportation awaited their transfer to the Holy Land. The crusade fractured. One group went from Genoa to Marseilles, another to Rome, while still another appeared in Brindisi, where the wise bishop forbade them from further attempting to reach the Holy Land.[23] Some of the crusaders even seem to have secured boats for the Mediterranean crossing, although the *Chronicon Eberheimense* reports that no sooner had these set sail than they were captured by Muslim pirates and sold into slavery.[24] A few returned to the Rhineland, but most seem to have disappeared from the historical record. Even Nicholas' fate is unknown. Only two sources comment on him once he left Genoa: one, the *Gesta Treverorum* suggests that he died in Brindisi, while a second, the *Annales Admuntenses*, claims that he survived this initial crusade and later, in 1217, took the cross and fought at Akirs and Damietta.[25]

So, warriors they were not, at least not in 1212. But exactly how old were these crusading 'children'? The original sources use the words *puer*, *puella*, or *puelle* to describe them. However, because these sources include them with *homines* and *feminae* and even *infantes lactantes*, several modern historians see this crusade less as one in which *only* children, or even *predominantly* children or even adolescents, participated.[26] They regard it, instead, more as a 'popular' or even 'poor'

Children's Crusade,' p. 520. Other contemporary French sources also report a popular crusading movement which began that year in Vendôme, but claim that, once it reached Paris, the crusaders were sent home by King Philip Augustus. See Raedt, 'The Children's Crusade,' pp. 292–93.

[21] Reiner of Liège, *Reineri annales*, p. 665; *Chronica regia Coloniensis*, pp. 191, 234.

[22] Panis, *Annales Ianuenses*, p. 131.

[23] *Gesta Treverorum*, p. 399.

[24] *Chronicon Eberheimense*, p. 450.

[25] *Annales Admuntenses*, p. 592.

[26] See especially Miccoli 'La "crociata dei fanciulli,"' p. 430 and Raedts, 'The

crusade, in other words as one designated more by class and wealth than by age. This assertion becomes even more convincing when the contemporary account of the Marbach annalist is examined. Not hiding his feelings of disgust nor his criticism for this crusade and its leaders, the Marbach annalist may be the most trustworthy source in which to research the question of age as he does not embellish what occurred in 1212. And this source claims that not only were these crusaders not teenagers or younger children, but that they were adult and married 'children.'[27] Other contemporary sources seem to indicate no age for them. Only medieval chronicles written long after the crusade insist on the youth of these crusaders.[28]

Furthermore, according to Georges Duby and Philippe Ariès, the word *puer* was often used during the Middle Ages to indicate an agricultural labourer or wage-earner.[29] (A somewhat analogous semantic situation occurred in the pre-Civil War American South where slave-owners often referred to their adult male slaves as 'boy.') Without firmer contemporary information, one must agree that the 'Children's Crusade' was not a military undertaking by adolescents.

What, then, of the Black Prince and Joan of Arc? In their cases, it is almost certain that they were teenagers. For the Black Prince, there is no doubt. He was born on 15 June 1330 as the first child of King Edward III of England and Philippa of Hainault. Joan of Arc's exact age cannot be determined from the sources available; she never revealed it nor was she asked at her trial how old she was. Unfortunately, without a clear answer to such a question, Joan's age during the events of her military career cannot be known for sure. Some believe she was born in 1412, which would make her seventeen years old when she began her military adventures. Others give 1414 or 1411 as her birth year. Since none of these dates is based on the least amount of original source evidence, scholars, such as Régine Pernoud and Jules Quicherat, have simply not discussed her age, except to say that she was still a teenager, even at her death in 1431.[30]

---

Children's Crusade,' pp. 295–300.

[27] *Annales Marbacenses*, pp. 82–83.

[28] Raedts, 'The Children's Crusade,' pp. 296–97.

[29] Duby, 'Les pauvres des campagnes,' p. 30; Ariès, *L'enfant et la vie familiale*, pp. 14–15; Raedts, 'The 'Children's Crusade',' p. 296.

[30] For a further discussion on this see DeVries, *Joan of Arc*, p. 202 n. 8.

What were these two teenagers doing, fighting in a war which seemed to know no chronological bounds, especially if, as was shown above, it might have been unusual for teenagers to have fought in medieval wars? Indeed, not only were they fighting, but they were also leading other soldiers far older and more veteran than they. And why did adult men follow them into these and other military engagements? The answer is quite simple: their youth did not matter. Should they have failed in their military tasks, their age might have mattered. What mattered was their victories, which most contemporary commentators and eye-witnesses credit to their bravery, leadership, and military skills.

Because of the tumultuous times, provoked for the most part by his father, the young Prince of Wales was active in warfare at a younger age than most sons of even the most bellicose of medieval leaders. While too young to participate in his father's early efforts at the battle of Sluys and at the siege of Tournai (1340) or in the Breton civil war (1342), once King Edward III was again able to attack the French in 1346, the young prince not only went with him, but also supplied him with men and revenues from his English holdings.[31] Whether the noble youth could have anticipated what awaited him in France cannot be known; it was to be quite the introduction to warfare.

The speed and scope of the English march from their landing at Saint-Vaast-la-Hogue to Crécy was impressive. Between 11 July and 26 August, not only did the English manoeuvre across a large amount of enemy territory, but they also captured many towns and fortifications, including the historical capital of Normandy, Caen.[32] The sources do not say what the Black Prince's role in the affair was to this point, but no doubt he was getting an education in how to lead an army from one of the best generals of the medieval world, his father, King Edward III.[33] In turn, he must have inspired such trust that his father gave him heavy responsibilities in the battle to follow.

---

[31] Barber, *Edward*, p. 45.

[32] On the English army's movement from the Seine to the Somme see Barber, *Edward*, pp. 59–61, and DeVries, *Infantry Warfare*, pp. 157–158.

[33] Admittedly, while there is no doubt as to Edward III's later success as a military leader (see Rogers, 'Edward III and the Dialectics of Strategy,' pp. 83–102), at this point in his career he had seen personal victory only at the battle of Halidon Hill and at the naval battle of Sluys, while he had been defeated at the siege of Tournai and in numerous other engagements associated with this siege.

On the morning of 26 August, with King Philip VI's army quickly approaching the battlefield, King Edward III ordered his troops in a defensive formation. All troops were to fight on foot, the cavalry dismounting to stand alongside the rest of the infantry. Even the Black Prince, who was placed in command of the centre line, was dismounted. Why was Prince Edward placed in this position of responsibility when still so young? It is difficult to say without being able to look into Edward III's psyche; if his son failed in his task at Crécy, his future military leadership would be largely ineffective. The Black Prince, however, would not fail.

After a largely one-sided archery duel, in which the English longbowmen clearly proved their strength against Genoese crossbowmen fighting in the employ of the French, Philip VI ordered his cavalry to charge the English position, directly at the centre of the line commanded by the Black Prince. Although the archery exchange had proved a failure for the French army, its main body, the cavalry, armed with lance and sword, was still an impressive and formidable force which in the past had often caused infantry foes to flee in panic even before encountering them. The French cavalry could still carry the day, especially if the Black Prince's position were to fail.

It was a brutal fight, described by the bourgeois of Valenciennes as 'very perilous, murderous, without pity, cruel, and very horrible.'[34] The Herald of Chandos agrees: 'That day was there battle so horrible that never was there a man so bold that would not be abashed thereby.'[35] The French cavalry made a number of attacks on the English line. These charges became directed at the centre of the English front line, the section commanded by the Black Prince. Indeed, the Prince himself became the target of many direct attacks, but despite on one occasion being 'compelled to fight on his knees,' he and his men held their position.[36]

Although having previously been knighted when the English landed at Saint-Vaast-la-Hogue, it was in this battle experience that the teenaged Edward, the Black Prince, 'earned his spurs.' Praise for his performance at Crécy was almost unceasing. The following day, when the English king conducted a funeral service for all those who had fought and died on both sides, the Black Prince stood by his side.[37] On

---

34 *Récits d'un bourgeois de Valenciennes*, p. 232.

35 *The Life and Campaigns of the Black Prince*, p. 9.

36 Geoffrey le Baker, *Chronicon*, p. 84.

37 John Arderne, the English army's (and perhaps the royal family's) surgeon

12 October 1347, back in London after the successful siege of Calais, and despite his age, Prince Edward became one of the first inductees in the chivalric Order of the Garter, established by his father to honour those nobles who had performed well in their military escapades in France; he was by far the youngest inductee. Also inducted were many others who had stood near him in that centre position and who, impressed by his strength of leadership, would continue to be his companions for the rest of his life.[38] His adolescence had not mattered, for he had performed his military task well, and even much older soldiers honoured that.

Joan of Arc did not have the wealth, education, nor the advantages of Edward III's eldest son. Nor, it should be said, did she have the responsibilities. The only similarity she had with the Black Prince, aside from her age, was her ability to make followers of much older troops, soldiers who seemed not to have considered her too young to lead them once she had proven her capabilities on the battlefield.

Born in Domrémy, Lorraine, of comparatively wealthy peasant parents,[39] Joan had a relatively normal young girl's rural life until the fall of 1428 when she approached the castle of Vaucouleurs with her now famous tale of having heard heavenly voices, most often those of Saints Michael, Margaret, and Catherine. Their message, spoken to her since childhood, was that she was to seek out Charles, Dauphin of France, and he would give her an army with which she would deliver France from its English occupiers.[40] Why the castellans at Vaucouleurs did not turn her away is undoubtedly one of the great mysteries of history, surpassed only by the mystery of why later at Chinon the Dauphin actually provided her with her desired army. Yet, Joan still had to

---

leaves the best record of this funeral and the Black Prince's place in it: see his *Treatises of Fistula in Ano*, p. xxvii. See also Barber, *Edward*, pp. 68–69 and pl. 16. It is also here that the Black Prince may have taken up his famous motto, *Ich d(i)ene*, impressed either by his Flemish allies or by the bravery of the dead King of Bohemia, whose blindness had not kept him from playing a role in the Crécy battle; see Barber, *Edward*, p. 69.

38 Barber, *Edward*, pp. 80–93.

39 DeVries, *Joan of Arc*, pp. 35–36.

40 On Joan's voices and their message see DeVries, *Joan of Arc*, pp. 38–39. This is largely based on Joan's own trial testimony in *Procès de condamnation*, 1:51–53, 171, and several testimonies of her friends and neighbours in her rehabilitation trial, as found in *Procès en nullité*, 1:253–310.

perform some great military feat to validate the faith the Dauphin had placed in her. Her chance came at Orléans.

Joan joined the French army at Orléans in April 1429. It was a demoralized force, led by Jean, Bastard of Orléans who, only two weeks before, had led his troops to an extremely embarrassing defeat at the battle of the Herrings. The Bastard of Orléans was reluctant to attack the English in their well armed and fortified siegeworks; instead, he wished to retreat from the city and leave it to the English.[41] Joan would have none of this, for her voices had told her that a victory at Orléans must precede the crowning of the Dauphin. A new strategy was undertaken, with the French attacking several of the boulevards surrounding the town. Finally, on 7 May, Joan herself led her soldiers against the most fortified and well armed boulevard held by the English, the boulevard of the Augustins, which had been erected to add protection to the Tourelles.

There was never any question in Joan's mission about her need to relieve the siege of Orléans. This had always been one of her tasks and she had talked unceasingly about it during her time at Vaucouleurs and Chinon. No one would have forgiven her had she shunned it on the morning of 7 May 1429. As for herself, Joan was adamantly opposed to caution and promised to lead the main attack in a direct assault of the fortress. She knew this would be risky; in fact, she prophesied to her confessor that she herself would be wounded.[42] Despite the risks, Joan was certain that she would be supported by her troops in an undertaking for which she felt some urgency.

In the midst of the battle, Joan was wounded, precisely as she had predicted. Yet, this did not stop her from carrying on the battle. Her fellow leader, the Bastard of Orléans, recalled the event as follows:

On May 7, early in the morning, when the attack was beginning against the enemy who were within the boulevard of the bridge [the Tourelles], Joan was wounded by an arrow which penetrated her flesh between her neck and her shoulder, for a depth of half a foot. Nevertheless, her wound not

---

[41] On the Bastard of Orléans at the siege of Orléans see DeVries, *Joan of Arc*, pp. 63–65. For an alternate view see *The Retrial of Joan of Arc*, p. 101 n. 1, where Pernoud defends the Bastard's military leadership at Orléans.

[42] According to the testimony of Pasquerel, in *Procès en nullité*, 1:394–95. Joan also testified (in *Procès de condamnation*, 1:79) that she knew that she would be wounded in the attack on the Tourelles.

restraining her, she did not retreat from the conflict, nor did she take medication for her wound. (my translation)[43]

When other leaders, including the Bastard of Orléans, became fatigued and wished to retreat from the fight to rest until the following day, Joan refused. The Bastard continued his testimony:

> The attack lasted from early morning until the eighth hour of vespers [eight o'clock in the evening], so that there was almost no hope of victory on this day. On account of this, this lord [the Bastard of Orléans] chose to break it off and wanted the army to retreat to the city. And then the Maid came to him and requested that he wait for a little while, and at that time she mounted her horse and retired alone into a vineyard at a distance from the crowd of men. In this vineyard she was in prayer for a space of seven minutes. She returned from that place, immediately took her standard in her hands and placed it on the side of the ditch. And instantly, once she was there, the English became afraid and trembled. The soldiers of the king regained their courage and began to climb [up the ramparts], making an attack on those against the boulevard, not finding any resistance. And then the fortification was taken and the English in it were put to flight. (my translation)[44]

Joan corroborates this testimony when she testified at her own trial that she 'was the first to put her ladder on the boulevard of the Tourelles.'[45]

Joan's military career was far from over. Although it would last less than a year longer, her relieving of the siege of Orléans with the attack of the Tourelles was recognized by both the French and the English as the defining moment in the way the Hundred Years War would fare. John, Duke of Bedford and Regent of England, wrote to his nephew, King Henry VI:

> And all things prospered for you until the time that the siege of Orléans was undertaken . . . At which time . . . by the hand of God, as it seemed, a great offense upon your soldiers who were assembled there in great number, caused to a large party of them . . . by a disciple and follower of the Fiend, called the Pucelle, who used false enchantments and sorcery. This offense and destruction not only lowered by great party the number of your soldiers there, but as well removed the courage of the remnant in a marvellous way,

---

43 Dunois, in *Procès en nullité*, 1:320.
44 Dunois, in *Procès en nullité*, 1:320–21.
45 Joan, in *Procès de condamnation*, 1:79.

and encouraged your opponents and enemies to assemble themselves afterwards in great number. (my translation)[46]

The French were more positive about what had occurred. The Dauphin's secretary, Alain Chartier, writing to an unnamed prince at the end of July 1429, could not help but extol Joan's virtues in raising the siege:

This Maid, whom divine precept burns to satisfy, immediately asked him to give her an army to succour the Orléanais who were then in danger. He [the Dauphin], to whom she showed no fear, at first denied her request, but finally conceded to it. This having been accepted, she took a huge amount of foodstuffs to Orléans. Crossing under the enemy camps, they perceived nothing hostile . . . Leaving the victuals in the city and attacking these camps, which in a way was a miracle, in a short space of time she captured them, especially that which was erected almost in the middle of the bridge [the Tourelles]. It was so strong, so well armed with all types of weapons, and so fortified that, if all people, if all nations fought against it, they could not capture it . . . Here is she who seems not to come from anywhere on earth, who seems to be sent from heaven to sustain with her neck and shoulders a fallen France. She raised the king out of the vast abyss onto the harbour and shore by labouring in storms and tempests, and she lifted up the spirits of the French to a greater hope. By restraining the ferocity of the English, she excited the bravery of the French, she prohibited the ruin of France, and she extinguished the fires of France. O singular virgin, worthy of all glory, worthy of all praise, worthy of divine honours! You are the honour of the reign, you are the light of the lily, you are the beauty, the glory, not only of France, but of all Christendom. (my translation)[47]

Neither side seemed to focus on the fact that she was a woman, or even a teenager.

It would be folly to suggest that the above information proves that either many or few teenagers participated in medieval combat. Because of the scantiness of age-related evidence on medieval soldiers, such a

---

[46] In *Procès de condamnation*, 5:136–37. See also DeVries, *Joan of Arc*, p. 95, and Pernoud, *Joan of Arc*, pp. 100–1. Quicherat dates this letter to the end of July 1429, but Pernoud dates it, in my opinion more accurately, to 1434. If this is correct, it is a particularly interesting document in that it reveals that Bedford, the leader of the English forces in France during this time, believed that the relief of the siege of Orléans was the turning point of this phase of the Hundred Years War.

[47] *Procès de condamnation*, 5:131–36.

suggestion is not defensible. Perhaps more importantly, this discussion reveals that when one encounters what seem to be historical examples of adolescent warriors fighting in the Middle Ages, caution must be followed: were they truly teenagers and, if so, did their youth seem to affect their fighting skills or leadership? Perhaps the only conclusion that can be reached is that in the Middle Ages when teenagers participated in a military engagement if they performed their task well their youth did not seem to matter to their contemporaries.

*Loyola College*
*Baltimore, Maryland*

## Cited Works

Alberic of Troisfontaines, *Chronicon*, ed. Paul Scheffer-Boichorst. Monumenta Germaniae Historica, Scriptores, 23. Hanover: Impensis Bibliopolii Hahniani, 1874.

*Annales Admuntenses*, ed. Wilhelm Wattenbach. Monumenta Germaniae Historica, Scriptores, 9. Hanover: Impensis Bibliopolii Hahniani, 1851.

*Annales Marbacenses*, ed. Hermann Bloch. Monumenta Germaniae Historica, Scriptores Rerum Germanicarum, 9. Hanover: Impensis Bibliopolii Hahniani, 1907.

Arderne, John. *Treatises of Fistula in Ano: Haemorrhoids and Clysters*, ed. D'Arcy Power. Early English Text Series, Original Series, 139. London: Kegan Paul, Trench, Trubner, 1910.

Ariès, Philippe. *L'enfant et la vie familiale sous l'Ancien Régime*, 2nd ed. Paris: Editions du Seuil, 1973.

*Armour from the Battle of Visby, 1361*, ed. Bengt Thordeman. 2 vols. Stockholm: Kungl. vitterhets historie och antikvitets akademien, 1939–40.

Baker, Geoffrey. *Chronicon Galfridi le Baker de Swynebroke*, ed. Edward Maunde Thompson. Oxford: Clarendon Press, 1889.

Barber, Richard. *Edward: Prince of Wales and Aquitaine: A Biography of the Black Prince*. New York: Scribner, 1978.

Boylston, Anthea, Malin Holst, and Jennifer Coughlan, 'Physical Anthropology' pp. 45–59 in *Blood Red Roses: The Archaeology of a Mass Grave from the Battle of Towton, AD 1461*, ed. Veronica Fiorato, Anthea Boylston, and Christopher Knüsel. Oxford: Oxbow, 2000.

*Chronica regia coloniensis*, ed. Georg Waitz. Monumenta Germaniae Historica, Scriptores Rerum Germanicarum, 18. Hanover: Impensis Bibliopolii Hahniani, 1880.

*Chronicon Eberheimense*, ed. Ludwig Weiland. Monumenta Germaniae Historica, Scriptores, 23. Hanover: Impensis Bibliopolii Hahniani, 1874.

Codagnello, Giovanni. *Annales Placentini*, ed. Oswald Holder-Egger. Monumenta Germaniae Historica, Scriptores rerum Germanicarum, 23. Hanover: Impensis Bibliopolii Hahniani, 1901.

DeVries, Kelly. *Infantry Warfare in the Early Fourteenth Century: Discipline, Tactics, and Technology*. Woodbridge, Suffolk/Rochester, NY: Boydell Press, 1996.

DeVries, Kelly. *Joan of Arc: A Military Leader*. Stroud: Sutton, 1999.

Duby, Georges. 'Les pauvres des campagnes dans l'occident médiévale jusqu'au XIIIe siècle' *Revue d'histoire de l'église de France* 52 (1966): 25–32.

*Gesta Treverorum*, ed. Georg Waitz. Monumenta Germaniae Historica, Scriptores Rerum Germanicarum, 24. Hanover: Impensis Bibliopolii Hahniani, 1879.

Gilchrist, John. 'The Erdmann Thesis and the Canon Law, 1083–1141' pp. 37–45 in *Crusade and Settlement: Papers Read at the First Conference of the Society for the Study of the Crusades and the Latin East and Presented to R. C. Smail*, ed. Peter W. Edbury Cardiff: University College Cardiff Press, 1985.

Giraldus Cambrensis (Gerald of Wales). *Opera*, ed. J.S. Brewer. 8 vols. London: Longman & Co., 1861–91.

Ingelmark, Bo Eric. 'The Skeletons' 1:149–210 in *Armour from the Battle of Visby, 1361*, ed. Bengt Thordeman. 2 vols. Stockholm: Kungl. vitterhets historie och antikvitets akademien, 1939–40.

Knüsel, Christopher and Anthea Boylston. 'How Has the Towton Project Contributed to Our Knowledge of Medieval and Later Warfare?' pp. 169–88 in *Blood Red Roses: The Archaeology of a Mass Grave from the Battle of Towton, AD 1461*, ed. Veronica Fiorato, Anthea Boylston, and Christopher Knüsel. Oxford: Oxbow, 2000.

Madden, Thomas F. *A Concise History of the Crusades*. Lanham, MD: Rowman & Littlefield, 1999.

McKern Thomas W. and T.D. Stewart. *Skeletal Age Changes in Young American Males*. Matick, MA: Quartermaster Research and Development Center, 1957.

Miccoli, Giovanni. 'La "crociata dei fanciulli" del 1212' *Studi medievali* 3 (1961): 407–43.

Munro, D.C. 'The Children's Crusade' *American Historical Review* 19 (1913–14): 516–24.

Murimuth, Adam. *Continuatio chronicarum*, ed. Edward Maunde Thompson. London: Eyre and Spottiswoode, 1889.

Panis, Ogerius. *Annales Ianuenses*, ed. Georg Heinrich Pertz. Monumenta Germaniae Historica, Scriptores Rerum Germanicarum, 18. Hanover: Impensis Bibliopolii Hahniani, 1863.

Pfeiffer, Susan. 'Estimation of Age at Death' pp. 167–75 in *Snake Hill: An Investigation of a Military Cemetery from the War of 1812*, ed. Susan Pfeiffer and Ronald F. Williamson. Toronto: Dundurn Press, 1991.

Powell, James M. *Anatomy of a Crusade, 1213–1221.* Philadelphia: University of Pennsylvania Press, 1986.

*Procès de condamnation et de réhabilitation de Jeanne d'Arc, dite la Pucelle*, ed. Jules Quicherat. Société de l'histoire de France. 5 vols. Paris: Jules Renouard, 1841–49.

*Procès en nullité de la condamnation de Jeanne d'Arc*, ed. Pierre Duparc. 5 vols. Paris: C. Klincksieck, 1977–89.

Raedts, Peter. 'The Children's Crusade of 1212' *Journal of Medieval History* 3 (1977): 279–324.

*Récits d'un bourgeois de Valenciennes (XIVe siècle)*, ed. Kervyn de Lettenhove. Louvain: Impr. de P. et J. Lefever, 1877.

Reiner of Liège, *Reineri annales S. Jacobi Leodienses*, ed. Georg Heinrich Pertz. Monumenta Germaniae historica, Scriptores 16. Hanover: Impensis Bibliopolii Hahniani, 1859.

Richardson, Thom. 'The Bridport Muster Roll of 1457' *Royal Armouries Yearbook* 2 (1997): 46–52.

Rogers, Clifford J. 'Edward III and the Dialectics of Strategy, 1327–1360' *Transactions of the Royal Historical Society*, 6th ser., 4 (1994): 83–102.

Sciuli P.W. and R.M. Gramly. 'Analysis of the Fort Laurens, Ohio, Skeletal Sample' *American Journal of Physical Anthropology* 80 (1989): 11–24.

Steegmann, A.T. 'Eighteenth Century British Military Stature: Growth Cessation, Selective Recruiting, Secular Trends, Nutrition at Birth, Cold and Occupation' *Human Biology* 57 (1985): 77–95.

Stroud G. and R. L. Kemp, *Cemeteries of the Church and Priory of St. Andrew, Fishergate.* The Archaeology of York: The Medieval Cemeteries, 12. York: Council for British Archaeology, 1993.

Tallett, Frank. *War and Society in Early-Modern Europe, 1495–1715.* London and New York: Routledge, 1992.

*The Life and Campaigns of the Black Prince, from Contemporary Letters, Diaries and Chronicles, including Chandos Herald's Life of the Black Prince*, ed. and trans. Richard Barber. Woodbridge, Suffolk: Boydell, 1979.

*The Retrial of Joan of Arc: The Evidence at the Trial for Her Rehabilitation*, ed. Régine Pernoud, trans. J. M. Cohen. London and New York: Harcourt, Brace, 1955.

Wrottesley, George. *Crecy and Calais from the Original Records in the Public Records.* London: Harrison & Sons, 1898.

Zacour, Norman. 'The Children's Crusade' 2:325–43 in *A History of the Crusades*, ed. Kenneth Setton. 6 vols. Philadelphia: University of Pennsylvania Press, 1962.

# Sex and the Medieval Adolescent

## Fiona Harris Stoertz

According to *The Book of St. Gilbert*, the serious conflict of adolescence (*grauius adolescentiae certamen*) was lust, for adolescence was 'the age when because the body, which perishes, oppresses the soul, the growing heat of sensual desire consumes mortal hearts to their increasing danger.'[1] Such concerns were not unique. A barrage of comments about the tendency for adolescents to be consumed utterly by lust can be found in French and English sources throughout the eleventh, twelfth, and thirteenth centuries. Bernard Silvestris, for example, in the twelfth century said 'a youth having been snared by passion, does not know "what is beautiful, what is disgraceful, what is useful, what is not."'[2] While this discourse was particularly widespread among monastic authors, it was not limited to them. In the poem 'The Parlement of the Thre Ages' Youthe was characterized as a lover.

> With ladys full louely to lappyn in myn armes,
> And clyp thaym and kysse thaym and comforthe myn hert;
> An than with damesels dere to daunsen in thaire chambirs.[3]

Likewise an Anglo-Norman book of courtesy and nurture warned a youth about the folly of spending all his money on women who would subsequently cast him away.[4]

It can be argued that the high medieval perception of adolescents as slaves to lust, an idea that while present in the early Middle Ages was far less prominent in most writings, was encouraged by such factors as the emergence of monastic and clerical reform movements that sought to raise religious standards and remove children and adolescents from monasteries and clerical positions; increased literacy

---

[1] 'Ille nempe etate, qua iuxta quod corpus corruptibile aggrauat animam, estus feruentior libidinum grauius depascit corda mortalium.' *The Book of St. Gilbert*, p. 14.

[2] 'Non revocant eum turpia preconia fame quia iuventus libidine irretita nescit "quid pulchrum, quid turpe, quid utile, quid non."' *The Commentary on . . . the Aeneid*, p. 24.

[3] *Parlement of the Thre Ages*, 6:246–49.

[4] Parsons, 'Anglo-Norman Books of Courtesy,' p. 394.

enabling people to read newly retrieved classical literature in which
the image of the lustful adolescent was a common feature; and the
growth of towns and trade, which provided new vocational opportunities
for young people and centers in which schools could grow.

The question I want to examine, however, is not so much why this
image of the adolescent governed by irresistible desires became so
prominent in the high Middle Ages—that is a question that I am
currently pursuing in a much larger context—but rather how this
widespread perception affected the treatment and experience of real
adolescents. Specifically I wish to look at four major groups: monks,
royalty and nobles, apprentices, and university students.

I will argue that monasteries in this period developed a harsh
approach to adolescence, attempting to suppress adolescent sexuality
by constant vigilance, careful training, symbolic and actual segregation
of adolescents from adult monks, and ultimately exclusion from many
orders. Reactions to royal and aristocratic sexuality were far more
ambivalent. While some writers of advice literature recommended
abstinence for both male and female adolescents, courtly literature
often celebrated premarital sexual activity between young couples. In
reality, aristocratic young men seem to have been expected to be
sexually active, and those who preferred to remain chaste could be a
source of grave concern to their families. Excessive sexual activity, on
the other hand, was considered potentially fatal and 'unnatural' sexual
acts were condemned by some authors. Aristocratic young women, in
contrast, considered to be as lustful as their male counterparts, were
supposed to be kept chaste through careful vigilance and early marriage. Consummation of a marriage, however, might be delayed if the
bride was too young, for excessively early conception was sometimes
deemed dangerous to both mother and child. The manifold sexual
transgressions of adolescent apprentices and university students were
a concern to urban authorities, yet young males in these groups were
discouraged from marrying early. University students, despite their
clerical status, arguably enjoyed more freedom than their apprentice
contemporaries, since the position of apprentices under the moral
supervision of a master probably limited their sexual freedom to some
degree.

The notion of adolescence as an age of lust was widespread in
Greco-Roman literature.[5] Ptolemy, in the second century CE, discuss-

<hr>

5 On this topic see Eyben, *Restless Youth in Ancient Rome* and Rouselle, *Porneia.*

ing a model of the stages of life based on planetary influences, claimed that individuals between fourteen and twenty-two were governed by the planet Venus with the result that 'At this time particularly a kind of frenzy enters the soul, incontinence, desire for any chance sexual gratification, burning passion, guile, and the blindness of the impetuous lover.'[6] These ideas were absorbed by influential Christian writers in the Latin West, such as Jerome (c. 345–419/20) and Augustine (354–430), who both portrayed adolescence as a time when lust was almost irresistible. In a letter to Nepotian, Jerome insisted that 'adolescence . . . has to cope with the assaults of passion and, amid the allurements of vice and the tinglings of the flesh, is stifled like a fire among green boughs, and cannot develop its proper brightness.'[7] Augustine, in his spiritual autobiography, the *Confessions*, gives what is perhaps the most compelling account of adolescent sexual stirrings:

> Once in adolescence, I was inflamed with a desire for a surfeit of inferior things, and dared to run wild with manifold and shady passions, and in your eyes my beauty wasted away and I putrefied, yet I was pleased with myself and wished to please the eyes of men. And what was there that pleased me but to love and be loved? But I loved not in the manner of mind to mind, as on the luminous path of friendship, but filthy lusts of the flesh and the bubblings of puberty were exuded like mist, which clouded over and obscured my heart so that the serenity of true love could not be distinguished from the darkness of lust.[8]

Augustine and John Chrysostom (d. 407) both suggested that the almost impossible feat of keeping adolescents chaste could best be achieved by marrying men off at fifteen when their passions erupted.[9] As

---

6 As cited in Eyben, *Restless Youth*, p. 35.

7 'adulescentia multa corporis bella sustineat, et inter incentiua uitiorum et carnis titillationes, quasi ignis in lignis uiridioribus suffocetur, et suum non possit explicare fulgorem.' Jerome, *Epistulae*, letter 52.3, p. 417.

8 'Exarsi enim aliquando satiari inferis in adulescentia et silvescere ausus sum variis et umbrosis amoribus, et contabuit species mea et conputrui coram oculis tuis placens mihi et placere cupiens oculis hominum. Et quid erat, quod me delectabat, nisi amare et amari? sed non tenebatur modus ab animo usque ad animum, quatenus est luminosus limes amicitiae, sed exhalabantur nebulae de limosa concupiscentia carnis et scatebra pubertatis et obnubilabant atque obfuscabant cor meum, ut non discerneretur serenitas dilectionis a caligine libidinis.' Augustine, *Confessiones*, 2.1–2, p. 29–30.

9 Eyben, *Restless Youth*, p. 26; Augustine, *Confessiones*, 2.2, pp. 30–31. For the

Flandrin has suggested, the decrees of Church councils from the early sixth century likewise imply that young people would find it difficult or impossible to remain chaste.[10]

On the whole, in the early medieval German west, while the propensity of adolescents to sin sexually remained a subtext, it does not appear to have been such an issue of concern. Thus, Caesarius of Arles (c. 469/470–542) in two of his sermons rejected adolescence as an excuse for lack of chastity. When *adulescentes* cried 'We are *iuvenes*, we cannot contain ourselves,' Caesarius told them that their problems arose from eating and drinking too much and being unwilling to control their thoughts and actions.[11] He does not appear to have believed that the young were particularly prone to misdeeds (he himself became a cleric at the age of eighteen), and argued that they were entirely capable of being chaste.[12] Thus, while Caesarius recognized classical ideas about adolescence, he also rejected them. Isidore of Seville (c. 560–636) similarly identified adolescence as an age where boys would be sufficiently grown up to beget offspring, and claimed that the word *adulescentia* was derived from the Latin verb 'to burn,' but did not pursue the negative implications of this idea.[13]

In early medieval monasteries, where literacy and classical traditions were strongest and adolescents abounded thanks to the widespread practice of child oblation, one does find in a few rules some slight concern about adolescent sexuality.[14] For example, Donatus of Besançon (d.c. 660) insisted in his rule for virgins that the beds of adolescent sisters (*adolescentes sorores*) be mixed with those of their elders.[15] Similarly, another seventh-century rule for virgins more explic-

---

development of sexual renunciation as an ideal, see Brown, *The Body and Society* and also, although the work should be read with caution, Pagels, *Adam, Eve, and the Serpent.*

[10] Flandrin, 'Repression and Change,' pp. 29–30.

[11] 'Iuvenes homines sumus, continere nos non valemus.' Caesarius of Arles, *Sermones*, sermon 43.1, 1:189–90. Virtually the same words are used in sermon 44.4, p. 197. The idea that excess food and drink produced excess semen and thus lust was a common one in classical medicine.

[12] Caesarius of Arles, *Sermones*, sermons 43.1 and 44.4, 1:181–90 and 197 respectively. In writing a monastic rule for his sister, Caesarius likewise made no allowances for adolescence.

[13] Isidore, *Medical Writings*, pp. 49–50.

[14] For a more detailed discussion of monastic legislation concerning adolescents, see Stoertz, 'Adolescence and Authority,' pp. 119–40.

[15] Donatus of Besançon, *Regula ad virgines*, ch. 65, p. 293.

itly forbade young women (*iuvenculas*) from sharing a bed, lest their warmth lead them into sin.[16] The sixth-century rule of St. Benedict, which is unusual in including a number of references to adolescents, also includes these rules.[17] Thus these ideas were enshrined in monastic discourse when Benedict's rule was widely adopted in the Carolingian period and beyond. Early commentators such as Smaragdus and Hildemar had little to add to Benedict's advice for adolescence. The tenth century *Regularis concordia*, the earliest surviving English customal, warned monks not to embrace or kiss adolescents or children and requested them to express only spiritual affection for them; this advice, however, appears to be concerned more about protecting young people from sexual predators, than controlling adolescent sexuality itself.[18]

Monastic attitudes towards adolescent sexuality changed dramatically in the eleventh century, particularly at Cluny. The *Liber tramitis*, which is thought to record Cluniac customs in the 1030s and 1040s under Abbot Odilo, subjected adolescents to close supervision by a guardian and limited their association with other young people.[19] Significantly, the rule provided liturgical directions for adolescents, symbolically separating them from children and adult monks, something that had not normally been done in the past.[20] Later eleventh-century Cluniac customals by Bernard of Cluny and Ulrich of Cluny enlarged upon adolescent liturgical rituals, and provided even stricter rules, carefully limiting the contact of adolescents with anyone but their guardians and ensuring that they were always watched. Bernard forbade adolescents from associating with other young people, speak-

---

[16] *Regula cujusdam patris ad uirgines*, ch. 14, p. 1065. Migne identifies this work as being Irish, but it has been suggested that this rule was written by Waldebert of Luxeuil; see McNamara and Halborg, *The Ordeal of Community*, p. 75.

[17] Benedict of Nursia, *Benedicti regula*, ch. 22, p. 78.

[18] *Regularis concordia Anglicae nationis monachorum*, p. 11.

[19] That the customs of Farfa reflect customs under Odilo has been shown by Hourlier, 'St. Odilo's Monastery.' In the rule, a distinction is made between adolescents under custody and those not under custody. For rules restricting adolescents, see *Liber tramitis*, pp. 225, 279; *Consuetudines Farfenses*, pp. 155, 199. Note that the term used to refer to adolescents in this rule is *iuvenes*, a term that in Roman literature was used interchangeably with *adolescentes*, although not in formal models of the stages of life. Although it represents a break from Benedictine tradition, this language would become standard in all future Cluniac rules.

[20] See *Liber Tramitis*, pp. 68, 78, 223, 225; *Consuetudines Farfenses*, 1:43, 51, 154.

ing with them, helping them dress, or even making a sign to them, unless it was about a necessary thing and under the supervision of the guardian who was ordered to sit between them. More mature and trustworthy people could talk to adolescents about necessary and useful things, but always with the guardian listening. If they rose at night, they had to carry a light lest they sin under the cover of darkness.[21] Hugh of Cluny, founding around 1055 the convent of Marcigny for women, forbade the entrance of women under the age of twenty entirely, considering even this to be a lascivious age.[22]

The prestige of Cluny meant that similar rules designed to constrain adolescent sexuality would quickly appear in other customals, such as that of Lanfranc, (d. 1089), Archbishop of Canterbury. Composed in the 1070s, Lanfranc's work was modeled after Bernard's customal, which likewise segregated adolescents from their peers and placed them under continual supervision. Lanfranc's fears of the dangers created by the presence of adolescents led him additionally to forbid even older monks to communicate in any way with adolescents without the permission of the abbot or prior and without the presence of the master sitting between them.[23] That adolescent sexuality was prominent among his concerns is indicated by a 1173 letter to his old student Anselm, the prior of Bec, asking him to give special attention to his young nephew, a monk at Bec:

> Because he is a newcomer to the service of God and at an age when man is lacerated inwardly by many and varied temptations through the suggestions of spirits assailing him, and tormented by many and diverse titillations of the flesh, both inwardly and outwardly . . .[24]

---

[21] Bernard of Cluny, 'Ordo Cluniacensis,' especially ch. 28, pp. 210–12. See also Ulrich of Cluny, *Antiquiores consuetudines Cluniacensis monasterii*, pp. 747–48.

[22] Hugh of Cluny, *Commonitorium ad successores suos*, PL 159, p. 951. See also Hugh of Cluny, *Exhortatio ad sanctimoniales*, pp. 947–50. For discussions on Marcigny, see Hunt, *Cluny under St. Hugh*, pp. 186–94; Thompson, *Women Religious*, pp. 83–93; McNamara, *Sisters in Arms*, pp. 217–20. Ulrich used the same phrase to refer to young monks.

[23] Lanfranc, *Decreta Lanfranci*, 1951, pp. 3, 10, 28, 113, 117–18. Lanfranc rarely separated adolescents liturgically as the Cluniacs did.

[24] 'Sed quia accedens ad seruitutem Dei et maxime id aetatis homo multis uariisque temptationibus per temptatorum spirituum suggestiones intrinsecus laniatur, multis diuersisque carnis titillationibus intus et exterius cruciatur' Lanfranc, *The Letters*, no. 18, pp. 96 and 98.

As the high Middle Ages progressed, in monastic writings adolescence and young manhood would increasingly be portrayed as ages in which it was difficult, if not impossible, to avoid sexual lapses. In the twelfth century Walter Daniel (fl. 1150–70) found it surprising that Aelred of Rievaulx, a novice in his early twenties, was able to resist sin, for he believed this to be an age when the heat of the blood prevented young men from behaving well.[25] Aelred, a Cistercian, himself felt that young monks represented a sexual temptation for older monks and warned mature individuals to be wary of forming spiritual attachments with outstanding youths, since such attachments could insidiously become 'vice-prone.'[26]

While some monastic authorities, like Lanfranc and the Cluniacs, reacted to the perceived dangerous sexuality of adolescent monks by emphasizing their careful training and supervision, more and more orders, such as the Cistercians,[27] Carthusians,[28] Granmontines,[29] and Dominicans[30] began to delay the admission of adolescents until they were eighteen or even twenty, a move that was encouraged by papal decrees in the twelfth and especially the thirteenth century. Pope Gregory IX (r. 1227–41), for example, decreed that the Black Monks should be at least fifteen and then eighteen at profession.[31]

Rules for women sometimes echoed the concerns of male houses about adolescent sexuality. For example, both Aelred's rule for recluses and the early thirteenth-century *Ancren Riwle*, warned that young anchoresses were especially at risk of sexual temptation.[32] Aelred commented that 'never is chastity sought or protected by adolescents without great contrition of heart and torture of the flesh.'[33] However, despite this

---

[25] Daniel, *The Life of Ailred of Rievaulx*, pp. 16–18.

[26] Aelred of Rievaulx, *The Mirror of Charity*, 3.28, pp. 266–67.

[27] The age of entry into the Cistercian order was initially fifteen, but by 1157 it had been raised to eighteen; *Statuta Capitulorum Generalium Ordinis Cisterciensis*, vol. 1, ch. lxxviii, 1134; ch. 16, 1154; and ch. 28, 1157. A very useful study of Cistercian decrees regarding young people is Lynch, 'The Cistercians and Underage Novices.'

[28] Guigo I, *Consuetudines*, ch. xxvii, pp. 691–92.

[29] Stephen of Muret, 'Regula,' ch. xliv, p. 88.

[30] 'From the Ancient Constitutions of the Order of Friars Preachers,' 1.xiv.3 and 1.xv.1, p. 192. This rule was in place by 1238 and probably earlier.

[31] Doran, 'Oblation or Obligation?' pp. 138–40. On papal regulations on age of entry in general see also: Metz, 'L'entré des mineurs,' pp. 195–96; Edwards, 'Canonistic Determinations of the Stages of Childhood.'

[32] *The Ancren Riwle*, pp. 7, 52–54, 424. Various other versions of this rule can be found in the Early English Text Society series.

[33] 'Numquam ab adolescentibus, sine magna cordis contritione et carnis afflictione

fear and the example of Marcigny, most female houses continued to accept girls aged twelve or younger, claiming that it was necessary for purposes of education, and then delayed formal profession for several years. Thus in female monasteries, adolescent sexuality was clearly not a sufficient threat to outweigh the conveniences of enclosure in childhood and adolescence.

Aristocratic attitudes towards adolescent sexuality were far more ambivalent. Courtly romances and courtly poetry often, but not exclusively, focused on the love affairs of the young.[34] In such stories, sexual gratification was often a reward for the brave and reckless daring of young knights, and youthful affairs were not usually condemned unless the woman was married, in which case punishment or suffering sometimes occurred. In this popular literature, the young were clearly expected to be lustful.

Courtly circles, however, were exposed to other theoretical perspectives. Giles of Rome (c. 1243–1316), in his thirteenth-century treatise for King Philip IV of France, suggested that early intercourse was morally dangerous to both men and women because it would make them lecherous. He claimed that 'each person has a great desire and great talent for the thing that they become accustomed to in youth.'[35] In accordance with Greek treatises on medicine, Giles also claimed that young women would have a more difficult time in childbirth and were more likely to die, an idea supported by a miracle of Thomas Becket in the twelfth century that portrayed a knight feeling remorse for his wife's sufferings in childbirth because 'she was not yet of the age that she ought to become a mother.'[36] Giles further suggested that children would be feeble in body and lacking in wit and reason if their parents had not yet achieved their full growth, an idea also advanced by Hildegard of Bingen (1098–1179).[37] Giles recommended that girls

---

castitas conquiritur uel seruatur.' Aelred of Rievaulx, 'De institutione inclusarum,' ch. 17, p. 653.

[34] For the close association between youth and love in troubadour poetry, see Denomy, 'Jovens,' pp. 4–6. For youths and French romans, see the article by Marion Rothstein in this volume.

[35] 'For eche persoun hath greet desire and greet talent to thyng that he vseth in greet youthe.' Giles of Rome, The Governance of Kings and Princes, bk. 2, pt. 1, ch. 16, p. 195.

[36] Materials for the History of Thomas Becket, 1:469–70.

[37] Cited in Amundsen and Diers, 'The Age of Menarche,' p. 365.

be at least eighteen and boys twenty-one before they begin having sexual relations.[38]

In reality, it generally seems to have been taken for granted that royal and aristocratic young men would be sexually active. The mistress of William Clito, for example, was mentioned without condemnation.[39] Only rarely were adolescents criticized for lack of chastity in the chronicles. William of Roumare, given to too much lust in his *adolescentia*, was divinely punished by an illness that caused him to mend his ways.[40] The chronicler of the house of Amboise did comment that Lisois lived to a great age because he was chaste in adolescence, something which the chronicler implied was unusual.[41]

Elites sometimes displayed concern when a youth did not engage in sexual adventures. William the Conqueror's chastity *in prima adolescentia* was so unexpected for his contemporaries that he was considered impotent, a serious flaw in the ruler of a duchy.[42] The story of Malcolm, King of Scotland (1153–65), who succeeded to the throne, *adhuc impuberem*, suggests that sexual activity was considered to be a normal part of adolescent development.[43] As Malcolm entered puberty (*pubertatis*), men tried to entice him to experience the pleasures of the flesh, but he insisted on remaining celibate. His mother, somewhat alarmed at this, advised him that he was a king, not a monk, and that the embraces of girls were appropriate to his age and physical development (*aetati et corpori eius*). He feigned agreement and she sent a beautiful, nobly born virgin (*virginem*) to sleep with him. Malcolm, however, gave up his bed to the virgin and slept on the floor wrapped in his cloak.[44] In telling the story, William of Newburgh (c. 1136–98?) commented that 'We should prefer the miracle of the young king's virginity, thus besieged but impregnable, not only to giving sight to the blind, but even to raising the dead.'[45] While chaste saints were

---

[38] Giles of Rome, *The Governance of Kings and Princes*, bk. 2, pt. 1, ch. 16, p. 196.

[39] Orderic Vitalis, *Ecclesiastical History*, 12:374. The young woman warned William of a plot against him as she was washing his hair, 'as was her custom.' As a reward, the woman was sent in the care of an abbot to a fellow knight whom William instructed to find an honourable marriage for the woman.

[40] Orderic Vitalis, *Ecclesiastical History*, 12:380.

[41] Duby, *The Knight, the Lady, and the Priest*, p. 247.

[42] William of Malmesbury, *De gestis regum Anglorum*, 2:331.

[43] William of Newburgh, *The History of English Affairs*, p. 100.

[44] William of Newburgh, *The History of English Affairs*, p. 108.

[45] 'Plane ego illud in rege iuvenculo sic impugnatae sed inexpugnatae integritatis

admired in the high Middle Ages, youthful sexual activity proved a young man to be a fully functional male, able to produce offspring.

While premarital sex was sometimes accepted and even encouraged for young men, chroniclers did not approve of young men who engaged in what theologians defined as 'unnatural' acts. Eadmer, Orderic Vitalis, and William of Malmesbury all condemned the behaviour of the dissolute court of William II, King of England, claiming that the courtiers, particularly the young men, were given to unrestrained debauchery and sodomy, a term which at this time could refer to a wide range of non-procreative acts. The court, again particularly the young, was also given to extremes of fashion, including a mincing gait; long hair, sometimes shaved in the front and curled; short beards; long tight shirts and tunics; and shoes with long curved points, all of which tended to symbolically reinforce their sexual transgressions.[46]

In contrast, elite girls were watched carefully to preserve their chastity, something emphasized by the interchangeable use of the terms *virgines* and *puellae* to describe all unmarried elite girls. Young women, like young men, were thought to be rather foolish and inclined to lust, but they were allowed less license. Most educational theorists urged close supervision, since girls possessed weaker intellects than boys and thus easily fell into sin.[47] Giles of Rome insisted that it was most important that girls be continent, chaste, abstinent, and sober. To achieve this, he urged they be kept from straying and running about so that they might remain shamefast and chaste. He also urged that they be taught to be silent and submissive so that their marriages would be happy.[48] Vincent of Beauvais (d.c. 1264), too, recommended that girls be taught good morals and manners, especially chastity, modesty, humility, and silence, claiming that lust became a great danger once

---

miraculum praeferendum censeo non solum illuminationi caecorum sed etiam suscitationi mortuorum.' William of Newburgh, *The History of English Affairs*, p. 110. For another case where good behaviour was a matter of surprise, see Orderic Vitalis, *The Ecclesiastical History*, 10:298.

[46] Eadmer, *History of Recent Events in England*, p. 49; William of Malmesbury, *De gestis regum Anglorum*, 2:369–70; Orderic Vitalis, *Ecclesiastical History*, 7:186–90. Around the time of the first crusade, long hair had been banned upon threat of excommunication. See Orderic Vitalis, *Ecclesiastical History*, 9:22.

[47] Shahar, *Childhood in the Middle Ages*, pp. 174–75; Stoertz, 'Young Women in France and England,' pp. 22–46.

[48] Giles of Rome, *The Governance of Kings and Princes*, bk. 2, pt. 2, ch. 19–21, pp. 245–49.

girls reached the nubile age, and they must be kept at home to protect their chastity.[49] On the whole, young girls had little personal freedom. Orderic Vitalis (d.c. 1142) commented that monks lived peacefully in enclosed cloisters, like the daughters of kings.[50] In the castle of the counts of Guines, separate wings were reserved for adolescent boys and adolescent girls, but whereas the girls were expected to sleep in their wing nightly, the boys could come and go as they pleased.[51] In the law code attributed to Ranulf de Glanville (d. 1190), heiresses in wardship guilty of sexual incontinence were to be disinherited.[52]

In some sense it is not entirely appropriate to discuss adolescent sexuality for elite girls, since they are so rarely called adolescents in the sources and since a very large proportion of royal girls were married near the minimum age of twelve and thus may not have reached menarche— that is, be capable of conception—before marriage.[53] How does this accord with the advice of Giles of Rome? John Parsons has argued convincingly that in the case of young marriages noble English families between 1150 and 1500 sometimes delayed regular cohabitation until the later teens, though marriages may have been consummated immediately because of the idea, increasingly important in canon law, that consummation as well as consent was necessary for a valid marriage.[54] This is supported both by the marked tendency of most English and French queens to bear children only in their late teens or early twenties,[55] although contemporaries estimated that menarche usually

---

[49] Gabriel, *The Educational Idea of Vincent of Beauvais*, pp. 40–44.

[50] Orderic Vitalis, *Ecclesiastical History*, 8:320.

[51] Shahar, *Childhood in the Middle Ages*, p. 221.

[52] Glanville, *Treatise . . . Commonly Called Glanvill*, 7:12.

[53] These include Matilda, daughter of Henry I of England; Matilda, wife of William, son of the same Henry I; Joanna and Matilda, daughters of Henry II of England; Blanche of Castile, wife of Louis VIII of France; Eleanor of Castile, wife of Edward I of England; Isabel of Angoulême, wife of John of England; Joan, daughter of the same John; Eleanor of Provence, wife of Henry III of England; Margaret, daughter of the same Henry III; and Jeanne of Champagne, wife of Philip IV of France.

[54] Parsons, 'Mothers, Daughters, Marriage, Power,' pp. 66–68.

[55] Matilda, daughter of Henry I, bore no children to Emperor Henry V. Isabel of Angoulême bore her first child seven years after her marriage to John. Eleanor of Castile's first documented child was born at least seven years after her marriage to Edward I (although Parsons speculates on an earlier pregnancy resulting from early consummation). Margaret, daughter of Henry III of England had her first child at

began between the ages of twelve and fifteen,[56] and by a number of cases where we know that regular relations were delayed for an extended period, as happened, for example, in the case of two daughters of Edward I of England; Eleanor daughter of Henry II of England; Margaret daughter of Henry III of England; Aveline de Forz, wife of Edmund, son of Henry III; and Sibyl, wife of Robert Curthose duke of Normandy.[57] Occasional fears that young brides might be barren, as in the case of Eleanor of Provence, wife of Edward I of England, and her sister Marguerite, wife of Louis IX of France, however, suggest that this practice was not universal.[58]

The position of adolescent apprentices was likewise somewhat ambiguous. Lengthy apprenticeship contracts often left male apprentices

---

twenty. Eleanor of Aquitaine miscarried shortly after her marriage to Louis VII of France, suggesting immediate consummation, and gave birth to her first daughter only after eight years of marriage when she was approximately twenty-three. Adele, Louis VII's third wife, gave birth to an heir after five years of marriage at about twenty years of age. Blanche of Castile, wife of Louis VIII of France, had her first child, stillborn, at the age of seventeen after five years of marriage. Marguerite of Provence, wife of Louis IX of France, was childless for six years. I have not discovered when Louis, the first son of Isabella of Aragon and Philip III of France, was born, but their second child Philip was born after six years of marriage. Jeanne of Champagne, wife of Philip IV of France, bore an heir only after five years of marriage. Exceptions to this pattern are Constance of Castile, second wife of Louis VII of France, and Marie of Brabant, second wife of Philip III of France, neither of whose ages I have been able to determine, but both of whom had children soon after they were married.

[56] For discussions of menstruation in the Middle Ages see: Amundsen and Diers, 'The Age of Menarche,' pp. 363–69; Wood, 'The Doctors' Dilemma'; Bullough and Campbell, 'Female Longevity and Diet in the Middle Ages'; Post, 'Ages at Menarche and Menopause.' The relatively low ages of first menstruation found by medieval scholars have proven confusing in the face of the work of J.M. Tanner who, in his *Growth at Adolescence*, claimed that the age of first menstruation declined from age 17.5 only in the 1830s. Laslett provides a useful solution to this problem by pointing out that Tanner's figures were based on Finnish and Norwegian data; in the U.S.A., France, and England the situation was different, as he himself discovered—there, in the nineteenth century the average ages of first menstruation were 14 or 15. Thus, he suggests, the medieval data makes sense; 'Age at Menarche in Europe,' p. 30.

[57] Most of these examples are those of Parsons, 'Mothers, Daughters, Marriage, Power.' For Sibyl, see Orderic Vitalis, *Ecclesiastical History*, 10:278 and 300.

[58] Eleanor of Provence was fifteen and had been married two years. Matthew Paris, *Chronica Majora*, 3:340; Parsons, *Eleanor of Castile*, p. 20.

with the choice between celibacy or consorting with prostitutes or concubines. Although some male apprentices did marry, many contracts contained clauses explicitly forbidding them marriage. The difficulties imposed by apprentice marriages are shown by such adjustments for married apprentices as payments in lieu of three meals per day.[59] Most masters would not be willing to have one or more extra people join the household, so they insisted that their male apprentices remain single. Yet, the imposition of such sexual restrictions on members of the age group characterized as most libidinous by medieval schemes of the stages of life must have created tensions within household and workshop. These tensions were heightened by the fact that guilds and contracts often ordered masters to oversee their apprentices' morals and to care for them like their own sons or like bourgeois children.[60] Masters attempted to restrain the tendency of apprentices to gamble, drink, stay out nights, and frequent prostitutes through restrictions in contracts and statutes, but such behaviour appears to have been a frequent problem. For example, in 1392 an apothecary complained that his apprentice left the house nightly (leaving the master's door open) to be with his concubine upon whom he had lavished £20 of his master's money.[61] Rossiaud linked such tensions to the relative acceptance of gang rape and prostitution in late medieval society.[62]

In contrast to male contracts, some women's apprenticeship contracts centred around marriage. They called for payment of a dowry or termination of the apprenticeship upon marriage, thus reflecting the temporary role that servanthood and apprenticeship tended to play in the female life cycle.[63] Still, not all female apprentices would have married, and it is difficult to judge how much sexual freedom they would have had. Female apprentices, away from the protection of their families, were especially open to sexual misuse. In a 1311 case, a female master was punished for having prostituted her apprentice.[64]

---

[59] Epstein, *Wage Labor and Guilds*, p. 109 and Fagniez, *Études sur l'industrie et la classe industrielle*, p. 64.

[60] See Boileau, *Les métiers*, 50.13; Fagniez, *Études sur l'industrie et la classe industrielle*, pp. 64–65; Epstein, *Wage Labor and Guilds*, pp. 77–78 (for thirteenth-century Tournai).

[61] Hanawalt, *Growing Up in Medieval London*, p. 124. For another example, see pp. 155–56.

[62] Rossiaud, *Medieval Prostitution*, pp. 11–51.

[63] Fagniez, *Études sur l'industrie et la classe industrielle*, p. 74.

[64] Hanawalt, *Growing Up in Medieval London*, p. 122. I have found no examples

Students, although in minor clerical orders and technically celibate, also engaged in a variety of sexual transgressions. Peter of Poitiers attributed their open participation in fornication and other 'unspeakable' sexual vices to their being away from their native land and the scrutiny of family and neighbours.[65] Thus they did things they would never dare to do at home. Masters, who were to a certain extent expected to watch over the morals of their students, condoned or even contributed to this behaviour at least some of the time—Jacques de Vitry (d. 1240) complained of masters who held their schools in rooms above brothels.[66] University officials did sometimes take action against this problem. In 1234, public prostitutes and the concubines of clerks were ordered to leave Oxford within a week upon threat of imprisonment. Many women were in fact imprisoned when they did not leave, but were offered their freedom on the condition that they leave town or, in the case of concubines who owned property, promise to stay away from clerks and to behave 'honestly.'[67] The relative freedom of students, though, and the fact that they were strongly discouraged from marrying, tended to encourage illicit sexual behaviour, something that was openly celebrated in many student songs, such as the Archpoet's Confession:

> Hard beyond all hardness, this
> Mastering of Nature:
> Who shall say his heart is clean,
> Near so fair a creature?
>
> . . .
>
> Young are we, so hard a law,
> How should we obey it?
> And our bodies, they are young,
> Shall they have no say in it?[68]

---

of the sexual abuse of male apprentices.

[65] Ferruolo, *The Origins of the University*, p. 263.

[66] Ferruolo, *The Origins of the University*, p. 264; Baldwin, *Masters, Princes, and Merchants*, p. 133.

[67] *British Borough Charters, 1216–1307*, pp. 373–74.

[68] 'Via lata gradior / more iuventutis / inplico me vitiis / inmemor virtutis / voluptatis avidus / magis quam salutis / mortuus in anima / curam gero cutis. . . . Res est arduissima / vincere naturam / in aspectu viginis / mentem esse puram / iuvenes non possumus / legem sequi duram / leviumque corporum / non habere curam.' Waddell, *The Wandering Scholars*, pp. 168 and 252. The translation is Waddell's.

Thus students perpetuated the idea that the demands of lust were irresistible to the young.

Even though many students openly frequented prostitutes and concubines, other students appear to have directed their violence against those who misbehaved sexually in a kind of 'rough music.' The prostitutes of Paris complained that they were harassed by students who broke into their homes, beat them, tore off their clothes, cut off their hair, and committed other enormities.[69] This may have been a motive in the killing of a clerk who was attacked by unknown clerks lying in wait when he brought a prostitute into a school.[70] Could some of this behaviour be a reaction to condemnations of adolescent lust? It is hard to know.

In this study I have examined how perceptions of adolescent sexuality affected individuals in different social groups. Outside the monasteries it seems that adolescent men enjoyed considerable freedom to indulge their desires, despite various theoretical and actual restrictions. Women, however, did not on the whole enjoy the same freedom. What is left is the question of the extent to which the freedom granted to men was a product of, or a cause of, premodern perceptions of adolescent lust.

*Trent University*
*Peterborough, Ontario*

## Cited Works

Aelred of Rievaulx. *The Mirror of Charity*, trans. Elizabeth Connor. Kalamazoo: Cistercian Publications, 1990.

Aelred of Rievaulx, 'De institutione inclusarum' pp. 635–82 in *Aelred Rievallensis opera omnia*, eds. A. Hoste and C. H. Talbot. Corpus christianorum, continuatio mediaevalis, 1. Turnholt: Brepols, 1971.

Amundsen, Darrel W. and Carol Jean Diers. 'The Age of Menarche in Medieval Europe' *Human Biology* 45 (1973): 363–69.

*The Ancren Riwle*, ed. James Morton. Camden Old Series, 57. New York and London: Johnson Reprint Corporation, 1968; rpt of the 1853 Camden Series edition.

Augustine, *Confessiones*, ed. P. Knöll. Corpus scriptorum ecclesiasticorum latinorum, 33. Vindobonae: F. Tempsky, 1896.

Baldwin, John W. *Masters, Princes, and Merchants: The Social Views of Peter the Chanter and his Circle*. Princeton: Princeton University Press, 1970.

---

[69] Ferruolo, *The Origins of the University*, p. 263.

[70] *Select Cases from the Coroners' Rolls*, pp. 87–88 (22 Dec. 1296).

Benedict of Nursia. *Benedicti regula*, ed. Rudolf Hanslik. Corpus scriptorum ecclesiasticorum latinorum, 75. Vindobonae: Hoelder-Pichler-Tempsky, 1960.

Bernard of Cluny. 'Ordo Cluniacensis per Bernardum' pp. 133–365 in *Vetus Disciplina Monastica*, ed. Marquard Herrgott. Paris: 1726.

Boileau, Étienne. *Les métiers et corporations de la ville de Paris, 13ᵉ siècle. Le livre des métiers*, ed. René Lespinasse and François Bonnardot. Paris: Imprimerie Nationale, 1879.

*The Book of St. Gilbert*, ed. Raymonde Foreville and Gillian Keir. Oxford: Clarendon Press, 1987.

*British Borough Charters, 1216–1307*, ed. Adolphus Ballard and James Tait. Cambridge: Cambridge University Press, 1923.

Brown, Peter. *The Body and Society: Men, Women, and Sexual Renunciation in Early Christianity*. New York: Columbia University Press, 1988.

Bullough, Vern and Cameron Campbell, 'Female Longevity and Diet in the Middle Ages' *Speculum* 55 (1980): 317–25.

Caesarius of Arles, *Sermones*, ed. Germanus Morin, Corpus christianorum, series latina, 103–4. Turnholt: Brepols, 1953. 2 vols.

*The Commentary on the First Six Books of the Aeneid of Virgil Commonly Attributed to Bernardus Silvestris*, ed. Julian Ward Jones and Elizabeth Frances Jones. Lincoln and London: University of Nebraska Press, 1977.

*Consuetudines Farfenses*, ed. Bruno Albers. Consuetudines Monasticae, 1. Stuttgardiae et Vindobonae: Sumptibus Jos. Roth, 1900.

Daniel, Walter. *The Life of Ailred of Rievaulx*, ed. and trans. F.M. Powicke. London: Thomas Nelson and Sons, 1950.

Denomy, A.J. '*Jovens:* The Notion of Youth among the Troubadours, its Meaning and Source' *Mediaeval Studies* 11 (1949): 1–22.

Donatus of Besançon, *Sancti Donati Vesontionensis Episcopi regula ad virgines*. Patrologiae cursus completus, series latina, 87. Ed. J.P. Migne. Paris, 1844–64. Pg. 273–98.

Doran, John. 'Oblation or Obligation? A Canonical Ambiguity' pp. 127–41 in *The Church and Childhood*, ed. Diane Wood. Oxford: Blackwell Publishers, 1994.

Duby, Georges. *The Knight, the Lady, and the Priest: The Making of Modern Marriage in Medieval France*, trans. Barbara Bray. New York: Pantheon Books, 1983.

Eadmer. *History of Recent Events in England: Historia Novorum in Anglia*, ed. and trans. Geoffrey Bosanquet. London: Cresset Press, 1964.

Edwards, Glenn M. 'Canonistic Determinations of the Stages of Childhood' pp. 67–75 in *Aspectus et Affectus: Essays and Editions in Grosseteste and Medieval Intellectual Life in Honor of Richard C. Dales*, ed. Gunar Freibergs. New York: AMS Press, 1993.

Epstein, Steven A. *Wage Labor and Guilds in Medieval Europe*. Chapel Hill and London: University of North Carolina Press, 1991.

Eyben, Emiel. *Restless Youth in Ancient Rome*, trans. Patrick Daly. London and New York: Routledge, 1993.

Fagniez, Gustave. *Études sur l'industrie et la classe industrielle à Paris au XIIIᵉ et au XIVᵉ siècle*. New York: Burt Franklin, 1877.

Ferruolo, Stephen. *The Origins of the University: The Schools of Paris and their Critics, 1100–1215*. Standford: Stanford University Press, 1985.

Flandrin, Jean-Louis. 'Repression and Change in the Sexual Life of Young People in Medieval and Early Modern Times' pp. 3–26 in *Family and Sexuality in French History*, ed. Robert Wheaton and Tamara K. Haraven. Philadelphia: University of Pennsylvania Press, 1980.

'From the Ancient Constitutions of the Order of Friars Preachers' pp. 189–200 in *The Coming of the Friars*, ed. and trans. R.B. Brooke. London: George Allen & Unwin Ltd., 1975.

Gabriel, Astrik L. *The Educational Idea of Vincent of Beauvais*. Notre Dame: Medieval Institute, University of Notre Dame Press, 1956.

Giles of Rome. *The Governance of Kings and Princes: John Trevisa's Middle English Translation of the De regime principum of Aegidius Romanus*, eds. David C. Fowler, Charles F. Briggs, and Paul G. Remley. New York and London: Garland Publishing, 1997.

Glanville, Ranulf de. *The treatise on the Laws and Customs of the Realm of England, Commonly Called Glanvill*, ed. G.D.G. Hall. London: Thomas Nelson and Sons, 1965.

Guigo I. *Guigionis Carthusiae majoris prioris quinti: consuetudines*. Patrologiae cursus completus, series latina, 153. Ed. J.P. Migne. Paris, 1854. Pg. 634–760.

Hanawalt, Barbara. *Growing Up in Medieval London: The Experience of Childhood in History*. Oxford and New York: Oxford University Press, 1993.

Hourlier, Jacques. 'St. Odilo's Monastery' pp. 56–76 in *Cluniac Monasticism in the Central Middle Ages*, ed. Noreen Hunt. Hamden: Archon Books, 1971.

Hugh of Cluny, *Sancti Hugonis commonitorium ad successores suos pro sanctimonialibus Marciniacensibus*. Patrologiae cursus completus, series latina, 159. Ed. J.P. Migne. Paris, 1854. Pg. 949–52.

Hugh of Cluny, *Sancti Hugonis exhortatio ad sanctimoniales apus Marciniacum Deo servientes. Patrologiae cursus completus, series latina, 159. Paris, 1854. Pg. 947–50.*

Hunt, Noreen. *Cluny under St. Hugh, 1049–1109*. London: Edward Arnold, 1967.

Isidore of Seville. *The Medical Writings*, trans. William E. Sharpe. Transactions of the American Philosophical Society, 54. Philadelphia: American Philosophical Society, 1964.

Jerome, *Epistulae*, ed. Isidorus Hilberg. Corpus scriptorum ecclesiasticorum latinorum, 54. Vindobonae: F. Tempsky, 1910.

Lanfranc. *Decreta Lanfranci. Lanfranc's Monastic Constitutions and the Anonymous instructio noviciorum, the Instruction of Novices*, ed. and trans. David Knowles. London: Thomas Nelson and Sons, 1951.

Lanfranc. *The Letters of Lanfranc, Archbishop of Canterbury*, ed. and trans. Helen Clover and Margaret Gibson. Oxford: Clarendon Press, 1979.

Laslett, Peter. 'Age at Menarche in Europe Since the Eighteenth Century' pp. 29–45 in *The Family in History: Interdisciplinary Essays*, ed. Theodore Rabb and Robert I. Rotberg. New York: Harper and Row, 1971.

*Liber tramitis aevi Odilonis abbatis*, ed. Petrus Dinter. Corpus consuetudinum monasticarum, 10. Siegburg: Francis Schmitt Success, 1980.

Lynch, J.H. 'The Cistercians and Underage Novices' *Cîteaux: Commentarii cistercienses* 24 (1973): 283–97.

*Materials for the History of Thomas Becket*, ed. James Craigie Robertson and J.B. Sheppard. Rerum britannicarum medii aevi scriptores, 67. London: Her Majesty's Stationary Office, 1875–85. 7 vols.

McNamara, JoAnn. *Sisters in Arms: Catholic Nuns Through Two Millennia*. Cambridge, MA: Harvard University Press, 1996.

McNamara JoAnn and John E. Halborg, *The Ordeal of Community*. Toronto: Peregrina Publishing Co., 1993.

Metz, René. 'L'entré des mineurs dans la vie religieuse et l'autorité des parents d'après le droit classique' *Studia Gratiana* 20 (1976): 189–200.

Orderic Vitalis. *The Ecclesiastical History of Orderic Vitalis*, ed. and trans. Marjorie Chibnall. Oxford: Clarendon Press, 1969–80. 6 vols.

Pagels, Elaine. *Adam, Eve, and the Serpent*. New York: Random House, 1988.

Paris, Matthew. *Chronica majora*, ed. Henry Richards Luard. Rerum britannicarum medii aevi scriptores, 57. London: Longman, 1872–83.

*The Parlement of the Thre Ages: An Alliterative Poem on the Nine Worthies and the Heroes of Romance*, ed. Israel Gollancz. London: Oxford University Press, 1915.

Parsons, H. Rosamond. 'Anglo-Norman Books of Courtesy and Nurture' *The Publications of the Modern Language Association of America* 44 (1929): 383–455.

Parsons, John Carmi. *Eleanor of Castile: Queen and Society in Thirteenth-Century England*. New York: St. Martin's Press, 1995.

Parsons, John Carmi. 'Mothers, Daughters, Marriage, Power: Some Plantagenet Evidence, 1150–1500' pp. 63–78 in *Medieval Queenship*, ed. John Carmi Parsons. New York: St. Martin's Press, 1993.

Post, J.B. 'Ages at Menarche and Menopause: Some Mediaeval Authorities' *Population Studies* 25 (1971): 83–87.

*Regula cujusdam patris ad uirgines*. Patrologia cursus completus, series latina, 88. Ed. J.P. Migne. Paris, 1862. Pg. 1053–70.

*Regularis concordia Anglicae nationis monachorum sanctimonialiumque or The Monastic Agreement of the Monks and Nuns of the English Nation*, ed. and trans. Thomas Symons. London and New York: Thomas Nelson, 1953.

Rossiaud, Jacques. *Medieval Prostitution*, trans. Lydia C. Cochrane. Oxford and New York: Blackwell, 1988.

Rousselle, Aline. *Porneia: On Desire and the Body in Antiquity*, trans. Felicia Pheasant. Oxford and New York: Basil Blackwell, 1988.

*Select Cases from the Coroners' Rolls, A.D. 1265–1413*, ed. Charles Gross. Publications of the Selden Society, 9. London: Bernard Quaritch, 1896.

Shahar, Shulamith. *Childhood in the Middle Ages*. London and New York: Routledge, 1990.

*Statuta Capitulorum Generalium Ordinis Cisterciensis ab anno 1116 ad annum 1786*, ed. Joseph-Maria Canivez. Louvain: Bureaux de la Revue, 1933–41. 8 vols.

Stephen of Muret. 'Regula venerabilis viri Stephani Murentensis' pp. 63–99 in *Scriptores Ordinis Grandimontensis*, ed. Jean Becquet. Corpus christianorum, continuatio mediaevalis, 8. Turnholt: Brepols, 1968.

Stoertz, Fiona Harris. 'Adolescence and Authority in Medieval Monasticism' pp. 119–40 in *The Growth of Authority in the Medieval West*, eds. M. Gosman, A.J. Vanderjagt, and J.R. Veenstra. Groningen: Egbert Forsten, 1999.

Stoertz, Fiona Harris. 'Young Women in France and England, 1050–1300,' *Journal of Women's History* 12 (2001): 22–46.

Tanner, James Mourilyan. *Growth at Adolescence, with a General Consideration of the Effects of Hereditary and Environmental Factors Upon Growth and Maturation from Birth to Maturity*, Oxford: Blackwell Scientific Publications, 1964.

Thompson, Sally. *Women Religious: The Founding of English Nunneries after the Norman Conquest*. Oxford: Clarendon, 1991.

Ulrich of Cluny. *Antiquiores consuetudines Cluniacensis monasterii collectore Udalrico monacho Benedictino*. Patrologia cursus completus, series latina, 49. Ed. J.P. Migne. Paris, 1858. Pp. 634–778.

Waddell, Helen. *The Wandering Scholars: The Life and Art of the Lyric Poets of the Latin Middle Ages*. Garden City, NY: Doubleday & Company, 1961.

William of Malmesbury, *De gestis regum Anglorum*, ed. W. Stubbs. Rerum britannicarum medii aevi scriptores, 90. London: Printed for Her Majesty's Stationary Office by Eyre and Spottiswoode, 1887–89. 2 vols.

William of Newburgh, *The History of English Affairs*, ed. and trans. P. G. Walsh and M. J. Kennedy. Warminster: Aris, 1988.

Wood, Charles T. 'The Doctors' Dilemma: Sin, Salvation, and the Menstrual Cycle in Medieval Thought' *Speculum* 56 (1981): 710–27.

# 'Like One That Fears Robbing':
# Cuckoldry Anxiety and The Two Gentlemen of Verona

## Philip D. Collington

*The Two Gentlemen of Verona* features two of Shakespeare's youngest and most immature romantic leads, Valentine and Proteus.[1] When Valentine falls in love, his servant Speed includes on a list of behavioural traits adopted by his master, 'you have learned . . . to watch, like one that fears robbing.'[2] Indeed, Valentine spends much of his sojourn in the play's Milan not so much pursuing his beloved Silvia as guarding her from a bevy of rival suitors, including initially Sir Thurio and later Proteus himself. Valentine's 'fear' of robbing seems to contradict one axiom concerning male sexual anxiety as stated by Coppélia Kahn two decades ago: 'Cuckoldry is something that happens to husbands . . . because they are husbands. A man whose mistress is unfaithful does not become a cuckold.' Technically, Kahn is correct: unmarried Valentine cannot be cuckolded.[3] So why does this fact not prevent him from worrying about the humiliation of losing a loved-one to a sexual rival—in other words, from behaving like a jealous husband? And why does this courtship comedy featuring teenage protagonists nonetheless include jokes such as Speed's comment about his master, 'my horns are his horns' and his subsequent warning to Proteus that the latter should guard his own 'laced mutton,' Julia, lest she promiscuously stray (1.1.79–97)?[4]

---

[1] William E. Stephenson reminds us that 'no other work by Shakespeare shows us protagonists quite so immature'('The Adolescent Dream-World,' p. 165). One recent editor likens the two to 'sophomores,' about sixteen years old (Schlueter, Introduction to Shakespeare, *The Two Gentlemen of Verona*, New Cambridge edition, p. 5).

[2] Shakespeare, *The Two Gentlemen of Verona*, 2.1.17–24. All quotations from the plays are taken from the Arden Shakespeare editions and will be cited parenthetically in my text.

[3] Kahn, *Man's Estate*, p. 120; see the *OED* definition of cuckold, 'A derisive name for the husband of an unfaithful wife' (sb. 1).

[4] 'Mutton' was slang for whore, according to Leech's gloss to the Arden edition of Shakespeare, *The Two Gentlemen of Verona*, p. 8 (note to 1.1.96).

In what follows, I will outline processes by which early modern adolescent males were acculturated into the lore of cuckoldry and the accompanying suspicion of women. Drawing on recent studies of the social history of youth, representative broadside ballads, and using lovelorn Valentine and Proteus as examples, I will demonstrate that the sexual precocity of youth in this period was accompanied by the premature onset of anxieties that would plague males right through their life-span. In her recent study of the processes by which early modern males constructed, asserted, and sometimes lost their manhood, Elizabeth Foyster observes that since patriarchal masculinity was largely contingent upon the ability of males to control female sexuality, bachelors too were hyper-sensitive about the loss of face before peers that accompanied a loved-one's perceived uncooperativeness: 'Men's need to prove themselves sexually competent before marriage, and the sensitivity about sexual reputation at this stage in their life cycle, is shown by their reaction to rejection during courtship.' Such a reaction could entail insulting the loved-one, challenging the rival, and even harming the self.[5] Shakespeare's play suggests that misogyny and aggression were less assertions of male prerogative than admissions of the contingency and insecurity of the self, a view that is supported by other historicizing studies of English masculinity.[6] The play's explicit thematic concern—'were man/ But constant, he were perfect' (5.4.109–10)—has long overshadowed the underlying preoccupation of its bachelors with *female* constancy.[7]

It is significant that Speed observes that his master has 'learned' to watch like one that fears robbing. That early modern men were not innately suspicious, but were acculturated to suspect female fidelity is not in dispute. However, I believe that young male playgoers vicariously enjoying Valentine's first experience in love likely understood that he would have learned to watch, not upon arrival in Milan in the play's second act, but like them from a much, much earlier age. Sir Keith Thomas argues that early modern youngsters inhabited a distinctive 'subculture . . . a separate society with its own system of order and classification, its own perceptions and values' that were inconsistent

---

[5] Foyster, *Manhood in Early Modern England*, pp. 44–45.

[6] See Breitenberg, *Anxious Masculinity in Early Modern England*; Fletcher, *Gender, Sex and Subordination in England 1500–1800*; and Smith, *Shakespeare and Masculinity*.

[7] On male inconstancy in the play, see Ewbank, '"Were Man But Constant He Were Perfect,"' pp. 91–114.

with those of the adult dominant culture.[8] Yet, Shakespeare's teenagers seem to inhabit simultaneously Thomas's recovered world of childish roughhousing and anarchistic pranks and a more 'grown-up' world of self-conscious sexual bravado and its concomitant suspicion of women. As Ilana Krausman Ben-Amos observes, 'most youths had few values that truly distinguished them from adults.'[9] In other words, the years Valentine has spent playing the 'idle truant' (2.4.59) nonetheless likely included exposure to the adult lore of love, courtship, cuckoldry, and jealousy.

One example: while departing for Milan Valentine teases his love-lorn friend Proteus for reading 'some shallow story of deep love, / How young Leander cross'd the Hellespont' (1.1.21–22). Clifford Leech's gloss points to the possible allusion to the Hero and Leander made famous in Marlowe's poem, but we need not confine our search to such literary sources. These were popular figures in a range of printed ephemera consumed by young lovers, such as in one very a propos broadside ballad, *The Constant Lover*, that advises young men how to stay loyal to their loves during prolonged separations: 'I, to her, will be like Leander / if Hero-like shee'le prove to me.' Like Shakespeare's play, this ballad is ostensibly concerned with male fidelity, yet, like the play, it also expresses urgent concerns that she, too, remain faithful during his absence: '[I] wish that she as true may be, / as I to her will constant proue.'[10] Thus, when Valentine describes his friend by saying 'His years but young, but his experience old; / His head unmellow'd, but his judgment ripe' (2.4.64–65), his words confirm the existence of significant overlap between the concerns of the two ages. Teenagers did not 'grow up' quickly and acquire adult concerns about love; rather, such concerns were inculcated in them from the earliest age.[11]

That Valentine is always already worried is suggested by his cynical description of the lengths to which rival males might go to steal away a lady. In a comic exchange in which the duke of Milan uncovers Valentine's plot to elope with his daughter, the duke pretends to love

---

[8] Thomas, 'Children in Early Modern England,' p. 51.

[9] Ben-Amos, *Adolescence and Youth*, p. 205.

[10] Shakespeare, *The Two Gentlemen of Verona*, ed. Leech, p. 4 (note to 1.1.22). The ballad, *The Constant Lover, Who his affection will not move, Though he live not where he love* by L[awrence] P[rice] is reprinted in *Roxburghe Ballads*, 1:213–16 (vv. 49–50, 93–94).

[11] On the precocity of teenagers in other areas of life, see Ben-Amos, *Adolescence and Youth*, pp. 67–68 and *passim*.

a woman and asks for advice on how to overcome various obstacles
to his attainment of her:

> DUKE. . . . she I mean is promis'd by her friends
>     Unto a youthful gentleman of worth,
>     And kept severely from resort of men,
>     That no man hath access by day to her.
> VALENTINE. Why, then I would resort to her by night.
> DUKE. Ay, but the doors be lock'd, and keys kept safe,
>     That no man hath recourse to her by night.
> VALENTINE. What lets but one may enter at her window?
>                                        (3.1.106–13)

While Valentine's lesson results in the duke's discovery of the rope
ladder concealed beneath his tutor's cloak, the lesson also reveals the
ruthlessness of this callow teen; that is, even though the duke's hypo-
thetical lady is betrothed to a 'youthful gentleman of worth,' no
precontract is binding enough, no father's lock secure enough, no
chamber window high enough to protect her from a marauding rival
intent on seduction.

Popular analogues to Valentine's fabliau-esque scenario suggest the
extent to which broadside ballads provided an inexhaustible source of
warnings and advice to lovelorn bachelors. According to Anthony
Fletcher, ballads prescribed for youthful auditors 'tactics and strategies
for the performance of the male gender role,' including in matters such
as courtship and marriage.[12] For instance, in the comic collection of
variations on the number three, *Choice of Inuentions*, seduction and
abduction are among the 'tactics' recommended to young listeners:

> There was a Lasse had three Louers,
>     the one of them a Taylor,
> The second was a monied man,
>     the third a Iouiall Saylor:
> The Taylor gaue his Loue a Gowne,
>     in loue and kinde good will;
> The Vsurer, with his money-bags,
>     her purse did often fill;
> The Saylor in the Euening came
>     vnto his heart's delight,

---

[12] Fletcher, *Gender, Sex and Subordination*, p. 105. On the saturation of popular
culture with ballads, see Smith, *The Acoustic World of Early Modern England*, pp.
168–205.

> And brauely carried the wench away,
>     the childe and all, by night.[13]

Out of this trio of suitors, one can imagine Sir Thurio as the wealthy usurer, Proteus as the gift-giving tailor, and Valentine as the more resourceful sailor. Presumably the unborn child is the sailor's own, as another lesson reiterated *ad nauseam* in ballads was quite simple: 'Above everything else . . . avoid being made a cuckold.'[14]

The corollary to Valentine's cynical lesson to the duke on how a lady may be stolen is that Valentine's own lady may be stolen, resulting in the insupportable humiliation of being made the butt of jokes. 'Let every man who keepes a bride / take heed hee be not hornify'd,' warns the husband in another ballad with the ominous title *Cuckold's Haven, Or, The married man's misery.* Furthermore, stealing away a lady may set a kind of precedent in the ensuing relationship, prompting ladies 'stolen' during courtship later to take matters into their own hands and engage in a little subterfuge of their own:

> They haue so many wayes
>     by nights or else by dayes,
> That though our wealth decayes,
>     yet they our hornes will raise.[15]

Shakespeare alludes to youths being informed of just this sort of outcome in *Romeo and Juliet*, where Friar Lawrence excoriates Romeo for abandoning Rosaline in favour of Juliet by invoking the spectre of female infidelity in a maxim about setting precedents in love: 'art thou chang'd? Pronounce this sentence then: / Women may fall when there's no strength in men' (2.3.75–76). In other words, were man but constant, she were perfect. Valentine's familiarity with assertive male activities (secret assignations, midnight escapes, sexual escapades) and the corresponding potential female ones (disobedience, promiscuity, infidelity) is not surprising, therefore, given the prevalence of

---

[13] Anon., *Choice of Inuentions, or Seuerall sorts of the figure of three*, in *Roxburghe Ballads*, 1:105–10 (vv. 80–91). Opie and Opie reproduce the recto side of this ballad in *The Oxford Dictionary of Nursery Rhymes* because it 'contains lines still remembered in the nursery' (plate XXII, facing page 422).

[14] Fletcher, *Gender, Sex and Subordination*, p. 103.

[15] M[artin] P[arker], *Cuckold's Haven*, in *Roxburghe Ballads* 1:148–53 (vv. 5–6, 19–22).

such motifs in the popular culture early modern adults shared with teenagers and even younger children.

*   *   *

*The Two Gentlemen of Verona* is a coming-of-age play which demonstrates how a wealthy Renaissance family—to borrow Edmund Spenser's phrase—might fashion their adolescent son into 'a gentleman or noble person in vertuous and gentle discipline.'[16] Paul Griffiths points out early modern youth was understood to be 'a time of dependency and socialization; [a] preparation for adulthood' during which boys, teenagers, and young men gradually consolidated a gender identity which would not reach completion until marriage. Before marriage—that 'point of departure' from puerility to social and sexual maturity—youths of all social classes enjoyed a prolonged cultural immersion in songs, games, literature, and folklore that outlined the responsibilities, benefits, and potential pitfalls that awaited them at the altar.[17]

The process of acculturation began as early as the nursery, where mothers, wet-nurses, and other caregivers sang songs to the infants and children under their care. Nursery rhymes represented many boys' first exposure to poetry and to cuckold lore, particularly since many of these stemmed from street ballads not necessarily designed for children's ears. As John H. Long observes, the Elizabethan populace was 'nurtured . . . in the ballad tradition.'[18] In a much-cited episode in Jonson's *Bartholomew Fair*, Nightingale is shadowed by a local justice intent on protecting a youth both from this ballad-peddlar's 'debauch'd company' and from that 'terrible taint, poetry, with which idle disease if he be infected there's no hope.' Among the gathering crowd, two avid ballad collectors marvel at the lewd woodcuts adorning Nightingale's wares: 'O sister, do you remember the ballads over the nursery chimney at home o' my own pasting up? There be brave pictures. Other manner of pictures, than these, friend.'[19] While Jonson's characters may be careful not to include lewd ballads in their

<hr/>

16 Spenser's Letter to Ralegh, in *The Faerie Queen*, p. 15, italics omitted.

17 Griffiths, *Youth and Authority*, pp. 27–28.

18 Long, *Shakespeare's Use of Music*, p. 53. On the origins of nursery rhymes in adult street ballads, see Immel's doctoral dissertation '"Little Rhymes, Little Jingle, Little Chimes,"' pp. 39–40 and *passim*; and the introduction to Opie and Opie's *Oxford Dictionary of Nursery Rhymes* (especially pp. 3–4, 19–22).

19 Jonson, *Bartholomew Fair*, Revels edition, 3.5, lines 2–7, 45–47.

nursery decorations, the 'taint' of adult songs did infiltrate other nurseries in the form of taunts similar to that still-popular rhyme concerning Peter the Pumpkin eater and the wife he couldn't keep.[20]

Nursery rhymes preserved in miniature stock figures and episodes found in more adult-oriented ballads, merry tales, and stage plays: jealous husbands, lusty wives, mocking neighbours. One rhyme rarely heard in its unexpurgated form after the eighteenth century mocks: 'Blackamoor, Tawnymoor, suck a bubby / Your father's a cuckold, your mother told me.'[21] The anonymous seventeenth-century ballad *The Country-man's Lamentation for the Death of his Cow* describes the many uses to which the carcass could be put: the Tanner buys the hide, the Chandler buys the tallow, the Butcher buys the meat, the Huntsman buys the horn, and so forth. The song's repetitive structure is reminiscent of familiar nursery rhymes about repairing London bridge or building Jack's house, and the whole song builds to the farmer's punch-line in the last stanza: 'Some say I'm a cuckold, but I'le swear I am none, / For how can it be, now my horns are gone?' To emphasize this point, the printed song is accompanied by woodcut illustrations depicting a man being gored by a bull and a troop of soldiers following their 'Ambassador,' a cuckoo.[22] One last rhyme prepares children for the camaraderie that awaits them at the pub when they're older:

We are all a dry,
With drinking on't;
We are all a dry,
With drinking on't;
The Piper kissed
The Fiddler's Wife,
And I can't sleep
For thinking on't.[23]

---

[20] For a useful collection of excerpts from moralizing and literary documents related to ballads, see Würzbach's Appendix to *The Rise of the English Street Ballad 1550–1650*, pp. 253–84; for example, Jonson's scene is quoted extensively on pp. 265–69.

[21] Quoted in its unexpurgated form in Immel, '"Little Rhymes, Little Jingle, Little Chimes,"' p. 164. Bowdlerized versions can be found in Baring-Gould and Baring-Gould, *The Annotated Mother Goose*, pp. 35–36 (rhyme n. 19 and note 44).

[22] Both animals, of course, are symbols of cuckoldry. The ballad is reprinted in *Roxburghe Ballads*, 3:601–3 (vv. 40–41).

[23] Cited in Baring-Gould and Baring-Gould, *The Annotated Mother Goose*, p. 37

A more indelicate version of such bar-room jests about local cuckold-triangles can be found in *An excellent new Medley*:

> The cuckow sung hard by the doore,
> Gyll brawled like a butter-whore,
> Cause her buckeheaded Husband swore
>     the Miller was a knave.[24]

In his important early essay about ballads, Hyder E. Rollins cites contemporary references to children 'hoot[ing] at' the misfortunes of adults, such as one educator who 'found himself flouted with ballads sung through the streets by boys and young children.'[25] After the laughter dies down, the sleepless speaker in the first poem (and children exposed to such rhymes) may have been struck by the sobering realization that any man could be subjected to such humiliation, both by his wife and by his neighbours and peers.

This cultural immersion in cuckold-lore continued at petty school, where children learned to read using what was known as a horn-book: a wooden paddle inscribed with alphabet letters and the Lord's Prayer and covered with a translucent film taken from animal horns.[26] Doubtless the name of this pedagogical innovation prompted giggles among pupils. One horn-book preserved in the Folger Shakespeare Library teaches vowel sounds using the sequence a-e-i-o-u, ba-be-bi-bo-bu, ca-ce-ci-*co-cu*, inadvertently producing the sound 'cocu' (French for cuckold) when recited out loud.[27] That such details were not lost on precocious schoolboys is suggested by Moth's derision of Holofernes in *Love's Labour's Lost*, where the boy says the schoolmaster teaches by the 'horn-book,' that his wit makes him a 'wit-old,' and that he could borrow the old man's 'cuckold's horn' to whip like a top (5.1.44–63).[28]

---

(rhyme n. 23).

[24] *An Excellent New Medley* by 'F.D.' (possibly a misprint for T[homas] D[eloney]) is reprinted in *Roxburghe Ballads*, 1:57–61 (vv. 65–68). This same medley complains that 'Young children now can sweare and curse' (v. 170). On teenagers' exposure to ballads and popular literature, see Ben-Amos, *Adolescence and Youth in Early Modern England*, pp. 192–93.

[25] See Rollins, 'The Black-Letter Broadside Ballad,' pp. 278–79.

[26] Abbott, *Life Cycles in England 1560–1720*, p. 67.

[27] *The Complete Works of Shakespeare*, ed. Bevington, p. liii (plate), emphasis added.

[28] The 'boy' Moth, incidentally, is consulted by Armado as a kind of authority on ballads, despite (or perhaps because of) his tender age; see *Love's Labour's Lost* 1.2.103–7. This latter passage is also excerpted in Würzbach's Appendix, p. 262.

When children graduated to their first spelling primer, they learned that A is for apple, B is for ball, C is for cat; but what about the letter 'X'? There were no xylophones or x-rays, so instead one resourceful pedagogical device, alphabet picture-cards, taught them that 'X' is for Xanthippe—the purportedly shrewish wife of Socrates.[29] A similar lesson appeared in *The Virgin's A, B, C; or, An Alphabet of Vertuous Admonitions for a Chaste, Modest, and Well-Govern'd Maid*:

> X.    Xantippe-like, the wife of Socrates,
> Affect not thou thy husband to displease;
> Nor with a rayling tongue pursue him still,
> But in humility obey his will.[30]

Incidentally, girls were also admonished by the letter 'E' to remain faithful to their future husbands: 'Exchange no love, but always constant be' (v. 17). Thus, veiled warnings about wifely rebellion and infidelity went hand-in-hand with fundamental lessons about the alphabet and spelling, prompting perhaps another item in Speed's catalogue of traits exhibited by lovelorn Valentine: '[you have learned] to sigh, like a schoolboy that had lost his ABC' (2.1.21–22).

According to Alice Bertha Gomme's monumental survey of early English games and pastimes, during their precious unsupervised hours (after school, on weekends, during holidays) youths would play a popular variant of tag called 'hornie' in which the child who was 'it' would chase his fellows, 'having his hands clasped and his thumbs pushed out before him in resemblance of horns,' while they egged him on by chanting 'hornie, hornie.'[31] Griffiths lists a number of other popular games with evocative names like prison bars, cat and trap, and cudgels, and observes that 'child's play rehearsed adult concerns' such as marriage, honour codes, and personal reputation.[32] Unfortunately, they rehearsed anti-social adult concerns as well.

To supplement their informal education in social mores and gender roles, parents who could afford tuition sent their boys on from petty

---

[29] See Abbott, Life Cycles in England 1560–1720, pp. 270–71 (plate 16).

[30] *Roxburghe Ballads*, 2:651–54 (vv. 85–88).

[31] Gomme, *The Traditional Games of England, Scotland, and Ireland*, 1:227–28.

[32] Griffiths, *Youth and Authority*, pp. 135–38. For a discussion of the kind of shadow-culture of children in which 'rigorous' codes of honour were enforced with elaborate 'ritual punishments' akin to those employed by adults, see Thomas, 'Children,' pp. 60–63 and sources cited there.

school to board at grammar and preparatory schools until around age 16, and from there to universities. Other options included service in neighbouring households or apprenticeship. Whatever the case, however, the final phase of youth involved living away from home for a minimum of one year, and frequently for much longer. As Keith Wrightson points out, 'service, like apprenticeship, was part of the child's preparation for an independent existence in the adult world.'[33] These prolonged absences from home often coincided with the onset of puberty, which intensified youths' fascination with the delights and dangers of the opposite sex. Indeed, during this life-stage, many adolescents fell in love for the first time and became avid consumers of ballads which, Margaret Spufford notes, depicted 'marital and extramarital intercourse or cuckoldry' for frustrated bachelors seeking prurient thrills as well as a kind of unofficial sex-education about what marriage held in store.[34]

One ballad, *Advice to Batchelors; Or, The Married Man's Lamentation* presents a characteristically dire warning to young men about the perils of giving up their 'happy life' of social and sexual freedom to become a 'slave' and 'cuckold':

> You batchelors that single are
>     may lead a happy life;
> For married men are full of care,
>     and women oft breed strife.

Besides being shrewish and a spendthrift, the unhappy narrator's wife is physically abusive and sexually unfaithful; but, worst of all, she has destroyed his credit and good name:

> She oftentimes doth tell me plain
>     that I do wear the horns;
> Sure ev'ry man doth this disdain,
>     and wise men meerly scorns.[35]

Another ballad, *The Batchelor's Delight, Being A pleasant new Song, shewing the happiness of a Single Life and the miseries that do commonly attend Matrimony*, cites biblical examples of 'tormented' husbands such as Adam, Samson, and Job to drive home the familiar warning, that 'He that doth suddenly marry a wife / will surely repent

---

33 Wrightson, *English Society 1580–1680*, p. 113.
34 Spufford, *Small Books and Pleasant Histories*, pp. 157–58.
35 *Roxburghe Ballads*, 3:376–79 (vv. 79, 80, 2, 41–44).

it at leisure.'[36] Demographic research suggests that few did marry in haste; in fact, most had plenty of time to read such materials and weigh their marital options, since in England men married on average in their late twenties.[37] In his useful survey, *Gender, Sex and Subordination in England 1500–1800*, Fletcher points out that many such ballads were designed to be satirical, not descriptive; yet they too contributed to what Foucault referred to as 'the imaginary landscape of the Renaissance' by generating anxiety in impressionable young batchelors who were acculturated to dread the stigma of cuckoldry and the figure of the abusive or adulterous wife.[38]

In *The Winter's Tale*, Shakespeare's Old Shepherd famously complains that between the ages of ten and twenty-three 'there is nothing . . . but getting wenches with child, wronging the ancientry, stealing, fighting' (3.3.59–63). What is remarkable about his observation is that he starts the boys so young with aggressive, sexual, and anti-social behaviour. Yet if games played by youths degenerated into teasing, fighting, and vandalism, these young offenders were merely imitating the examples set by older role models. For youths, one more important (if unofficial) rite of passage entailed their initiation into what Griffiths refers to as England's 'rough nocturnal culture' of drinking, singing, gambling, fighting and whoring—one which 'showed off the excessive and violent aspects of manhood' and through which 'young men distanced themselves from the cosy domestic world of childhood and their mother's care, and staked a claim for a place in the ranks of adult men.'[39] Both Griffith's observation and the Old Shepherd's complaint are supported by the confessions proffered by the band of outlaws Valentine encounters in exile in the woods outside Milan:

> 3 Outlaw. Know, then, that some of us are gentlemen,
>     Such as the fury of ungovern'd youth

---

[36] *Roxburghe Ballads*, 3:423–26 (vv. 73–74).

[37] Wrightson, *English Society 1580–1680*, p. 68.

[38] Foucault's phrase is taken from *Madness and Civilization*, p. 7. On ballads, see Fletcher, *Gender, Sex and Subordination*, pp. 101–25 and *passim*. In his dissertation, Ken Stahl argues that ballads should be interpreted less as descriptive documents produced by the people, than as prescriptive documents produced by dominant cultures intent on reinforcing gender stereotypes and the status quo: 'broadsides tell us not so much about what people actually thought, but about what they were supposed to think' ('Broadside Ballads of the English Renaissance,' p. 6).

[39] Griffiths, *Youth and Authority*, p. 207.

> Thrust from the company of awful men.
> Myself was from Verona banished,
> For practising to steal away a lady . . .
>
> (4.1.44–48)

Fighting, stealing, getting wenches with child: 'awful' adults condemned such liminal rough-housing, but sent the younger generation conflicting messages. According to Foyster, the immediate examples set by elders and peers were more instrumental than moral conduct-books in shaping teens' developing sense of masculine selfhood.[40] In fact, much youthful misbehaviour simply imitated socially-sanctioned adult rituals which boys either witnessed or in which they themselves participated.

Documents transcribed by Toronto's Records of Early English Drama Project illustrate just how disruptive such extra-legal activities could prove for the inhabitants of a town or parish. In the first document taken from Langport circa 1615, a certain William Thomas was charged with hindering the apprehension of his friend, 'one William Hayne whoe was often drvnke and did diuerse foule misdemeanors in his said house playinge vppon a Crowde & singeinge filthie and vncyvell songes to the terror of the neare inhabitantes.' Doubtless Hayne's disruptive antics were popular among his drinking companions, such as when 'he would davnce with a paire of hornes and a Codpeece before them all'; however, when the riotous behaviour spilled into the streets and Hayne threatened to 'frye them [his neighbours] and Cut them to small peeces,' the fun quickly dissipated and officers were brought to the scene.[41] In a second document dated two years later, the vicar of High Littleton and his son complain to the justices of the peace that three habitual drunkards named Hill, Bedford, and Tanner, 'verie leaude [lewd] and Idle fellowes,' were vandalizing gates, stiles, and bridges, and generally disturbing the peace:

> for Hill and his companie by night in theire dronkennes did teare & rent the towne-pouynd of Hallowtrow, & neare that pounde did break vp or unhange a barns doore wher poore women were that night lodged & did fright and fowlly abuse the saide poore women, and goinge vpp and doune the streete did crie Cookholdes Cookholdes as loud as they coulde.[42]

---

[40] Foyster, *Manhood in Early Modern England*, pp. 39–40.

[41] *Somerset, Including Bath*, 1:156. I have silently expanded abbreviations indicated by italics in the REED transcriptions.

[42] *Somerset, Including Bath*, 1:138.

In his seminal study of skimmingtons, charivaris, and other forms of rough music, E. P. Thompson points out that cuckolds and hen-pecked husbands were such a popular target for scornful neighbourhood rituals, because 'boys . . . found in a riding a superb occasion for legitimised excitement and aggression, directed against adults.'[43] In these rituals, youths simultaneously internalized anxieties about cuckoldry and projected these outward onto hapless neighbourhood victims.

Shakespeare's England was not experiencing an epidemic of female infidelity—ballad moralizing and midnight drunken escapades notwithstanding. The irony of recovering this statistically inaccurate portrait of female sexual mores in popular culture is that it shows the extent to which Shakespeare turned this imaginary landscape on its head. In his plays depicting courtship leading to marriage, it is usually young women who are chaste and true, and young men who prove promiscuous or inconstant. His dramatic depictions of youthful courtship seem designed to reassure men that women are largely constant and that fears to the contrary are therefore largely unfounded. To be fair, for every satirical ballad warning of the inevitability of cuckoldry, there survives a ballad extolling the pleasures of married life; the importance of marrying for love; and the imperative that men, too, remain sexually faithful. Serious works also attempted to counter the misinformation about married life circulating in English popular culture. For example, prefaced to Robert Tofte's translation of *The Blazon of Jealousie* is a short dedicatory poem that recommends a sustained consideration of sexual jealousy. Again, contrary to Kahn's statement quoted in my introduction, the poem contends that jealousy is everyone's concern—young and old; male and female; married and single. The poem reads in part:

> The Man or Wife from this pollution free,
> (For detestation thereof) here may see,
> The substance and successe of Iealousie.
> Vnmarryed Youth (of eyther sexe) are here
> Prescrib'd a Caution, and a course to cleare
> Themselues of this. The auncient may collect
> Prime Principles to dispossesse Suspect,
> No ouer-growne in any hee or shee,
> Discouering but th'Effects of Iealousie.[44]

---

43 Thompson, 'Rough Music,' pp. 490–91.

44 'The Censure of a Friend, vpon this Translation, done by R. T. Gentleman' by 'Anth. Mar.,' in Varchi, *The Blazon of Jealousie*, sig. [B3v].

Undoubtedly more youngsters heard scurrilous ballads than read Benedetto Varchi's erudite book; for if Shakespeare's plays are any indication, the folklore of cuckoldry and the melodrama of sexual jealousy remained among the more popular destinations in English adolescents' imaginary landscape.

*    *    *

*The Two Gentlemen of Verona* begins with Proteus and Valentine poised on the verge of that important event of privileged adolescence: finishing abroad. The play opens with Valentine saying farewell to his 'Home-keeping' friend, Proteus (1.1.2), though their emotional leave-taking barely conceals the fact that these childhood friends have recently become alienated from one another by Proteus's infatuation with Julia in Verona: 'I leave myself, my friends, and all, for love' (v. 65). Because of this attachment to Julia, Proteus does not welcome the prospect of a trip abroad, even to a city as exciting as Milan, and has evidently refused to go on previous occasions. His father and uncle, on the other hand, ignorant of Proteus's romantic involvement with Julia, decide that Proteus 'cannot be a perfect man, / Not being tried and tutor'd in the world' (1.3.20–21) and that it is time that he travel to Milan for finishing as well:

> There shall he practise tilts and tournaments,
> Hear sweet discourse, converse with noblemen,
> And be in eye of every exercise
> Worthy his youth and nobleness of birth.
> (vv. 30–33)

In spite of the personal sacrifices he has already made for love—jeopardizing his friendship with Valentine and declining such a gentlemanly rite-of-passage in Milan—Proteus's relationship with Julia is not entirely secure. She is beset with other suitors, 'the fair Sir Eglamour' and 'the rich Mercatio' (1.2.9–12); and after she seemingly rejects one of Proteus's letters, Speed informs him, 'I think you'll hardly win her' (1.1.128). When she finally accepts Proteus, their relationship lacks parental approval (1.3.48–49). Then, just as Proteus successfully gains 'her oath for love, her honour's pawn' (1.3.47), parental authority arbitrarily separates the two. Proteus compares his impending trip to a kind of romantic eclipse:

> O, how this spring of love resembleth
> The uncertain glory of an April day,

Which now shows all the beauty of the sun,
And by and by a cloud takes all away.
(vv. 84–87)

The image of the cloud suggests that Proteus fears that in his absence
a rival suitor will come between him and his 'uncertain glory,' Julia.
Shortly before Valentine's departure, Proteus did quibble with Speed
in a passage containing the play's only explicit reference to cuckoldry
(mentioned above): 'my horns are his horns' (1.1.79). Furthermore, if
Launce's bawdy quibble about his master's premarital sex with Julia
are truthful ('when it stands well with him, it stands well with her'
[2.5.20–21]), then the lovers may have made some considerable emotional and physical commitment in addition to their exchange of verbal
vows. If even the currently unattached Valentine risks being cuckolded
'*in posse*,'[45] what fate awaits Proteus *in esse* when Julia is left alone? The
seeds of suspicion have been sown.

In an ironic fulfilment of Antonio's earlier order that the teen depart
without packing—'Look what thou want'st shall be sent after thee'
(1.3.74)—Julia disguises herself as a page and pursues her lover to Milan.
Proteus may not 'want' (i.e., 'desire') Julia, but he certainly 'wants' (i.e.,
'needs') the reassurance of his masculinity that her selfless devotion to
him would provide. When she arrives in disguise as Sebastian, Proteus
unwittingly engages her/him as a go-between, saying 'I have need of
such a youth, / That can with some discretion do my business' (4.4.63–
64). Of course, that 'business' is to carry a love-token from him to Silvia.
Now Julia can monitor his behaviour, but her ingenuity nearly backfires
in the final scene when Proteus discovers that Sebastian is sporting Julia's
ring, confirming what he earlier suspected, Julia's constancy: 'How! let
me see. / Why this is the ring I gave to Julia' (5.4.91–92). For a brief but
suggestive moment, Proteus fears that that very Sebastian whom he
engaged 'with some discretion [to] do [his] business' (4.4.63–64) has in
his new master's absence engaged in 'business' (i.e., 'coitus') with Julia.[46]
Here Proteus illustrates the phenomenon Keith Thomas identified years
ago as the 'double-standard' of sexual morality: that unchastity, promiscuity, or premarital sex are peccadillos for men, but unpardonable
crimes for women.[47] Proteus is betrothed to, and expects fidelity of, Julia.

---

[45] Shakespeare, *The Two Gentlemen of Verona*, ed. Leech, p. 7 (note to 1.1.79).
[46] On 'business' as slang for sexual intercourse, see Williams, *A Dictionary of
Sexual Language*, 1:179–80.
[47] Thomas, 'The Double Standard,' pp. 446–67.

The vows he has made to her are known widely enough to have reached Silvia's ears in neighbouring Milan, yet he attempts to seduce her and possibly other women with impunity: '[Thou] hast deceiv'd so many with thy vows,' Silvia complains (4.2.95). That such a man expects constancy from a woman he describes to others as being 'dead' (4.2.103) suggests that female infidelity obsesses even callous lovers. He would not be a cuckold *in absentia*.

Female inconstancy also worries Valentine, who vacillates between showing off his treasured Silvia and worrying that she will be stolen away. He tactlessly boasts of Silvia's virtues to Proteus prompting the latter to complain of his friend's 'braggardism' (2.4.149); yet at the same time Valentine is consumed with 'jealousy' and would keep rivals away, especially Sir Thurio (v. 173). His anxiety is heightened by the competitive atmosphere in Milan, where just as Julia was beset with rival suitors in Verona, Silvia is likewise the toast of Milan's bachelors. In fact, her first scene on-stage involves a flirtatious request that Valentine compose a letter to one of his supposed rivals, a 'secret, nameless friend' (who is actually Valentine himself [2.1.98]). Out of his depth in this sophisticated court, Valentine misunderstands her subtle invitation and pens a terse missive to his imagined rival, prompting Speed to mock the misperceptions of a master blinded by jealousy and inexperience in love. Speed's comment on this abortive epistolary exchange underscores the extent to which young men fell back on popular literature to guide their comportment during the bewildering experience that is courtship:

> For often have you writ to her, and she in modesty,
>    Or else for want of idle time, could not again reply,
>    Or fearing else some messenger, that might her mind discover,
>    Herself hath taught her love himself to write unto her lover.
>    All this I speak in print, *for in print I found it.*
>                  (2.1.155–59, emphasis added)

Leech does not identify the source of this obscure comment except to say that the lines were quoted from 'a printed book'; and numerous critics have documented the play's indebtedness to literary and homiletic sources, as well as to the manuscript culture of letter-writing.[48]

---

[48] Shakespeare, *The Two Gentlemen of Verona*, ed. Leech, p. 30 (note to 2.1.159). On the play's literary and homiletic sources, see Sargent, 'Sir Thomas Elyot and the Integrity of *The Two Gentlemen of Verona*,' pp. 33–48; and Slights, '*The Two*

Yet Speed's obscure quatrain of fourteeners also recalls the 'print' of courtship and marriage ballads, as these lines could easily be transposed into the ballad stanza form of alternating iambic tetrameter and trimeter (and, more importantly, sound like such in performance).

To a certain extent, Valentine's fears are not unfounded, as Sir Thurio does pose a very real threat inasmuch as he is Silvia's father's choice for his daughter's hand in marriage. After Sir Thurio 'frowns' on Valentine, Speed eggs on his master, "Twere good you knocked him.' The men then exchange insults, prompting Silvia to exclaim, 'A fine volley of words, gentlemen, and quickly shot off' (2.4.1–31). Shortly thereafter, Proteus is enjoined by his friend to admire Silvia, but from a respectful distance—for Valentine claims her as his treasured possession, one which he vows to watch with 'twenty pairs of eyes' (2.4.90). Here Valentine echoes the misogynous advice repeated in street ballads; for example, the second part of *The Merry Cuckold* warns that 'If a man had all Argus his eyes, / A wife that is bad will something deuise / To gull him to 's face.'[49] And *Cuckold's Haven* describes the futility of trying to avoid being 'hornify'd' by a lusty wife:

> Though narrowly I doe watch,
>     and vse lock, bolt, and latch,
> My wife will me o'rematch,
>     my forehead I may scratch.[50]

Granted, Valentine and Silvia have not yet exchanged marital vows or secured parental permission; yet he boasts to Proteus of the wealth and social prestige her love bestows upon him—inadvertently alerting a rival male to her great value:

> Why, man, she is mine own
> And I as rich in having such a jewel
> As twenty seas, if all their sand were pearl,
> The water nectar, and the rocks pure gold.
>                                         (2.4.164–67)

---

Gentlemen of Verona and the Courtesy Book Tradition,' pp. 115–32. On letters, see Kiefer, 'Love Letters in *The Two Gentlemen of Verona*,' pp. 133–52.

49 *Roxburghe Ballads*, 2:5–8 (vv. 5–7).

50 *Roxburghe Ballads*, 1:148–53 (vv. 6, 7–10).

Thus Silvia is the possession Valentine must guard against marauding thieves. 'For love,' he explains, 'is full of jealousy' (v. 173). Not surprisingly, when Proteus later brings word of Valentine's banishment, he quickly assumes the worst: 'Hath she forsworn me?' he asks, 'No Valentine if Silvia have forsworn me' (3.1.212–14).

Prompted in part by lust, in part by envy of his friend, Proteus forgets Julia and starts to court Silvia as well, thus betraying his friend and breaking his initial vow of constancy. Silvia's rejection of Proteus's amorous advances is as devastating to his self-esteem as her acceptance of Valentine's is beneficial to his. Proteus complains that she 'twits' him for leaving Julia and 'spurns [his] love' (4.2.8–14), reducing his self-esteem to a low ebb. Abashed, he admits, 'Silvia is too fair, too true, too holy, / To be corrupted with my worthless gifts' (4.2.5–6). Like his gifts of a 'false' (i.e., out of tune) song (4.2.57) and a comically incontinent dog (4.4.1–57), Proteus himself is also esteemed worthless by her. Most devastating is her ridicule of his speech: 'Thou subtle, perjur'd, false, disloyal man, / Think'st thou I am so shallow, so conceitless, / To be seduced by thy flattery' (4.2.92–94). In light of Valentine's ringing pronouncement to the duke, 'That man that hath a tongue, I say is no man, / If with his tongue he cannot win a woman' (3.1.104–5), Proteus is a colossal failure.

Proteus's dogged attempts to woo Silvia with words, poetry, and music reflect the importance English culture attached to verbal seduction as an informal rite of passage for young males: 'young men judged each other's sexual prowess by their ability to be so sexually attractive and skilful that force became wholly unnecessary.'[51] Humiliated by his inability to prove himself a man in this manner, Proteus acts out of desperation in the play's final scene. When Proteus 'rescues' Silvia from the outlaws, he asks for some self-affirming praise from her: 'Vouchsafe me for my meed but one fair look' (5.4.23). Her refusal to grant him even this small 'boon,' however, re-iterates her loyalty to Valentine and her contempt of Proteus: 'Had I been seized by a hungry lion, / I would have been a breakfast to the beast, / Rather than have false Proteus rescue me' (vv. 24, 33–35). Furthermore, her assertion that 'All men but Proteus' respect friendship and loyalty (v. 54) singles him out, by implication, as the only one in Milan who is not manly. Proteus's attempted sexual assault therefore becomes a kind of desperate assertion of masculinity when all other avenues have been exhausted:

---

[51] Foyster, *Manhood in Early Modern England*, p. 10.

Nay, if the gentle spirit of moving words
Can no way change you to a milder form,
I'll woo you like a soldier, at arm's end,
And love you 'gainst the nature of love: force ye.
(vv. 55–59)

The final blow to Proteus comes, not so much when he is foiled in his attempted rape of Silvia or when he is rebuked for this by his incredulous friend (vv. 62–72), but when Valentine makes a gesture of self-aggrandizing largesse that further humiliates Proteus: 'that my love may appear plain and free, / All that was mine in Silvia I give thee' (vv. 82–83). This gift is a stinging reminder that Proteus has failed to woo Silvia with his own words. He is only rescued from utter annihilation by Julia, who earlier in the play foresaw her reparative function when reassembling the parts of his torn love letter:

And here is writ 'love-wounded Proteus'.
Poor wounded name: my bosom, as a bed,
Shall lodge thee till thy wound be throughly heal'd;
And thus I search it with a sovereign kiss.
(1.2.114–17)

In the end she searches and repairs Proteus's wounded self-esteem and he at last rediscovers a reliable source of masculinity-confirming devotion and affection: 'What is in Silvia's face but I may spy / More fresh in Julia's, *with a constant eye?*' (5.4.113–14, emphasis added). Because she is constant, he is perfect once again.

Critical opinion regarding Valentine's gift to Proteus is divided, but I believe that the most common explanations—that Valentine is testing Proteus's loyalty or educating him about magnanimity with Silvia and Julia acting as accomplices—accord more generosity to Valentine than the scene bears out.[52] Brimming with confidence, Valentine thinks that he no longer needs to prove himself using Silvia; indeed, as Foyster observes, more than monogamous love-relationships, what teenagers really needed was 'to seek continually the approval of their peers as they took their first steps towards manhood.'[53] Valentine's successes (and, more importantly, Silvia's and Proteus's validation of these successes)

---

[52] For example, see Lindenbaum, 'Education in *The Two Gentlemen of Verona*,' pp. 238–41 and Sargent, 'Sir Thomas Elyot and the Integrity of *The Two Gentlemen of Verona*,' pp. 45–47.

[53] Foyster, *Manhood in Early Modern England*, p. 45.

have enabled him to consolidate his masculine identity. Paradoxically, in seeming to give Silvia away, Valentine is also testing Silvia's constancy, her willingness to be given away. To be sure, she has spent much of his absence surrounded by would-be suitors and untrustworthy men (Thurio, Proteus, and Eglamour): will she accept Valentine's attempt to bestow her upon another? From Valentine's anxious perspective, the test is motivated and even rather shrewd, though critical responses usually condemn the gift as an act of 'unbelievable stupidity' and a dramatic blunder on Shakespeare's part.[54] We never find out whether it is or not, for the action is interrupted by Julia's swoon, and Silvia has no lines to indicate her reaction to Valentine's gesture. However, Valentine is in a win-win situation: if she accepts the terms, then she is inconstant and not worth having; if Proteus refuses (as he does), Valentine's willingness to sacrifice his love proves him to be an adherent to the friendship cult. With one self-aggrandizing gesture, 'Valentine is no longer the almost hopelessly aspiring lover but is the dispenser of magnanimity.'[55] William E. Stephenson also sees this gift as an act of one-upmanship: 'Valentine can rise above [Proteus] again by an even greater display of nobility, a towering act of self-sacrifice.'[56] Valentine would discard Silvia in order to secure praise from his defeated, contrite, ingratiated friend. Valentine nearly dispenses with her like a jewel, portrait, ring, or other prized object. Yet there is one final plot twist.

In a turn of events frequently overshadowed by the controversial gift episode, Thurio bursts onto the scene and declares, 'Silvia's mine' (5.4.123). In a flash, Valentine's magnanimity disappears and he issues this terrible warning:

> Thurio, give back; or else embrace thy death;
> Come not within the measure of my wrath;
> Do not name Silvia thine. If once again,
> Verona shall not hold thee. *Here she stands,*
> Take but possession of her with a touch:
> I dare thee but to breathe upon my love.
> (5.4.124–29, emphasis added)

---

54 Ewbank, '"Were Man But Constant He Were Perfect,"' p. 105.

55 For a discussion of the friendship cult, see Leech's introduction to the Arden *Two Gentlemen of Verona*, pp. liv–lvi (quotation on p. lxviii); and Small's seminal discussion, 'The Ending of *The Two Gentlemen of Verona*,' pp. 21–32.

56 Stephenson, 'The Adolescent Dream-World,' p. 167.

Sounding like a jealous husband, Valentine frightens his cowardly rival into abandoning all claim to Silvia. This speech recalls Petruchio's bold pronouncement at the wedding feast in *The Taming of the Shrew*:

> I will be master of what is mine own.
> She is my goods, my chattels, she is my house,
> My household stuff, my field, my barn,
> My horse, my ox, my ass, my any thing,
> *And here she stands.* Touch her whoever dare.
> (3.2.227–31, emphasis added)

Petruchio's warning echoes the Tenth Commandment, 'thou shalt not couet thy neighbours house, neither shalt thou couet thy neighbors wife . . . nor his oxe, nor his asse nor any thing that is thy neighbours.'[57] Valentine is likewise warning would-be seducers not to covet his future wife. Silvia's almost complete silence, combined with the outlaws', Proteus's, and Thurio's submission to Valentine, suggests that this is a dream-come-true for Valentine.[58] Of the two would-be gentlemen come from Verona for finishing, Valentine proves victorious. In the words of Milan's Duke, 'Sir Valentine, / Thou art a gentleman' (5.4.143–44).

Thus the two young women in the play are unassailably constant to the young men who are unforgivably inconstant. Valentine in particular anxiously guards his possession from Thurio, but blithely bestows her as a gift to Proteus. There is no shame in giving away a love-object, only in having her stolen away; there is no shame in betraying a woman, only in being betrayed or duped by one. This double standard is reflected in the popular ballad literature, where countless songs advocate premarital abstinence for women; but, where men are concerned, the ballads merely recommend a degree of restraint.[59] Ironically, Proteus is frequently excoriated by commentators for leaving Julia for Silvia, yet elsewhere in the canon Romeo is excused for leaving Rosaline for Juliet.

---

[57] Quotations are taken from the Bishops' Bible, Exodus 20:17.

[58] Stephenson, 'The Adolescent Dream-World,' pp. 167–68.

[59] For example, *Slippery Will: Or, The old Batchelor's complaint* boasts of one man's exploits in seducing and abandoning a bevy of women, only to conclude with a mild warning to younger bachelors not to wait until they are old and grey: 'I must confesse that I did amisse / In loving of so many; / O but now what a plague is this, / I am not beloved of any!' *Roxburghe Ballads*, 2:503–8 (vv. 127–30).

Amid all this adolescent male inconstancy, there is one constant: that cuckoldry anxiety—the fear of infidelity in one's wife and the resultant scorn from one's peers—is not something that arrived on an early modern Englishman's emotional landscape *ex nihilo* the day he got married. In *Troilus and Cressida* it is unmarried Troilus, 'the youngest son of Priam . . ./ Not yet mature' (4.5.96–97) who is one of Troy's most outspoken critics of cuckolds 'gor'd with Menelaus' horn' (1.1.112). Likewise, in *Romeo and Juliet* it is the unattached Mercutio who fantasizes about the seduction of Romeo's Rosaline (see 2.1.23–27), prompting his friend to comment: 'He jests at scars that never felt a wound' (2.2.1). These young men share a preoccupation with sex and infidelity that Martin Ingram agrees is not limited to husbands: 'mocking rhymes and the like involved a prurient or even pornographic element which suggests that they sometimes served as a *proxy form of sexual indulgence* rather than a clear-cut condemnation of it.' During that long decade from the onset of puberty to the socially delayed entrance into marriage, who better than teenage boys and unmarried twenty-something men to indulge in this 'proxy' sexual indulgence and its concomitant social anxieties?[60] This is why Valentine watches like one who fears robbing. The dread of emotional abandonment and social ridicule affected English males long before their wedding day; indeed, as I have argued elsewhere, from the cradle to the grave.[61]

*Niagara University*
*Lewiston, New York*

The author wishes to acknowledge the financial support of a Social Sciences and Humanities Research Council of Canada Doctoral Fellowship and a Niagara University Research Council Academic Year Research Grant, and to thank University of Toronto Professors Alexander Leggatt and Konrad Eisenbichler for their input and encouragement at various stages of this work.

## Cited Works

Abbott, Mary. *Life Cycles in England 1560–1720: Cradle to Grave*. London: Routledge, 1996.

Baring-Gould, William S. and Ceil Baring-Gould. *The Annotated Mother Goose: Nursery Rhymes Old and New, Arranged and Explained*. New York: Bramhall House, 1962.

---

[60] Ingram, *Church Courts, Sex and Marriage*, p. 165 (emphasis added).

[61] See Collington, "O Word of Fear," *passim*.

Ben-Amos, Ilana Krausman. *Adolescence and Youth in Early Modern England*. New Haven: Yale University Press, 1994.

Breitenberg, Mark. *Anxious Masculinity in Early Modern England*. Cambridge: Cambridge University Press, 1996.

Collington, Philip David. "'O Word of Fear': Imaginary Cuckoldry in Shakespeare's Plays' Ph.D. Dissertation. University of Toronto, 1998.

Ewbank, Inga-Stina. '"Were Man But Constant, He Were Perfect": Constancy and Consistency in *The Two Gentlemen of Verona*' pp. 31–57 in *Shakespearean Comedy*, ed. Malcolm Bradbury and David Palmer. Stratford-upon-Avon Studies, 14. New York: Crane, Russak, 1972. Rpt. pp. 91–114 in *Two Gentlemen of Verona: Critical Essays*, ed. June Schlueter. New York: Garland, 1996.

Fletcher, Anthony. *Gender, Sex and Subordination in England 1500–1800*. New Haven: Yale University Press, 1995.

Foucault, Michel. *Madness and Civilization: A History of Insanity in the Age of Reason*, trans. Richard Howard. New York: Vintage—Random House, 1973.

Foyster, Elizabeth A. *Manhood in Early Modern England: Honour, Sex and Marriage*. London: Longman, 1999.

Gomme, Alice Bertha. *The Traditional Games of England, Scotland, and Ireland*. 2 vols. London: David Nutt, 1894.

Griffiths, Paul. *Youth and Authority: Formative Experiences in England 1560–1640*. Oxford: Clarendon Press, 1996.

Immel, Andrea L. '"Little Rhymes, Little Jingle, Little Chimes": A History of Nursery Rhymes in English Literature before *Tommy Thumb's Pretty Song Book*' Dissertation. University of California, Los Angeles. 1994.

Ingram, Martin. *Church Courts, Sex and Marriage in England, 1570–1640*. 1987. Rpt. Cambridge: Cambridge University Press, 1994.

Jonson, Ben. *Bartholomew Fair*, ed. E. A. Horsman. The Revels Plays. London: Methuen, 1960, 1968.

Kahn, Coppélia. *Man's Estate: Masculine Identity in Shakespeare*. Berkeley: University of California Press, 1980.

Kiefer, Frederick. 'Love Letters in *The Two Gentlemen of Verona*' *Shakespeare Studies* 18 (1986): 65–85. Rpt. pp. 133–52 in *Two Gentlemen of Verona: Critical Essays*, ed. June Schlueter. New York: Garland, 1996.

Lindenbaum, Peter. 'Education in *The Two Gentlemen of Verona*' *Studies in English Literature* 15 (1975): 229–44.

Long, John H. *Shakespeare's Use of Music: The Histories and Tragedies*. Gainesville: University of Florida Press, 1971.

Opie, Iona and Peter Opie, eds. *The Oxford Dictionary of Nursery Rhymes*. Oxford: Clarendon Press, 1951, 1969.

Rollins, Hyder E. 'The Black-Letter Broadside Ballad' *Publications of the Modern Language Association*. 34 (1919): 258–339.

Sargent, Ralph M. 'Sir Thomas Elyot and the Integrity of *The Two Gentlemen of Verona*' *PMLA* 65 (1950): 1166–80. Rpt. pp. 33–48 in *Two Gentlemen of Verona: Critical Essays*, ed. June Schlueter. New York: Garland, 1996.

Shakespeare, William. *Love's Labour's Lost*, ed. R. W. David. Arden Shakespeare. London: Routledge, 1951, 1994.

Shakespeare, William. *Romeo and Juliet,* ed. Brian Gibbons. Arden Shakespeare. London: Methuen, 1980, 1986.

Shakespeare, William. *The Complete Works of Shakespeare*, ed. David Bevington. 4th edition. New York: Longman, 1997.

Shakespeare, William. *The Taming of the Shrew*, ed. Brian Morris. Arden Shakespeare. London: Routledge, 1981, 1989.

Shakespeare, William. *The Two Gentlemen of Verona*, ed. Clifford Leech. Arden Shakespeare. London: Routledge, 1972, 1989.

Shakespeare, William. *The Two Gentlemen of Verona* ed. Kurt Schlueter. New Cambridge Shakespeare. Cambridge: Cambridge University Press, 1990.

Shakespeare, William. *The Winter's Tale*, ed. J. H. P. Pafford. Arden Shakespeare. London: Routledge, 1963, 1993.

Shakespeare, William. *Troilus and Cressida*, ed. Kenneth Palmer. Arden Shakespeare. New York: Routledge, 1982, 1991.

Slights, Camille Wells. '*The Two Gentlemen of Verona and the Courtesy Book Tradition*' *Shakespeare Studies* 16 (1983): 13–31. Rpt. pp. 115–32 in *Two Gentlemen of Verona: Critical Essays*, ed. June Schlueter. New York: Garland, 1996.

Small, S. Asa. 'The Ending of *The Two Gentlemen of Verona*' *PMLA* 48 (1933): 767–76. Rpt. pp. 21–32 in *Two Gentlemen of Verona: Critical Essays*, ed. June Schlueter. New York: Garland, 1996.

Smith, Bruce R. *The Acoustic World of Early Modern England: Attending to the O-Factor*. Chicago: University of Chicago Press, 1999.

Smith, Bruce R. *Shakespeare and Masculinity*. Oxford: Oxford University Press, 2000.

Spenser, Edmund. *The Faerie Queen*, ed. Thomas P. Roche, Jr. and C. Patrick O'Donnell, Jr. New Haven: Yale University Press, 1978, 1981.

Spufford, Margaret. *Small Books and Pleasant Histories: Popular Fiction and its Readership in Seventeenth-Century England*. London: Methuen, 1981.

Stahl, Ken. 'Broadside Ballads of the English Renaissance: The Politics of Celebration and Social Criticism' Ph.D. Dissertation. Claremont Graduate School, 1989.

Stephenson, William E. 'The Adolescent Dream-World of *The Two Gentlemen of Verona*' *Shakespeare Quarterly* 17 (1966): 165–68.

Stokes, James and Robert J. Alexander, eds. *Somerset, Including Bath*. Records of Early English Drama. 2 vols. Toronto: University of Toronto Press, 1996.

*The Roxburghe Ballads*, ed. W. Chappell. Vols 1–3 (The Ballad Society, 1869–1880). Rpt. New York: AMS Press, 1966.

*The Holy Bible, Conteyning the Olde Testament and the Newe*. Bishops' Bible. London, 1595.

*The Oxford English Dictionary*. 1971. Compact Edition. 3 Vols. Oxford: Oxford University Press, 1987.

Thomas, Keith. 'Children in Early Modern England' pp. 45–77 in *Children and Their Books: A Celebration of the Work of Iona and Peter Opie*, ed. Gillian Avery and Julia Briggs. Oxford: Oxford University Press, 1989.

Thomas, Keith. 'The Double Standard' *Journal of the History of Ideas* 20 (1959): 195–216. Rpt. with rev. pp. 446–67 in *Ideas in Cultural Perspective*, ed. Philip P. Wiener and Aaron Noland. New Brunswick, NJ: Rutgers University Press, 1962.

Thompson, E. P. 'Rough Music' pp. 467–538 in *Customs in Common*. New York: The New Press, 1991.

*Two Gentlemen of Verona: Critical Essays*, ed. June Schlueter. New York: Garland, 1996.

Varchi, Benedetto. *The Blazon of Jealousie*, trans. Robert Tofte. London, 1615.

Williams, Gordon. *A Dictionary of Sexual Language and Imagery in Shakespearean and Stuart Literature*. 3 vols. London: Athlone, 1994.

Wrightson, Keith. *English Society 1580–1680*. London: Hutchinson, 1982, 1984.

Würzbach, Natascha. *The Rise of the English Street Ballad, 1550–1650*, trans. Gayna Walls. Cambridge: Cambridge University Press, 1990.

# Greensickness in Romeo and Juliet: Considerations on a Sixteenth-Century Disease of Virgins

## Ursula Potter

In a lecture to undergraduate students at the University of Sydney, Visiting Professor Michael Best commented on the difficulties that producers of *Romeo and Juliet* encounter in handling the disjunctions in Capulet's behaviour towards his daughter.[1] For an Elizabethan or Jacobean performance, however, these difficulties may not have existed. For a contemporary audience, the clues to Capulet's abrupt change of heart towards his daughter may be found in an outburst that is all too frequently cut from modern stagings of the play: 'Out, you green-sickness carrion! Out, you baggage / You tallow-face!' (III.v.156–57).[2] The greensickness reference may be brief, but the connotations for an Elizabethan audience are considerable. Editors of the play have generally footnoted greensickness as a form of anaemia common in young girls, suggesting it draws attention to Juliet's pale face, or noting greensickness as a disease of unmarried girls and proposing that its use by Capulet signifies Juliet's unwillingness to marry. In an article by David Bergeron specifically exploring the images of sickness in *Romeo and Juliet*, Juliet's greensickness is glossed only as anaemia.[3] More recently, Sasha Roberts has gone some way towards making a connection with the virgin's melancholy.[4] Greensickness was well known in Shakespeare's time, and indeed well into the 1920s, and a fuller understanding of the disease will illuminate Capulet's fatal decision to rush his daughter into marriage.

When Juliet defiantly rejects marriage to Paris, her father reacts first with confusion and then with anger. On the surface, this appears a typically autocratic response to filial defiance, yet it can also be seen

---

[1] University of Sydney, Australia, 9.8.99. Professor Best is with the Department of English, University of Victoria, BC, Canada.

[2] All references are to *The Riverside Shakespeare*.

[3] Bergeron, 'Sickness in *Romeo and Juliet*,' p. 357.

[4] Roberts, *William Shakespeare: Romeo and Juliet*, pp. 20–21.

as an expression of a father's fear that his daughter is showing symptoms of a disease common in adolescent girls in Elizabethan England, and particularly in girls from affluent families. Capulet had every expectation that Juliet would be proud to have so worthy a gentleman as Paris as her bridegroom. He therefore interprets her outright rejection and the ambiguous wording of her response as evidence of an irrational state of mind, a familiar symptom of greensickness:

> Capulet. How how, how how, chopp'd logic! What is this?
> 'Proud,' and 'I thank you,' and 'I thank you not,'
> And yet 'not proud.'
>
> (III.v.149–51)

As Capulet continues, a note of panic enters his voice:

> Fettle your fine joints 'gainst Thursday next
> To go with Paris to Saint Peter's Church,
> Or I will drag thee on a hurdle thither.
> Out, you green-sickness carrion! Out, you baggage!
> You tallow-face!
>
> (III.v.153–57)

Only a few scenes earlier, Capulet was resisting early marriage for his daughter, claiming she was too young at not even fourteen, and asking Paris to wait a further two years. Juliet's age was indeed well below the norm for marriage, as several historians have pointed out.[5] Now, Capulet has done an about face. He is reading into Juliet's behaviour, that is her weeping and her pale face, the symptoms of greensickness, the potentially fatal disease of virgins. Her inexplicable resistance and her 'chopp'd logic' in the face of his concern to do the right thing for her only confirm, in his mind, how far the condition has progressed.

'Greensickness carrion' is a direct reference to diseased flesh and to a corpse-like pallor; it conveys the dual nature of Capulet's fears for Juliet's life and for the onset of sexuality in her.[6] He condemns the 'young baggage' to 'graze' where she will, to 'hang, beg, starve, die in the streets' (III.v.192), signifying the life of prostitution.[7] Even Juliet's emotionally inarticulate mother is shocked at her husband's language, 'fie, fie, what, are you mad?' she exclaims (III.v.157). Capulet has no

---

[5] See Young, 'Haste, Consent' and Laslett, *Family life and illicit love*, pp. 40, 218.

[6] See 'thou most ill-shrouded rottenness' used to describe a promiscuous woman in Beaumont and Fletcher's *Philaster or Love Lies a-Bleeding*, II.iv.137.

[7] Rubenstein, *A Dictionary of Shakespeare's Sexual Puns*, p. 116.

reason to suspect Juliet of sexual activity, yet he has good precedents for his fears. Greensickness was not only well documented in the medical theory of the time, but also reflected in popular literature. In Robert Greene's prose work, *Mamillia* (1583), another well-meaning father follows similar reasoning:

> In the meantime *Gonzago* perceiving his daughter to be marriageable, knowing by skill and experience, that the grass being ready for the siethe, would wither if it were not cut; and the apples beeing ripe, for want of plucking would rotte on the tree; that his daughter beeing at the age of twentie yeeres, would either fall into the greene sicknes for want of a husband, or else if she scaped that disease incurre a farther inconvenience: so that like a wise father he thought to foresee such daungers [by devising a meet match].[8]

Gonzago and Capulet were followed in seventeenth-century literature by a host of other fathers fretting over the health of their virginal, pubescent daughters.

The onset of puberty in girls was regarded with considerable apprehension, it being commonly held that 'generally women begin to sprout hairs [*Pubescere*], as they call it, or yearn for a male . . . at fourteen years old, then they do offer themselves, and some plainly rage. [Without husbands such girls] do not live, but linger.'[9] Medical theory put the start of menstruation at about twelve;[10] at fourteen a girl was considered sexually mature and legally *hors du guard* [outside wardship].[11] Thus, in *The Winter's Tale*, Antigonus swears that if Hermione proves an adulteress he will geld his three daughters when they reach fourteen, 'fourteen they shall not see / To bring false generations' (II.i.147–48). The emphasis in the play on Juliet's age (see I.ii.9; I.iii.2; I.iii.10–21), signposts her entry into puberty, and although she can hardly be accused of raging, as Burton warns, sexual desire is prominent in her characterisation.

For Juliet to die of greensickness, or to lose her virginity outside marriage, or for her never to marry, would be a disaster for the House of Capulet. Romeo had earlier argued along similar lines that Rosaline,

---

8 Greene, *Mamillia*, 2:36.

9 Burton, *Anatomy of Melancholy*, p. 656.

10 See, for example, De Ketham, *The Fasciculus Medicinae*, p. 52, or *The 'Sekeness of wymmen'*, p. 12.

11 'The Law's Resolutions of Women's Rights (1632),' in *Daughters, Wives, and Widows*, p. 33.

who had sworn to live chaste, was making 'huge waste' and cutting off her posterity (I.i.218–20). The Montagues similarly fear for the health of the melancholic Romeo; the future of both families rests with an only child: 'Earth has swallowed all my hopes but she,' Capulet informs the audience early in the play, 'she's the hopeful lady of my earth' (II.ii.15). Juliet's virginity is a precious commodity, but one which can only be realised in its transfer into lawful marriage and motherhood, and Capulet's reasoning that he must get her married in haste or put his lineage in jeopardy, is neither naive nor purely comic. Capulet is, in fact, operating well within the bounds of common medical perceptions of greensickness at the time. As he sees it, he is taking measures to save Juliet's life, yet, as the audience sees it, he is making a tragic mistake.

## Greensickness: clinical history and background

Greensickness has a well-documented clinical history. Until very recently, it has been generally defined as 'chlorosis,' a term which connotes greenness, or a form of anaemia, a disease of young girlhood occurring at or soon after the period of puberty. Chlorosis reached epidemic proportions in the eighteenth and nineteenth centuries and then declined dramatically early in the twentieth century. In a 1927 home health journal, greensickness was still listed as a potentially deadly disease of young girls.[12] More recently a correlation with *anorexia nervosa* has been suggested, based on the psychogenic nature of the disease rather than on clinical anaemia.[13] The physical symptoms of chlorosis were those most often associated with anaemia: a pale complexion, general weakness, headaches, palpitations, eating disorders, amenorrhoea. To a late sixteenth-century audience, however, the psychological symptoms were of greater significance, encompassing weeping, sighing, anxiety, depression, violent mood swings, and either a strong sexual urge 'to comyn with man and doon' or an extreme distaste for sexual relations, 'they hafe no corage to man.'[14]

Interest in the sickness grew in medical circles in the sixteenth century. In 1544 the gynaecological writings of the medieval author Trotula of Salerno were published. Trotula associated the disease with

---

[12] *Health Knowledge*, pp. 80–84.

[13] Loudon, 'Chlorosis, anaemia,' pp. 1673–75.

[14] *The 'Sekenesse of wymmen'*, pp. 29–31. For a detailed and beautifully illustrated history of this condition see Dixon, *Perilous Chastity*, p. 13.

the onset of menstruation, an event that was held to coincide with the first stirrings of sexuality. Trotula's work was instrumental in contributing to the sixteenth-century understanding that sex was the appropriate cure. The Latin name of *morbus virgineus*—the disease of virgins—was coined, also in 1544, by the physician Johann Lange, and the more common name 'greensickness' appears to have originated later in the century.[15] The term is assumed to embrace not only the greenish pallor of the girl's complexion, but also the concept of an immature female state of mind. According to Robert Burton in *The Anatomy of Melancholy* (1621), greensickness girls display 'perverse conceits and opinions, dejection of mind, much discontent, preposterous judgement. They are apt to loath, dislike, disdain, . . . they pine away, void of counsel, apt to weep and tremble.'[16] These are the symptoms Capulet is reading into his daughter's behaviour. Other Renaissance terms for similar conditions in women not specific to virgins identify the presumed cause of this disease: womb-fury, uterine suffocation, uterine strangulation, uterine fits, *passione hysterica* and fits of the mother (the matrix). These and various other names were applied to a set of symptoms and associations that connoted a disordered womb and led to gynocentric models of hysteria.[17] Shakespeare has Lear exclaim at a moment of extreme stress: 'O! How this mother swells up toward my heart; / [*Hysterica*] *passio!*, down, thou climbing sorrow, / thy element's below.' (II.iv.56–58) Lear fears his degeneration into a feminine state of hysteria.

Although humoral theory had much to do with treatment and with susceptibility to the condition, greensickness was unequivocally attributed to the existence of the womb. The 'Maids', Nuns', and Widows' Melancholy' is a distinct condition, states Burton, 'for it much differs from that which commonly befalls men and other women, as having only one cause proper to women alone.'[18] The condition was thought to be brought on either by a frustrated desire for sexual intercourse, or by emotional stress. It could be triggered by 'a vexation of the mind

---

[15] OED cites Greene's *Mamillia* as the earliest example.

[16] Burton, *Anatomy of Melancholy*, p. 354.

[17] See Dixon, *Perilous Chastity*, p. 15; see also Mendelson/Crawford, *Women in Early Modern England*, pp. 18–30; Jacquart/Thomasset, *Sexuality and Medicine*, pp. 173–77.

[18] Burton, *Anatomy of Melancholy*, p. 353; see also 'Many of the grevaunce that wymmen hafe ar caused of the mother that we calle the matrix,' *The 'Sekenesse of wymmen'*, p. 27.

[or] a sudden sorrow.'[19] The womb was regarded as highly susceptible to the emotions, which caused it to rise up and compress the diaphragm, leading to breathlessness (*globus hystericus*), faintness, and paleness of skin amongst other symptoms. Juliet's grief at the death of Tybalt is deemed dangerously excessive in her parents' eyes: 'Some grief shows much of love, / But much of grief shows still some want of wit' (III.v.72–73), warns Juliet's mother. Paris also explains 'her father counts it dangerous that she do give her sorrow so much sway' (IV.i.10), and the Friar makes the same point at the end of the play: 'you, to remove that siege of grief from her, / Betroth'd and would have married her perforce' (V.iii.237–38).

The various terms used for the condition all stemmed from the prevailing understanding of the womb as an unstable and unrestrained organ within the body, afflicting both mind and body through pressure on other organs. The physician Johann Lange believed that corrupt menstrual blood caused the patient to become foolish and delirious, and he pointed to the obvious cure: 'I instruct virgins afflicted with the disease that as soon as possible they live with men and copulate, if they conceive they recover.'[20] Burton likewise understood that:

> a fallen uterus & spoilt menstrual blood are general causes, for, in a word, the whole malady proceeds from that inflammation, putridity, black smoky vapours, etc., from thence comes care, sorrow, and anxiety, obfuscation of spirits, agony, desperation, and the like . . . But the best and surest remedy of all is to see them well placed, & married to good husbands in due time; hence these tears, that's the primary cause, and this the ready cure.[21]

It is this Renaissance theory of the humours rising through the body to affect the mind that leads Romeo to define the nature of love through medical imagery:

> Love is a smoke made with the fume of sighs,
> Being purg'd, a fire sparkling in lovers' eyes,
> Being vex'd, a sea nourish'd with loving tears.
> What is it else? A madness most discreet,
> A choking gall, and a preserving sweet.
> (I.i.190–94)

---

[19] Burton, *Anatomy of Melancholy*, p. 354.
[20] Quoted in Loudon, 'Chlorosis, anaemia, and anorexia nervosa,' pp. 1670–71.
[21] Burton, *Anatomy of Melancholy*, pp. 353–55.

Recommended treatment for an afflicted woman was generally either to satisfy the unruly womb with sexual intercourse, or to stabilise it through diet, purging, bloodletting, rigorous exercise, and a novel form of aromatherapy, known as 'subfumigation,' intended to entice the womb back to its proper location by the use of sweet or foul smells. 'Apply evil smels to [the patient's] nostrils,' writes one physician, 'and sweet smels beneath and tie their legs hard with a garter for revulsion sake.'[22]

Although married women could suffer similar symptoms, maidens and widows were regarded as the most afflicted for want of 'benefit of marriage'—a euphemism for sexual intercourse, sometimes also referred to as 'hymeneal exercises.'[23] For virgins an early diagnosis was essential to avoid a worsening condition, as explained by Lazarus Riverius, a sixteenth-century physician:

> It is very good advice in the beginning of the Disease, before the Patient begins to manifestly rave, or in the space between her fits, when she is pretty well, to marry her to a lusty young man. For so the Womb being satisfied, and the offensive Matter contained in its Vessels being emptied, the Patient may peradventure be cured.[24]

In *Romeo and Juliet,* Capulet assuredly has the lustiness of the noble and youthful Paris in mind when he describes Paris to Juliet as positively 'Stuff'd, as they say, with honorable parts, / Proportion'd as one's thought would wish a man' (III.v.181–82). In *The Winter's Tale*, Perdita shows the same understanding, likening the sun to the virile, male, life-giving force beneficial to virgins, whom she compares with 'pale primeroses, / That die unmarried, ere they can behold / Bright Phoebus in his strength (a malady / Most incident to maids)' (IV.iv.122–25).

Of course, it was not always possible for an afflicted virgin to be married in haste, nor did everyone agree with this simple remedy. Paracelsus (1493–1541), far from recommending sex as a cure, aimed to 'expel lewd thoughts by shutting [the victims] in dark unpleasant places with bread and water without mercy.' Paracelsus also suggested that a 'good beating' would quickly return a raving woman to her

---

22 *The 'Sekenesse of wymmen'*, pp. 71 and 53; Jorden, *A Disease Called the Suffocation of the Mother*, f. 24v.

23 Jorden, *A Disease*, f. 23v (pagination incorrect).

24 Lazarus Riverius, *The Practice of Physicke* (1668) quoted in Loughlin, *Hymeneutics*, p. 40.

senses.[25] Some authors advocated keeping victims out of the company of men altogether. In one of the Paston letters, from the mid-fifteenth century, Elizabeth Clere writes to John Paston to urge him to arrange a marriage for his sister. The severe treatment his sister is currently receiving at the hands of her mother sounds suspiciously like a Paracelsian form of treatment for greensickness:

> for she was never in so great sorrow as she is nowadays; for she may not speak with no man, whosoever come, ne not may see ne speak with my man, ne with servants of her mother's, but that she beareth her on hands otherwise than she meaneth. [i.e. unless she deceives her mother] And she hath since Easter the most part been beaten once in the week or twice, and sometimes twice on a day, and her head broken in two or three places.[26]

We are fortunate to have access to some case notes (Observations) written by Shakespeare's son-in-law, John Hall, who practised in and around Stratford in the early 1600s.[27] Hall's notes are useful indicators of contemporary, regional medical practice. Out of 178 case histories well over 100 deal with women's health, including his wife, Susanna Shakespeare, and his daughter, Elizabeth. In the 'Alphabetical Table of Diseases and Medicines' which heads the case notes, 'Green Sickness' is listed under Observations 189, 190 and 245; it is unfortunate that these are among the seventy or so case notes which are missing. Hall's treatment of his fifteen-year-old daughter Elizabeth suggests greensickness, as does his cure of thirteen-year-old Mary Comb of Stratford whose 'Lunar evacuations' had stopped and who had become 'cruelly vexed with the Mother.'[28] Menstruation problems, premenstrual tension and related emotional afflictions feature frequently in Hall's notes, of which the following entry is an example:

> Editha Staughton, aged 17, was miserably afflicted with Melancholy, her Courses as yet not having broken forth, as also with the Mother; she was very easily angry with her nearest Friends, so that she continually cried out that her Parents would kill her . . . she had been purged well by expert

---

25 Dixon, *Perilous Chastity*, pp. 40–41.

26 *Paston Letters*, pp. 23–24.

27 At the time of writing *Romeo and Juliet*, circa 1595, Shakespeare was the father of two daughters approaching puberty: Susanna born on 6 May 1583 and Judith born in February 1585.

28 Hall, 'Select Observations,' pp. 33, 132.

Physicians, yet her Father desired my counsel, whether she was curable; to which I answered, Very hardly, being her Constitution was Melancholy.[29]

Such case notes give evidence of a father's real concern and point to the class of society deemed to be most at risk. It was a French surgeon Ambrose Paré (1517?–1590), who pointed out that the condition seemed to occur more in upper-class urban families. He believed that:

maids that live in the country are not so troubled with those diseases, because there is no such lying in wait for their maiden-heads, and also they live sparingly and hardily, and spend their time in continual labor.[30]

The belief that greensickness was a disease of the leisured classes was standard by the seventeenth century. One early eminent example could have been the teenage Queen of Scots. The English ambassador to France reported in 1559 when Mary was sixteen, that 'the Scottish Queen in my opinion looked very ill on it, very pale and green, and withal short breathed, and it is whispered here among them that she cannot live long.'[31] For well-to-do Renaissance fathers, rebellious, emotional, or irrational behaviour in a teenage daughter was not treated lightly, but regarded as potentially life-threatening.

Capulet is indeed a careful and caring father, but he might have done better to call upon a professional physician rather than prescribe his own cure. Capulet's characterisation as a 'cot-quean,' i.e. as usurping the role of his wife in running the household, is a contributory factor to the domestic nature of the tragedy. Not only does he run 'every thing in extremity' (I.iii.102), meaning in a disorganised and ad hoc fashion, but he deprives his wife and daughter of their natural domestic roles.[32] Lange claimed uterine fury never occurred 'in married women occupied in house cleaning,' an opinion supported by other contemporary authors who regarded a physical occupation as essential to a healthy and virtuous wife or daughter.[33] A rich diet was a further risk factor, for certain foods increased a woman's seed and there were dangers in having 'hote metys and drinkys, and lyuoun yn mych rest.'[34] Capulet's

---

[29] Hall, 'Select Observations,' pp. 174–175.

[30] Quoted in Dixon, *Perilous Chastity*, p. 44.

[31] Fraser, *Mary Queen of Scots*, p. 111.

[32] See also the opening lines of Act One, Scene Five for further evidence of a disorganised household.

[33] Quoted in Dixon, *Perilous Chastity*, p. 135.

[34] *The 'Sekenesse of wymmen'*, pp. 27, 55; see also Chapter VIII, 'Of the Ordering

household is noted for its generous provision of meats and spices (IV.iv.1–6).

## Theatre audiences and popular culture

This, then, is some of the medical background to greensickness in Shakespeare's time. What could a public theatre audience be reasonably expected to understand by Capulet's greensickness diagnosis? Anyone familiar with Shakespeare's source, Arthur Brooke's *The Tragical History of Romeus and Juliet* (1562), would have been aware that Juliet's sickness is made much of by Brooke, who articulates the parents' fear that their languishing daughter will die. Brooke includes many references to Juliet's symptoms and behaviour and to marriage as the cure.[35] His daughter's refusal is read in part by the father as an aversion to sexual relations:

> . . . and yet thou playest in this case
> The dainty fool and stubborn girl, for want of skill
> Thou dost refuse thy offered weal, and disobey my will.[36]

Brooke does not use the term greensickness, which seems to have entered the English vocabulary only later in the sixteenth century; instead he calls it 'envys faint disease,' that is, the envy of married girls (this suggests that green for envy may have been another possibility in coining the term greensickness).[37] Similarly, in Shakespeare's play, Capulet, having just alluded to Paris' 'honorable parts,' likewise presumes Juliet is showing symptoms of sexual aversion:

> a wretched puling fool,
> A whining mammet, in her fortune's tender
> To answer, 'I'll not wed, I cannot love;
> I am too young, pray you pardon me.'
> (III.v.183–86)

---

of the Body in a Virgin' in Juan Luis Vives, 'Instruction of a Christian Woman,' pp. 63–71.

35 Brooke, *Tragical History*, p. 100. Juliet's symptoms include sighing, weeping, reckless heed of meat, of sleep, of clothes, face changed, her doings strange, shut up alone, and her bold behaviour (pp. 100–2).

36 Brooke, *Tragical History*, p. 109.

37 Brooke, *Tragical History*, p. 103.

In *Pericles,* a similar male interpretation is made of Marina's resistance to Boult's sexual advances, 'Now the pox upon her green-sickness for me!' cries Boult in frustration (IV.vi.13–14).

Beyond the medical treatises, aspects of greensickness filtered through into Elizabethan popular culture through contemporary advice manuals and even through school curricula. During the course of their Latin exercises, many thousands of grammar school boys in England were introduced to the understanding that girls were usually healthier for a good dose of sex. In Erasmus' colloquy 'Courtship,' a young suitor varies the *carpe diem* trope to persuade of the health benefits of sex. The girl he is wooing puts the case for chastity:

> *Maria:*    Which is the more pleasing sight, a rose gleaming
> white on its bush or plucked and gradually withering?
> *Pamphilus:* In my opinion the rose that withers in a man's hand,
> . . . is luckier than one that grows old on a bush. . . .
> But a girl's flower doesn't fade the instant she marries.
> On the contrary, I see many girls who before marriage
> were pale, run-down, and as good as gone. The sexua
> side of marriage brightened them so much that they
> began to bloom at last.[38]

Romeo is evidently familiar with such advice since he says of Juliet:

> Be not [Diana's] maid, since she is envious
> Her vestal livery is but sick and green,
> And none but fools do wear it; cast it off.
> (II.ii.7–9)

Such arguments had apparently failed with his first love, Rosaline, who was well armed with 'Dian's wit' (I.i.209).

The majority of English authors, both medical and lay, concurred with Erasmus in accepting marriage as the answer to incipient green-sickness.[39] Henry Swinburne, in *A Treatise of Spousals* (ca. 1600), argues that because girls ripen sooner than men 'to these persons, albeit very young, the remedy against lust is not to be denied.'[40] Cecil

---

38 Erasmus, *Colloquies,* p. 95.

39 For further evidence from Renaissance physicians see Loughlin, '"Love's Friend and Stranger to Virginitie."'

40 Swinburne, *A Treatise of Spousals,* pp. 47–48. Burton also asserts that the 'best and surest remedy of all is to see [the girl] well placed, and married to good husbands in due time,' *Anatomy of Melancholy,* p. 353.

Burghley's well known precept, which endorses such advice, was commonly copied into commonplace books: 'Marry thy daughters in tyme least they marry themselves.'[41]

Juan Luis Vives, a prominent humanist authority on childrearing and education, took the approach that prevention was better than cure. Because Vives was wholly committed to the concept of chastity and celibacy as the ultimate expression of Christian piety, his advice to parents is grounded entirely in suppressing sexuality in the girl. He agreed that upper class daughters were particularly at risk for they 'follow pleasures and delicacies, unto which pleasures whoso is given, we see be pale and consumed.'[42] Parents should ensure their daughter attends no banquets, plays or dancing. Dancing in particular was a risky pastime for young women, conducive to hysteria, and a threat to chastity. Vives warns parents that 'these dances, plays, banquets [are] the enemies of quietness, the very pestilence of chastity.'[43] 'I will entreat of this dancing that nowadays is much used,' he writes, 'what good doth all that dancing of young women, holden up on men's arms, that they may hop the higher? What meaneth that shaking unto midnight, and never weary,' yet apparently too weak to go to church except on horseback or by coach. Vives adopts the Paracelsian view of dancing as conducive to hysteria when he maintains that: 'yet to say good sooth, who would not reckon women frantic when they dance?'[44] Perhaps there were indeed moral grounds for concern; in the 1604 comedy *The Wit of a Woman* a concerned father voices his reservations towards his daughter's dancing lessons:

> yet indeed these dancers, sometimes do teach [our daughters] tricks, above trenchmore, yea and sometimes such la voltas, that they mount so high, that you may see their hey nony, nony, nony no.[45]

## Capulet and Vives

Shakespeare's audience would be aware that Capulet has transgressed all the parenting rules Vives lays down. Juliet's parents have been most remiss in their choice of nurse and slack in their subsequent supervi-

---

[41] See, for example, the commonplace book MS V.a. 381 at the Folger Shakespeare Library.

[42] Vives, 'Instruction of a Christian Woman,' p. 69.

[43] Vives, 'Office of an Husband,' in *Daughters, Wives, and Widows*, p. 132.

[44] Vives, 'Instruction of a Christian Woman,' pp. 102–3.

[45] *The Wit of a Woman*, lines 432–35.

sion. Having been alerted to the vulgar nature of the nurse and to the absence of parental supervision in the household, the audience then follows Juliet's introduction, at the hands of her father, into the adult world of society and sexuality. Juliet is brought into contact with an indiscriminate throng of men through the worst possible means: a banquet, dancing, feasting, drinking, flirting, with the result, as Vives would have anticipated, of putting fire and tow together.

The most significant flaw in Capulet's judgement as a parent however, is to misread Juliet's grief as symptomatic of ill health. There has been much in the play to encourage his diagnosis, incorrect though it may be. Weeping and signs of grief and melancholy were among the most common symptoms of greensickness. Shakespeare's audience is continually reminded of Juliet's grief-stricken behaviour. Her weeping and confinement to her bedroom is repeatedly brought to the fore: by her nurse (III.iii.99), by her mother (III.v.69–70), by Paris 'Poor soul, thy face is much abus'd with tears' (IV.i.29), and by herself when Juliet tells her mother, 'Madam, I am not well.' (III.v.68). It is when Lady Capulet tells her husband and Paris that 'tonight [Juliet] is mewed up to her heaviness' (III.iv.11) that Capulet decides to call back Paris (the stage directions, taken from Q1, are specific), and 'make a desperate tender' (III.iv.12) of his child's love. In his wisdom, Capulet diagnoses sex as the remedy for his languishing daughter, and hurries the marriage plans forward. 'Thou hast a careful father, child,' Lady Capulet tells Juliet, 'one who to put thee from thy heaviness, / Hath sorted out a sudden day of joy' (III.v.107–9). Juliet's response is entirely logical, 'I wonder at this haste, that I must wed / Ere he that should be husband comes to woo' (III.v.118–19). Only a day or two earlier Capulet had made Juliet's consent a condition of the marriage and was asking Paris to wait until Juliet reached sexual maturity, 'let two more summers wither in their pride, / Ere we may think her ripe to be a bride' (I.ii.10–11). Within two days of that statement Capulet has revised his opinion of Juliet's ripeness.

Indicators of Capulet's understanding of Renaissance humoral theory are embedded in his moving expression of love and sympathy for his daughter:

> How now, a conduit, girl? What, still in tears?
> Everymore show'ring? In one little body
> Thou counterfeits a bark, a sea, a wind:
> For still thy eyes, which I may call the sea,
> Do ebb and flow with tears; the bark thy body is,
> Sailing in this salt flood; the winds thy sighs,

> Who raging with thy tears and they with them,
> Without a sudden calm will overset
> Thy tempest-tossed body.
>
> (III.v.129–37)

For Shakespeare's audience, the watery imagery used by Capulet reflects Renaissance theories on the fluid nature of a woman's physiology. The conduit pipe recalls the arteries and veins in the body and the term conduit draws on notions of women's bodies as incontinent feminine sites.[46] Gail Kern Paster draws on Renaissance proverbs and medical texts to document extensively and convincingly the representation of the fluid female body in Renaissance drama, and to reveal the anxiety this generated in men struggling to contain these leaky vessels. When she writes that the 'conventional Renaissance association of women and water is used not only to insinuate womanly unreliability but also to define the female body . . . even when it is *virgo intacta*, as a crucial problematic in the social formations of capitalism,' she could well be writing of Capulet faced with an incontinent daughter threatening his own domestic capitalism.[47]

The tempest-tossed imagery could also have significance. The ship as metaphor for the soul is a known Renaissance literary usage, but when used of a woman it may well signify the unruly womb in its watery environment. In Jorden's treatise on the suffocation of the mother, he uses the simile of 'shippes tossed in the sea, exposed to all maner of assaults and daungers' to express the perturbations of the mind.[48] Similarly, in *Philaster or Love Lies a-Bleeding* (1609), the dramatist draws on ocean imagery to represent the promiscuous female body: 'Thou troubled sea of lust.'[49]

'The sudden calm' that Capulet conceptualises for his daughter mirrors his wife's image of 'a sudden day of joy.' It is not just the romance of a wedding that will stabilise her, but rather plain and wholesome sex. Capulet's actions are in line with current theory that parents may endanger the life of a daughter by waiting too long for marriage. Burton urged parents to consider the miseries of long engagements: 'Virgins must be provided for in season, to prevent many

---

46 See for example: Spencer's description of the body (the Castle of Alma) in *The Faerie Queene* (2.9.32); Harris, 'This is not a Pipe,' p. 215.

47 Paster, *The Body Embarrassed*, p. 25.

48 Jorden, *A Disease*, f. 23v (pagination incorrect).

49 Beaumont/Fletcher, *Philaster*, II.iv.137.

diseases . . . And therefore as well to avoid these feral maladies, 'tis good to get them husbands betimes, as to prevent other gross inconveniences.'[50] The irony is, as the audience knows, but not Capulet, that Juliet is no longer a virgin, indeed she has just risen from a bed of passion. To the audience therefore, Capulet's behaviour is comically naive, but also poignantly real.

## Juliet's symptoms

Shakespeare's characterisation of this thirteen-year-old allows the possibility that Juliet is indeed showing symptoms of greensickness. A number of critics have read Juliet's powerful expression of desire for Romeo as a transgression of Renaissance theories on female behaviour, as they are generally prescribed in Renaissance conduct manuals.[51] Certainly, in school texts Tudor schoolboys received the lesson that 'it's [the man's] job to woo; that isn't appropriate to [girls]. We girls like to be swept off our feet, even if sometimes we're deeply in love.'[52] William Harvey's description of male and female roles in courtship also pithily epitomises contemporary cultural mores: 'Male *woo, allure, make love*; female *yield, condescend, suffer*; the contrary *preposterous*.'[53] As a thirteen year-old whose behaviour is impeccable towards her parents before she meets Romeo, Juliet's boldness after meeting Romeo may have signified to the audience a physiological rather than a social disorder. The reversal of gender roles, emphasised through the falconry imagery (II.ii.158–59, II.ii.182) renders Juliet the seducer who offers herself to the Romeo in the manner Burton forecasts: 'at fourteen years old, then they do offer themselves, and some plainly rage.'[54] Few of Shakespeare's older heroines voice the erotic desires this thirteen-year-old confidently articulates:

> Learn me how to lose a winning match,
> Played for a pair of stainless maidenhoods.
> Hood my unmann'd blood, bating in my cheeks
> (III.ii.12–14)

---

[50] Burton, *Anatomy of Melancholy*, p. 805.
[51] See Roberts, *William Shakespeare: Romeo and Juliet*, p. 53.
[52] Erasmus, *Colloquies*, p. 98.
[53] Quoted in Loughlin, *Hymeneutics*, p. 86.
[54] Burton, *Anatomy of Melancholy*, p. 656.

The 'pair of stainless maidenhoods,' indicates Juliet's assumption that Romeo is also a virgin and she is the one who will possess him:

> O, I have bought the mansion of a love,
> But not possess'd it, and though I am sold,
> Not yet enjoy'd
>
> (III.ii.26–28)

The audience has been privileged to witness in Juliet a level of sexual desire that could be construed as symptomatic of incipient greensickness and also to witness her own provision of a cure.[55]

## Coma or Syncope

One further feature of greensickness deserves consideration in relation to this play, and it is one that generates more questions than answers. A number of the sixteenth-century medical treatises indicate coma as a symptom of uterine fits, either for several hours or even for days. In discussing *suffocacio matricis*, the author of *The 'Sekenesse of wymmen'* points out that 'yn this sekenes wymmen fal doune to ground as they had the fallyng evyll and are swollen at the hert. And this accyse [attack] endurethe sum tymes too dayes or iij.'[56] Edward Jorden also notes how common this symptom is in uterine fits and warns of misreading coma, *syncope*, as death:

> syncope or swounding, the very image of death . . . lying like a dead corpse three or foure houres togither, and sometimes two or three whole dayes without sense, motion, breath, heate, or any signe of life at all . . . there have been laws enacted, *Mercurialis* reporteth, that no woman which was subject to this disease should be buried until she had beene three dayes dead.[57]

There was an anecdote circulating in Elizabethan England, which told of the physician, Vesalius, who commenced a dissection of a female corpse, only to find the body regain consciousness, causing him such trauma that he never performed surgery again. Coma in fact becomes a

---

55 The influence of Juliet's erotic fluency on subsequent comic heroines is discussed by Mary Bly, 'Bawdy Puns and Lustful Virgins: the Legacy of Juliet's Desire in Comedies of the Early 1600's,' 'Romeo and Juliet' *and its Afterlife*, ed. Stanley Wells, *Shakespeare Survey: An Annual Survey of Shakespeare Studies and Production*, 49 (Cambridge: Cambridge UP, 1996) 97–109.

56 *The 'Sekenesse of wymmen'*, p. 49.

57 Jorden, *A Disease*, ff. 9–11 (pagination incorrect).

major feature of a later play that echoes *Romeo and Juliet*. Gail Kern Paster has noted the similarity of plot in *A Chaste Maid in Cheapside*, where another parent diagnoses her daughter's weeping as a symptom of greensickness and promptly determines a husband is the answer. The daughter pretends to sicken and die, since by undergoing a false funeral she hopes to escape her parents' demands. Paster points out that the counterfeit illness was fully diagnosable by current medical and popular thinking as suffocation of the mother and suggests Middleton's audience might recognise both the literary allusion (presumably to Juliet) and the gynaecological symptom.[58] This prompts the likelihood that at least some in Shakespeare's audience were expected to be aware of this possible effect of uterine fits, while the parents in drama remained apparently ignorant of it. Perhaps Shakespeare is here intensifying the tragic irony of incompetence in a father who considers himself aware, but is shown to be inadequate in governing either his family or his household, or in his self-appointed role as physician to his daughter. Had he been up-to-date with medical theory he would have delayed the funeral a day or two.

## Greensickness in Jacobean Literature

It was of course natural that a female condition that was thought to be cured by sexual intercourse would become a topic for humour, and bawdy humour at that, in male circles. In Campion's *Fourth Book of Ayres* (1618) Ballad XXIII opens with the lines:

> Faine would I wed a fair young man, that day and night could please me:
> When my mind or body grieved, that had the power to ease me.
> Maids are full of longing thoughts, that breed a bloodless sickness,
> And that, oft I hear men say, is only cured by quickness.[59]

Two early seventeenth-century poets, Lord Herbert and Thomas Carew, wrote poems on greensickness, using the theme as vehicles for the *carpe diem* motif, but each gives evidence of medical knowledge. In Herbert's *The Green-sickness Beauty*, the first stanza identifies the four most common symptoms:

> Though the pale white within your cheeks compos'd,
> And doubtful light unto your eye confin'd,

---

58 Paster, *The Body Embarrassed*, pp. 52, 61, 62.
59 Campion, *The Third and Fourth Book of Airs*, Ballad XXIII.

> Though your short breath not from itself unloos'd,
>     And careless motions of your equal mind,
>     Argue your beauties are not all disclos'd;[60]

Herbert has picked out the pallor, the dull eye (also commonly noted as a symptom), the shortness of breath and the distracted mind, to demonstrate that this girl is still a virgin, that her 'beauties are not all disclos'd.' The treatment Elizabethan dramatists give to greensickness is usually humorous, a trope for characterising fathers as well meaning but naive. In *The Wit of a Woman* (1604) one credulous father hires his daughter's lover who is disguised as a doctor:

> Father: Master Doctor, I thank you for your kindness, . . . there is a young gentlewoman, somewhat given to the green sickness, and if you can cure her, I tell you she hath a father that will soundly recompence your pains.[61]

In John Ford's *Tis Pity She's a Whore* (1633) another naive father of an ailing daughter thinks along the same lines as Capulet:

> Doctor:                    I rather think
>     Her sickness is a fulness of her blood—
>     you understand me?
> Father:                    I do, you counsel well,
>     And once within these few days will so order't
>     She shall be married, ere she know the time.
>                                 (III.iv.7–11)

Like Shakespeare, Ford plays up the dramatic irony of a father grieving over his daughter's refusal to marry, while the audience is aware she is already pregnant—in this instance to her brother. These fathers are characterised as both naive and out-of-touch with youth; the significance of Capulet's age—he has to be close to sixty (I.v.33–39)—emphasises the generation gap. Possibly, there are also implications of pretentions to status: these fathers are quick to diagnose greensickness in an out-of-sorts daughter and perhaps anxious to claim evidence of upper-class status, of their own diagnostic skills, and of course proof of their daughter's virginity.[62]

---

[60] Herbert, *Minor Poets*, p. 47.

[61] *The Wit of a Woman*, lines 549–54.

[62] Loughlin has argued that in drama the symptoms of greensickness provided the only epistemological surety of virginity available to fathers or suitors; see her *Hymeneutics*, pp. 39–41.

# Conclusion

How, then, does the greensickness reference influence a reading of *Romeo and Juliet?* It supports the views of scholars who see adolescence as a major theme in the play.[63] It explains the relevance of the age of fourteen, lower than in Shakespeare's source, it throws light on Capulet's behaviour as a father; and it further focuses attention on male perceptions of female sexuality. This latter effect is important for the play as a whole; *Romeo and Juliet* is a highly sexed play that opens on a scene of crass male sexual bravado, with extensive punning on maidenheads and naked weapons.

The play deals with emerging sexuality in an adult world which fails to value sex as love, seeing it only as a genital drive to be satisfied or joked over. Romeo and Juliet's young passion is located in a social climate that has reduced lovemaking to sex making, and women's anatomy to a fearful handicap. Bawdy sex is what characterises the nurse; the aging Capulet views sex as escapades in a long gone past; and an absence of sex is what characterises his young wife. For most of the young men it is all talk and no action (II.iv.147–49). Roberts and other critics have commented that the play presents masculinity in a culture of phallic violence.[64] I would suggest that Shakespeare's use of the greensickness trope endorses this view; it goes beyond the humorous to point to the limitations of male attitudes towards sexuality and to locate an aged father's inadequate handling of the onset of puberty in his only daughter in poignantly domestic terms.

*University of Sydney*
*Sydney, Australia*

## Cited Works

Beaumont, Francis and John Fletcher. *Philaster or Love Lies a-Bleeding*, ed. Andrew Gurr. The Revels Plays. London: Methuen & Co. Ltd., 1969.

Bergeron, David M. 'Sickness in *Romeo and Juliet*' *CLA Journal* 20 (1977): 356–64.

Brooke, Arthur. *The Tragical History of Romeus and Juliet*. London: Cassell & Co. Ltd., 1890.

---

[63] For example Kahn, 'Coming of Age in Verona,' and Cox, 'Adolescent Process in *Romeo and Juliet.*'

[64] Roberts, *William Shakespeare: Romeo and Juliet*, p. 61.

Burton, Robert. *The Anatomy of Melancholy* (1621), eds. Floyd Dell and Paul Jordan-Smith. New York: Tudor Publishing Co., 1938.

Campion, Thomas. *The Third and Fourth Book of Airs* (1618). Menston: The Scolar Press, 1973.

Commonplace book. MS V.a. 381. Folger Shakespeare Library, Washington, DC.

Cox, Marjorie. 'Adolescent Process in *Romeo and Juliet*.' *The Psychoanalytic Review* 63 (1976): 379–92.

*Daughters, Wives, and Widows: Writings by Men about Women and Marriage in England, 1500–1640*, ed. Joan Larsen Klein. Urbana: University of Illinois Press, 1992.

De Ketham, Johann. *The Fasciculus Medicinae of Johannes de Ketham* (Venice 1491), trans. Charles Singer. English trans. Luke Demaitre. Birmingham, AL: The Classics of Medicine Library, 1988.

Dixon, Laurinda S. *Perilous Chastity: Women and Illness in Pre-Enlightenment Art and Medicine*. Ithaca: Cornell University Press, 1995.

Erasmus, Desiderius. *Colloquies*, trans. Craig R. Thompson. Chicago: University of Chicago Press, 1965.

Ford, John. *'Tis Pity She's a Whore* (1633), ed. Simon Barker. London: Routledge, 1997.

Fraser, Antonia. *Mary Queen of Scots*. London: Weidenfeld & Nicolson Ltd., 1969.

Greene, Robert. *Mamillia: Parts I and II* (1583). *The Life and Complete Works in Prose and Verse of Robert Greene, M.A*, ed. Alexander B. Grosart. Vol. 2. New York: Russell & Russell, 1964.

Hall, John. 'Select Observations on English Bodies or Cures both Empirical and Historical performed upon Eminent Persons in Desperate Diseases (1657)' pp. 104–320 in *Shakespeare's Son-in-Law: John Hall Man and Physician,* ed. Harriet Joseph. Hamden, CT: Archon Books, 1964.

Harris, Jonathan Gil. 'This is not a Pipe: Water Supply, Incontinent Sources, and the Leaky Body Politic' in 203–28 *Enclosure Acts: Sexuality, Property, and Culture in Early Modern England*, eds. Richard Burt and John Michael Archer. Ithaca and London: Cornell University Press, 1994.

*Health Knowledge: A Thorough and Concise Knowledge of The Prevention, Causes, and Treatments of Disease, Simplified for Home Use*, ed. J.L. Corish. New York: Medical Book Distributors, Inc., 1927.

Herbert, Edward. *Minor Poets of the Seventeenth Century.* Everyman's Library 873. London: Dent and Sons, 1953.

Jacquart, Danielle and Claude Thomasset. *Sexuality and Medicine in the Middle Ages*, trans. Matthew Adamson. Princeton, NJ: Princeton University Press, 1988.

Jorden, Edward. *A Disease Called the Suffocation of the Mother* (1603). The English Experience 392. Amsterdam: Da Capo Press, 1971.

Kahn, Coppélia. 'Coming of Age in Verona' pp. 171–93 in *The Woman's Part: Feminist Criticism of Shakespeare*, eds. Carolyn Ruth Swift Lenz, Gayle Greene, Carol Thomas Neely. Urbana: University of Illinois Press, 1980.

Loudon, I.S.L. 'Chlorosis, anaemia, and anorexia nervosa' *British Medical Journal* 281 (1980): 1673–75.

Loughlin, Marie H. *Hymeneutics: Interpreting Virginity on the Early Modern Stage*. Lewisburg, PA: Bucknell University Press, 1997.

Loughlin, Marie H. '"Love's Friend and Stranger to Virginitie:" The Politics of the Virginal Body in Ben Jonson's *Hymenaei* and Thomas Campion's *The Lord Hay's Masque*' *English Literary History* 63:4 (1996): 833–49.

Mendelson, Sara and Patricia Crawford. *Women in Early Modern England 1550–1720*. Oxford: Clarendon Press, 1998.

Paster, Gail Kern. *The Body Embarrassed: Drama and the Disciplines of Shame in Early Modern England*. Ithaca, NY: Cornell University Press, 1993.

*The Paston Letters*, ed. Norman Davis. The World's Classics 591. London: Oxford University Press, 1963.

Roberts, Sasha. *William Shakespeare: Romeo and Juliet*. Writers and their Work. Plymouth, MA: Northcote House Publishers Ltd., 1998.

Rubenstein, Frankie. *A Dictionary of Shakespeare's Sexual Puns and their Significance*. London: MacMillan Press, 1984.

*The 'Sekeness of wymmen' A Middle English Treatise on Diseases in Women*, ed. M.-R. Hallaert. Scripta 8. Brussel: Omirel, UFSAL, 1982.

Shakespeare, William. *The Riverside Shakespeare*, ed. G. Blakemore Evans. Boston: Houghton Mifflin Co., 1974.

Swinburne, Henry. *A Treatise of Spousals, or Matrimonial Contracts*. New York: Garland Publishing, 1985.

Vives, Juan Luis. 'Instruction of a Christian Woman' pp. 29–136 in *Vives and the Renascence Education of Women*, ed. Foster Watson. London: Edward Arnold, 1912.

*The Wit of a Woman* (1604). Malone Society Reprints. Oxford: Oxford University Press, 1913.

Young, Bruce W. 'Haste, Consent, and Age at Marriage: Some Implications of Social History for *Romeo and Juliet*' *Iowa State Journal of Research* 62:3 (1988): 459–74.

# Girls in Trouble in Late Medieval Bologna

## Carol Lansing

In late medieval Italy, patrician males passed through an adolescent or youth phase that was sometimes a very prolonged one.[1] This was a stage of life in which young men were no longer children but carried no adult responsibilities. As Christiane Klapisch-Zuber pointed out in 1973, the adolescent stage for elite Florentines was defined not by sexual maturation, but by social and economic dependence. Adolescence ended with autonomy, which meant release from submission to *patria potestas*, the authority of the father and household head. The long and often irksome dependence of young male elites has been the subject of fascinating studies.[2]

Girls were different. They were not allowed a similar transitional phase. Women were always subjected to *patria potestas*: their subordination to paternal authority was not temporary.[3] No transitional stage eased the passage to adult roles. Girls were expected, instead, to move straight from childhood to marriage and adult life.[4] Ideally, families whisked their daughters off to marriage soon after puberty. Family honour after all was closely linked to the control of female sexuality and family status commodified in the dowries families paid for their daughters and received with their brides. Young men could pass through a transitional phase that might well include sexual escapades; young women could with honour be only virgins or married matrons. In effect, elite boys could be allowed time to experiment and get into a bit of trouble, but girls could not.

Despite the lack of a formal youth stage, the adolescent daughters of the elite are everywhere in late medieval Italy. If girls were not supposed to go through a painful transition from childhood to adulthood, the society was nevertheless fascinated with those who did. Many of the

---

[1] See *Infanzie*, and especially the article by Andrea Zorzi, 'Rituali di violenza giovanile nelle società urbane del tardo Medioevo,' pp. 185–209.

[2] Klapisch-Zuber, 'Childhood in Tuscany.'

[3] See Bellomo, *La condizione giuridica della donna*, pp. 53–54.

[4] See for example the discussion of adolescence in Shahar, *Childhood in the Middle Ages*, pp. 27–31.

most powerful representations in late medieval Italian culture were young women in this transitional stage, including the idealized love objects of poets as well as female *brigate* or youth bands such as the young women narrators in Boccaccio's *Decameron*. The most popular saints were often rebellious teenage girls, either virgins who refused marriage (like Clare of Assisi and Catherine of Siena), or young brides who battled to escape the married role (like Umiliana dei Cerchi of Florence).[5] If elite families and the law defined adolescence in terms of economic and legal dependency, the larger society also understood that adolescence was about sexual maturation. For many saints, puberty led to crises of identity as girls resisted the demands of family and society to pursue a religious ideal.[6] This was a struggle about sex and identity as young women sought to claim identities that precluded sexual relations and the social expectations for married elite women.[7] Adolescent rebellion meant the control of sexuality, the choice to remain virginal or, if married, to escape the marriage debt. Saints' lives portray a runaway girl such as Clare clutching an altar as her male relatives try to drag her back to a socially advantageous marriage. Other young women married and then repudiated all the elaborate trappings of young brides: Umiliana gave away pieces of her clothing, as well as feathers from her marriage bed. These strong-willed young women captured society's imagination. When Umiliana's corpse was carried out of the family tower, a crowd jostled for pieces of her clothing or hair. A society that imposed strict controls on women, including their very mobility outside the home, also venerated adolescent girls who battled against just those demands.[8] Marriageable girls embodied a set of social values, values commodified in their dowries and displayed when young brides were elaborately dressed for their weddings. When girls like Clare or Catherine repudiated the marriages planned by their families, their actions spoke to a profound cultural ambivalence about a secular culture that valued wealth and rank.

What of adolescent girls who did not have propertied families and represented no one's honour or status? A compelling picture of the experience of girls is suggested by Klapisch-Zuber's 1973 account of the late medieval treatment of female children. Working from the

---

[5] See *Women and religion in medieval and Renaissance Italy*. On Catherine's family, see Luongo, 'The Politics of Marginality'; on Umiliana, Papi, 'Umiliana dei Cerchi' and *'In castro poenitentiae.'*

[6] On child and adolescent saints, see Weinstein/Bell, *Saints and Society*, chs. 1–2.

[7] See Elliott, *Spiritual marriage*.

[8] Chabot, '"Sola, donna, non gir mai."'

analysis of the Tuscan catasto of 1427, she concluded that families were more attached to their male children and tended to view daughters as disappointments. There was a striking imbalance in the sex ratio for children under the ages of 14 or 18, the age when males started to pay taxes and when most girls married. This implies not only that young girls were undercounted in tax returns, but that they were more apt than boys to be abandoned, to be put out to distant wetnurses, and to receive poorer care in general.[9] It was only when girls reached a marriageable age that they became the centre of anxious attention. This evidence derives from fifteenth-century Tuscany, but female children were probably even less welcome in the late-thirteenth-century towns, when rapid demographic growth put great economic pressure on families, so that providing for daughters could be particularly burdensome.[10]

Sources for adolescent girls outside the elite, particularly girls without dowries, are elusive. Late medieval Italian society deplored the fact that some adolescent girls lacked dowries, so much so that the provision of funds to enable them to marry honourably was considered an act of piety. Occasionally, tax records provide some indirect evidence. In Bologna in 1329, as many as a quarter to a third of households declared themselves indigent, which meant they would be unable to pay dowries. Families with modest resources complained on their returns of the high cost of dowries. Widows in particular were hard-pressed. A widow with a 43 lire patrimony stated that her 20-year-old daughter 'could not marry because of her lack of dowry.'[11] Another widow implausibly hoped to give each of her three daughters a 50 lire dowry, though her declared patrimony was only 36 lire.

Girls without marriage prospects do occasionally appear directly in contemporary court records. Adolescent girls were directly questioned in judicial inquests as victims, as suspected criminals, and also as witnesses. People also testified to the court about adolescent girls. That testimony offers a rare look at thirteenth-century ideas about female adolescents. An extensive collection of thirteenth-century Italian court records survives in Bologna. They include inquests, both state-initiated

---

[9] Klapisch-Zuber, 'Childhood in Tuscany.'

[10] On Bolognese demography and family structure see Pini, 'Problemi demografici bolognesi del Duecento,' and 'Un aspetto dei rapporti tra città e territorio nel Medioevo'; and Ortalli, 'La famille à Bologne au XIIIe siècle.'

[11] See Matassoni, 'Piangere Misera,' pp. 416–19.

inquiries and inquests sparked when an individual made a notification or accusation to the court. In either case, the court questioned witnesses not only on the details of the accusation, but on the *fama* or public reputation of the accused, and their relations with the other witnesses. That testimony can reveal aspects of contemporary attitudes and practice that are available in no other thirteenth-century source.

The use of court records to recover social experience is controversial. Depositions after all are formulaic sources: witnesses answered specific questions shaped by the requirements of the law and then notaries translated their statements into Latin. Further, legal scholars argue that the judicial process had a logic of its own and the highly formalized representations made to the court can be used to study court procedure, but bear little resemblance to experience outside the court. As Massimo Vallerani has argued, the court was a *theatrum mundi* in which individuals and events played narrow roles as legal *persone* and *atti* in the fictive reality created by court process.[12]

If the court was a theatre, it was one in which people represented aspects of their social experience. Witnesses told little stories about recent events and about their friends, their enemies, and their neighbours. Often, people made statements designed to manipulate the courts. However, at a basic level their stories had to be credible, since they were intended to persuade a judge or notary of the truth about an individual or an event. If one concocts a story for the court, it had better be plausible. To give an example, men were at times described as being of 'mala fama,' bad repute, because they were inveterate gamblers who even gambled away their trousers in the town square. This does not imply that every man characterized in this way actually had lost his pants gambling, but it does mean that there were men who had done so: the accusation was credible.[13] For this reason, the tales told in inquests are not really strictly accurate, but they do reveal contemporary attitudes and practice. The evidence may be anecdotal, but revealing. Further, while some Bolognese tried hard to manipulate the courts, the courts in turn pursued inquiries into false testimony or instruments with energy. In sum, while the stories people told surely were not all true, they are nonetheless useful as representations of social practice.

---

[12] See Vallerani, 'L'amministrazione della giustizia a Bologna in età podestarile,' p. 292.

[13] For an example of a man accused of gambling away all his clothing see Bologna, Archivio di Stato, Curia del podestà, Ufficio Corone ed Armi 7, 1, fol. 4r.

Inquests from thirteenth-century Bologna—like medieval court records more generally—are endlessly full of cases of violence against women: assault, rape, homicide. The stories told to the court are at times horrific: a little girl abused by her stepmother, a woman pregnant with twins clubbed to death by her husband in their bed, a woman whose husband slit her throat because her father failed to pay her dowry.[14] At times, these victims can be identified as adolescent girls or young women. In some circumstances, the court was careful to inquire about age. The penalty for some offenses could be mitigated if the person who committed a crime was a minor and thus without full legal capacity. If a person convicted of homicide was under the age of fourteen or a *furioso*, for example, the podestà could decide the penalty.[15] In other cases the penalty was more severe if the victim was underage. This meant that the accuser, accused, and witnesses might have reason to lie about a girl's age, if in fact they knew it. The notaries recording a legal notification or testimony often took care to indicate that the case involved a girl, terming her a *mamula*, which meant a younger child, a *puella* or a *domicella*. This corresponded to traditional medieval accounts of the stages of life, derived from Isidore of Seville. These differentiated between infancy, *pueritia*, which ended at 14 and *adolescentia*, which lasted into the 20s.

In practice, determining a girl's age could be very imprecise. People guessed at ages. In one rape inquest, three different witnesses estimated the boy's age at 14, at 15–16, and at 16–18, and the girl's age at 14, at 15–16, and over 12.[16] The terms used by the court's notaries did not indicate whether a girl had undergone puberty. A girl who is termed a *mamula* or a *puella* could be post-pubescent. Elisabeth Crouzet-Pavan found that in Venice before 1360 the term *puella* was used by the courts only for minor girls, girls under twelve; after that date it was sometimes extended to victims aged fourteen.[17] This was evidently not true in

---

[14] For the pregnant wife, Bologna, Archivio di Stato, Curia del podestà, Libri Inquisitionum et testium 47 II, 1, fol. 16r; another pregnant wife murdered, Libri Inquisitionum et testium 30, 13, fols. 43r–45r. For a protest over the way a woman beat her stepdaughter, who is termed a 'puella parva,' Libri Inquisitionum et testium 5, 4, fol. 22v (paginated backwards). The inquest into the enraged husband killing his wife in Serravalle over her dowry is Libri Inquisitionum et testium 21, 5, fol. 17r.

[15] *Statuti di Bologna dell'anno 1288*, book 4, rubric 38, p. 204. See also *Statuti di Bologna dall'anno 1245 all'anno 1267*, vol. 3, book 10, rubric 5, p. 276.

[16] Bologna, Archivio di Stato, Curia del Podestà, Libri Inquisitionum et testium 44, 1, fol. 75r–v.

[17] Crouzet-Pavan, 'A Flower of Evil,' p. 176. On Italian discussions of the stages

Bologna. In practice, a girl called a *mamula* also was not necessarily pre-pubescent, judging from cases in which witnesses speculated that a girl they termed a *mamula* might be secretly married. In 1295 a man confessed to the rape of two girls who are termed *mamulae*: one was a virgin aged 14 and the other a 15-year-old girl who then became a prostitute.[18] Occasionally, the notaries took care to term a girl a *puella parva*, a small girl, which did clearly indicate that she was a child. Further, it can be difficult to distinguish between a girl in her teens and a young woman in her twenties. If male, she would have been termed a *iuvenis*, a youth. Occasionally, this term was applied to women. In a 1299 inquest concerning a woman named Strella who was suspected of prostitution, a witness in response to a question about her age and appearance termed Strella a female youth ('una iuvenis femina') and very beautiful.[19]

The carefully protected daughters of the elite appear in these records only rarely. Public talk about a marriageable girl could mean dishonour. In one inquest, a servant was accused of 'verba iniuriosa,' defamation, because he had told people that he was secretly married to his employer's daughter Billina, so that no one else would be willing to marry her. Witnesses termed her a *bona mamula*, a good girl, though some speculated otherwise.[20] Again, if secret marriage implied sexual relations, this suggests that the term *mamula* was probably being used for a post-pubescent girl. It is striking that her mother pursued a case that encouraged public speculation about her daughter's character and sexual reputation. At the same time, the anti-magnate laws of the late thirteenth-century attacked elite lineages by limiting the ways they could display status and honour, including the clothing and marriages of their daughters. The law of 1288 did permit certain ornaments to marriageable adolescent girls, termed *domicelle non maritate*, but not to males over twelve or girls once they were married.[21] The courts did take the trouble to pursue elite young women for violations of the

---

of life, see Klapisch-Zuber, 'Childhood in Tuscany,' esp. pp. 96–97.

[18] Bologna, Archivio di Stato, Curia del Podestà, Libri Inquisitionum et testium 35, 2, fols. 38v–39r.

[19] Bologna, Archivio di Stato, Curia del Podestà, Libri Inquisitionum et testium 46, 5, fols. 2r–5r. The issue was whether she was a prostitute and lived in a neighbourhood from which prostitution was banned.

[20] Bologna, Archivio di Stato, Curia del Podestà, Libri Inquisitionum et testium 47 I, 6, fols. 1r–4r.

[21] *Statuti di Bologna dell'anno 1288*, book 4, rubric 95, p. 250.

sumptuary laws: wearing tiaras in church or long trains on their dresses.[22] Their marriages also could become the subject of court inquiries. Bologna banned marriages with the Lambertazzi faction, and the courts occasionally inquired into the subterfuges families used to marry their daughters in violation of the ban. Nevertheless, for the most part, elite women of marriageable age do not appear in court cases.

Instead, the young women who show up in court records generally came from the working poor. Often, they appear in court as victims. Tales of rape or attempted rape are usually simple: so-and-so broke in the house and threw a girl to the ground, or attacked her on the road. Nevertheless, the incidental references in these cases can be revealing and even surprising. In 1295, a man was begged not to harm a girl, termed a *puella,* because 'she was an orphan and stayed with Sister Blaxia in order to learn.'[23] Probably, Sister Blaxia was a tertiary and the *puella* was learning a trade. Another example is a case that described an adolescent female servant operating quite independently. In 1286, the court held an inquest in response to a notification of an attempted rape. A servant named Divitia described the attack in a deposition to the court. Divitia reported that she was passing along the street on her way to visit a friend when a man named Rolandino called to her. Would she consider working in his household? He lacked a servant and his wife was Sienese and incompetent. He knew Divitia's brother-in-law Bernardino, he reassuringly added. Divitia replied that she would gladly stay with any woman who was a 'bona persona,' a person of good repute. Rolandino led her to his house, offering to show it to her, but once she was inside he closed the door, shoved her off the stairs into a horse's stall and tried to raise her skirts. His attempt at forcible rape failed because she fought him off, she reported, but in his frustrated rage he beat her with his fists and tore her hair. When she emerged from the house injured, weeping, her hair loose, two clerics in a nearby church helped her. Without two witnesses Divitia could not meet the requirements for legal proof, and Rolandino was allowed to go unpunished.[24]

---

[22] See Bologna, Archivio di Stato, Curia del Podestà, Libri Inquisitionum et testium 8, 16, fol. 38r for an inquiry into the length of a train on a woman's dress; for testimony concerning tiaras and garlands, Libri Inquisitionum et testium 7, 11, fols. 4r–6r. For four married women accused of wearing illegal tiaras, Corone ed armi, 4, fols. 21v–22r.

[23] Bologna, Archivio di Stato, Curia del Podestà, Libri Inquisitionum et testium 35, 3, fol. 35r.

[24] Bologna, Archivio di Stato, Curia del Podestà, Libri Inquisitionum et testium 8,

Divitia is termed a *puella* and surely was an adolescent girl. In response to the judge's question, she said that she was not a virgin and volunteered that she had refused an offer of marriage. What do we make of her tale to the court? She certainly represented herself as an independent young female servant. Poor families placed daughters as young as eight years of age as domestics, perhaps for a covert price, with the understanding that the girl would live and work under her master's authority.[25] Steven Epstein has reported a Genoese contract of 1256 in which a woman placed her daughter as a household servant for fourteen years, in exchange for food and clothing.[26] This, as Epstein points out, seems close to domestic slavery and was evidently a way for a very poor household to get a daughter housed and fed. In other arrangements, a female servant worked to earn a dowry and then was to be married with the aid of her master, perhaps at age eighteen. Divitia does not fit this pattern because she portrays herself as more independent, making decisions without reference to the authority of an employer or a kinsman. She sketches herself as a girl who had turned down an offer of marriage and cheerfully (if foolishly) agreed to a new employer on her own. She also seems without protectors, despite a married sister and brother-in-law. It is perfectly possible that something entirely different had happened and Divitia's story was a fabrication intended to dupe the court. Again, to do so Divitia had to be credible: her account could not be too much at variance with practice.

Another, very common role for adolescent girls was work as an *amasia*, or concubine, a woman who exchanged sex and other services with a man for resources. Some lived with their lovers as concubines and provided domestic work. The role of household servant and the role of concubine could easily blur. In other cases, the relationship was not co-residential: an *amasia* lived with other women and served a man termed her *dominus* or lord. These were apt to be university students who paid what were termed 'expenses.' One man is said to have brought bread and wine when he visited his *amica*.[27] The relationship also could overlap with that of pimp and prostitute: a man might keep a lover and profit from her sexual relations with others. A

---

1, fols. 1r–2r.

[25] See Klapisch, 'Childhood in Tuscany' and 'Female Celibacy and Service.'

[26] Epstein, *Genoa and the Genoese*, p. 102.

[27] Bologna, Archivio di Stato, Curia del Podestà, Liber inquisitionum et testium 33 II, 3, fols. 4r–9r. See my 'Concubines, lovers, prostitutes.'

man named Corsino kept Lucia, who is termed a *iuvenem*, as his *amasia* and servant. She lived not with him but in a house kept by a woman, where there were prostitutes. Lucia, he reported, washed students' hair for pay.[28] These were impermanent relations; the women and any offspring had no legal or economic claims on the man. *Amasie* were often questioned in inquests into prostitution and also appeared in other sorts of cases. Numbers are elusive, but the arrangement was common. I have found discussions of roughly 65 *amasie* in the extant thirteenth-century inquests.

It was dishonourable for adolescent girls to end up as amasie. Witnesses told the court stories about how girls became concubines and prostitutes that are revealing of contemporary attitudes about female adolescence. In a few cases, witnesses blamed the girl's family, reporting that a family gave their daughter to a man to be his concubine 'for a price;' one girl was said to have been given to Tuccio the priest for thirty pounds.[29] In other cases, girls were described as kidnapped by men. Kidnap accusations were common, and some were fictive. Many accusations and notifications to the court described dowered girls kidnapped in the hopes of a forced marriage. The motive could be simply the hope that the family would accept a fait accompli, pay the girl's dowry, and salvage honour. For example, in 1288, two men carried off Billina, who is termed a *iuvencula mulier*, literally a little youth who is a woman. Ugolino placed a ring on her finger and then told her to state that she wanted him as her husband. Instead, Billina's witnesses reported, she kept her mouth shut. Then, when friends rode up, Billina ran to a sheep shed and hid, emerging only when she heard her mother call her name.[30]

The testimony of witnesses often complicated kidnap cases by blaming the adolescent girl. In a number of cases, the court was initially told that a girl had been kidnapped and raped. Then, witnesses testified that she had in fact run away by choice. In that circumstance, a kidnap accusation could be a way for a girl's family to gain some leverage over the young man. Rape or carnal knowledge accusations similarly could be used for leverage.[31] Families also might accuse a

---

[28] Bologna, Archivio di Stato, Curia del Podestà, Libri Inquisitionum et testium 7, 12, fol. 6v.

[29] Bologna, Archivio di Stato, Curia del Podestà, Liber inquisitionum et testium 2, 6, fol. 28r is an example.

[30] Bologna, Archivio di Stato, Curia del Podestà, Libri Inquisitionum et testium 12, 3, fols. 20r–24v.

[31] For an example of an accusation of carnal knowledge withdrawn because of

daughter's lover of theft. An inquest was launched because the court was notified that Bunalello had gone to the house of a widow and her son and carried off her daughter Giliola, together with the clothing on her back. He took her to the house where he lived and had carnal knowledge of her. Bunalello was absolved. Cambio, the first witness, responded to the court that 'he had heard it said that this Giliola certainly separated herself from the house of this lady Armegarda her mother, and certainly went to the house of Bunalello and that Bunalello certainly kept her for his woman and knew her carnally by the will of Giliola, not violently or through violence but just as a woman who freely and by her will separated herself from her house and went to the same Bunallelo.'[32] Cambio sketched a young woman who freely chose to leave her mother's household and live with her lover. Twelve more witnesses were questioned and most stated that Giliola had chosen to be Bunallelo's *amasia*, or concubine. The question at issue was not kidnap, but theft: had Bunallelo and Giliola stolen her clothing by taking it with her when she left her mother's home?

In other cases witnesses took the view that girls were not kidnapped, but ran off because of pregnancies, as was the case with Tomaxina, who ran away with a man to the city because she was pregnant by a priest and feared her father and brothers.[33] And people believed that male kinsmen did kill girls over dishonourable pregnancies. In one lurid case from the contado, a man killed his sister Ymelda and his illegitimate brother Rolandino because the pair had had incestuous relations and Ymelda was pregnant, at least according to the neighbours.[34] There were also cases in which young lovers simply ran off together and married, like Benasay and Bartholomea, who exchanged vows and a ring in a tavern without the permission of her father, mother, or *parenti*.[35]

---

a dowry notification, see Bologna, Archivio di Stato, Curia del Podestà, Libri Inquisitionum et testium 8, 12, fol. 10r.

[32] Bologna, Archivio di Stato, Curia del Podestà, Libri Inquisitionum et testium 11, 4, fol. 3r.

[33] Bologna, Archivio di Stato, Curia del Podestà, Libri Inquisitionum et testium 27, 3, fols. 13r–14v. See Inquisitionum et testium 48, 1, 16r–19r for another example of an inquest into whether a girl in the contado was kidnapped or ran away because she was pregnant and feared her father and brothers.

[34] Bologna, Archivio di Stato, Curia del Podestà, Libri Inquisitionum et testium 27, 3, fols. 4r–6v.

[35] Bologna, Archivio di Stato, Curia del Podestà, Libri Inquisitionum et testium

The thirteenth-century court maintained a sharp dichotomy between girls of *bona fama*, good public reputation, and those of *mala fama*. Often, however, this did not fit the social experience of witnesses. People could not decide about the character of an adolescent girl because the difference hinged on the intangible question of choice. In many of these cases, people speculated that perhaps the girl had not been victimized, but had rebelled. Was Billina really kidnapped or could she have chosen to run off with the two men? In response to a question about how the episode was viewed by neighbours one witness answered that Billina's friends claim that she was kidnapped by force 'and some say yes, some say no.' The family and friends had a strong incentive to maintain that Billina was a young woman of good fame who had been the innocent victim of an attempt at kidnap and forced marriage. She had not dishonoured the family and her value on the marriage market was undiminished. Some neighbours speculated instead that she had chosen to go with Ugolino but had been prevented and that the family sought to cover up her rebellion with a kidnap accusation.

In another case, a couple was accused of kidnapping a teenage girl from her guardian's house and refusing to return her. Their guilt or innocence depended on whether she had rebelled or been forced. Witnesses suggested that the *puella* had in fact run away from her guardians to stay with her mother's sister. Despite her aunt and uncle's pleading, the girl refused to return to her legal guardian. The beleaguered uncle, faced with a kidnapping charge, even resorted to a bit of theatre for the neighbours. He marched her out into the street and told her to go back to her guardian. She simply refused.[36] This vignette of the irritated uncle's public display of a stubborn adolescent girl who refused to accede to adult authority illustrates how difficult it could be for Bolognese and the courts to cope with female adolescents.

A different kind of runaway girl appears in a theft inquest. It is a puzzling glimpse of the rebellion of a young girl who was apparently without marriage prospects. Johana confessed that she stole a collection of items including clothing, a gold ring and a purse from the house of a notary named Gherardo, then with her neighbour and friend Gisina took the goods to the house of a woman named Bonissima,

---

45, 2, fol. 20r–v.

[36] Bologna, Archivio di Stato, Curia del Podestà, Libri Inquisitionum et testium 30, 13, fols. 48r–53v.

whom Gisina knew. After the robbery, Johana stayed in Bonissima's house and Gisina fed her there. Johana intended the property to go to a man named Gregory 'who,' she said, 'lay with me and is my *amicus* [*amasio*] and promised to take me as a wife.' After eight days, they divided the goods and Johana slipped out of town after dark with a man from Piacenza. This was apparently arranged by Bonissima's household. The Placentino was to lead Johana to Ravenna and carried a letter introducing her to a certain man who, she was told, was the *amicus* of Gisina, but instead, once they were out of Bologna, a group of rustics captured the pair and delivered them to the court. In response to a question Johana reported that she was ten years old.

Gherardo, the notary she had robbed, gave a revealing deposition. Johana was in fact his niece; her mother had been his sister. The girl had turned ten in May. He valued the stolen property at nine libras, more or less. Johana thus was a girl without living parents who probably lived with her maternal uncle. He was a prosperous and respectable notary, judging from the stolen goods, which included valuable clothing and a gold ring. Nothing in the case suggests that Johana had a dowry and there is little to suggest that Gherardo had much concern for the girl's welfare. Against this background of family disinterest, Johana appears independent, rebellious, and very unwise. On Gisina's advice, Johana ran away, stealing valuable goods which were divided by members of Bonissima's household and then recovered by the court. It is not obvious whether she was actively duped by her friend Gisina or perhaps by her *amicus* Gregory. She implied that she had been Gregory's lover before she left her uncle's household and stole the goods as a dowry so that he would marry her. When Johana was sent off to Gisina's *amicus* in Ravenna, she must have been slated for domestic service or, more probably, for prostitution. Could Johana have been a prepubescent child of ten? Perhaps: children certainly worked as servants and prostitutes. However, Johana's relations with Gregory and her marriage plans suggest that she was more probably an adolescent. There was an incentive to tell the court that she was well under twelve in hopes of mitigating any judicial punishment. The judge handed Johana over into the keeping of a religious house while her case was pending and then banned her.[37]

---

[37] Bologna, Archivio di Stato, Curia del Podestà, Libri Inquisitionum et testium 45, 2, fol. 13r; see also 45, 8, fols. 7r–8r.

One thread that runs through this inquest as it does through the court registers and contemporary statutes is the idea that older women trap young girls into concubinage and prostitution.[38] These tales explained girl prostitutes not in terms of runaway teenagers and familial neglect, but in terms of the exploitation of girls by older women.[39] There was some truth to this. Some mothers surely were supported by teenage daughters, judging from prostitution inquests that described girls who were *amasie* or prostitutes and lived with their mothers. In one case, a woman named Maria was said to have been a priest's concubine and then her daughter's pimp.[40] The priest would have no economic responsibility for Maria or their illegitimate daughter; given the bleak alternatives, prostitution was a reasonable economic choice.

People used this picture of the sexual corruption and exploitation of teenaged girls by older women in efforts to manipulate the courts. In 1298 a woman named Blonda notified the court that her neighbour Meglior, a Florentine, was a well-known pimp and a receiver of prostitutes, pimps, and sodomites who publicly kept a brothel in her house. She was 'a woman who steals small girls [*puellas parvas*] and has them corrupted of their virginity for money.' In particular, she had stolen Blonda's own young daughter, Dulce, kept her against her mother's will, and prostituted her.[41] The defense witnesses, a series of neighbours, dramatically characterised the relations between the two women and the motives underlying Blonda's charge. They pointed out that Blonda's son had recently been banned for an assault on Meglior. It was notorious in the neighbourhood that in response Blonda had threatened Meglior with the courts. If she did not relax the young man's ban, Blonda had said, then she would lodge notifications and accusations that would get Meglior burned.

The witnesses were suggesting then that the lurid charge of stealing and prostituting girls and so forth was intended to get Meglior into serious trouble. Yes, they said, Dulce does live with her and, one

---

[38] See Alexandre-Bidon/Lett, *Children in the Middle Ages*, p. 101.

[39] See for example Bologna, Archivio di Stato, Curia del Podestà, Libri Inquisitionum et testium 22, 2, fol. 6v, in which an older woman is accused of persuading *puellas* to come to her house and then prostituting them.

[40] Bologna, Archivio di Stato, Curia del Podestà, Libri Inquisitionum et testium 1, 3, fol. 1v.

[41] Bologna, Archivio di Stato, Curia del Podestà, Libri Inquisitionum et testium 46, 2, fols. 41r–47v.

suggested, is a man's *amasia*. They did not address whether Dulce was in fact a *puella parva*, a prepubescent child. It is clear that these witnesses thought that the fate of the girl was not the mother's real concern. Blonda sought not to rescue Dulce from concubinage or prostitution but rather her son from jail. A son after all would be more valuable to a mother than a daughter.

Witnesses were suspicious not only of mothers corrupting teenaged girls but of young wives betraying their husbands. In the stories witnesses told in depositions, the roles of young women switched easily from innocent victim to criminal mastermind. In an inquest into the murder of a man named Pietro Orbi, the witnesses both male and female tended to blame his death on his young, pregnant wife Margarita. ('You whore! You had your husband killed,' people reportedly said to her.) The pair had been staying at an inn and men tended to come there to drink because of her presence. One young man, identifiable because he dressed in green, was in love with her and came often. Witnesses thought that he had managed to sneak back into the inn that night and kill Pietro in his bed. His name, it turned out, was Guido Bonati. Guido neatly fits the pattern of a late medieval male youth, a young adult with a living father and without responsibilities. Witnesses termed him and his companion youths (*iuvenes*) and in response to a question estimated their ages at twenty-five. His father testified. Guido had not slept at home for many nights; his father knew nothing of his actions and considered him a bad man, a gambler who did not abide by his father's views ('non stat ad sensum patris') and was an habitue of taverns and prostitutes. Another son agreed. His brother Guido Bonati was an unstable man ('hominem instabilem') who frequented taverns and prostitutes, did not abide by his father's views and had not slept in his father's house for the past ten nights. Nevertheless, the witnesses suggested that it was Margarita who had somehow planned her husband's death. They mentioned evidence suggesting that she had been unhappy: she had been on the stairs weeping that evening because of a sharp exchange with Pietro. According to one female witness, she only pretended to weep after her husband was killed, but produced no tears. It was Margarita, the young pregnant wife who described herself in her deposition as frightened and persecuted by Guido's attentions, who had arranged her husband's murder.

What can be concluded from these scattered vignettes of teenaged girls, drawn from legal testimony? Adolescent girls without marriage prospects do appear neglected, of little interest to their kin, male or female. At times, there was a sad discrepancy between their given names, which connoted high value, and the apparent disinterest of their uncles, mothers, and brothers.[42] Divitia, the unprotected young servant girl who fought off rape, was named 'riches.' Dulce, whose mother pretended to be concerned about her prostitution in order to get her brother out of jail, was named 'sweetness.' There was also a discrepancy between the categories employed by the courts and how witnesses represented the actions of adolescent girls. A dichotomous understanding in terms of *bona* or *mala fama,* good or bad public reputation, often was not useful. Further, accusations and notifications to the court tended to represent adolescent girls as victims, raped, kidnapped, or duped. In many cases that picture of victimization did not hold up once local witnesses were questioned. They speculated instead that these girls in fact might have rebelled: perhaps Billina was not kidnapped but chose to go with Ugolino, and Giliola with Buna-lello. And, in fact, some adolescent girls did rebel against social norms and family expectations. If poor girls appear neglected, they also appear independent and resourceful. Some teenaged girls evidently chose to get themselves into trouble. Johana chose to commit theft and run off with a lover rather than work in her uncle's household, without prospect of marriage and independence. To others, to be a man's concubine might well have seemed preferable to a more respectable existence living as a poor, unmarried daughter with a widowed mother.

*University of California*
*Santa Barbara, California*

## Cited Works
## Manuscript Sources

Bologna, Archivio di Stato, Curia del podestà,
    Libri Inquisitionum et testium 1–2, 5, 7–8, 11–12, 21–22, 27, 30, 33 II, 35,
    44–48
    Ufficio Corone ed Armi 4, 7

## Published Sources

Alexandre-Bidon, Danièle and Didier Lett. *Children in the Middle Ages,* trans. Jody Gladding. Notre Dame, IN: Notre Dame University Press, 1999.

---

[42] On changing naming patterns, see Herlihy, 'Tuscan Names.'

Bellomo, Manlio. *La condizione giuridica della donna in Italia*. Turin: Eri, 1970.

Chabot, Isabelle. "'Sola, donna, non gir mai'": Le solitudini femminili nel Tre-Quattrocento' *Rivista di storia delle donne* 18:3 (1986): 7–24.

Crouzet-Pavan, Elisabeth. 'A Flower of Evil: Young Men in Medieval Italy' 1:173–221 in *A History of Young People*, ed. Giovanni Levi and Jean-Claude Schmitt, trans. Camille Naish. 2 vols. Cambridge and London: The Belknap Press of Harvard University Press, 1997.

Elliott, Dyan. *Spiritual Marriage: Sexual Abstinence in Medieval Wedlock*. Princeton, NJ: Princeton University Press, 1993.

Epstein, Steven A. *Genoa and the Genoese, 958–1528*. Chapel Hill, NC: University of North Carolina Press, 1996.

Herlihy, David. 'Tuscan Names, 1200–1530' *Renaissance Quarterly* 41:4 (1988): 561–82.

*Infanzie: Funzioni di un gruppo liminale dal mondo classico all'Età moderna*, ed. Ottavia Niccoli. Florence: Ponte alle Grazie Editori, 1993.

Klapisch-Zuber, Christiane. 'Childhood in Tuscany at the beginning of the Fifteenth Century' pp. 94–116 in *Women, Family and Ritual in Renaissance Italy*, trans. Lydia Cochrane. Chicago: University of Chicago Press, 1985.

Lansing, Carol. 'Concubines, Lovers, Prostitutes: Infamy and Female Identity in Medieval Bologna,' forthcoming in *Beyond Florence; Rethinking Medieval and Early Modern Italy*, ed. Paula Findlen, Michelle Fontaine, Duane Osheim. Palo Alto: Stanford University Press, 2002.

Luongo, F. Thomas. 'The Politics of Marginality: Catherine of Siena in the War of the Eight Saints (1374–78)' Ph.D. Dissertation, University of Notre Dame, 1997.

Matassoni Iole. '"Piangere Miseria." Le motivazioni dei Bolognesi per impietosire gli ufficiali addetti all'estime del 1329' *Atti e memorie della Deputazione di Storia patria per le province di Romagna*, n.s. 46 (1996): 413–27.

Medici, Maria Teresa Guerra. *L'Aria di città. Donne e diritti nella città medievale*. Naples: Edizioni scientifiche italiane, 1996.

Ortalli, Gherardo. 'La famille à Bologne au XIIIe siècle, entre la réalité des groupes inférieurs et la mentalité des classes dominantes' pp. 205–23 in *Famille et parenté dans l'Occident médiéval*, ed. Georges Duby and Jacques LeGoff. Collection de l'École française de Rome 30. Rome: École française de Rome, 1977.

Papi, Anna Benvenuti. 'Umiliana dei Cerchi: Nascita di un culto nella Firenze del Dugento,' *Studi francescani* 77 (1980): 87–117.

Papi, Anna Benvenuti. *'In castro poenitentiae': santità e società femminile nell'Italia medievale*. Italia sacra, 45. Rome: Herder, 1990.

Pini, Antonio. 'Problemi demografici bolognesi del Duecento' *Atti e memorie della Deputazione di storia patria per le provincie di Romagna, n.s. 16–17 (1969): 147–222*.

Pini, Antonio. 'Un aspetto dei rapporti tra città e territorio nel Medioevo: la politica demografica "ad elastico" di Bologna fra il XII e il XIV secolo' 1:365–408 in *Studi in memoria di Federigo Melis*. Naples: Giannini, 1978.

Shahar, Shulamith. *Childhood in the Middle Ages*. London and New York: Routledge, 1990.

*Statuti di Bologna dall'anno 1245 all'anno 1267*, ed. Luigi Frati. Bologna: Regia Tipografia, 1877 [i.e. 1880]

*Statuti di Bologna dell'anno 1288*, ed. Gina Fasoli and Pietro Sella. 2 vols. Rome: Biblioteca Apostolica Vaticana, 1937.

Vallerani, Massimo. 'L'amministrazione della giustizia a Bologna in età podestarile' *Atti e memorie delle Deputazione di storia patria per le provincie di Romagna*, n.s. 43 (1993): 291–316.

Vallerani, Massimo. 'I processi accusatori a Bologna fra Due e Trecento' *Società e storia* 78 (1997): 741–88.

Weinstein, Donald and Rudolph Bell, *Saints and Society*. Chicago: University of Chicago Press, 1982.

*Women and Religion in Medieval and Renaissance Italy*, ed. Daniel Bornstein and Roberto Rusconi, trans. Margery J. Schneider. Chicago: University of Chicago Press, 1996.

# The Medieval Aristocratic Teenaged Female: Adolescent or Adult?

## John Carmi Parsons

Considerations related to the life course loom large today in the study of women's history but, with regard to medieval women, the lack of an 'ages of women' literature similar to that for men raises many questions about medieval views on women's life course. At what age were medieval women held to have reached adulthood or, more to the point, what constituted 'adulthood' for women: chronological age, biological capacity, social status, or social behaviour? While most women's lives passed as unremarked as did most men's, we may be able to distil some ideas from the lives of the most eminent of women whom their sovereign spouses and clerics alike cast as exemplary figures to society in general and to other women in particular.[1] Examining noble consorts' behaviour, the ways in which society observed it and male authors portrayed it, may open fresh paths for discussion. As a preliminary line of inquiry, I will consider two historical cases that suggest how male writers, and society at large, might react to the behaviour of especially young aristocratic wives.

The first case dates from March 1184. Isabelle of Hainaut, first wife of King Philip II of France, was a month off her fourteenth birthday when, at Senlis, she heard that Philip had gathered his nobles to announce their divorce. Modern historians suggest that Philip's motives were diplomatic: a threatened divorce might scare her father,

---

[1] For clerical letters exhorting or scolding queens to set a proper example, J.C. Parsons, 'The Queen's Intercession,' pp. 150–51 and, e.g., Peter of Blois in Migne *PL*, 207, cols. 448–49; C. Casagrande, 'The Protected Woman,' esp. pp. 78–79. A 1292 instruction manual for a royal prince, believed to have been written by King Sancho IV of Castile, states that 'queens . . . must be more virtuous than other women in all things . . .; for as others see them do, so shall they all do' (*Castigos e documentos*, p. 217). The Bourgeois of Paris ca. 1393 offered Valois queens as models to his wife: 'Since such high and honored ladies do this, lesser women . . . should do so as well' (*Le Ménagier de Paris*, p. 56). See also La Tour Landry, *The Book of the Knight of the Tower*, pp. 23–25; D. Bornstein, *The Lady in the Tower*, esp. 76–93.

Count Baldwin V of Hainaut, into closer compliance with Philip's wishes. Medieval sources, however, imply that Philip feared Isabelle was barren and hoped to take another wife who could bear his heir. Whatever the case, the young queen seized the initiative and, on the day fixed for the divorce, left the royal residence in Senlis, barefoot and wearing only a penitential shift. Carrying lighted tapers and distributing alms as she went, she walked through the streets to every church in the town, weeping and praying for deliverance from the evil counsel of those who sought her ruin. Realizing her dilemma, the town's poor and lepers rushed to the royal residence. As the royal council was meeting, the mob rioted so loudly in the king's hearing, asking God to help the queen, that Philip's uncle and cousins were quickly able to induce him to abandon the divorce. The earliest chronicle accounts of this incident are reliable, but we may well ask if Isabelle's own advisors (perhaps supplied by her father) might have suggested this course of action to her. Even if that were true, however, my focus is on chroniclers' attitudes in recording her actions and the popular reaction to them. If advisors were present, the chroniclers saw no reason to mention them; nor would an advisor's role have been evident to those who reacted so strongly to Isabelle's actions on that March day. For all the indigent of Senlis knew, and for aught the chroniclers tell us, Isabelle was acting on her own.[2]

The second case dates from a century later. In January 1297, Elizabeth, the fourteen-year-old daughter of King Edward I of England, married Count John of Holland, two years her junior. The young count was still in the tutelage of a regent, Frank van Borselen, whose self-seeking rule had alienated John's subjects. A year after Elizabeth reached Holland, the people rose against Borselen, who fled with the count to the seacoast. Abandoned in The Hague, Elizabeth wandered her empty chambers bewailing her fate. She contemplated an armed expedition to rescue John, but Borselen's son-in-law urged her instead to appeal to the people for help. Distraught and dishevelled as she was, Elizabeth rushed to The Hague's marketplace and with many tears and sighs begged the people to save her husband. The regent and count had taken ship for Sweden, but their becalmed vessel was seized, Borselen summarily beheaded, and the count returned to his wife. John's youth, however, meant that formal guidance for his

---

[2] This incident and its reports are discussed in Parsons, 'Violence, the Queen's Body and the Medieval Body Politic.'

domains was still needed. Elizabeth's role in the crisis had enhanced her stature so she used her persuasive powers to induce John to accept his cousin, the count of Hainaut, as regent. This settlement was anomalously proclaimed in both John and Elizabeth's names. Sad to say, John did not long survive these events and left Elizabeth a childless widow soon after her seventeenth birthday.[3]

Young noblewomen like Isabelle and Elizabeth belonged to a group of women often called upon to perform public ritual acts potentially of great significance to their male kin's dominion. Schooled in that group's customs by mothers or other female relatives, young noblewomen could undertake such ritual acts, and marriage, at a very early age.[4] Clearly, however, Isabelle and Elizabeth were not ritualizing in that sense. Both young women exploited desperate situations to leave a wife's domestic sphere as subject agents who were able, albeit temporarily, to affect events around them. They achieved their ends by manipulating an imagery of mediation and penitence that enacted their own weakness even as they turned events in their favour: in a patriarchal society, the actions of a female intercessor or mediator, whatever her rank, acknowledged that she could only solicit male authority—or, as in these cases, the brute power of his subjects, be they French beggars or Dutch burghers. As Catherine Brown observes, the manipulation of such 'authoritative (and "oppressive") constructs through the artifice of performance . . . can be an active, nay aggressive, means of rewriting those very constructs to the pragmatic benefit of the (re)writing subject.'[5]

It is the appeal to the popular evident in Isabelle and Elizabeth's actions that affords these incidents subversive undertones. Isabelle

---

[3] Elizabeth was born in August 1282; see Parsons, 'The Year of Eleanor of Castile's Birth,' p. 265. Count John's birth year is variously reported, but 1284 is the most likely year; see Dek, *Genealogie der graaven van Holland*, p. 80). For the events described here, see Green, *Lives of the Princesses of England*, 3:21–30. The widowed Elizabeth returned to England and in 1302 wed Humphrey de Bohun VIII, earl of Hereford and Essex (1276–1322); she died at the birth of her tenth child in May 1316.

[4] Stanley Chojnacki, 'Measuring Adulthood,' pp. 371–95, posits a 'social' adulthood that did not coincide with chronological age. On the training of aristocratic women by older female family members, see Parsons, 'Mothers, Daughters, Marriage, Power,' pp. 63–78; for a specific instance see Caviness, 'Patron or Matron?' pp. 31–60, and J. Holladay, 'The Education of Jeanne d'Evreux,' pp. 585–611.

[5] Brown, 'Muliebriter.'

saved Philip from the sin of adultery, which would have set his subjects a bad example and left him vulnerable to charges of violating his coronation oath. By praying openly against those who sought her downfall, she implicitly condemned those of Philip's advisors who had approved the divorce and constituted herself a more worthy counsellor than they. Even as she compelled Philip to retain her as his wife, she assured his good governance and so implied a relationship between herself and the right order of the realm, as witnessed by the response of Senlis' indigent. Countess Elizabeth's tearful popular appeal likewise invited her husband's subjects to find a political voice and established a similar association between them and herself as a proponent and protector of order. An advisor did urge Elizabeth's appeal to the people, but in itself this shows that the advisor—the regent's own son-in-law, a renegade within the prevailing male aristocratic power structure of the moment—saw this course of action as appropriate to Elizabeth's rank, age, and circumstances (and we would have to admit the same for any who may have advised Isabelle at Senlis).

Whatever the impetus to their actions, both women had a direct and significant impact on the reality around them. Elizabeth's role in ending one regency so heightened her profile that she was, it seems, able to smooth the path for another. Isabelle's successful resistance to Philip's wish to divorce her raises the possibility that he was sufficiently impressed by her actions that during his protracted attempts after 1193 to divorce his second wife, Ingeborg of Denmark, he kept her imprisoned precisely to stop her mounting a popular appeal as Isabelle had done.[6]

Given the resistance and sophistication of these two women's actions, it is remarkable that the chroniclers who so matter-of-factly record these events say nothing of the ages at which these young wives so decisively influenced events around them. Writing in the 1190s, Gislebert of Mons, the first author to describe the 1184 events at Senlis, was the only contemporary to record Isabelle's birth in April 1170 (as her father's chancellor he was in an excellent position to know); but even he did not remark her age when reporting her dramatic walk through Senlis. Nor does the Dutch writer mention Elizabeth's age, though her husband was clearly still too young to rule in his own right. The asymmetry between Elizabeth's commanding public action and the deficiencies of John's

---

[6] On Ingeborg, see Damsholt, 'Medieval Women's Identity in a Postmodern Light' and G. Conklin, 'Ingeborg of Denmark.'

youth returns me to the questions with which I began. What can these incidents suggest to us about the age at which medieval women left what we would now consider childhood or adolescence, and enter adulthood? To paraphrase Joan Kelly, can we say that medieval aristocratic women *had* an adolescence? A change of clothing, for example, might visually mark a moment in the transition from childhood to maturity, but that was only a stage of physical growth not necessarily determined by either chronological or intellectual maturity.[7] In any event, such a change of clothing for a woman did not merit the same ceremonial as a knight's assumption of the trappings of his calling. The only comparable point of transition for a woman was the wedding that marked her passage from daughter to wife. The moment at which a maturing aristocratic girl was ready for marriage was often decided by her mother or a grandmother, and a not infrequent criterion was whether the girl was yet of an age to bear children safely. While this suggests some chronological sense, the older female members of such a young woman's family were concerned not with specifically adult behaviour, but only with the wifely act of childbearing, which in the Middle Ages was not necessarily limited by chronological adulthood.

In the present context, we might well ask whether women's ages were perhaps more likely to be reckoned relationally than chronologically or biologically. Isabelle of Hainaut must have understood that her status depended on a continuing spousal relationship; she had known one failed betrothal before she wed Philip in 1180 and was surely aware of herself as a pawn in matrimonial diplomacy. In this sense, she was perhaps trying to preserve her marriage since, if divorced, she would be left neither wife, maid, nor widow, and hence outside any relational reckoning of her status. Exactly the same observation is valid for Elizabeth Plantagenet who, had van Borselen succeeded in carrying off the young count to Sweden, would have been left without a male partner to define her status.

There was, also, the practical matter that if single Isabelle could not produce the legitimate children upon whom an aristocratic woman's fate might ultimately depend. She was fighting for the right to bear the child Philip feared she could not bear. Isabelle and Elizabeth were young *and childless* when they made their dramatic gestures. Again,

---

[7] I build here on ideas from Taglia, 'The Cultural Construction of Childhood,' pp. 255–87. See also the helpful essays in *Constructions of Widowhood and Virginity in the Middle Ages*, esp. the editors' introduction, 'Constructions of Widowhood and Virginity,' pp. 1–21.

it was marital status that mattered, not their age at marriage nor their maternity. As neither adolescent had borne a living child at the time of these incidents, maternity itself cannot have determined either wife's life status at the time of the incidents discussed here.[8]

In fact, we rarely if ever hear of unwed aristocratic teenaged women behaving as Isabelle and Elizabeth did. Only *wives* laudably exert themselves in public to assure their husbands' rule or their children's rights (and by extension their own positions and rights). So while marriage in one sense marked a woman's transfer from paternal to conjugal authority, it could also enable a kind of social liberation, albeit one that authorized such actions only in support of husband or children. To factor in a classic aspect of adolescence identified by modern sociologists, Isabelle's tearful prayers at Senlis for salvation from those who sought her ruin suggest a kind of generational struggle against adult (male) royal counsellors who approved her divorce and thus menaced a teenager's claim to the adult status that depended on her marriage.[9]

This line of reasoning could carry important implications for our understanding of all medieval women. Chroniclers refer to Isabelle and Elizabeth not as *puella* or *mulier*, but as *comitissa* and *regina*—that is, their personal or chronological identities had been subsumed in the official personae they had acquired by marriage. I argue elsewhere for the existence of 'The Queen's Two Bodies'—a natural, reproductive body that ages and dies, and an official, counselling body identified with an advisor's timeless functions.[10] Of course, few women married reigning noblemen. However, the exemplary role in which male rulers' wives were cast, as noted above, meant that noble consorts' behaviour resonated throughout society, as implied by countless sermon *exempla* and other texts, among which the *Ménagier de Paris* is possibly the best known. Thus the extent to which a queen's ageless counselling body displaced her aging biological body implies that other women's

---

[8] On comparative ages at marriage and first childbirth, Parsons, 'Mothers, Daughters, Marriage, Power.' At fourteen, Isabelle of Hainaut possibly had already delivered a stillborn or very short-lived daughter, an event that may have sparked Philip II's fears that they would not have a son; see Parsons, 'Violence, the Queen's Body, and the Medieval Body Politic.'

[9] Parsons, 'Violence, The Queen's Body, and the Medieval Body Politic'; Hanawalt, 'Historical Descriptions and Prescriptions for Adolescence.'

[10] Parsons, ''Never was a body buried in England with such solemnity and honour,' p. 333, and 'The Pregnant Queen as Counsellor,' pp. 52–53.

reproductive bodies, despite their importance to patriarchal society, might also have been subsumed by other roles, including the mediating or advisory roles that many women performed within their families, between husbands and children, and at any age—often in an overtly generational sense because so many women married men significantly older than themselves.[11] Thus, if women's life course was relationally reckoned, any woman might, like Isabelle and Elizabeth, assume at marriage behaviour associated with adulthood regardless of their chronological age—or their husbands', given that John of Holland could not rule in his own right even after his wife so dramatically intervened to save him from an evil regent.

To consider briefly the other end of the life scale, older women were often depicted in literature as hideous schemers, poisoners, or witches. These were, of course, male figurations probably related to the prejudices against widows common to many traditional societies. But some old hags in literature are revealed as wise counsellors; others, most eminently in the 'Marriage to Sovereignty' myth, are revealed as beautiful young women who confer wealth, power, or knowledge on their husbands.[12] Again, the capacity of aged women to perform the same functions as younger women implies that precisely the functions of married women that male writers foregrounded in preference to biological functions were unrelated to chronological age or biological role. Despite what literary representations of their advanced age may suggest, many historical aging noblewomen took part in crucial diplomatic negotiations, or were prominent and influential as mediators and intercessors. These are all strongly male-supportive activities, of course, but few women would have failed to realize the extent to which their status depended upon that of their husbands or sons. Such behaviour would, again, suggest that women's ages and behaviour in medieval Europe were perhaps reckoned on relational and not exclusively chronological bases. The deciding factor was not age, but the woman's demonstrated loyalty to husband or children, a loyalty that could be manifest at any age. Approached from another angle, a woman's

---

[11] Herlihy, *Medieval Households*, pp. 120–22.

[12] Harper, 'Fear and the Status of Women.' The most familiar version of the Marriage to Sovereignty myth, in which a youth sleeps with, or marries, an aged hag later revealed as a young and beautiful woman who bestows upon him the sovereignty of her domains, is most probably that found in Chaucer's Wife of Bath's Tale, for which see especially *Geoffrey Chaucer: The Wife of Bath*. Again, the essays in *Constructions of Widowhood and Virginity* are helpful here.

capacity to act not in her own self-interest but altruistically was in no sense limited by her chronological age.[13]

Intimately familiar medieval Christian imagery may also have contributed to shaping understandings of women's ages. Christ's age, thirty-three, was deemed the 'perfect' age—some thought that in Heaven, everyone was thirty-three. As a male, however, Christ was not an entirely valid model for women. That maidenhood was, in contrast, considered the 'perfect' age for women leads us to consider in these contexts the impact of the Church's most authoritative model for women, the Virgin Mary.[14] The Virgin's eternal disdain for the passage of time meant that she was always the same and her role as the supreme intercessor was itself timeless. As noted above, earthly women could perform that role at any age, whether in early youth or maturity. And of course, 'no man has known me' can be true for a woman at any age, not in her youth alone. Thus a woman could remain a maiden (in the physical sense) at any chronological age, just as she might mediate or intercede at any time during her mortal lifespan. It might well be asked, then, if maidenhood, the 'perfect' age for a woman, might not be reckoned in ways other than chronologically.

In common with scholars who long contested the belief that childhood was not recognized in the medieval period as a distinct phase of human existence, Barbara Hanawalt has cogently argued that the Middle Ages did so recognize adolescence.[15] The examples I have discussed show, however, that some aristocratic female behaviour that today might be reckoned 'adult' could, in the Middle Ages, take place at a very early age, during what now would be defined as 'adolescence,' and could as well continue into old age without noticeable interruption. Such behaviour patterns suggest that while certain phases of life were acknowledged in theory, their definition in practice may have been fluid, not linked inflexibly to chronological or biological criteria. We cannot of course assume, let alone insist, that the patterns indicated here for aristocratic young women held true for all medieval women. Among the lesser nobility, merchant classes, or peasants, there were any number of variants related to class or economic status—for one thing, most women would have had neither

---

13 Parsons, 'Pregnant Queen as Counsellor,' pp. 52–53.

14 See Phillips, 'Maidenhood as the Perfect Age of Woman's Life.'

15 Hanawalt, 'Historical Descriptions and Prescriptions for Adolescence.' For debate on medieval perceptions of childhood, see literature cited in Parsons, '"Que nos in infancia lactauit,"' pp. 291–92, notes 3–5.

opportunity nor need for such dramatic public displays as those enacted by Isabelle of Hainaut and Elizabeth Plantagenet (though we might recall here the wives of Weinsberg who in 1140, allowed by Emperor Konrad III to take from the besieged town only what they could carry on their backs, saved their husbands by bearing them out on their shoulders).[16] That changes in clothing, the celebration of marriage, and the onset of motherhood could take place at a wide range of naturally or artificially reckoned points in a woman's life suggests strongly that we might think twice about drawing life boundaries for medieval women based on chronology or biology alone. Given the early ages at which medieval noble girls were initiated into public ritual behaviour, and the ages at which they could engage in non-ritual behaviour that may appear startling today but which was then regarded as laudable, can we say that such transitional periods as adolescence really existed for teenaged aristocratic medieval women?

If there was a more fluid scale of ages and behaviours for women than for men—if women were capable of some functions all their lives without reference to a fixed age scale—were they able to think of themselves (and, more importantly, were they in consequence able to function) independently of male-centred time scales? For younger women, this could be as empowering a concept as it seems to have been for Isabelle and Elizabeth, and might have allowed older women to exercise power at a time in their lives when we are often told they were despised or ridiculed as past all usefulness. In this respect, it is worth noting too that elderly males were often portrayed in 'Ages of Man' schemes as doddering fools, but at the same time their white locks were taken as signs of experience and wisdom, many older men were renowned as hardy warriors, and more than a few fathered children into their sixties. Medieval society sought the *auctoritas* embodied in 'The Ages of Man' literature, but that same society was, by every necessity, a rigorously pragmatic one in which most women might well never have recognized themselves reflected in the 'Ages of Man.'

*Melbourne, Florida*

---

[16] *Chronica regia coloniensis*, p. 77. I owe this reference to Madelyn Dick of York University, Toronto.

# Cited Works

Bornstein, Diane. *The Lady in the Tower: Medieval Courtesy Literature for Women*. Hamden, CT: Archon Books, 1983.

Brown, Catherine. 'Muliebriter: Doing Gender in the Letters of Heloise' pp. 25–51 in *Gender and Text in the Later Middle Ages*, ed. Jane Chance. Gainesville, FL: University Press of Florida, 1996.

Casagrande, Carla. 'The Protected Woman' pp. 70–104 in *Silences of the Middle Ages*, ed. C. Klapisch-Zuber, trans. A. Goldhammer. A History of Women in the West, 2. Cambridge, MA: Harvard University Press, 1992.

Caviness, M. 'Patron or Matron? A Capetian Bride and a Vade Mecum for Her Marriage Bed' *Speculum*, 68 (1993): 333–62; repr. pp. 31–59 in *Studying Medieval Women: Sex, Gender, Feminism*, ed. Nancy F. Partner. Cambridge, MA: Medieval Academy of America, 1993.

Chojnacki, Stanley. 'Measuring Adulthood: Adolescence and Gender in Renaissance Venice' *Journal of Family History*, 17 (1992): 371–95.

*Chronica regia coloniensis (Annales maximi colonienses) cum continuationibus in Monasterio S. Pantaleonis scriptis aliisque historiae coloniensis monumentis*, ed. Georgius Waitz. Scriptores rerum germanicarum in usum scholarum ex monumentis Germaniae historicis recusi, 18. Hannoverae: Impensis Bibliopolii Hahniani, 1880.

Conklin, G. 'Ingeborg of Denmark, Queen of France, 1193–1223' pp. 39–52 in *Queens and Queenship in Medieval Europe*, ed. Anne J. Duggan. Woodbridge, Suff. / Rochester, NY: Boydell Press, 1997.

*Constructions of Widowhood and Virginity in the Middle Ages*, eds. Cindy L. Carlson and Angela Jane Weisl. New York: St. Martin's Press, 1999.

Damsholt, Nana. 'Medieval Women's Identity in a Postmodern Light: The Example of Queen Ingeborg' pp. 225–41 in *The Birth of Identities: Denmark and Europe in the Middle Ages*, ed. Brian Patrick McGuire. Copenhagen: Reitzel/Medieval Centre, University of Copenhagen, 1996.

Dek, Adriaan W.E. *Genealogie der graaven van Holland*. The Hague: Uitg. Excelsier, 1954.

*Geoffrey Chaucer: The Wife of Bath*, ed. Peter G. Beidler. Case Studies in Contemporary Criticism. Boston: Bedford Books of St. Martin's Press, 1996.

Green, Mary Anne Everett. *Lives of the Princesses of England from the Norman Conquest*. 6 vols. London: Henry Colbourn, 1850–55.

Hanawalt, Barbara 'Historical Descriptions and Prescriptions for Adolescence' *Journal of Family History*, 17 (1992): 341–51.

Harper, Edward B. 'Fear and the Status of Women' *Southwestern Journal of Anthropology*, 25 (1969): 81–95.

Herlihy, David. *Medieval Households*. Cambridge, MA: Harvard University Press, 1985.

Holladay, J. 'The Education of Jeanne d'Evreux: Personal Piety and Dynastic Salvation in her Book of Hours at the Cloisters' *Art History*, 17 (1994): 585–611.

La Tour Landry, Geoffroy de. *The Book of the Knight of the Tower, Translated by William Caxton*, ed. M.Y. Offord. 2 vols, Early English Texts Society, Second Series 2. London and New York: Oxford University Press, 1971.

*Le Ménagier de Paris*, ed. Georgine E. Brereton and Janet M. Ferrier. Oxford: Clarendon Press, 1981.

Parsons, John Carmi. 'Mothers, Daughters, Marriage, Power: Some Plantagenet Evidence, 1150–1500' pp. 63–78 in *Medieval Queenship*, ed. John Carmi Parsons. New York: St. Martin's Press, 1993.

Parsons, John Carmi. '"Never was a body buried in England with such solemnity and honour": The Burials and Posthumous Commemorations of English Queens to 1500' pp. 317–37 in *Queens and Queenship in Medieval Europe*, ed. Anne J. Duggan. Woodbridge, Suff. / Rochester, NY: Boydell Press, 1997.

Parsons, John Carmi. 'The Pregnant Queen as Counsellor and the Medieval Construction of Motherhood' pp. 39–61 in *Medieval Mothering*, ed. John Carmi Parsons and Bonnie Wheeler. New York: Garland Publishing, 1996.

Parsons, John Carmi. 'The Queen's Intercession in Thirteenth-Century England' pp. 147–77 in *Power of the Weak: Studies on Medieval Women*, ed. Jennifer Carpenter and Sally-Beth MacLean. Champaign-Urbana: University of Illinois Press, 1995.

Parsons, John Carmi. '"Que nos in infancia lactauit": The Impact of Childhood Care-givers on Plantagenet Family Relationships in the Thirteenth and Early Fourteenth Centuries' pp. 289–324 in *Women, Marriage, and Family in Medieval Christendom*, ed. Constance M. Rousseau and Joel T. Rosenthal. Kalamazoo, MI: Medieval Institute Publications, Western Michigan University, 1998.

Parsons, John Carmi. 'Violence, the Queen's Body and the Medieval Body Politic' forthcoming in *A Great Effusion of Blood: Varieties of Medieval Violence*, ed. Mark Meyerson and Oren Falk. Toronto: University of Toronto Press, 2001.

Parsons, John Carmi. 'The Year of Eleanor of Castile's Birth and Her Children by Edward I' *Medieval Studies*, 46 (1984): 245–65.

Peter of Blois. *Petri Blesensis epistola 154* in Jacques-Paul Migne, *Patrologia Latina*, 207, cols. 448–50.

Phillips, K.M. 'Maidenhood as the Perfect Age of Woman's Life' pp. 1–24 in *Young Medieval Women*, ed. Katherine J. Lewis, Noel James Menuge, and Kim M. Phillips. Phoenix Mill: Sutton Publishing Ltd., 1999.

Sancho IV of Castile. *Castigos é documents del rey don Sancho*, pp. 79–228 in *Escritores en prosa anteriores al siglo XV*, ed. Pascual de Gayangos. Biblioteca de autores españoles desde la formacion del lenguaje hasta nuestros dias, 51 Madrid: Ediciones Atlas, 1952.

Taglia, Kathryn Ann. 'The Cultural Construction of Childhood: Baptism, Communion, and Confirmation' pp. 255–87 in *Women, Marriage and Family in Medieval Christendom*, ed. Constance M. Rousseau and Joel T. Rosenthal. Kalamazoo, MI: Medieval Institute Publications, Western Michigan University, 1998.

# Leaving Town to Work for the Family:
## The Counter-Migration of Teenaged Servants in Fourteenth-Century England

### John Leland

When considering the work experience of medieval teenagers, it is usual to think either of service within the family group or service as apprentices. There were, however, also medieval adolescents who left their family homes, often rural ones, and took positions as paid servants with other households, often in the cities. As Barbara Hanawalt pointed out, 'Service, like apprenticeship, was a phase in the life cycle that moved the adolescent from the natal home to that of a master. It was a threshold period in which the young people learned skills, accumulated capital, and dreamed of moving on to adult, non-dependent roles.'[1] Similarly, Penn and Dyer say 'A craftsman or peasant experienced life as a wage earner in early life, and eventually could have become an employer in later years as his workshop or holding grew in size.'[2] This view has been confirmed in detail by P.J.P. Goldberg's study of servants, especially female servants, in northern England. Considering servants coming into towns, chiefly York, he concluded that 'service must have accounted for a significant proportion of migrants of both sexes.' These would be 'individuals hired by the year who lived with their employers' and 'such servants were invariably young and unmarried, though it is true that a few servants probably remained as such through most of their working lives.' Exactly how young these servants were varied, of course, but he found that they were generally older than twelve and rarely older than twenty.[3]

---

[1] Hanawalt, *Growing Up in Medieval London*, p. 173.

[2] Penn and Dyer, 'Wages and Earnings,' p. 363.

[3] Goldberg, 'Female Labour, Service and Marriage,' p. 21; Goldberg, 'Marriage, Migration, Servanthood,' p. 151 (Table 3: Age Distribution of Female Servants over Time). Although there is some evidence for older male servants, Goldberg believes most male servants were also young; *Women in England*, pp. 6–7. On the younger end, there were cases of children aged four and seven who were claimed as

Not all these servants were teenagers in the strict sense, but many were. When their personal life cycles moved them back from the homes of their masters to the natal homes before they had completed the terms of service agreed upon between their masters and themselves, these youths came within the purview of the Statute of Labourers. The Statute contained what Musson calls 'a form of restraint of trade clause—that if X left employment prematurely, no one else could hire or retain him.'[4] The servants who fell within this group may have had a variety of motivations for returning home, but these generally revolved either around the pull of family loyalties in the former home or the push of unsatisfactory treatment in the employer's home.

Regarding the pull, some servants who returned home said they did so to see a relative who had taken ill.[5] The most important factor in prompting families to encourage their young people to come home and stay, however, may have been the need for more rural labour after the Black Death.[6] As Hanawalt says in discussing apprenticeships, 'So desperate was the demand for labour in the countryside that kin and parents who would normally have encouraged careers in London for younger sons and daughters kept them home to work for the family in their fields and businesses.'[7] The motives that kept some potential apprentices at home could also lead to families of servants who had already gone to the city to encourage them to return home and employ them there when they did return.

Besides the positive need for their services at home, runaway servants might also have felt the push of negative experiences in their extrafamilial positions. Servants sometimes complained of being mistreated or cheated by their employers or by others. Anthony Musson

---

servants, but these claims were rejected by the courts. (*Women in England*, pp. 84–85 has the case of Joan, aged four, while Hanawalt, *Growing Up in Medieval London*, pp. 176–77 has the case of Ellen Chamberlain, aged seven). On the older end, Goldberg found a female servant aged twenty-six and a few older male servants; see Goldberg, 'Marriage, Migration, Servanthood,' *passim*.

[4] Musson 'New Labour Laws, New Remedies?' p. 78. See *Statutes of the Realm*, 1:307 for the actual text of the statute.

[5] Hanawalt, *Growing Up in Medieval London*, p. 189.

[6] The historiographical debate on the economic impact of the Black Death is reviewed in Hatcher, 'England in the Aftermath of the Black Death.'

[7] Hanawalt, *Growing Up in Medieval London*, p. 21. She adds that 'The low rural population also increased opportunities to purchase or rent land and made alternatives to a career in trade more attractive' (p. 136).

cites a case in Durham in which 'Thomas Leward complained that his servant had removed himself on the grounds of harsh treatment'—in fact, Leward complained that one Roger Neuman had so beaten Leward's servant that the servant had fled.[8] In another case, it was admitted that an employer had struck his servant, though he maintained he did so to punish her properly for disobedience.[9] Other servants complained that masters had failed to pay them the promised wages, or had unjustly extended their contracts.[10] Penn and Dyer believe many young servants simply preferred to avoid the restrictions on their lives implied by the customary year-long contracts, and cared more for their freedom than for the economic security that might matter more to older married workers. It even appears that young servants who earned enough to marry and settle down chose not to do so, deliberately remaining in a prolonged 'adolescence.'[11] Whatever the reason might have been, the cases studied in this article point to a reversal of the conventional flow of young people from country to city.

This renunciation of the new urban ties and the return to earlier family ties is particularly noticeable when the second employer specified is a kinsman, especially a parent of the young servant. In such cases it may be deduced that the servant's grounds for leaving employment in the city and returning to the natal family were probably not purely a matter of an offer of higher wages as the statute assumed. Such cases may be found in the pardons granted for not answering complaints of violating the Statute of Labourers recorded in the *Calendar of Patent Rolls*. Some of these pardons, of course, involve workers who were not adolescents. There are two groups for which it can be argued, with varying degrees of probability, that they were young people.

The first and most probable group is that of the servants who left a first employer for a second employer explicitly described in the record as a parent or relative, usually a father. The second group includes the servants who shared a surname with their second employers, though the latter are not explicitly described as kin of the servants they

---

[8]Musson, 'New Labour Laws, New Remedies?' p. 81. The source, *Durham Halmote Rolls* 1:159 (not 59 as in Musson) says 'Dies datus est Ranulpho de Kitchin *and others* ad inquirend. et praesentand. ad prox. cur. si Rogerus Neuman verberavit famulum Thomae Leward ita quod praed. famulus elongavit se de servicio praed. Thomae.'

[9] *Women in England*, pp. 94–95.

[10]Hettinger, 'Defining the Servant,' pp. 213–15.

[11]Penn and Dyer, 'Wages and Earnings,' pp. 366 and 374.

employed. Fully adult workers might occasionally be identified by reference to a parent, or be employed by a probable kinsman of the same surname, but scholars familiar with the evidence believe that servants identified as the sons or daughters of specified parents were generally adolescents in a broad sense. The formula X child of Y was usually used for those who had not yet married and established households of their own. Pre-adolescent children were not bound by the statute.

The most credible cases of employment within the family as grounds for leaving previous employment are those in the first group, where the family relationship between the servant and the second employer is specified. For example, William Sherman of Wodehouse (Wood-house, Yorks.) was pardoned on 17 November 1380 for not answering the complaint of Nicholas Witteby of London that William had employed Richard Williamson Sherman after he prematurely left the service of Nicholas.[12] It is extremely probable that Richard was the son of William Sherman and left Nicholas in London to serve his own father in Yorkshire. In a second case, both the parent and the child were pardoned: Walter Smith of Stevenhache (Stevenage, Hertfordshire) was pardoned on 3 May 1382 for not answering William Albon of London for employing Walter's son Thomas, while Thomas was also pardoned a few days later (12 May) for leaving William's service before the agreed time. As William is described as a citizen and smith of London, it appears that Thomas Smyth was intending to follow the trade from which his family took its name, but decided to do so with his father in Hertfordshire rather than with an established London smith. William Albon is listed as a master of the Smith's Guild in London records in 1364 and 1372, and of the Bladesmiths and Blacksmith's Guild in 1376, and as a juror the same year. He may be the man of the same name who appears in records as early as 1350.[13]

---

[12] *CPR 1377–81*, p. 554.

[13] *CPR 1381–85*, p. 115; *PMR*, 1:236; 2:146; 3:31; the last is definitely the smith; *CLB*, Letter Book G, pp. 174, 291; Letter Book H, pp. 25n., 45. *CPR 1381–85*, pp. 108, 115 (case). There are numerous possible references to a Thomas Smyth, and a few to a Walter, but no definite references to these particular two men. The references include *CPR 1388–92*, p. 407, *CPR 1391–96*, p. 291; *CPR 1399–1401*, pp. 414–15; *CLB* Letter Book H, p. 419; Letter Book I, p. 120 (all Thomas), and *CPR 1391–96*, p. 81; *CLB* Letter Book G, p. 82; Letter Book I, p. 173 and *CCR 1360–64*, p. 437 (Walter). It is interesting that one Thomas Smyth appears as a servant of Mathilda, Countess of Oxford.

Another servant who left a London craftsman was Henry Berry the younger of Holm by Sea (Holm next the sea, Norfolk), whose father Henry was pardoned on 4 July 1383 for not answering John Blakeman, citizen and goldsmith of London, for 'taking his son Henry out of service before the term agreed.'[14] The wording in this case indicates that it was the father's decision rather than the son's to end the son's London service, which tends to confirm the view that Henry the younger was not yet fully adult. John Blakeman was not as prominent as William Albon was, but he might be the John 'Blakman' of Farndon (Faringdon) Ward who was among those who appeared to support the mayor Nicholas Brembre against John (of) Northampton in 1386. Other references to the Berri or Berry family suggest they were minor landed gentry in Norfolk.[15]

Besides these cases where the second employer is explicitly a parent, there is also an example of a probably related employer who was not a parent. This involved the Costyn family of Hanam (Hanham, Gloucestershire). John Costyn of Hanam was pardoned on 17 May 1394 for not answering John Weston of Hampton for employing Alice, daughter of Walter Costyn, she having left Weston's service before the time agreed. The shared Costyn surname makes it likely that Alice was kin to John, though not his daughter. The most likely explanation would be that John Costyn was Walter's brother and Alice's uncle, simply on the grounds that Alice's employer would be likely to be of the generation older than her own, though other relationships are possible (e.g. Walter could be Alice's grandfather). John Weston here can be identified with the John Weston 'of Hampton' who was a tax collector in Gloucestershire in 1392 and 1398, presumably also the John Weston 'Junior' who served in similar offices in the same shire from 1373 to 1384, and was 'Junior' to the earlier John (de) Weston of that county who had served as sheriff in 1352 and a variety of other county offices, in a career recorded by Nigel Saul. Alice Costyn's service to the younger John Weston may not have been voluntary: on 24 June 1390, a commission had been appointed to investigate the complaint of Joan Peshale, a member of a leading Staffordshire family,

14 *CPR 1381–85*, p. 302.

15 *CLB* Letter Book H. pp. 279–82; the master in this case might be connected with the John Blakenden, goldsmith, whom Sylvia Thrupp mentions as an alderman who died in 1422–23; Thrupp, *The Merchant Class of Medieval London*, p. 324. Other Berris or Berrys in Norfolk (not Henry): *CCR 1360–64*, p. 548; *1369–74*, p. 564.

that a party of men including John Weston had robbed her and abducted not only her daughter Mathilda but also one of her servants, Alice 'Costayne.' If this is the Alice of the pardon, as the names of both abductor and victim suggest, then Alice's return to her father may have been more an escape than a conventional breach of contract.[16]

Setting aside its colourful aspects, this case is on the borderline between the first type, in which the family relationship is specified, and the second, in which the family connection can only be assumed from the identical surnames of the servant and the servant's second employer. Sometimes the surname in question is sufficiently distinctive that a family relationship is probable. For example, when John Nightgale of Thirnham (Thornham?) was pardoned on 29 October 1377 for not answering Hugh de Malton for employing Agnes Nightgale before the end of her term of service to Hugh, it is a fair assumption that John was a kinsman, most likely the father, of Agnes.[17] This case was unusual in that the complainant was not a citizen of London or another major city.

The London pattern returned, however, in the case of Richard Lovekyn of Storteford (Bishop's Stortford, Hertfordshire) pardoned on 27 June 1379 for not answering Robert Somervyll, saddler of London, for taking John Lovekyn into his service before the end of the term

---

[16] *CPR 1391–96*, p. 402. John Weston 'of Hampton' *CFR 1391–96*, pp. 26, 263; John Weston Junior, *CFR 1368–77*, pp. 230, 269; *CFR 1377–83*, pp. 54, 187; *CFR 1383–91*, p. 69. John de Weston the sheriff in Saul, *Knights and Esquires*, pp. 65, 118, 161–62. Other John Weston references are in *CCR 1354–60*, pp. 4, 8, 13 (London), 16 (London), 28, 79 (London), 90 (Hunts.), 413 (London), 417 (Hunts.), 469–70, 611 (London), 660; *1360–64*, pp. 112, 323; *1364–68*, pp. 73 (Ely), 121–22, 391; *1369–74*, pp. 80 (Shaftsbury), 527; *1374–77*, p. 84. Abduction of Alice 'Costayne' by party including John Weston, *CPR 1388–92*, pp. 339–40. Two Joan Peshales (mother and daughter) appear in the *VCH Staffordshire*, 4:119. Note that Adam de Peshale held land at Weston (under Lizard) *V.C.H. Staffordshire*, 5:155–56. There was also a John Weston in Norfolk, *CPR 1368–77*, pp. 191, 198, 204, 251, 264, 272, 280; *CCR 1360–64*, pp. 16, 56; *CCR 1369–74*, pp. 493–94, 504, etc. This John de Weston who held county offices in Norfolk and Suffolk for many years acted as escheator in a case of 12 February 1373 involving John Costyn. *CFR 1377–83*, p. 207. A John Coston, chaplain, appears in several records in Gloucestershire at an earlier period, and a John Coston Junior who might more probably be the man involved in this case. *CCR 1354–60*, pp. 430, 545–46, 610, 611, 616–17; *1364–68*, pp. 9, *1374–77*, p. 185; John Costyn Junior, in Surrey, *CCR 1374–77*, p. 465.

[17] *CPR 1377–81*, p. 33.

John had agreed with Somervyll. As with Nightgale, the surname is unusual enough to make it likely that Robert and John were kin, probably father and son. There had been a John Lovekyn mayor of London in 1349, but there is no evidence of a connection. Somervyll may have been the man of that name supplied by the city of London as a man-at-arms for the defence of Calais in 1369. (It seems less likely he was the Robert son of William de Somervylle who appears in Melton Mowbray the same year.)[18]

Another London case was that in which Thomas Barbour the elder of Newark was pardoned on 9 February 1382 for not answering William Kirkeby citizen of London for retaining John Barbour as his servant after John had prematurely left the service of Kirkeby. Although the name John Barbour is unfortunately common, kinship between Thomas and John is still probable in these circumstances. More doubtful, but more interesting is the possibility that this John Barbour could be identified with the John Barbour 'dwelling without Bishopsgate' who was on the list of those reported by the aldermen of London in August of 1381—the year before this case—as suspected of sympathizing with the Peasants' Revolt of that June, a revolt in which many Londoners were active, particularly those from the journeyman/servant class whose rebellious tendencies Strohm, Hilton, and Tardif have described.[19] If this connection is correct, John Barbour might have had very good reason for leaving London at this time. William Kirkeby, John Barbour's former master, may have also been involved in the turbulent politics of the time, on the other side. He could be identified with the William Kirkeby, tailor, 'who came to the Guildhall at the mayor's election contrary to the proclamation' and was released on bail on 18 November 1384 under the heavy penalty of 200 pounds. His presence at this election would indicate that he was a follower of John (of) Northampton, the former mayor convicted that year of stirring up

---

[18] *CPR 1377–81*, p. 365 (case); *CLB*, Letter Book G, p. 244 (Calais). There are numerous references to the earlier mayor, e.g. *CCR 1354–60*, pp. 5, 15, 97, 355, 600, 608, 622, 633, 644, 652, 657; *1360–64*, pp. 83–84, 318, 108. *CCR 1364–68*, p. 501. Somervyll in Melton Mowbray.

[19] *CPR 1381–85*, p. 89 (the case); *CPMR*, 2:200 (rebel). For London involvement in the revolt, see Strohm, *Hochon's Arrow*, p. 37; Hilton, *Bond Men Made Free*, pp. 186–92; Tardif, 'The Mistery of Robin Hood,' does not focus on the revolt as such but on the general rebellious tendency of the urban underclass. John Barbour appears as a mainpernor in 1386 in *CPMR* 3:69.

further trouble in the city after he failed to gain re-election. Northampton was allied with John of Gaunt, duke of Lancaster, and had accused his opponents of assisting the rebels who destroyed Lancaster's town house in London (the Savoy) during the revolt. If John Barbour was in fact favourable to the rebels, and William Kirkeby his master was against them, they would have been on opposing sides in the crisis, which might have been John's reason for returning to his family in Newark.[20]

A less dramatic London case of persons with a shared surname was unusual in that the servant was female, as was one of her employers. John Reydon of Mildenhale (Mildenhall, Suffolk) was pardoned on 22 October 1402 of his outlawry in London for not appearing to answer James Bynde and Joan his wife for admitting to his service Alice Reydon of Mildenhale after she left the service of Joan in London. The shared surname and home town make it likely that Alice was John's daughter, though there is no explicit indication of a relationship; she might have been John's wife or other kinswoman. There are several references to other Reydons holding modest amounts of property in Suffolk, and a John Reydon sold land in Essex to some Londoners.[21]

In another London case, the shared-surname parties are specified as elder and younger, rendering a father-son relationship more probable. On 18 June 1365, Thomas Hale the younger was pardoned of his outlawry in the court of husting of London for not answering Nicholas Coupere of London, 'sporiere' (spurier), touching a trespass contrary to the Ordinance of Labourers done by him, Thomas Hale of Edesburgh (Edlesborough, Buckinghamshire), the elder, and William Cook. It appears likely that the younger Thomas Hale was returning to

---

[20] *CPMR* 3:66 (William Kirkeby at Guildhall). For discussions of these events see McKisack *The Fourteenth Century*, p. 435; Goodman, *John of Gaunt*, pp. 78–79, 97–101; *Westminster Chronicle*, pp. 90–97 (Northampton). A William Kirkeby was a mainpernor in 1390; *CPMR* 3:170 and a William Kirkeby of London was mainpernor in 1373, *CCR 1369–74*, p. 595; another was a pie baker in 1392—presumably not the earlier tailor, *CLB* Letter Book H, p. 389; this might be the royal purveyor of 1358: *CLB* Letter Book G, p. 107. Other John Barbours appear in *CCR 1354–60*, p. 78 (Bucks.); *1364–68*, pp. 161 (already dead), 302 (Dunstable); *1369–74*, pp. 328 (Shorham), 571 (Colbroke), 585 (Cambridge) and *1374–77*, pp. 65–66 (London: John son of William Barbour—definitely not the one pardoned, but perhaps the one in the rebel reference.)

[21] *CPR 1401–05*, p. 163. *CCR 1360–64*, pp. 152–53, 477–78 (Reydons in Suff.); *CCR 1374–77*, p. 116 (John Reydon in Essex).

Edlesborough from London, but whether Thomas the elder employed Thomas the younger there is not specified. It may be that both Hales men had worked for Nicholas Coupere in London and then transferred their service to William Cook.[22]

Such a joint service by father and son apparently occurred with John Devenshire the elder and John Devenshire the younger. On 29 January 1354, Walter le Kene and Richard le Kene were pardoned for not appearing to answer Adam de Shareshull, knight, for retaining the two Devenshires, formerly servants of Shareshull.[23] Adam de Shareshull was himself serving on the commission to enforce the Statute of Labourers in the county of Oxford later in 1354, as well as on various other judicial commissions. A special commission was appointed to investigate his own abduction in 1358, together with attacks on his servants. If this hostility to Shareshull and his household had already been manifest in 1354, it might have given the Devenshires a motive for leaving Shareshull's service.[24]

Another father and son pardoned for 'trespasses of labourers, servants and artificers' were John de Bateley and John his son, who were pardoned on 6 November 1355, for not appearing in the West Riding of Yorkshire to answer 'touching divers excesses.' In the context of a violation of the labour rules, the most likely interpretation of this is that they were both workmen and were demanding higher wages that were considered excessive.[25]

---

[22] *CPR 1364–67*, p. 129; unfortunately William Cook was a common name; there are references in *CFR 1368–77*, pp. 167, 391 and *CCR 1369–74*, p. 391 to William Cook as a merchant of Hull and a collector of the lay subsidy in Boston; in *CCR 1354–60*, pp. 401 to a William Cook in Beds., 414 in Derby; in *CCR 1354–60*, pp. 506 and *1360–64*, p. 522 in Essex; in *CCR 1364–68*, p. 280 in Agmundesham; in *CCR 1369–74*, p. 385 to a dead William Cook in Chesterton; there is also a William Cook who was pardoned for not appearing to answer for having retained Richard Kyng who had left the service of John Rede, but the date of this pardon (29 Jan. 1403) makes it unlikely that it is the same man; *CPR 1401–05*, p. 193. There were also a variety of references to persons named Thomas de Hale or variations thereof; *CCR 1354–60*, pp. 518, 623; *CCR 1364–68*, pp. 35–36; *CFR 1347–56*, pp. 148–49.

[23] *CPR 1354–58*, pp. 3–4.

[24] *CPR 1354–58*, pp. 57, 67, 122, 123; *CCR 1354–60*, p. 341; *CPR 1358–61*, p. 149 (the abduction), 153; *CCR 1360–64*, pp. 201–4; *CCR 1369–74*, pp. 156–57; *CCR 1370–74*, p. 145 and *CFR 1368–77*, pp. 73, 103 (his death in 1370). *VCH Oxfordshire*, 7:19.

[25] *CPR 1354–58*, p. 304.

A possible London case involving a shared surname is that of Robert Neel of Caysho (Keysoe, Bedfordshire), pardoned on 30 November 1385 for not answering John Bisshop for taking Henry Neel into his service and refusing to return him. Here Bisshop's residence is unspecified, but he may be the John Bishop, mercer of London, who as late as 1388 was suing one Simon Brown for leaving the service of his wife Katerine back in 1375. It should be noted that there are references to other John Bisshops elsewhere.[26]

A shared surname case whose London link is not obvious at first sight is that of Robert Kyneman, who was pardoned on 15 October 1389 for not answering for retaining John Kyneman, who had left the service of Thomas Heywode of Glastyngbury (Glastonbury, Somerset). However, Robert is identified by the *Calendar of Patent Rolls* index with Robert Kyngman of Somerset, who was yeoman of the pantry and therefore served at court in Westminster.[27] Thus, it is likely that John was a kinsman of Robert's who left the service of a Somerset neighbour for the service of his kinsman in the capital, reversing the usual geographical trend of these cases.

The youthful career of another royal officer may appear in the case of Richard son of Nicholas Ters, pardoned on 26 October 1356, in the county of York for not appearing to answer the justices appointed there to keep the Ordinance and Statute of Labourers. He may be identified with the Richard Ters pardoned on 13 May 1376 for various abuses committed while he was one of the king's foresters in Whittlewood (Northamptonshire).[28] Although there is a geographical difference, the name is unusual enough that it may well be the same man at a later stage of his career. An active forester in 1376 would plausibly be an adolescent servant twenty years before. If so, this case is unusual

---

[26] *CPR 1385–89*, p. 33; *CPRM* 3:143 (Bishop in 1388); other John Bishops include a goldbeater in 1396 and others from 1355 to 1412. *CLB* Letter Book H, p. 429 (1396), Letter Book G, pp. 58–59 (1355); Letter Book I, p. 105 (1412); see also *CCR 1364–68*, p. 329. A Robert Neel was mentioned in the will of one Walter Neel c.1353–55; Thrupp, *The Merchant Class*, p. 357, and another Robert Neel in Kent in 1366; *CCR 1364–68*, p. 302.

[27] *CPR 1388–92*, p. 75 (case); *CFR 1368–77*, p. 85; *CPR 1377–81*, p. 541; *CPR 1388–92*, p. 332 (yeoman of the pantry); *CPR 1391–96*, pp. 409, 450; *CPR 1396–99*, p. 423; *CPR 1399–1401*, p. 342 (grants for his service to Richard II, Richard II's father Prince Edward, and Henry IV). A Thomas Heywode was sued over property in Southampton *CCR 1374–77*, p. 548.

[28] *CPR 1354–58*, p. 463; *CPR 1374–77*, p. 267.

for giving some information about the career of the unhappy servant after he was pardoned for his violation of the labour laws.

Another possibly rural case is that of Andrew Gull, pardoned on 14 June 1399 for not answering Thomas de Maldon for employing Nicholas Gull, who had left Thomas before the agreed term. Thomas de Maldon was a landed gentleman in Essex who performed various county duties (despite an exemption from such work in 1380) and also appears in the records having some debtors outlawed. There was also a Thomas de Maldon, mercer of London, who would have fit the usual urban pattern, but all references to him are some thirty years before this case.[29] Also outside the London area was the case of John Buknale of Lincoln, pardoned for not answering for having admitted to his service William Buknale, formerly servant of Thomas Heley of Newark.[30]

Another non-London case offered a striking reversal of the typical pattern of family member as the second employer of a servant who had left another master was the case of John Serle, mason, of Surrey, pardoned on 1 February 1404 for not appearing to answer John Blachynden, mason, the elder, for having admitted to his service John Blachynden, mason, the younger, who had left the elder John Blachynden's service at Lyndefeld (Lindfield, Sussex.) . Thus instead of leaving employment elsewhere to return home and take employment with a kinsman, John the younger apparently left employment with a kinsman, probably a father, to take employment in the same craft with a nonkinsman in a different county. This is a useful reminder that despite the result of most of the cases discussed here there were still those who preferred to go away from their homes and families in search of other opportunities.[31]

Although this last case is not typical, overall these records do show certain general tendencies: the youths involved generally came from smaller places to the larger cities, especially to London; they tend to be in the service of established craftsmen in the city, and they tend to return home to take up positions working with kinsfolk, probably in

---

[29] *CPR 1396–99*, p. 399 (Case); *CFR 1377–83*, pp. 57, 147; *CFR 1383–91*, p. 72; *CPR 1377–81*, p. 497 (Essex positions of Thomas de Maldon); *CPR 1377–81*, p. 316; *CPR 1391–96*, p. 315 (debts); Thomas de Maldon of London, *CCR 1360–64*, p. 525; *1364–68*, pp. 200, 293; *1374–77*, p. 89.

[30] *CPR 1413–16*, p. 79.

[31] *CPR 1401–05*, p. 339. A John Serle was yeoman of the wardrobe in 1359, but it seems unlikely this could be the same man. *CCR 1354–60*, p. 574.

most cases with parents, though that can be said confidently only of the first group studied here, whose relationships are explicitly recorded. These decisions to return challenged the customary pattern which had been established in the pre-plague period but still largely continued, a well-known pattern described by Barbara Hanawalt: 'Medieval cities did not replace their populations, but relied instead on recruits from the countryside, market towns, and younger sons of gentry and nobility. In addition to the apprentices, a large number of foreigners came to London, as did poorer people from the countryside looking for service positions.'[32] Since the cities survived and grew largely by attracting young people from the country to replace those who succumbed to the higher mortality of the cities, most of the cases described in this article form an interesting series of exceptions to the expected pattern. It may be that the willingness of their families to receive and employ these servants when they returned home encouraged these unsung Whittingtons to turn their backs on London or the other towns where they had first been employed.

*Salem International University*
*Salem, West Virginia*

## Cited Works

CCR. *Calendar of Close Rolls Preserved in the Public Record Office*, ed. H.C. Maxwell Lyte. 62 vols. London: H.M.S.O., 1892–1963.

CFR. *Calendar of Fine Rolls*, ed. H.C. Maxwell Lyte. 22 vols. London: H.M.S.O., 1911–62.

CLB. *Calendar of Letter Books Preserved among the Archives of the Corporation of the City of London*, A–L (1275–1497) ed. R.R. Sharpe. 11 vols. London: Francis, 1899–1912.

CPMR. *Calendar of Plea and Memoranda Rolls Preserved Among the Archives of the Corporation of the City of London, 1323–1482*, ed. Arthur Herman Thomas and Philip E. Jones. 6 vols. Cambridge: Cambridge University Press, 1926–61.

CPR. *Calendar of Patent Rolls Preserved in the Public Record Office*, ed. J.G. Black et al. 73 vols. London: H.M.S.O., 1891–1986.

*Halmonata Prioratus Dunelmensis Containing Extracts from the Halmote Court of Manor Rolls of the Prior and Convent of Durham, A.D. 1296–A.D. 1384*, ed. John Booth. Surtees Society, 82. Durham, Surtees Society, 1889.

---

[32] Hanawalt, *Of Good and Ill Repute*, p. 46.

Goldberg, P.J.P. 'Female Labour, Service and Marriage in the Late Medieval North' *Northern History* 22 (1986): 18–38.

Goldberg, P.J.P. 'Marriage, Migration, Servanthood and Life-Cycle in Yorkshire Towns of the later Middle Ages: some York Cause Paper Evidence' *Continuity and Change* 1 (1986): 141–69.

Goodman, Anthony. *John of Gaunt. The Exercise of Princely Power in Fourteenth-Century Europe*. New York: St. Martin's Press, 1992.

Hanawalt, Barbara A. *Growing Up in Medieval London. The Experience of Childhood in History*. Oxford and New York: Oxford University Press, 1993.

Hanawalt, Barbara A. *Of Good and Ill Repute. Gender and Social Control in Medieval England*. Oxford and New York: Oxford University Press, 1998.

Hatcher, John. 'England in the Aftermath of the Black Death' *Past and Present* 144 (August 1994): 3–35.

Hettinger, Madonna J. 'Defining the Servant: Legal and Extra-Legal Terms of Employment in Fifteenth-Century England' pp. 206–28 in *The Work of Work: Servitude, Slavery and Labour in Medieval England*, ed. Allen J. Frantzen and Douglas Moffat. Glasgow: Cruithne Press, 1994.

Hilton, Rodney Howard. *Bond Men Made Free. Medieval Peasant Movements and the English Rising of 1381*. New York: Viking Press, 1973.

McKisack, May. *The Fourteenth Century, 1307–1399*. Oxford: Clarendon Press, 1959.

Musson, Anthony. 'New Labour Laws, New Remedies? Legal Reaction to the Black Death Crisis' pp. 73–88 in *Fourteenth Century England I*, ed. Nigel Saul. Woodbridge, Suff.: Boydell Press, 2000.

Penn, Simon A.C. and Christopher Dyer, 'Wages and Earnings in Late Medieval England: Evidence from the Enforcement of the Labour Laws' *Economic History Review*, 2nd Ser. 43 (1990): 356–76.

Saul, Nigel. *Knights and Esquires: The Gloucestershire Gentry in the Fourteenth Century*. Oxford: Clarendon Press, 1981.

*The Statutes of the Realm*. 11 vols. London: G. Eyre and A. Straham, 1810–28; rpt. London: Dawson of Pall Mall, 1963.

Strohm, Paul. *Hochon's Arrow. The Social Imagination of Fourteenth-Century Texts*. Princeton, NJ: Princeton University Press, 1992.

Tardif, Richard. 'The Mistery of Robin Hood' pp. 345–61 in *Robin Hood: An Anthology of Scholarship and Criticism*, ed. Stephen Knight. Woodbridge, Suff. / Rochester, NY: D.S. Brewer, 1999.

Thrupp, Sylvia. *The Merchant Class of Medieval London, 1300–1500*. Ann Arbor: University of Michigan Press, 1976, rpt. 1992.

VCH. *Victoria History of the County of Stafford*, ed. William Page et al. London: Constable / Oxford University Press, 1908–90.

VCH. *Victoria History of the County of Oxford*, ed. L.F. Salzman et al. 13 vols. London: Oxford University Press, 1907–96.

*The Westminster Chronicle, 1381–1394*, ed. and trans. L.C. Hector and Barbara F. Harvey. Oxford: Clarendon Press / New York: Oxford University Press, 1982.

*Women in England, c. 1275–1525. Documentary Sources*, ed. and trans. P.J.P. Goldberg. Manchester: Manchester University Press / New York: St. Martin's Press, 1995.

# Index